Challenging Times

Challenging Times

The Women's Movement in Canada and the United States

EDITED BY

CONSTANCE BACKHOUSE

AND

DAVID H. FLAHERTY

McGill-Queen's University Press
Montreal & Kingston • London • Buffalo

© McGill-Queen's University Press 1992
ISBN 0-7735-0910-0 (cloth)
ISBN 0-7735-0919-4 (paper)

Legal deposit third quarter 1992
Bibliothèque nationale du Québec

Printed in Canada on acid-free paper

Canadian Cataloguing in Publication Data

Main entry under title:
Challenging Times
    Includes index.
    ISBN 0-7735-0910-0 (bound) – ISBN 0-7735-0919-4 (pbk.)
    1. Feminism – Canada. 2. Feminism – United States.
    I. Backhouse, Constance, 1952–   . II. Flaherty,
    David H.
    HQ1154.T54 1992   305.42'0971   C92-090235-9

Typeset in Palatino 10/12 by
Caractéra production graphique inc., Quebec City.

Contents

Preface

The Centre for American Studies and the Centre for Women's Studies and Feminist Research, both at the University of Western Ontario, are respectively engaged in the two areas from which the present volume initially drew its major scholarly resources: the study of the United States from a Canadian viewpoint and the study of women's issues. The conference in May 1989 that led to this volume was a product of a collaborative consultation among faculty and students at Western who are associated with these two centres and who do research and teach on aspects of the women's movement in Canada and the United States.

Begun in 1984, the Centre for American Studies is an interdisciplinary working unit of scholars at the University of Western Ontario, primarily in the fields of history, law, business, political science, geography, and economics, who are interested in studying the United States. The Centre for Women's Studies and Feminist Research was established in 1987. Its purpose is to promote scholarly research and teaching in the field of women's studies and feminist research.

The central objective of the present volume is to examine the women's movements in Canada and the United States with a particular emphasis on the last generation, since the movements became highly visible. At the most general level, two questions are explored: what have been the achievements and experiences of the women's movements to date, and what remains to be accomplished?

Reliance on a comparative perspective between Canada and the United States is one attractive and informing aspect of the present volume, especially since so little comparative work has been done on the women's movement in general. One way of outlining the volume intellectually is as an assessment of the similarities and differences among Canadian and American feminists who live on the North American continent. It contributes to greater communication between academic feminists in North America with a direct examination of commonalities and differences in their respective experiences. As the following pages demonstrate, contributors from Canada are more likely than Americans to have knowledge of the development of the recent women's movement in both countries. This collection of essays may assist, at least in part, in redressing the balance.

As a joint project of the Centre for Women's Studies and Feminist Research and the Centre for American Studies, the co-editors are grateful to the then directors of the respective centres, Kathleen Okruhlik and David H. Flaherty, for their contributions to the enterprise. The administrators of the centres, Julie Ashford and Frances Kyle, made similarly essential contributions. Fran Kyle, in particular, handled the multiplicity of chores associated with dealing with individual authors and producing this book; her contribution was invaluable. Kirstin Fogg helped with the details of organization for the 1989 conference at the University of Western Ontario.

Essential financial support came from the Social Sciences and Humanities Research Council of Canada; the Renaissance Campaign of the University of Western Ontario; the Naruth Foundation, courtesy of Nancy Jackman; the u.s. Information Service, through the good offices of the American Embassy in Ottawa; the Human Rights Fund of the Canadian Department of Justice; and two partners of Lerner and Associates in London, Ontario.

The co-editors appreciate the personal, intellectual, and financial contributions of all of those involved in the shaping of this volume, including, in particular, the participants in our 1989 conference. They also wish to acknowledge the valued assistance of the reference librarians of the D.B. Weldon Library at the University of Western Ontario; they responded to innumerable queries with their customary professionalism.

Contributors

CONSTANCE BACKHOUSE is Associate Professor of Law, University of Western Ontario. She is the author of *The Secret Oppression: Sexual Harassment of Working Women*, with Leah Cohen (1979); *Sexual Harassment on the Job*, with Leah Cohen (1981); and *Petticoats and Prejudice: Women and Law in Nineteenth-Century Canada* (1991).

THE HONOURABLE MONIQUE BÉGIN, a sociologist, is Dean of the Faculty of Health Sciences at the University of Ottawa. She held the Joint Chair in Women's Studies at the University of Ottawa and Carleton University from 1986 to 1990. In the government of Pierre Trudeau, she served as minister of national revenue (1976–77) and then as minister of national health and welfare from 1977 to 1979 and then from 1980 to 1984. She served as executive secretary and director of research for the Royal Commission on the Status of Women in Canada. Her recent publications include *Medicare: Canada's Right to Health* (1988); "Debates and Silences – Reflections of a Politician," in *Daedalus* (Fall, 1988); and several texts on women and health.

NAOMI BLACK is Professor of Political Science at York University. Her publications include: *Canadian Women: A History*, with Alison Prentice, Paula Bourne, Gail Cuthbert Brandt, Beth Light, and Wendy Mitchinson (1988); *Social Feminism* (1989); and "The Canadian Women's Movement: The Second Wave," in Sandra Burt, Lorraine Code, and Lindsay Dorney, eds., *Changing Patterns: Women in Canada* (1988).

MARJORIE GRIFFIN COHEN is an economist who is Professor of Political Science and Women's Studies at Simon Fraser University. She has held various executive positions in NAC and is the author of *Women's Work, Markets, and Economic Development in Nineteenth-Century Ontario* (1988); and *Free Trade and the Future of Women's Work: Manufacturing and Service Industries* (1987).

MICHELINE DE SÈVE is Professor in the Département de science politique, Université du Québec à Montréal. She has written *Pour un féminisme libertaire* (1985) and *L'Echappée vers l'Ouest* (1991).

MICHELINE DUMONT is Professor in the Département de sciences humaines, Faculté des lettres et sciences humaines, Université de Sherbrooke. She is an author of *Women of Quebec: A History* (1987); and has written *Le Mouvement des femmes hier et aujourd'hui* (1986); and *The Women's Movement, Then and Now* (1986).

MARGRIT EICHLER is Professor of Sociology, Ontario Institute for Studies in Education and the University of Toronto. She has written *The Double Standard: A Feminist Critique of Feminist Social Sciences* (1980); *Nonsexist Research Methods: A Practical Guide* (1988); and *Families in Canada Today: Recent Changes and Their Policy Consequences* (1988).

SARA M. EVANS is Professor and Chair, Department of History, University of Minnesota. She is the author of *Born for Liberty: A History of American Women* (1989); and *Wage Justice: Comparable Worth and The Paradox of Technocratic Reform*, with Barbara J. Nelson (1989).

MARIANNE A. FERBER is Professor of Economics at the University of Illinois at Urbana-Champaign. She has written *Women and Work, Paid and Unpaid: An Annotated Bibliography* (1987); and *The Economics of Women, Men and Work*, with Francine D. Blau (1986); and edited *Work and Family: Policies for a Changing Workplace*, with Brigid O'Farrell and LaRue Allen (1991).

DAVID H. FLAHERTY is Professor of History and Law at the University of Western Ontario, where from 1984 to 1989 he directed its Centre for American Studies. His writings include *Protecting Privacy in Surveillance Societies: The Federal Republic of Germany, Sweden, France, Canada, and the United States* (1989); and "Who Rules Canada?" in *Daedalus* (Fall, 1988). He also co-edited *Southern Exposure: Canadian Perspectives on the United States* (1986), with William R. McKercher.

M. PATRICIA FERNÁNDEZ KELLY is Research Scientist, Institute for Policy Studies and Associate Professor of Sociology, Johns Hopkins University. Her writings include *For We Are Sold, I and My People: Women and Industry in Mexico's Frontier* (1983); "Broadening the Scope: Gender and International Economic Development," in *Sociological Forum* 4, no. 4 (1989); and *Women, Men, and the International Division of Labor*, edited with June Nash (1983).

LORRAINE GREAVES is Professor of Sociology at Fanshawe College in London, Ontario. She is currently completing her Ph.D. at Monash University in Melbourne, Australia. She is the author of *Taking Control: An Action Handbook on Women and Tobacco* (1989); and "Reorganizing the National Action Committee on the Status of Women, 1986–1988," in Jeri Wine and Janice Ristock, eds., *Women and Social Change: Feminist Activism in Canada* (1991).

MARJORIE HEINS is Director of the American Civil Liberties Union's Arts Censorship Project. She was director of the Civil Rights Division for the Attorney-General's office in Massachusetts in 1990–91 and staff counsel with the Massachusetts Civil Liberties Union until 1989. In 1987–88, she was a visiting professor of law, Boston College Law School. Her writings include *Cutting the Mustard: Affirmative Action and the Nature of Excellence* (1987).

CATHARINE A. MACKINNON is Professor of Law at the University of Michigan. Her books include *Sexual Harassment of Working Women: A Case of Sex Discrimination* (1979); *Feminism Unmodified: Discourses on Life and Law* (1987); *Pornography and Civil Rights: A New Day for Women's Equality*, with Andrea Dworkin (1988); and *Toward a Feminist Theory of the State* (1989).

PATRICIA A. MONTURE-OKANEE is Assistant Professor at the University of Ottawa Law School; she received her LL.B. from Queen's University in 1988. Her writings include "Ka-Nin-Heh-Gah-E-Sa-Nonh-Yah-Gah," in the *Canadian Journal of Women and the Law* 2, no. 1 (1986); and "A Vicious Circle: Child Welfare and the First Nations," in the *Canadian Journal of Women and the Law* 3, no. 1 (1989).

ARUN MUKHERJEE is Assistant Professor in the Department of English at York University. One of her major research interests is the issue of race in feminist literary theory. She is the author of *The Gospel of Wealth in the American Novel: The Rhetoric of Dreiser and His*

Contemporaries (1987); and *Towards an Aesthetic of Opposition: Essays on Literature, Criticism, and Cultural Imperialism* (1988).

GRETA HOFMANN NEMIROFF holds the Joint Chair of Women's Studies at the University of Ottawa and Carleton University. She has edited two books on women in Canada: *Women and Men: Interdisciplinary Readings on Gender* (1987); and *Celebrating Canadian Women: Poetry and Prose by and about Women in Canada* (1989). Her latest book is *Reconstructing Education: Towards a Pedagogy of Critical Humanism* (1992).

JEAN F. O'BARR is Associate Professor (Adjunct) in the Department of Political Science, Duke University. She is the editor of *Signs: Journal of Women in Culture and Society*. She has written *Restructuring the Academy: Women's Education and Women's Studies*, with Elizabeth Minnich and Rachel Rosenfeld (1988).

CHRISTINE OVERALL is Associate Professor of Philosophy at Queen's University. She has edited *The Future of Human Reproduction* (1989) and *Perspectives on AIDS: Ethical and Social Issues* (1991); and is the author of *Ethics and Human Reproduction: A Feminist Analysis* (1987).

GLENDA SIMMS has chaired the Canadian Advisory Council on the Status of Women since December 1989. A teacher in her native Jamaica, she moved to Canada in 1966. She has taught at the University of Lethbridge and the Saskatchewan Indian Federated College, and is currently on leave from the Faculty of Education at Nipissing University College. Simms was a founding member of the National Organization of Immigrant and Visible Minority Women of Canada and has served as president of the Congress of Black Women of Canada.

MARIANA VALVERDE is Associate Professor of Sociology at York University. She is the author of *Sex, Power and Pleasure* (1985); and *The Age of Light, Soap and Water: Moral Reform in English Canada 1880s–1920s* (1991).

JILL VICKERS is Associate Vice-President (Academic) and Professor of Canadian Studies and Political Science at Carleton University. Her publications include *Taking Sex into Account: The Policy Consequences of Sexist Research* (1984); and *An Examination of the Scientific Mode of Enquiry in Politics* (1991).

Abbreviations

ACLU	American Civil Liberties Union
AFEAS	Association féminine d'éducation et d'action sociale
B&B	Royal Commission on Bilingualism and Biculturalism
CBC	Canadian Broadcasting Corporation
CCF	Co-operative Commonwealth Federation, Canada
CECM	Commission des écoles catholiques de Montréal
CEW	Committee for the Equality of Women, Canada
Clio	Collectif Clio, Quebec
CR	Consciousness raising
CRIAW	Canadian Research Institute for the Advancement of Women
CRTC	Canadian Radio-television Commission (now the Canadian Radio-television and Telecommunications Commission)
DAWN	DisAbled Women's Network of Canada
DOB	Daughters of Bilitis
EEOC	Equal Employment Opportunity Commission, U.S.
ERA	Equal Rights Amendment, U.S.
FFQ	Fédération des femmes du Québec
FLQ	Front de libération du Québec
HUAC	House Un-American Activities Committee, U.S.
ILO	International Labour Office
IVF	*In vitro* fertilization
MP	Member of Parliament

NAC	National Action Committee on the Status of Women, Canada
NDP	New Democratic Party, Canada
NOW	National Organization for Women, U.S.
POW	Participation of Women Committee, Canada
PTA	Parent-Teacher Associations
RCSW	Royal Commission on the Status of Women in Canada
SDS	Students for a Democratic Society, U.S.
SNCC	Student Non-Violent Co-Ordinating Committee, U.S.
UAW	United Auto Workers
VOW	Voice of Women, Canada
WAM	Women's Action Movement, Montreal
WCTU	Woman's Christian Temperance Union
WEAL	Women's Equity Action League, U.S.
WJC	Women's Joint Committee, Canada
WLG	Women's Liberation Group, Toronto
WLM	Women's Liberation Movement
WSP	Women's Strike for Peace, U.S.
YWCA	Young Women's Christian Association

Challenging Times

1 The Contemporary Women's Movements in Canada and the United States: An Introduction

CONSTANCE BACKHOUSE

The contributors to this volume of essays were all participants at a conference held at the University of Western Ontario in London, Ontario, Canada in May of 1989.[1] The theme of the colloquium was a comparison between the contemporary women's movements in Canada and the United States. As presenters of papers or as commentators, all attempted to answer pressing questions about the nature of feminism in its current forms, the interrelationship and tensions between different portions of the movement, and prospects for future growth.

As an exercise in purely comparative analysis, it would be inaccurate to suggest that this volume of essays constitutes a definitive examination. The feminist movements in each country are sufficiently complex and unwieldy to defy the sweeping generalizations and categorizations which necessarily precede detailed comparison. Furthermore, although many of the Canadian contributors make valiant efforts to draw comparative conclusions, the American authors tend to be somewhat more insular in their writing. The articles do, however, offer extremely useful implicit comparisons, allowing readers to draw conclusions of their own regarding the distinctive originating forces, factors shaping the direction of feminist philosophy and activism, and issues provoking unity and dissension within the women's movement in each country. Furthermore, it becomes obvious from the text of some of these essays that certain political and theoretical issues transcend international borders, ebbing and flowing between the two countries in symbiotic fashion.

The critical starting question, of course, must be how to define "the contemporary women's movement." This perplexing matter is far from a pedantic query. Scores of women, young and old, who have freshly discovered their own affinity to feminism face the bewildering prospect of trying to find answers to such questions as "Where is the women's movement?" and "How do I sign up?"

On some level, the question is unanswerable. Naomi Black suggests that the women's movement is a complicated web of consciousness-raising groups, task forces, collectives, women's caucuses, women's centres, women's studies programs, and feminist publishing houses. One could easily expand this list to include women's conferences, feminist marches, feminist cultural events such as music/theatrical/film festivals, feminist bookstores, and women's shelters. Inclusion of "direct action" initiatives would require listing the countless "everyday acts and outrageous rebellions" where women individually and in concert have triumphed over oppression.[2]

Intriguingly, Micheline Dumont suggests that the search to define "the women's movement" may be entirely misplaced. Perhaps we would do better to examine the perspectives of women who disclaim the movement. "Thousands of women say 'I am no feminist, but ... ' Why? We must learn about their motives, not about our interpretations," claims Dumont. Women who define themselves as being outside of the feminist movement could indeed tell us a lot about the nature of our work and the gaps it conceals.

And as Lorraine Greaves cautions, the subjectivity of the women doing the defining is typically determinative. She correctly reminds us that when those giving meaning to the term are "predominantly white, apparently heterosexual, usually educated, articulate, verbal women," they tend to locate the women's movement within their own ranks. This volume must, then, be considered a very partial presentation. It is important to emphasize that the writings collected here represent the views of only some of the participants and members in the women's movement, who are attempting to review the past and analyse prospects for the future from their own individual points of reference. There is no detailed examination, for example, of lesbianism or the role of organizations for women with disabilities in either the Canadian or American setting. The treatment of racism is not sufficiently integrated throughout the volume, undoubtedly reflecting the reality of the women's movement in both countries as well. The essays here represent only a beginning and they discuss only a few portions of the larger web, slowing to scrutinize some of the rents and some of the seams along the way.

Yet despite all of the necessary disclaimers, the enterprise in which the contributors to this volume are engaged is of fundamental importance. The current wave of feminist activity began in the 1960s in the United States according to Sara M. Evans, in the same decade in English Canada according to Jill Vickers, and in the 1940s in Quebec according to Dumont. Today we constitute a relatively mature, extensively institutionalized movement, with a rich history behind us. Many of the contributors have lived through and personally shaped this unfolding drama. It would be unreflectively short-sighted for us not to attempt to scrutinize the terrain of these past decades, to set down our account of the central events.

New generations of feminists will soon be replacing us. We had the luxury, however misguided, of thinking that we worked on a fresh slate, that we stood exhilaratingly as the first feminists of this current wave. Many of those who join us now find our knowledge, our process, and our structures to be confusing and, at times, intimidating and silencing. We have an obligation to set down how we think we have arrived at this place, documenting our sense of victories, challenges, and defeats. The greater the access to these recollections, the more quickly incoming feminists will be able to take their place as full participants, questioners, and challengers to our understandings and ideas.

To this end, Dumont and Micheline de Sève provide remarkably helpful background on the feminist movement in Quebec. For unilingual anglophones, these essays collectively furnish some of the only such work accessible. Challenging commonly held myths that, owing to the stranglehold of the Roman Catholic church, feminism in Quebec was late in appearing, Dumont describes the stubborn refusal of the rural women's groups, les Cercles des Fermières, to obey the edicts of the bishops in the 1940s. Women's study-groups, some defiant and some compliant with church demands, broke much new ground between 1940 and 1960. They paved the way for the explosion of feminist activity after the Quiet Revolution of the early 1960s.

The centrality of nationalism for Quebec women is a matter beyond debate. Even Greta Hofmann Nemiroff, a bilingual Quebec "Anglophone," who argues from personal conviction that "nationalism of any sort is anathema," concedes that the cause of nationalism is inextricably woven into current realities. Nationalism is "part of our identity," explains de Sève, "and an important form of self-assertion, just as it is for a Black woman to define herself as Afro-American or a Native woman to become a member of the Assembly of First

Nations. All are ways for a feminist living under Canadian rule to claim full recognition of her own specific voice inside the women's movement."

Both Dumont and de Sève attempt to correct the erroneous understandings of many English Canadians about the Quebec scene. Feminists both nourish and oppose the nationalist movement, they note. As one example, they cite the position of women on the Quebec referendum, held in 1980 to determine whether Quebec should seek to alter the constitutional framework with the rest of Canada by implementing an arrangement for "sovereignty-association." At the "Yvette rally" in Montreal in 1980, well publicized in English-Canada, fourteen thousand Quebec women congregated to support the No vote. Ten days later, at Place Desjardins, fifteen thousand women chanted "Yes" in a rally that was given much more subdued coverage in English-language media. Feminists were active on both sides.

Since that time, the position of Quebec feminists has become more unified, as the recent debate on the Meech Lake constitutional amendment so dramatically illustrates. The ratification of Meech Lake, with its recognition of Quebec as a "distinct society," became the cornerstone of demands almost universally put forward by Quebec feminists. As Dumont notes, this principle was simply "indispensable" for women who wished to remain both feminists and Quebecers. The reluctance of many English-Canadian feminists to accept it created severe blockages between "the two solitudes," which require our most urgent attention now that the Meech Lake accord has failed and constitutional reform is again on the national agenda. Unless English-Canadian feminists become significantly better versed on the perspectives of Quebec women, something which has been more the exception than the rule to date, the outlook for future relations is bleak.

The English-Canadian feminist movement often recognizes the gulf between the Quebec and Canadian perspectives, even as it seems unable to bridge it. Vickers suggests that Canadian political culture is built upon the recognition of division and differences between people. She identifies "a belief in dialogue," "a willingness to engage in debate," and an acceptance of those differences that are "not dissolvable" as hallmarks of the current feminist movement. Vickers points to the strength of feminist umbrella groups which represent ideologically diverse interests and linguistic groups as proof of her assertion. Whether francophone Québécoises would agree with this assessment is somewhat problematic. And Vickers herself concedes that our alleged tolerance of diversity may fail to withstand the challenge of women of colour, immigrant women, and women of the First Nations.

Vickers argues that home-grown influences were quite likely strong at the origin of the Canadian women's movement. She credits particularly the women's caucuses of the Co-operative Commonwealth Federation (CCF) party (the predecessor to the current New Democratic Party [NDP]), which dated from the 1920s, and the women's peace movement (Voice of Women), from the 1950s, as true antecedents of contemporary Canadian feminism. Documenting the unusual case of Marlene Dixon, a radical American feminist transplanted from Chicago to Montreal in the 1960s, Vickers suggests that American influences were dramatic, but unlikely to take root. For Canadians nurturing their own nationalist apprehensions vis-à-vis the overweening American culture, this will be reassuring.

The Canadian-American similarities are more obvious in the accounts of the two governmental commissions on the status of women: the Presidential Commission in the United States reported in 1963, the Royal Commission in Canada in 1970. Sara Evans credits the American commission with politicizing large numbers of women to the extensiveness of sex discrimination. Monique Bégin notes that the hearings and discussions surrounding the Canadian commission "played a key role in creating and accelerating the process of a feminist evolution in Canadian women's associations."

Naomi Black also attempts a direct comparison when she juxtaposes the failure of the American Equal Rights Amendment campaign and the success of Canadian women's fight to have equality provisions enshrined in the Canadian Charter of Rights and Freedoms in 1982. This was not a case of superior feminist strength in Canada, she asserts, but merely the result of two quite different battles. The sheer length of the process in the United States permitted a mobilization of ideological right-wing factions that was not duplicated in Canada. By contrast, within a relatively short time framework, a self-appointed elite group of Canadian feminists was able to mobilize pressure on executives who could move without consulting their legislatures. Black asserts that the machinery of the American National Organization of Women would have been superbly effective had they been engaged in a similar enterprise south of the border.

The explicitly comparative approach is a topic that seems to hold the attention of Canadian writers rather more obviously than their American counterparts. In her analysis of the contemporary women's movement in the United States, Evans cites various factors of influence, all of them American-based. She describes the clash between changing labour force participation of women and the stultifying domestic ideology, the "grass-roots" community activism of women against the House Un-American Activities Committee, and the anti-segregation efforts of the African-American women, as events which came together in the late 1950s to repoliticize American women as a group. While Evans notes the parallels with Canada in the important role played by the President's Commission on the Status of Women appointed by President John F. Kennedy, the American commission preceded the Canadian one by a full six years. "The influence has been largely if not entirely one-way," postulates Black, noting the earlier visits of Canadian feminists such as Emily Howard Stowe and Letitia Youmans to seek training and inspiration south of the border. Perhaps one can be forgiven for wondering whether or not such powerful women might have left behind some nuggets of insight or strategic advice that served their American sisters well, unattributed though this foreign influence may have been.

One obvious locus for cross-fertilization between the women's movements in Canada and the United States is the academic field of women's studies. Both countries boast a burgeoning complement of women's studies courses, instructors, and programs. Margrit Eichler notes that women's studies has achieved "some degree of institution-alization in the Canadian university and college system," while Jean F. O'Barr states that approximately half of American campuses have courses on women and programs in women's studies. Certainly Canadians are well versed in the texts and periodical literature coming from the American movement. American feminist journals such as *Signs* have Canadian feminists on their board of international correspondents.

The ultimate assessment of the importance of academic women's studies to the mission of feminism is difficult. Are we sufficiently powerful, sufficiently learned, and sufficiently visionary to claim to be training the next generation? We can document our rites of passage, with research and courses on women at first segregated – often viewed as "fringe" to central academic matters – and then integrated into previously "malestream" curricula and research. The prospects of remaining true to feminism despite the "institutionalizing" tendencies of the academy are unquestionably problematic. The barrenness of the environment plagues all of us, and tenuous feminist networks often provide the only slender ties to reality that exist.

The scholarly agenda which drives us is, according to O'Barr, typically borrowed from personal involvement in the wider women's movement. Eichler analyses Canadian data which show that women's studies instructors are unusually active within an array of women's organizations, and that they see a high degree of mutual interdependence between the academic process and the activist movement. Lorraine Greaves questions whether feminist activists who are not within the colleges and universities feel the same. The elitism of Canadian and American higher education is undoubtedly a grave barrier to most women. Feminist researchers must make their work accessible, according to Greaves, and she lists a spectrum of possibilities from video and theatre to pamphlets and Braille.

The importance of recognizing diversity within the women's movement is a theme which is clearly prominent in both countries. It is tempting to suggest that the current wave of feminism is more sensitive to this than earlier manifestations. Nancy Cott, in *The Grounding of Modern Feminism*, has reminded us that nineteenth-century women consistently used the singular word *"woman,"* symbolizing their conception of the unity of the female sex. The very language used by "the *women's* movement" which sprang to life in the 1960s and 1970s encompassed greater potential to comprehend "plural forms."[3]

Yet O'Barr suggests that it has taken us well into the current wave to begin to "shift away from an undifferentiated concept of women." Arun Mukherjee describes the "invisibility" of Black women and other women of colour in American women's studies courses and programs, and the failure of white feminists to critique feminist writing that is racist. Mariana Valverde calls for a transformation of women's studies curricula away from ethnocentric bias. "Gender does not transcend race," claims Patricia Monture-OKanee.

Valverde asserts that "racism is [currently] the major issue of the women's movement," and this is surely a phenomenon shared by both Canada and the United States. "Canadians pride themselves on being polite racists," claims Glenda Simms, but the roots of both countries go back to the enslavement of peoples of colour. Research in both countries must become more "race-conscious" in approach.

The response of the (largely white) women's movement to the claims of racism is instructive to those attempting to gauge its durability and strength. Mukherjee writes that, when "plurality and difference" split "feminism" into "feminisms" sometime in the 1980s, it was initially heralded as a sign of maturity. As the full implications began to sink in, however, white women reacted with guilt, denial, and hostility. Without question, as Mukherjee claims, this has culminated in a "crisis of legitimation," something that has greatly amused those most strongly opposed to feminism, whether or not they are anti-racist themselves.

But there are some encouraging signs of heightened sensitivity to racism, as more and more feminists become committed to taking account of the wide diversity of race among women. Valverde calls for white feminists to critique our earlier work from a racially conscious perspective and provides a model re-examination of her own research on sexuality. Greaves calls for a policy of affirmative action within the movement, to provide places and resources for women who have been excluded – because of race, class, disability, and heterosexism. Mukherjee urges the hiring of more Black women and women of colour in women's studies programs, the reformulating of anti-racist guidelines for feminist journals, and the inclusion of more writing by Black women. The extent to which we heed these calls over the coming years will be critical to the growth and survival of our movement.

Another hallmark of the current wave has been the focus on violence against women. There were antecedents from the turn of the century, of course, as Sheila Jeffreys has so clearly documented in *The Spinster and Her Enemies*.[4] The second wave began in the 1960s without much reference to violence. As Monique Bégin has reminded us, the Canadian Royal Commission made no mention of the issue. But by the 1980s, Catharine A. MacKinnon argues, a "distinctive feature of the contemporary women's movement is its focus on making sexual abuse visible."

Over the past several decades both Canada and the United States have witnessed the phenomenal growth of feminist-based rape crisis centres, battered women's shelters, and, incipiently, incest survivors' groups. The delivery of services to women and children who suffer from violence has been one of the prime goals of the women's movement. Our ability to continue and expand access to these services, and to do so within a feminist-defined framework, resisting the intrusion of the "professionalized" social service agencies, poses a critical challenge for the future.

Juxtaposed against service delivery have been twin efforts in the two countries to reform the law to reflect women's experience. Catharine MacKinnon surveys the results of these campaigns with respect to the law of rape. Despite the fact that criminal law in Canada is federal, while it is largely formulated state by state in the United States, the legal changes in both countries have been similar. In most jurisdictions rape has been redefined as "sexual assault" and the law has been rendered "gender-neutral." Conviction rates have not improved significantly, notes MacKinnon, who takes issue with much of this reform. "The problem is not gender-neutral, so the solution may not be either," she argues.

The place of law reform within the feminist agenda is a matter for some reflection. Feminism is a highly visible force in law schools in both countries, nurtured by a small group of dedicated female professors; feminist lawyers frequently take a central role within feminist organizations; much feminist energy has been directed into legal analysis. Disturbing questions remain about the representativeness of those who set the law reform agenda, however, and the prospect of achieving satisfactory results when working through classist, racist, male-dominated structures. As Monture-OKanee cautions, if rape laws are harshened, "First Nations men are going to be ... serving the sentences."

The questionable wisdom of a legal focus for feminists is underscored by Marjorie Heins's research on American Supreme Court jurisprudence. She dissects the seeming inability of the court under Chief Justice William Rehnquist to comprehend the historical and continuing racism of the United States. Heins suggests that we need sweeping changes to concepts of "excellence," "merit," and "qualifications" in order to deconstruct their current discriminatory application. The likelihood of accomplishing such tasks through law is a topic that bears further examination. Major dilemmas centre upon whom courts will recognize as authoritative witnesses and how enthusiastically judges will engage in second-guessing the hiring and promotion decisions of predominantly white, male institutions. The extraordinary cost and time commitment involved in litigation, not to mention the personal sacrifice demanded from litigants, will undoubtedly continue to limit the gains possible through these avenues.

Heins also describes the recent Supreme Court treatment of an affirmative action program designed to aid racial minorities in the City of Richmond case in 1989.[5] There the American court invalidated the program, subjecting it to the same sort of tests used to scrutinize discrimination directed against racial minorities. As Heins notes, this indicates an inability to appreciate the difference between the "hateful, invidious racial discrimination against Black citizens that stains United States history, and remedies designed in some small measure to correct the continuing effects of that past discrimination."

In Canada, affirmative action has had a significantly longer history. From the nineteenth century, attempts have been made to secure special status for Roman Catholic education and the French language. Regional representation was the cornerstone of Senate and Supreme Court appointments. In the twentieth century, the federal government has developed policies to integrate Francophones into the public service. A "Canadians-first" hiring policy for universities has been in effect since 1981 as part of a response to concerns about the "Americanization" of post-secondary education. Canadian human rights legislation and the Charter of Rights and Freedoms make specific accommodation for affirmative action. Whether this will result in more benign treatment of affirmative action programs in Canadian law awaits further examination.[6]

Marjorie Cohen argues that economic issues should be central to the current feminist agenda. She notes that obvious problems, such as the wage gap between men and women, have traditionally occupied feminist attention, but suggests that since the 1980s, a more sophisticated feminist movement in Canada has begun to address broader economic policy such as the budget, trade policy, privatization, deregulation, and the general economic structure. Citing earlier disagreements between feminists over whether these matters are really feminist issues, Cohen suggests that the Canadian women's movement has become more aware of the "structural nature of women's oppression." She places the locus of this change within the executive of the National Action Committee on the Status of Women, where an increased number of "left-oriented" women have come to power.

In direct contrast, Marianne A. Ferber documents the perspectives of American feminists on economic issues. The two countries obviously share many problems, such as occupational segregation by sex and race, disparity in wages, insufficient child-care facilities, and the burden of housework falling predominantly to women. Both feminist movements labour mightily to secure greater equality in pay and access to a wider array of occupations. Both allocate some (if not enough) attention to the status of women working without pay in the home. Yet there the similarity stops. While Canadian feminists begin to tackle wider economic issues, such as the free trade policies implemented by the Mulroney government, American feminists are visibly halted by the strident resistance of "determined advocates of the free market" who oppose such preliminary measures as pay equity.

Perhaps this explains the amazement with which many Canadian women watched the unfolding of the emotional debate between American feminists over the question of pregnancy leave. In 1986 the United States Supreme Court heard the California Federal Savings case, which considered whether a law requiring employers to offer four months' pregnancy leave to women was discriminatory.[7] Before the law was eventually upheld, some American feminists (significantly, those who controlled the National Organization of Women) argued that such leaves offended the concept of equality and would inhibit the hiring of women. The different economic and social context in Canada has fostered an entirely different feminist climate. Here, pregnancy leaves have been a matter of law for decades, funded through government-administered unemployment insurance benefits. The feminist focus in Canada was on the expansion of the leaves and their funding, rather than a debate over the potential difficulties of programs directed entirely to women. Perhaps this explains the ferocity with which many Canadian feminists opposed free trade with the United States, fearing that the extensive (if insufficient) net of welfare provisions which we have come to expect would be at risk as businesses from the two culturally different countries began to compete directly.

Reproductive freedom has also been a central preoccupation of the contemporary women's movement in Canada and the United States, as Christine Overall notes. Access to birth control and abortion has mobilized thousands of women on both sides of the border to challenge government legal prohibitions and male-dominated medical circles. The historic *Roe* v. *Wade* decision in the United States in 1973 predated the Canadian *Morgentaler* ruling of 1988 by some fifteen years. It created a one-way flow of women from Canada seeking abortions, who obtained the procedure in one of hundreds of American abortion clinics dotting border cities from coast to coast. Now, as Americans witness continued challenges to *Roe* v. *Wade*, speculation has begun that the border traffic will reverse, with anxious Americans seeking, in Canadian clinics and hospitals, facilities that may soon be lost to them in their own nation. However the two countries weather the tenacious attempts to encroach upon access to abortion, their mutual dependence could not be starker.[8]

Thus Patricia Fernández Kelly's plea to re-examine the class roots of pro-choice and pro-life positions is important to feminists on both sides of the border. She argues that modern pro-choice discourse was formulated by a women's movement largely insensitive to class differences. Pro-life ideology has fed upon the mistrust that working-class women have long felt about feminism, and has staked out a high moral ground against allegedly individualistic, self-indulgent feminist claims.

Fernández Kelly takes issue with the feminist tendency to dismiss pro-lifers contemptuously as reactionary forces bent on maintaining women's subordination. She documents a profoundly anti-establishment strand of the pro-life movement and urges the women's movement to recapture this strand through a broadened redefinition of reproductive choice. "We should inquire about the conditions that make pregnancy and motherhood into a calamity for a large number of women," she insists. This class dissection of abortion politics is a thought-provoking piece of work, which has important implications for women in both countries. Despite the claims of the Canadian women's movement to greater sensitivity on economic and class issues, we show no marked superiority in this field. The receptivity of Canadian and American feminists to Fernández Kelly's critique may prove the key to unlocking the polarization and deadlock over abortion in our two nations.

Christine Overall's contribution provides a philosophical examination of the concept of "reproductive rights," a phrase which she claims encompasses two notions. Discussions of the "right to reproduce" have recently complemented the traditional focus on the "right not to reproduce." In its most obvious forms, according to Overall, the "right to reproduce" includes the right not to be interfered with in such ways as forced sterilization or coercive birth control programs. The current wave of the women's movement has witnessed many breaches of this right in Canada, the United States, and throughout the Third World. Glenda Simms refers to the discriminatory sterilization and birth control practices visited upon Black women in North America and Africa.

In recent decades, the explosion of reproductive technology has created considerable concern in feminist circles. A host of techniques such as *in vitro* fertilization, embryo freezing, contract motherhood, and other mechanisms have been developed to combat "infertility." It is intriguing to recall that Shalumith Firestone published *The Dialectic of Sex* in 1970, right at the outset of the current movement. In her important classic, she called for the elimination of childbirth by natural means, arguing that pregnancy remained an insoluble barrier to women's equality. Marge Piercy, in her influential feminist novel *Woman on the Edge of Time*, published in 1976, postulated a feminist utopia in which all birthing took place through technological means.[9]

By the 1980s, the feminist perspective on reproductive technology in both countries had become far less sanguine. Overall notes the reluctance of feminists to advocate the end of infertility research and treatment, since they wish to allow infertile women to make autonomous decisions. However, she expresses concern with the perspective that children are "owed to each of us, as individuals or as members of a couple," and fears that some women's access to reproductive technology may require the violation of other women's right not to reproduce. Canadians who prize their medicare programs fear the "incursion of u.s.-style commercialization of reproduction and reproductive entrepreneurialism." And feminists from both countries decry the delivery of reproductive technology from a monopolized medical system riddled with sexism, racism, homophobia, and other shortcomings. The prospect that reproductive technology will contribute to feminist goals seems increasingly unlikely.

In the end we are left with two contemporary women's movements in the United States and Canada, which share much and differ significantly. In origins, in the selection of issues for discussion and activism, and in the understanding of those issues, there is much similarity and marked division. Mutual influence, if predominantly one-way, has a long tradition and a promising future. As feminist activists in both countries come to appreciate the roots and agenda of their neighbours more clearly, an even greater potential for enrichment will undoubtedly unfold.

PART ONE

The Origins of the Contemporary Women's Movement in Canada and the United States

THE FOUR ESSAYS IN THIS PART ATTEMPT TO EXAMINE THE
various factors that provided the originating impetus for the most
recent wave of the women's movements in Canada and the United
States. Monique Bégin and Jill Vickers describe the initial resurfacing
of the organized feminist movement in Canada in the 1960s, Sara
Evans portrays a similar burst of energy in the United States in the
same decade, and Micheline Dumont recounts the somewhat earlier
awakening of feminist activism in Quebec in the 1940s.

Monique Bégin writes from the perspective of one who lived in
the centre of the resurgence. As a young Quebec sociologist, she was
recruited to serve as the executive secretary of the Royal Commission
on the Status of Women (1967–70). Unlike many Canadian royal
commissions, this one did not prove to be a tedious retreading of
old ground, fulfilling the twin functions of diminishing expectations
and delaying reform. The hearings, research, and report of that
Commission raised unprecedented public awareness of feminism,
uniting English-speaking and French-speaking individuals and wom-
en's organizations from every corner of the country. With the passage
of twenty years, Bégin (now dean of health sciences at the University
of Ottawa) reflects upon the nature of that Royal Commission – its
strengths, its weaknesses, and ultimately its symbolic meaning for
the history of the Canadian women's movement.

Jill Vickers probes the less spectacular, more elusive "grass roots"
underlying the rise of the current wave of feminism in Canada, while
offering explicit comparison to the situation in the United States.
Emphasizing the high degree of intergenerational continuity in
Canada, she attributes an important role to the Voice of Women, the
anti-war organization active from the 1950s. Vickers documents the
gender struggles within the early women's caucuses of the Co-operative Commonwealth Federation (CCF). She stresses that the revitalized Canadian women's movement was committed to reform within
the ordinary political process, tolerant of diversity but anchored by
a fundamental belief in the welfare state. In contrast, she recounts
that the American women's movement was influenced to a larger
extent by a dynamic wave of grass-roots consciousness-raising
groups. Small but extraordinarily influential groups of radical feminists denounced the major institutions of u.s. government and
society, rejected reform through the traditional political process, and
opted for the building of a counterculture.

Sara Evans writes from the perspective of having been active
within one of the earliest consciousness-raising, women's liberation
groups in the United States. She cites the influx of women into
the paid labour force and their increasing antagonism towards the

pervasive ideology of domesticity as central factors in the revitalization of American feminism. Evans documents the spectacular activities of the Women's Strike for Peace in 1962, the founding of the National Organization for Women later in the decade, and the emergence of the women's liberation movement out of the civil rights movement and the New Left. She argues that these three distinct waves were ultimately to build on and influence each other, creating a mass movement which would offer fundamental challenges to the cultural definitions of masculinity and femininity by the 1970s.

Micheline Dumont provides a provocative inquiry into the roots of the Quebec feminist revival, admonishing English-speaking feminists for their apparent ignorance about the Quebec situation. "The Quebec movement is just as important as the Canadian movement and is important for the Canadian movement," she claims. The parallels between this cry and the complaints of English-speaking Canadians about the paucity of American feminists' knowledge about the Canadian women's movement will strike readers forcefully. Dumont locates the genesis of modern Quebec feminism in the activities of les Cercles des Fermières, rural and urban women's study groups which embodied consciousness-raising potential by the 1950s. She documents the explosive force of feminism in the 1970s, after the Quiet Revolution had restructured Quebec society, and recounts the painful and divisive debates over issues of sovereignty and constitutional ratification.

These essays collectively attempt to identify and account for the germinating influences responsible for the reawakening of organized feminism in the United States, Canada, and Quebec.

2 The Royal Commission on the Status of Women in Canada: Twenty Years Later*

MONIQUE BÉGIN

There have been enormous changes in our collective sensitivity to women's issues since the tabling of the Report of the Royal Commission on the Status of Women in Canada (RCSW) in the House of Commons on 7 December 1970, further to the private presentation of a copy, a week earlier, to Prime Minister Pierre Elliott Trudeau.[1] Among its many contributions to changing our society, feminism is now firmly engaged in reinterpreting and re-evaluating knowledge within almost all of the disciplines of the academy. There is, however, much work still to be done in making scholarship and knowledge accessible to and representative of women. The work of the royal commission also belongs to this long process of social change. Twenty years ago, when as executive secretary of the commission, I co-signed the report, we had no way of anticipating the fate of our recommendations. In fact, the report initiated far-reaching changes and has played a key role in making the situation and status of women part of the political agenda of the country.

In order to achieve a perspective on the RCSW, I would like to outline the concerns which led to its establishment. This includes briefly describing the political and cultural climate of the mid and late 1960s, as well as referring to accounts given by key political actors of the time. Then I will reflect on the actual experience represented by the work of the commission between 16 February 1967,

---

* I would like to thank my colleague Donna Jowett for her help in editing this text.

when it was established by Prime Minister Lester B. Pearson, and the tabling of its report three and a half years later. In retrospect, it is apparent that the commission lacked a clear theoretical focus, such as has emerged over the last two decades through the work of feminist activism and scholarship. I will address this more fully later in this essay. Finally, I will assess the impact and consequences of the report "twenty years after."

SETTING THE STAGE

Canadians, in the late 1960s, were in the wake of the famous "B&B" Commission (the Royal Commission on Bilingualism and Biculturalism, which released its reports in 1965 and 1967), and they were passionately discussing their national identity. The country was still elated at the memory of its Centennial celebrations and at the spirit of generosity of the Montreal Expo '67: "Man and His World" [sic]. A new prime minister, Pierre E. Trudeau, had been elected in April 1968, announcing a major change in political philosophy and style. Quebec was going through a resurgence of nationalism, and the first seven separatist deputies to the National Assembly (out of one hundred) had just been elected (representing 24 per cent of the ballots cast in the 1970 provincial election). Finally, in October 1970, Canadians had learned with horror of the kidnapping of British diplomat James Cross and of the death of provincial minister Pierre Laporte. They watched Ottawa's implementation of the War Measures Act in Quebec with mixed feelings.

Yet, when the report of the RCSW was tabled two months after these events, a respected journalist of the *Toronto Star*, Anthony Westell, wrote:

At 2:11 p.m. in the House of Commons Monday, the Prime Minister rose, bowed politely to the Speaker, and tabled a bomb, already primed and ticking. The bomb is called the Report of the RCSW in Canada, and it is packed with more explosive potential than any device manufactured by terrorists. As a call to revolution, hopefully a quiet one, it is more persuasive than any FLQ manifesto. And as a political blockbuster, it is more powerful than that famous report of the controversial commission on bilingualism and biculturalism.

This 488–page book, in its discreet green, white and blue cover, demands radical change not just in Quebec, but in every community across Canada. It is concerned not merely with relations between French and English, but between man and woman. The history of the problem it describes and seeks to solve is not 100 years of Confederation but the story of mankind.

First attention focussed naturally on the Commission's 167 proposals for practical action, from reform of the law to provide abortion on demand to rewriting of schoolbooks which teach sexual discrimination to our children.

But controversial as some of these proposals may seem now, they will quickly be accepted in substance, if not in every detail. They are reasonable answers to real problems which can no longer be ignored, and governments and public opinion are ready for reform.[2]

The immediate history preceding the creation of the RCSW has now been documented in several sources.[3] The events can be summed up as follows. Quebec women founded the new Fédération des femmes du Québec (FFQ) in April 1966. This followed on the heels of the enthusiastic celebration a year earlier (inspired by Thérèse Casgrain) of the twenty-fifth anniversary of the right of women to vote provincially. The FFQ joined forces, early in September 1966, with English Canada's Committee for the Equality of Women (CEW). The CEW was a regrouping of thirty-two women's organizations, which convened in May 1966 under the leadership of Laura Sabia in order to press for the creation of a royal commission on all aspects of the status of women in Canada. Working in a parallel way, women journalists attached to so-called "Women's Pages" in newspapers, to women's periodicals (Doris Anderson for the English-language *Chatelaine* and Fernande St-Martin for the French-language *Châtelaine*), and to women's radio and television programs ("Femmes d'aujourd'hui" on Radio-Canada television and "Take Thirty" on the Canadian Broadcasting Corporation [CBC]) promoted the idea, discussing it with their audiences and building support for it. Pressure began to bear on the federal government in September 1966 and, within six months, the commission was created.[4]

What is less well understood, however, is what was happening in Quebec and how joint action from coast to coast became a reality, making possible the move by the federal government. I would like to focus on the relationship between the Quebec and English-Canadian women's movements leading up to the RCSW. While considerable attention has been given to the English-Canadian women's movement, this relationship has been neglected.

In the aftermath of the B&B, organized without the full and equal participation of francophone women, a royal commission demanded by English-speaking women only was politically impossible. The women's movements in Quebec and English Canada operated within the context of "two solitudes," and, although there were channels that connected them, these have not been well documented. Most analyses of events represent either a francophone or an anglophone version (or an anglophone history, with a separate table listing, without any effort of reconciliation, some Quebec data). When the two versions are integrated into one text, recognition goes to the "national" history, and Quebec women seem to disappear from the account.

As far as I can tell, the "second wave" of Canadian feminism in the 1960s developed and organized through two separate entities, which followed two distinct dynamics, within the context of two distinct histories. The Quebec and English-Canadian women's movements did, however, share a similar agenda, and the movements connected later in the decade. This "second wave" corresponded in fact, for both movements, to the evolution of decades of struggles by women's associations for suffrage, social reforms, and equal pay.

The creation of a royal commission was an idea which came, culturally speaking, from English Canada. This can be documented through the archives of several large national women's associations: the Canadian Federation of Business and Professional Women's Clubs, University Women's Clubs, the Zonta Clubs, and the National Council of Women.[5] I also observed, in the course of our royal commission, how much the American presidential Commission on the Status of Women set up by President John Kennedy (the Eleanor Roosevelt Commission, 1961–63) had impressed anglophone colleagues, while, as a relatively young but interested Quebec sociologist, I had never heard of it.[6] What was happening in English Canada was the continuation, possibly with a renewed ardour and surely with new approaches, of a long-standing commitment by women's associations to reforms needed to obtain more simple justice for women, as well as a call for new social adjustments required by the buoyant 1960s. But in their commitment, national associations expressed, in practice, the wishes of women in only nine of the ten provinces, despite the fact that some associations did have one or more francophone branches (in addition to the anglophone ones) in Montreal or Quebec City. This observation also applies to the Voice of Women, despite the fact that Thérèse Casgrain was the president of its Quebec branch, La Voix des Femmes. This pacifist activist (and feminist) women's association, now regarded as the pioneer of the second wave of feminism, probably remained as marginal in Quebec as the New Democratic Party (NDP) with which it was often associated.[7]

In Quebec, women's associations were provincially oriented first. By the time English-Canadian women were requesting, as their common objective, the creation of a royal commission, women in Quebec were already involved in redefining what they wanted changed in their status and in the society around them. The political as well as the intellectual figures of the so-called Quiet Revolution had never associated women and women's concerns and issues to their crusade for accelerated social change. So women in Quebec were doing it their way, at the grass-roots levels of their respective associations, and through a broad provincial consultation launched to define the program and agenda of the future FFQ. (The new FFQ was also innovative in that it was a regrouping of both associations and individuals.) A good case in point is the evolution of one of these so-called traditional associations, the Association féminine d'éducation et d'action sociale (AFEAS), with some thirty-five thousand members, formed in 1966 from the integration of Les Cercles d'économie domestique and L'Union catholique des femmes rurales. Such associations, as well as the FFQ, had already taken action provincially on many fronts. Women seized every platform to demand changes, including the Parent Commission on Education, the centennial celebration of the Quebec Civil Code, and the initiatives in Quebec emanating from the Catholic church's second Vatican Council.

I recall sitting as a volunteer on a committee of the CECM (the Montreal Catholic schoolboard) as far back as 1963, devising retraining courses for married women re-entering the paid labour market. I also recall becoming a member of the Association des femmes diplômées des universités (University Women's Club) in 1964 to participate in the preparation of our brief and recommendations to the Parent Commission, clearly a feminist brief. Women's associations were busy preparing documents and recommendations for changes to family and property law, surrounding the celebration of the centennial of the Quebec Civil Code, in 1966. We had read Simone de Beauvoir's *Le deuxième sexe* (1949) in the late 1950s, and we felt part of history in the making, our history as women, which had its own universe, separate and apart from that of the society around us. When the English-Canadian women invited us to join them, through the newly founded FFQ, we did not have a royal commission in mind as an objective. Instead, we were busy using all the existing mechanisms for change opened to us in Quebec. In feminist solidarity we did, however, give our immediate support to the Committee for the Equality of Women. I wrote the press release, and Réjane Laberge-Colas, our president, along with Thérèse Casgrain, joined the delegation in Ottawa.

What were the channels of communication between the principal social actors involved here? There were no institutional lines of communication; there were, however, individuals who could, for one reason or another, bridge the two cultures on women's issues and concerns. The late Thérèse Casgrain was certainly one of them through her network of La Voix des Femmes/The Voice of Women. Another one was Laura Sabia, whom I had met in Montreal a few times when she was the national president of the University Women's Clubs. Fully bilingual and clearly interested in the new Quebec women's movement, she closely followed the activities of the FFQ. Newsletters of national associations with francophone branches in Quebec also played a limited support role in the same way that, in those years, the Montreal YWCA acted as a leader in integrating francophones, and feminists, to their committees and board. On the federal political scene, English-Canadian women had direct access to both the Honourable Judy LaMarsh and Grace MacInnis, respectively a Liberal cabinet minister and an NDP member of Parliament. But as yet no Quebec woman had been elected to the House of Commons (although we had our own Claire Kirkland-Casgrain in Quebec City, the first woman elected to the National Assembly).[8] So political communications between Quebecers were made through men of influence, whose wives and female family friends were active participants in the FFQ; Marc Lalonde and Pierre Juneau, then respectively special advisor to Prime Minister Pearson and vice-president of the Bureau of Broadcast Governors, were two of them.

Could the government have ignored the request for a royal commission, and if so, what would have happened? As Cerise Morris points out, the then Liberal government was a minority government, with the NDP holding the balance of power.[9] This, plus the culture of the 1960s – the B&B soul-searching, the emerging mobilization around human rights issues – made the decision a logical one in the circumstances, although women as a constituency were simply not part of the political agenda. It is fair to suspect that politicians did not quite understand, nor could they assess exactly what was happening, as is often the case when politicians are confronted with social movements. (The 1985 de- and re-indexation of the federal old age pension is a clear case in point.)[10]

The essential point is that women did not represent, towards the end of the 1960s, a constituency in the political agenda of the Canadian state. This was less true in Quebec, where women had intervened more forcefully into an only too male Quiet Revolution. In the rest of Canada, women's issues were absent from the political agenda, except for the bare minimum symbolized by the "Equal Pay for Equal Work" slogan. This adage suited the logic of the developing "equal rights" political philosophy around which the second wave of feminism coalesced. It was also in keeping with the demographic changes brought about by the ever-increasing re-entry into the paid labour force since 1960 of thousands of married women.

Anything that had to do with "the status of women" was chan-nelled to the Women's Bureau of the federal Department of Labour. First created in 1954 by the indefatigable Marion Royce, it was then directed by Jessica Findlay and Sylva M. Gelber. At the time of the royal commission, the bureau, in matters of public policy, seems to have nurtured itself, apart from the annual briefs and recommen-dations of women's associations such as the B & P (Business and Professional Women's Association), the Zonta Clubs, and the CFUW (Canadian Federation of University Women's Clubs), on the work of the International Labour Office (ILO) in Geneva.[11] The bureau's pub-lished documents are remarkable when studied in today's light.[12] The bureau, however small it was, at least anchored a pragmatic feminist viewpoint in the business of the state.

It is impossible to guess what would have happened if the govern-ment had not moved on the demand for a royal commission. My instinct is that reforms would have had to proceed anyway; in Quebec, they could not be stopped. Many women's associations and many individual women were both mobilized and determined. The more radical women's movement was at the door, and feminism was becoming a world-wide phenomenon as important for civilization as decolonization. By moving relatively rapidly and positively, the gov-ernment avoided the bitter atmosphere of constant confrontation that seems to exist, for example, between American feminists and the federal administration. Cerise Morris has analysed the Canadian government's response in this way:

The new social problem of definition of women's status was produced through the particular interaction of three sets of public participants: the claims-making groups (C.E.W.); the news media; and the federal government of Canada. The government played the role of initially unwilling, then con-vinced respondent in the process ... By deciding to establish the R.C.S.W., the federal government clearly, and at one point in time, accepted and thus legitimized the social problem definition of the status of women. ... the creation of this new social problem definition provided a conceptual frame-work and beginning vocabulary for the development and articulation of feminist analysis and ideology which was to come.[13]

We should also note that because the federal government moved to create the royal commission, some reforms took place relatively quickly and in a spirit of co-operation. As a consequence, some political parties and politicians benefitted in the process, demonstrating to others around them that "the status of women" was a good thing politically. This in turn set in motion an imitative process among the various levels of state activities in Canada, which worked in favour of women.

THE ROYAL COMMISSION

Elsie Gregory MacGill, one of the seven commissioners appointed by the Pearson government, was already a feminist, but, quite rapidly, the remaining four women sitting on the commission (Florence Bird, Lola M. Lange, Jeanne Lapointe, and Doris Ogilvie) became feminists in their own right. This politicization occurred through a process of group education: the reading of essays and existing research material, followed by the shared experience of the public hearings. It is difficult to assess the commitment to feminism of the two male commissioners, but they actively participated in the work of the commission, especially Jacques Henripin, who was a member for the whole duration of the commission (while John P. Humphrey came to it a year after its creation, replacing Donald Gordon Jr, who resigned shortly after his appointment). Some of the younger generation of commission staff were natural "Simone de Beauvoir" feminists, while older colleagues shared a commitment to legal, non-discriminatory reforms.

What were the intellectual foundations of the royal commission's feminism? At its inception, it should be recalled, the readily available modern feminist texts were limited, basically, to de Beauvoir's *The Second Sex* (published in French in 1949 and in English in 1952, but available in Quebec only ten years later, because of the Catholic church's censorship) and Betty Friedan's *The Feminine Mystique* (1963 in English; 1964 in French). Kate Millett's *Sexual Politics* and Germaine Greer's *The Female Eunuch* were respectively published in 1969 and in 1970, when the work of the commission was already completed.

The Canadian women's movement, inspired by the American women's liberation movement, came into being during the existence of the royal commission and could have informed and influenced its work. It did not. The commission did not benefit from discussions generated within the women's movement because we did not know what was going on, except through rare public demonstrations (such as one at the Toronto public hearings). These were often quite radical and difficult to understand from outside the movement and without the help of written manifestos. The radical women's movement started around 1967, this time in English Canada. Feminist historians trace the francophone movement to the women's demonstration of

November 1969 in Montreal over the issue of abortion, when women chained themselves to each other in protest against a new city by-law prohibiting all demonstrations. The police forces, stunned at facing female and not male opponents, retreated in disarray. The radical movement appealed to younger women, often students, who would not normally belong to women's associations.

In the vocabulary of 1980s feminist political thought, the commission would be labelled liberal or reform feminist, in contrast to the radical schools of thought that developed in the early 1970s, following the 1968 student revolutions. The commission did not have an explicit conceptual framework or a shared philosophy, other than its commitment to the "equal rights" approach, which coexisted with general notions of the value of a specifically "female culture." We survived as a group, and produced an almost unanimous report, by keeping to as pragmatic an approach as possible. Listening to what women themselves had to say and reporting their demands appeared, to most members of the commission, senior staff included, as an important process in itself and as the only legitimate course of action. This ideological debate between theory and process did, however, create such strong tensions in the commission that two academics resigned in the first months of operation: David Kirk, director of social science research, who wanted to see a major research program developed, and Donald Gordon, a commissioner.[14]

We were liberal and pragmatic feminists; yet, parts of the report were, and still are, purely utopian in the eyes of the Canadian state, although these sections appeared to the commissioners as plain common sense. I am referring here to two parts of the report, chapter four, "Women and the Family," and chapter five, "Taxation and Child-Care Allowances." One philosophical statement the commission strongly adhered to was that no one was equipped to pass judgment on women's sexual, reproductive, or work-related choices except women themselves. It was for women to decide if they would marry, have children and work in paid employment, or stay at home for a few years when children were below school age, or remain full-time at home, or combine all these elements. "Mothers at home vs mothers at work" (in paid employment) was hotly debated in the media at the time of the royal commission, reflecting the demographic changes then taking place among married women. If there was a single theme that was at centre stage during the period, it was this one.

As a consequence of these and other debates, the commission decided to make sure real choices were developed by society, and offered by the state, so that women could decide individually what was best for them. This meant that neither the recommendations made in the report nor existing government measures would be loaded one way or the other. The report therefore recognized explicitly the role and responsibility of the state vis-à-vis all children and recommended a gender-role neutral approach. The commission wanted to see day-care centres and other child-care programs offered across the country, including homemaker services. In addition, all mothers were to be provided with a taxable cash allowance for each child one hundred times larger than the then $6 per month family allowance. After the tabling of the report, these two sets of measures were discarded without a word by all the parties concerned, even by women, who appeared to be ashamed to ask for that much money on behalf of themselves and their children.

Another set of recommendations dismissed by the state were those concerning abortion (the very day we presented Prime Minister Trudeau with the report, it was obvious to me they would be rejected). It was one of the most difficult issues facing the commission, and we agonized trying to reach a consensus. I co-signed the report and the recommendations making abortion during the first three months of pregnancy the sole decision of the woman, but my real choice would have been to co-sign Elsie Gregory MacGill's minority report, an option I did not have as the executive secretary.[15] (As I said in the House of Commons a few years later, when I was a member of Parliament, abortion should be decriminalized and should be considered "a private medical matter between patient and doctor," quoting Elsie MacGill's minority statement.)[16] In fact, I realized recently that abortion should actually be listed under the Regulations of the *Canada Health Act* as one of the "medical services" deemed essential for any province to qualify for federal funding under the requirements of providing comprehensive health services contained in this legislation.

An important question to ask today is whether a strong feminist analysis of a woman's right over her body as a fundamental principle of physical integrity could have persuaded a significant segment of public opinion towards a pro-choice legislative framework. Had a clear and significant majority developed on this issue, the law might then have been modified during the 1970s. This will remain a hypothetical question. It was clear at the time, however, that although Prime Minister Trudeau recognized that women exercised a primary role in deciding on abortion, he believed that Canadian society was deeply divided on the issue and his 1969 reform was all that could be offered politically.[17]

The report contained weaker as well as stronger recommendations. I was, at the time, particularly sensitive to chapter seven on the

Participation of Women in Public Life. I knew nothing about political parties and electoral campaigns when we were drafting our report, but I could see that our recommendations were simply pious wishes and felt frustrated by our failure to deal thoroughly with the real problems underlying the absence of women from the public sphere.[18] It is now clear to me that we were lacking both a feminist analysis of power and the conceptual tools for such a study. At that time, discussion focused on whether gender was determined by nature or influenced by culture, but we lacked the framework necessary to move beyond this dichotomy. We had not heard of the concept of empowerment. Nor had we heard of the feminist process as an expression of the values shared specifically by women because of their socialization – such as nurturance and caring, service to others and self-abnegation, peace, co-operation, harmony in human relations and in one's environment – values so badly needed as an alternative to the ways power has traditionally been exercised.

Because of the absence of a general theory, the commission remained as close as possible to the women of Canada whose voices we wanted to amplify. This explains, in part, a missing dimension of the report. For example, we paid great attention to what housewives had to say about their plight and frustrations. We acknowledged that what they did was indeed work, unpaid work, which society should recognize. But we failed to offer an analysis of housewives' lack of economic recognition and low status by way of a theoretical development, using concepts such as production/reproduction or private/public sphere. Therefore, it is not surprising that the recommendations regarding housewives' participation in public pension plans and employers' recognition of voluntary work as "real" work experience were never acted upon: the report did not provide the framework for the necessary public debate.

The commission did not even identify violence towards women – physical, sexual, and psychological – as a feminist issue. Brutality, beating, rape, and incest were topics we might not even have heard, had they even been voiced during the public hearings. Of course, we all knew these facts, but they were regarded as social problems, not feminist issues.

I noted earlier that the state perceived chapter four, "Women and the Family," as purely utopian. This chapter proceeded in fact from a generous but gratuitous ideal view of the role of parents and the state vis-à-vis children, a view not grounded in a feminist analysis of marriage and of the family as an institution. Had the commission been able to conduct such a feminist analysis, it would have had to expose relationships of domination, abuse of power, and violence against women, demonstrating the element of coercion over women (and children) so often observed in families. At the writing stage of this chapter, the first domestic women's liberation texts were available and they are quoted in the report.[19] But their new radicalism, advocating "the complete breakdown of the present nuclear family," overshadowed for the commission the critical importance of their diagnosis.[20] If women had to be controlled by coercion, their so-called natural, second-class status was in fact a male social construction, and men's violence a feminist issue.

Underlying the nascent feminist analysis and the theoretical framework was the notion of social change and of the blueprint to achieve it. I have always been interested in theories of social change. It became clear to me during the work of the commission that there was no one integrated approach to engineering orderly social change; all avenues of reform had to be pushed to their limit in a parallel fashion. The commission had to recognize that there are many different expressions of social change. Individuals do not respond to the same dimensions of social change. For some women, and for some commissioners, the primary route and expression of change occurred through legal channels, visible in the amendment of legislation and the making of jurisprudence. For others, economic issues were the only measure of success, and, for still other groups, education and information made the difference. Finally, there were those for whom a change at the symbolic level was the only valid signal of improvement. Although all of this was reflected in our report and recommendations, the focus was on legal and economic changes.

The in-house research and the commissioned studies also expressed history in the making. Women's studies were about to start on the most modest scale in Canadian and American universities, but the expression "feminist scholarship" was unknown.[21] The "classics" at the time were such female academics as Mary Beard, Alice Rossi, Evelyne Sullerot, Alva Myrdal, Marie-José Chombart de Lauwe, Viviane Isambert-Jamati, Andrée Michel, Margaret Mead, or Jessie Bernard. They were not referred to as feminist scholars; they simply were the first to study women as legitimate subjects. Canadian researchers, often young professors, now famous feminist scholars, were given the opportunity by the commission to develop what were to become important feminist critiques and theory through research contracts and publication.[22] For example, Micheline Dumont of the University of Sherbrooke started writing the history of Quebec women for the commission. At that time she developed the now well known, original hypothesis on female religious orders as a channel for women to realize their intellectual and managerial potential through legitimate social roles other than those of marriage and motherhood.

On a lighter note, we rejected numerous esoteric and unsolicited research proposals. I must confess that given the state of the art at the time, we had to rely on common sense, intuition, and judgment more than on clear, objective criteria, when we turned away certain research and researchers. One instance was the now well known and controversial socio-biologist Lionel Tiger, a Canadian from British Columbia, who sought funding for his work on male bonding.[23]

By pragmatism and by belief, we did privilege what women had to say about themselves, their lives, and the society around them. We granted maximum importance to the process – the public's involvement through public hearings, briefs, and recommendations – that distinguishes royal commissions from "expert" studies and research. We immediately set up a team whose job was actively to seek participation from individuals and groups, decoding what had always been, in previous commissions, a rather legalistic process surrounded with an impressive apparatus of protocol and formality. We were the first commission to print a simple little pamphlet explaining our work and how to prepare a brief, listing questions about the status of women. These pamphlets were distributed to women's groups and in shopping centres across the country. We were also the first to hold hearings not only in major downtown hotels but also in church basements, community halls, and, again, shopping malls. The media followed us in all the provinces, amplifying what was being said by women for the general public.

As a young woman discovering Canada through other women, I found the experience of the public hearings – and of the whole commission for that matter – one of the most memorable of my life. What I discovered month after month, week after week, is how universal women's experiences were; this would be a lesson for life. Women in rural areas of Canada, women living and working in cities, native or immigrant women, young students as well as older women, francophone and anglophone women, all said the same things. They spoke of their aspirations and their lack of opportunities, the prejudices and stereotypes, the discrimination and injustice, the need to change marriages and families to attain real and equal partnership. They spoke of the children they cared for. They stressed how the current political, economic, and social structures of Canada were an insult to their dignity as women. What they had to say was most empowering, and it seemed to me that the intrinsic merit of their case was so obvious that society – the state – would have to understand and readjust as soon as the report and its recommendations, demonstrating what needed to be done, were released.

TWENTY YEARS AFTER

Texts still refer to the RCSW as a landmark in Canadian women's history. The fact is that the report, which we saw as an instrument of change for women and for all concerned in society, went through several printings and is still consulted. It has aged rather well. Because of its reformist, moderate approach, rooted in what the women of Canada had told the commission, the report gave credibility to a cause and appealed to a broad base of individual women and women's associations.

A central concern of some members of the commission was to make sure the report would not be shelved in the usual way. Our last chapter and recommendations dealt with structures to be established for future action: an interim immediate process of discussion inside the federal bureaucracy, Human Rights Commissions at all levels of government, and fully autonomous Status of Women Councils, again in all governments. Because the time had come to be concerned about the status of women, and because of the behind-the-scenes work of women civil servants (in senior management and more often in middle management) who espoused the recommendations of the report as rightful demands, the government started moving towards implementation.

A co-ordinator, Freda L. Paltiel, was appointed in the Privy Council Office, together with an interdepartmental committee with five "working parties" (that held over one hundred meetings), which was followed by an equal employment opportunities office in the Public Service Commission. On 7 May 1971, Trudeau appointed Robert Andras, minister of consumer and corporate affairs, to be "minister responsible for the status of women."[24] The interdepartmental committee did not want a distinct Department for Women's Affairs for fear of ghettoization. As a new civil servant (by then, I had started working at the Canadian Radio-Television Commission [CRTC] as assistant research director), I was a member of this committee, and, with others, we had decided that we wanted male ministers to be given the status of women as a responsibility, in addition to their regular portfolio, on a rotation basis. We wanted these men and their bureaucracies to educate themselves, and I recall pleading, at one of the committees, that it was as good a way as any to raise the consciousness of the state. Granted there was no woman in the Liberal caucus and government at the time, but some of us felt strongly that it was men's duty to do some learning and some readjustment.

I was the first woman to be offered ministerial responsibility for the status of women. After two years at the CRTC and a pressing invitation to run for office from the prime minister's office, I joined the Liberal Party and was elected to the House of Commons on 30 October 1972, one of the first three women from Quebec. In September 1976, after four years as a backbencher, Prime Minister Trudeau invited me to join the cabinet as minister for the status of women. I declined his offer, quite indignant that, contrary to the previous incumbents, I would be at a serious disadvantage, with no regular portfolio, no bureaucracy, and no budget, thus being a junior minister, not even second to a senior minister. All of this unfolded at the time the recession was starting, the Badgley report on abortion was imminent (with a cabinet which I knew would not move an iota on the issue), and following the expectations created by International Women's Year.[25] (Later that same day the prime minister called back, and I accepted his invitation to join the cabinet as minister of national revenue.)

During the time that the state was learning how to cope with our report and recommendations, women prepared themselves for new pressures on the government to promote its implementation. Two popular "guides for discussion" were prepared, one by the National Council of Women, the other by the Fédération des Femmes du Québec. Ex-commissioners and staff became speakers for women's associations. Regroupings of women appeared, culminating, especially in English Canada, with the foundation in 1973 of the National Action Committee (NAC), an umbrella group similar to the FFQ.

This is a major difference between Canadian and American women's movements. The very fact that a royal commission of inquiry is about the presentation of briefs by the public and the making of recommendations played a key role in creating and accelerating the process of a feminist evolution in Canadian women's associations. Hence, around 1967 most women's associations became more or less feminist. The political consequences of this are extraordinary and help to explain the powerful role played by NAC in its interaction with the federal government in later years. The young women's liberation movement did the rest with its radical concepts and dramatic demands, shaking public opinion and slowly permeating the collective psyche.

Issues of the status of women in Canada consequently met with a huge public constituency made up of large, grass-roots women's organizations, rural as well as urban, of different religious and ethnic backgrounds, both in Quebec and elsewhere in Canada, a constituency relatively unified through NAC and the FFQ. No politician, federal or provincial, could ignore this new electoral reality. This, more than anything else, accounts for the relative alacrity with which the federal and provincial governments competed to create structures representing women's interests in their bureaucracies. Ottawa created its Advisory Council on the Status of Women on 31 May 1973, followed by Quebec on 6 July 1973. In both cases, women had been requesting these measure since the tabling of the report of the commission three years earlier. Other structures also evolved, such as the Women's Programme in the Department of the Secretary of State.

CONCLUSION

An important contribution to post-commission history is a recent issue of *RFR/DRF*: "Feminist Perspectives on the Canadian State."[26] Its contributors criticize the federal government for having taken a long time to respond to the report of the RCSW.[27] Viewed from the perspective of radical politics, the criticism is not surprising. I myself felt quite frustrated at times that "nothing was happening." But looking at it from a distance, I would submit that, between 1971 and the recession (1976 on), the Canadian state quite rapidly adopted all the simple reforms requested, integrating women's issues in official discourse, and taking action on several fronts that did improve the daily lives of thousands of women in Canada. It did so exceptionally rapidly and smoothly when compared with state action in most industrialized countries, including the United States, with the exception of the Nordic European countries.

What the state failed to do was set in motion the radical changes requiring the transformation of society. At the level of the federal government, the dossiers which best illustrate this are the pay equity issue, the question of a day care program, and abortion. If we take "pay equity" to illustrate the point, all that the federal Liberal government was able to do on the subject, after bitter inside arguments, was to create a one-person royal commission in 1983 – at least keeping the issue alive. Judge Rosalie Abella reported to the new Conservative government of Brian Mulroney on equality in employment in October 1984 and made a series of specific recommendations against all aspects of systemic discrimination in the workplace: salary, seniority, job classification, training and development, special needs, career opportunities, promotion, and affirmative action.[28] Nothing of any consequence has since been discussed or implemented at the national level, and women's pay still lags behind men's salaries by roughly 30 per cent. At the provincial level, only Manitoba, Ontario, and Quebec have initiated modest readjustments in women's salaries. The case of Quebec is particularly interesting because of the trade union movement's recent aggressive – and relatively successful – feminist platform and strategy towards pay equity for "traditional" female jobs in the public sector, well illustrated by the nurses' and teachers' strikes of the fall of 1988. As to the other issues where radical change is needed, everyone knows the saga of the day-care policy (after commissions and committees, and a National Strategy on Child Care [December 1987], the Mulroney government tabled, on 25 July 1988, the Canada Child Care Act, a bill judged quite inadequate by all concerned and which died on the Order Paper just before the 1988 general election) and its sad fate in the 1989 budget of finance minister Michael Wilson, or the unacceptable Bill C-43, subsequently rejected by the Senate, recriminalizing abortion and taking the decision away from the pregnant woman, contrary to the Supreme Court's historic decision on abortion of 28 January 1988.[29]

The state has dismissed any attempt to fundamentally change the market rules or the family arrangements. However, I personally believe that a great number of citizens would welcome such fundamental social changes. As usual, politicians lag behind the voters, thinking, incorrectly, that they know them only too well. There are moments when I would not be surprised if, in today's House of Commons, one heard an honourable member stand up and speak in a manner similar to Mr F.G. Biggs, a Conservative member who represented Pembina (Alberta) in 1971, and who had this to say on Women's Day, three months after the commission had tabled its report to Parliament:

My grandfather was a gentleman and my grandmother did not feel like a slave ... I believe the basic rules still apply. Someone must bring home the bacon, someone must cook the bacon and raise the babies if the human race is to survive ... Women have not changed particularly in one very basic respect. They look for the good hunter, the good man to bring home the bacon. Before we rush in ... I think we should see what we are doing in respect of the male who has full responsibility.[30]

There is no doubt in my mind that the federal government has now deliberately backtracked on the issues of serious concern in the daily lives of women. I realize that dossiers calling for radical socioeconomic changes are difficult for any government, but it is nonetheless true that strategies could have been devised and leadership could have been provided. Instead, grants and programs have been cut or cancelled, ensuring that women's associations have been seriously affected in their work, if not in their very existence, and "the status of women" is now the pariah of both the bureaucrats and the politicians.

3 The Intellectual Origins of the Women's Movements in Canada

JILL VICKERS

Much current scholarship sees the contemporary women's movement as one of "the new social movements" which emerged after the Second World War in the ideological "space" made for them by critiques of the Old Left. This view directs us away from uncovering continuities of thought within a country between generations of women's movements over their century of existence. Canadian observers argued as recently as 1975 that "the current women's 'movement' ... really has no historical connection with the women's suffrage movement at the turn of the century. The two are separated by a half century of inactivity on the part of women."[1] I will reject this interpretation and argue that it is as important to understand the forces of continuity in those movements across time as it is to identify elements of novelty which increase the pace of mobilization and change. This is especially true as we come to understand that women's movements are engaged in projects which are multigenerational in nature.

The intellectual roots of the second wave of the Canadian movements which relate to the Canadian federal state display a high degree of intergenerational continuity.[2] Many ideas about how to practise feminist politics were transmitted to the New Feminists from a generation of Old Feminists with whom they interacted in a number of sites of activity. In particular, the Women's Peace Movement, especially the Voice of Women, and women's caucuses within the Co-operative Commonwealth Federation (CCF) were sites of interaction. The existence of a suffrage movement in Quebec until the mid-1940s also permitted an intergenerational exchange of ideas, which affected the pan-Canadian movement.

The influence of u.s. feminism in this account is more complex. Most of the available scholarship locates the origins of contemporary feminism in the u.s. in the reactions of leftist women against the sexism they found in organizations of the New Left. There is little doubt that u.s. feminist ideas had an impact in Canada. First, because our electronic media (except for radio) are dominated by u.s. sources, the women's movement projected to Canadians was the u.s. movement. Second, the women of the "draft dodger" generation who came to Canada, especially figures like Marlene Dixon, had a considerable initial influence on the formation of groups in the large cities where they located. What is less clear is the character of feminism within the indigenous New Left movement in Canada and its relationship to u.s. feminism. The Waffle Movement, which operated first within and then independently of the New Democratic Party (NDP), illustrates some of the differences.[3]

The anglophone women's movement in Canada inherited a set of ideas about how to do politics which I will label "radical liberalism." It embodied a commitment to the ordinary political process, a belief in the welfare state, a belief in the efficacy of state action in general to remedy injustices, a belief that change is possible, a belief that dialogue is useful and may help promote change, and a belief that service in terms of helping others is a valid contribution to the process of change.[4] Some of these ideas were shared between anglophone and francophone women through much of the 1960s.[5] It is less clear to what degree they remain shared. Some parts of the Native women's movement shared them in the 1960s, but a significant part does not share them now.

This political culture inherited by Canadian feminists of the 1960s significantly affected the development of the movement.[6] It also limited the influence of many of the ideas of the Women's Liberation Movement (WLM) and radical feminists, whose views of the politics of the state, drawn from the u.s. New Left, involved a rejection of the ordinary political process and were anti-statist in character. The commitment of feminists to the welfare state that Canadian women helped to create, and our movements' development of a multipartisan strategy in relation to the official politics of the state, illustrate that radical feminist ideas were of relatively little importance in shaping these aspects of the movement. Nonetheless, radical feminist ideas concerning the project of creating organizations which "bend the iron law of oligarchy" had considerable influence in Canada within feminist groups and in the development of feminist critiques of main-stream political institutions.[7]

In this essay, I will first outline the operational code which has characterized English Canada's second-wave women's movement. Second, I will sketch the ideas of the Women's Liberation Movement and radical feminists. Third, I will explore the ideas of the feminist political culture transmitted to the second wave through such groups as the Voice of Women. In each instance, I will focus on ideas which influenced how individuals and groups interacted with one another politically, their views of the state, and their theories of how change occurs.

THE OPERATIONAL CODE OF CONTEMPORARY WOMEN'S MOVEMENTS

The movements which currently relate to the Canadian and Quebec states are characterized by ideological diversity and a capacity for collaborative action despite such differences. This is manifested in the fact that their central institutions, the National Action Committee on the Status of Women (NAC) and the Fédération des femmes du Québec (FFQ), are umbrella organizations which regroup other organizations of diverse ideology, size, purpose, and operating style in enduring, if fragile, coalitions, primarily for the purpose of interacting with their respective states. I will focus primarily on the federal state, examining developments within Quebec only as they influence the pan-Canadian movement.

Monique Bégin has argued that the revitalization of traditional women's organizations which occurred during the 1960s, in part because of the Royal Commission on the Status of Women, meant that most existing women's associations became to some extent feminist and that New Feminist organizing could build on existing traditions, expertise, and membership.[8] The commission went across the country receiving briefs and presentations and creating grass-roots awareness. Many groups became feminist in purpose but remained traditional in their views of politics and organization.

By the early 1970s, "grass-roots feminism was already articulating a sense of itself as different from institutionalized feminism."[9] Self-defined liberationists claimed the grass-roots label, believing their movement "[differed] greatly from the middle-class women's rights groups which consist mostly of professional and church women."[10] In Canada, this did not prevent co-operation between women and groups from the two aspects. Bonnie Kreps explained to the commission that "Radical feminism is called 'radical' because it is struggling to bring about really fundamental changes in our society."[11] Her description of the women's liberation movement, however, was *inclusive* of other positions including liberal feminism. Describing the women's liberation movement as "a generic term covering a large spectrum of positions," she divided the movement into the three familiar ideological positions (liberal, left, and radical), adding that "all three broad segments have their own validity, all three are important. One belongs in one segment rather than another because of personal affinity with the aims being striven for."[12]

This early example of the Canadian tradition of integrative feminism is more characteristic than an anomaly. In the United States, the very word "feminism" was rigorously reserved for the ideas of young radical/revolutionary women. Many of those women Kreps included, such as liberal feminists, were defined by u.s. women as "traditional" because of their reformism. They were also denied the designation "feminist" because of their acceptance of ordinary political process and structures.[13] But as one u.s. scholar noted with bemusement, quite radical women and groups in Canada were willing to work with quite traditional groups in these formative years, just as they were willing to accept funding from the state for their projects.[14]

The sense of differentiation and the question of whether the old and new generations could work together is nowhere more evident than in accounts of the Strategy for Change Conference at which the National Action Committee on the Status of Women was formed. The assembly of between five hundred and seven hundred women represented groups ranging from the Communist party to the Imperial Order of Daughters of the Empire, from maternal feminist to radical feminist. Laura Sabia, who chaired and was later president, recalls: "The militants kept grabbing the microphones and shouting down the speakers, and the organizing committee didn't know what to do. We were ladies! ... And yet those radical women taught us a lot."[15] What only became fully apparent later was that NAC's umbrella structure, based on the membership of groups, would bring together four major ideological elements in the movement for collaborative action, while also maintaining representation from all of the political parties and both anglophone and francophone groups.

A 1984 survey of delegates to the NAC annual meeting showed a high degree of convergence (67.9 per cent) on most key feminist beliefs and issues and a high degree of intergenerational agreement.[16] The variance of 32.1 per cent was revealed by factor analysis to be composed of four distinct ideological forces, as indicated in table 1.

Table 1
Ideological Characteristics of the Anglophone NAC Delegate: Summer, 1984 Annual
General Meeting

Factor	Factor 2	Factor 3	Factor 4
10.2%	9.0%	7.2%	5.7%
Strong Feminist	Traditional	Economic	Liberal/Reform
Force	Force	Force	Force

Source: Appelle, MA Thesis, 1987:78–100; see note 15.

In 1984, NAC had 458 member groups, 70 of which were pan-Canadian organizations. Its evolution over the decades since its founding has involved the grafting of a grass-roots onto an original coalition of revitalized traditional groups. As Joan Richardson observed in her study of the 1970s anglophone movement in Montreal, the shared values about the political system "meant that there was not an unbridgeable gulf between women's rights and radical feminist organizations, such as there is in the United States." She also noted "an absence of the terrific fear and antagonism which characterized u.s. feminist activity in the 1960's and 70's" and the futility of applying the mutually exclusive categories characteristic of the u.s.[17]

What then are the ideas which made up the operational code of "second-wave" feminism in Canada? First, we can identify a belief in dialogue and a willingness to engage in debate, not just to try to dissolve differences but to understand those that are not dissolvable. Roberta Hamilton and Michele Barrett put it this way: "Canadians talk to each other – indeed shout at each other – across barriers of theory, analysis and politics that in Britain, for example, would long since have created an angry truce of silent pluralism." They argue that Canadian feminists "write from within a political culture built on the recognition rather than the denial of division and differences between people." Hamilton and Barrett conclude that "In Canada, this task [of apprehending diversity without becoming totally distracted by it] has been undertaken with greater solidarity and less suspicion between activists and intellectuals, academics and reformers than has been the case in Britain or the United States."[18]

A willingness to engage in dialogue is central to the ideas of radical liberalism inherited from the Old Feminists. The necessities of Canadian life also created practices supportive of exchange. For example, anglophone and francophone feminists maintained interchanges in the 1970s through a process of elite interaction, which is a familiar characteristic of Canadian politics. The next decade and a half saw some rupturing of that tradition as feminism in Quebec became intertwined with Quebec nationalism which increasingly aimed at autonomy and sovereignty. Nonetheless, a belief in debate and a commitment to engage in dialogue persisted in the creation of new organizations committed to bilingualism, such as the Canadian Research Institute for the Advancement of Women (CRIAW) in 1975. And, despite periods of withdrawal, FFQ's maintenance of symbolic involvement in NAC kept some lines of communication open. Split loyalties are well understood in feminist politics in Canada. As Hamilton and Barrett note, "A belief in undivided sisterhood was never very marketable in Canada," so the value placed on understanding and accommodating some if not all differences has always been considerable.[19]

The belief that "explaining will help" is also a feature of radical liberalism. Lynn McDonald, sometime president of NAC and more recently a New Democratic Party member of parliament (MP), saw it (negatively) involving "a commitment to the ordinary political process, public education and persuasion of politicians and parties within the system, conversely avoidance of partisan politics and radical political theory."[20] This bond to the ordinary political process is by no means a universal or eternal verity within the contemporary movement. Experience with right-wing governments in British Columbia, for example, has lessened this commitment and made Vancouver feminist groups much more anti-system than many of their eastern counterparts.[21] Moreover, the stance McDonald describes is less a matter of being anti-partisan than of being multipartisan. Since its founding, NAC has contained representatives from the three parliamentary parties and the Communist Party. NAC's choices for president have included a prominent Conservative (Laura Sabia), New Democrats (Lynn McDonald, Grace Hartman) and Liberals (Doris Anderson, Chaviva Hošek).

Another part of the operational code of the second-wave movement is the belief that change is possible and that state action is an acceptable way of achieving it. Caroline Andrew argues that Canadian women's organizations played a significant and active role in the creation of our welfare state.[22] We may have a greater sense of efficacy vis-à-vis the state as a result. But Canadians in general are more likely to view our state as a benign utility engaged in worthy redistributive efforts and necessary regulatory tasks. While neo-liberal debates about welfare state reform are under way in Canada, few feminists would seriously question the view that "the state is turning out to be the main recourse of women."[23]

Generally, then, most Canadian feminists perceive the state more as a provider of services, including the service of regulation, than as a reinforcer of patriarchal norms, and most seem to believe that services, whether child care or medicare, will help.[24] Certainly, most Canadian feminists believe that "helping others is a valid contribution which has intrinsic value."[25] This attitude towards the state, therefore, probably best explains the willingness of many women's groups, however apparently radical, to receive state funding.

The radical liberalism I have formulated as the operational code of the second-wave movement is balanced by a counterforce operating in some grass-roots groups and unions still influenced by the goals of participatory democracy of the New Left. Nonetheless, these counterforce elements are very different from their antecedents in that few are revolutionary in their goals, usually rejecting total isolation from the politics of the state and also rejecting the use of force. They work with a realization that "Feminists who act only as critics of the system, and create too much distance from social institutions, run the risk of being unable to reach and activate people."[26] There is also dissent concerning the orientation of umbrella groups like NAC. Almost on a regular cycle, women espousing an ideology of egalitarianism, anti-hierarchy, anti-leadership, and the ideals of participatory democracy demand a reorienting of the organization's purposes.[27]

The picture, then, is of an operational code which generally supports involvement in the ordinary political process, tolerance of ideological diversity, encouragement of dialogue and a service commitment, but with a strong strain of dissent "from the grass-roots." This dissent manifests itself most often in terms of approach or emphasis. As Nancy Adamson and her colleagues suggest, most women in the movement believe it must try to tread a path between the extremes of marginalization and co-option.[28]

THE IDEAS OF THE WOMEN'S LIBERATION MOVEMENT AND RADICAL FEMINISM: OR IN WHAT WAYS WAS RADICAL FEMINISM RADICAL?

Radical feminism is an important if little understood influence in Canada. The Clio Collective, for example, argues that "the radical-feminist message injected new energy into liberal feminism which had existed in Quebec for more than seventy years."[29] They trace the process whereby the "operations central" of the women's movement in Quebec, the FFQ, gradually became more radical as its member groups examined the oppression of women as a sex. In Quebec, Kate Millett, Shulamith Firestone, and Germaine Greer (all translated into French in 1971 or 1972) had an impact. These were also the major sources in English Canada along with Simone de Beauvoir (translated into English in 1952). Their books popularized ideas which were radical in two ways. They argued that sex oppression was first and primary and that all other oppressions sprang from it. Furthermore, they argued that all of the institutions in our society are permeated by and perpetuate male dominance; together they constitute a patriarchy. While much of the radical influence involved re-energizing existing institutions and traditions, the focus on personal and sexual relationships was crucial to the mobilization of young women. Beyond these general influences the picture is more complex.

Kreps's concept of the Women's Liberation Movement as "a generic term covering a broad spectrum of positions" obviously made sense to her in Toronto in the early 1970s. It was not acceptable, however, to Marlene Dixon, who moved to Montreal to teach sociology at McGill after her contract was not renewed by the University of Chicago, purportedly because of her feminist activities. To Dixon, as for Kreps, the Women's Liberation Movement was to be an autonomous movement. But to Dixon, there was no place in it for liberal or traditional feminists. She saw it as emerging out of the struggle within and against the sexism in organizations of the New Left, specifically Students for a Democratic Society (SDS) and the Student Non-Violent Co-Ordinating Committee (SNCC).[30]

Dixon identifies three early Women's Liberation Movement tendencies – the socialists, the consciousness-raising groups, and the WITCH group "with its wild and poetic imagery of Kings, Fairies, Witches and Powers [which] involved a litany of oppression and rebellion" – and which clearly prefigured contemporary cultural feminism. To confuse us further, the socialists in Dixon's account were also called radicals. She notes that at the 1965 Chicago conference, the basic division between women was "usually referred to as 'consciousness raising' vs 'radical' or 'bourgeois vs revolutionary.'"[31] Dixon harshly judged the socialists of pre-1970 radical groups for refusing to demand theoretical and organizational autonomy. Despite her description of the consciousness-raising women as "bourgeois," the borrowed "speak bitterness" techniques of Maoist practice formed the basis for the consciousness-raising.[32]

By 1969 Marlene Dixon was in Montreal acting as the prime mover in a group called WAM, the Women's Action Movement. It promoted rapid polarization within the emerging Women's Liberation Movement in Montreal and soon splintered, leaving considerable disagreement whether "the splinter" was made up largely of Young Socialists or of counterculture women, as consciousness-raising or radical feminist women were also called.[33] There is also discord over the causes of the splintering. Nancy Sullivan attributes it to a conflict over the question of a pro-independence stand for Quebec, but no Women's Liberation Movement group took an explicit stand on the crucial issue of Quebec independence.

Accounts of Toronto groups also describe the process of splintering.[34] Few explicit formative ideas characterized the Women's Liberation Group (WLG) founded in 1969. Its members were all women, although male leftists were involved as sympathizers. All had a preference for communal living and wished to avoid structure in the group's character. A second group, the New Feminists, broke away apparently because of the WLG's political orientation and its lack of structure.[35] Much more organized, the New Feminists were all female, and were required to adhere to a radical anti-male, anti-political constitution and to undergo a rigorous six-month indoctrination program. Internal conflict resulted in a mass exodus, at least in part because of the co-ordinating committee's anti-male and anti-lesbian dictates.[36] Small groups of women in various cities moved through this process of splintering and resplintering. Many went on to develop service collectives, caucuses within mainstream organizations, such as the YWCA (Montreal) and the NDP (Toronto), and single-issue campaign groups.[37]

By 1975 Marlene Dixon saw the conflict within the Women's Liberation Movement as one between the "so-called feminists" and "politicos." She identified a joining of forces in the U.S. between the liberal feminists (National Organization of Women) and radical feminists espousing an ideology which she describes as "reactionary feminism" because of its explicit "men are the enemy" premise. Seeing "reactionary feminism" as "an ideology of vengeance," she argues that "with the virtual expulsion of the left leadership, the 'radical feminists' assumed leadership over the portion of the movement not yet co-opted into the reformist wing." Finally, Dixon repudiated the methodology of consciousness-raising which she had taken in her missionary kitbag to Montreal, arguing that "the error ... was to substitute understanding psychological oppression for political education."[38] Seeing consciousness-raising used purely as a method of individualist self-realization (which of course made it attractive to white, middle-class American women who were not "objectively oppressed" except by men), Dixon rejects the program radical feminists constructed using it, especially "man-hating,

Lesbian Vanguardism, reactionary separatism, [and] virulent anti-communism."[39] Finally, in this article, Dixon announced that she had become a Marxist-Leninist.

Radical feminism was formed out of the conflicts within the u.s. New Left Movement. And because the u.s. was a vibrant imperial power, the universalizing doctrines of radical feminism spread quickly to other countries. The Left in Canada – Old and New – was different, however, because the Canadian state was different, because of the atypical history of the Left in Quebec, and because Canada was not at the centre of a vast and powerful empire at war in Vietnam. But the u.s. New Left shaped the ideas we now call radical feminism, and in that movement can be found the origins of the ideas which are so different from the radical liberalism outlined earlier.

The largely white u.s. New Left developed an indigenous radical discourse influenced by C. Wright Mills and Thorstein Veblen rather than by Marx. The civil rights movement unleashed an unprecedented quest for equality but increasingly excluded the young mobilized whites. Turning to the left, they sought a made-in-usa leftism from which they would not be excluded by the ideology of class: "It was not the cold war alone which had brought this about. It was a passion for a fundamental break with the radical past, with the sectarian debates, foreign subcultures and sterile programs."[40] The u.s. baby-boom generation wanted a radically new movement, and "the new movement was determined to resist the examples of its elders ... sds was the first organized expression of the postscarcity generation's new nationalism."[41] The theme of participatory democracy in which individuals would have control over their own lives was central to this innovative movement. The Old Left in the u.s. had been pro-statist, emphasizing only disciplined action for the individual. The New Left was fiercely anti-statist and radically individualist.

Two countercultures in the New Left in the 1960s successively influenced u.s. feminism. First, there was the political subculture, "those engaged in the politics of direct democracy, who organized traditional constituencies in new ways." This position parallels that of the Waffle in Canada. Then there were the cultural radicals who believed that "the struggle within the state and its institutions [was] hopeless and beside the point." They wanted freedom from the state and from social institutions, reflecting the trend in u.s. thought which sees liberty as the freedom of the individual from restraints. This libertarianism, which espouses an absolute sovereignty for individuals, merged with a Maoist theory of liberation and with other radical analyses that found nothing worthy of reform. Tom Hayden in the SDS "challenged politics itself as a form of domination infinitely more oppressive than economic exploitation." The goal of direct or participatory democracy was based on the belief that the power of the sovereign individual had "been systematically undercut by representative government, trade union bureaucracies and large, impersonal institutions."[42] These tendencies were absorbed by what we now know as radical feminism, initially in its politically engaged form, but far more profoundly in its politically disengaged version now described as cultural feminism.[43]

The u.s. Women's Liberation Movement reacted against the sexism of New Left men who exploited the sexuality and the labour of female members, denied them leadership roles, and denied status to their grievances. It eventually emerged as an independent movement but continued to share many of the ideas of the New Left, including the views of the cultural radicals. Certainly in terms of basic ideas about politics of the state, the Women's Liberation Movement groups shared more with the New Left than they discarded.

In the United States in the 1960s the project of improving women's rights through state action was under way with organizations like the National Organization of Women. The new feminism, by contrast, saw itself as reconstituting woman in a discourse of oppression and liberation. Largely white New Left women retained the sense of being oppressed by all of the large, impersonal institutions of u.s. society, as well as by men, as they struggled to define the sisterhood of oppressed women as a category which included them because of their sex. Many ideas about the nature of oppression and liberation were "in the air." Women's Liberation Movement women, like New Left men, borrowed freely. The process of consciousness-raising, adopted from Maoism, was the central method for women to uncover their oppression by speaking of their experiences. But it did not provide an analytic framework for theorizing about the nature of oppression. Most early radical feminists simply "adopted certain Marxist ideas and applied them to male-female relations." Maoism, however, "was instrumental in shaping radical feminist ideas about power and oppression."[44] Institutions were seen as "mere tools" of male dominance. The opposition to hierarchy in WLM groups was derived as much from experience as from theory, although it probably reflected Maoism filtered through the experiences of the French New Left.[45]

The New Left movement's theory of change assumed that it primarily involved alterations in the consciousness of individuals. The popular New Left notion of "the great refusal" – "Suppose they gave a war and nobody came?" – shows both the character and the short time-span that change was thought to take. Some groups in Montreal shared these views: "All value accrued to the individual. The transformation sought was that of the individual, not of the community, or of the society."[46] This put an enormous premium on the achievement of solidarity among women and left only the ideas of false consciousness or collaboration to explain women whose views differed.

Jo Freeman has argued that the frequent splintering and rapid formation of new groups created "a good deal of consciousness and very little concerted action."[47] But if a change in consciousness was the desired "product," then we must count the groups as highly successful. Certainly the fear of conflict often identified with old feminism was washed away to be replaced by a fear of women with different views who could only be accounted for by being viewed as collaborators, suffering from false consciousness or acting in bad faith. In short, because oppression was understood largely as the product of socialization, change was understood as a series of individual struggles to free the self from a captured consciousness. The enormous energy that was generated re-energized liberal feminism in both the U.S. and Canada and re-energized socialist feminism in Canada as well.[48] It did not allow structures to evolve, however, which could sustain over time something recognizable as the WLM.

The process of retreat from a politically engaged stance began as the New Left concluded that a spontaneous revolution in America was neither inevitable nor imminent; that is, when the realities of a political conception of change struck home. One feminist "revolutionary" said in 1971: "Long-term action is required … Most of us who have been in the movement *for more than two years* realized recently that we have to work for about ten or twenty years. You have to learn to live with that. It's scaring a lot of people."[49] M.L. Carden asserts that the cognitive restructuring which occurs as a result of consciousness-raising is like that involved in a conversion process. Women possessing a new world view with no corresponding new world on the horizon could not easily go back to a compromised life. Rather they became determined to create at least a fragment of a new world in which their consciousness would fit. The key was to create a feminist community within a patriarchal society and an imperialist state. The familiar areas of feminist health care, services, creativity, and scholarship emerged as part of that process of "Living Our Visions" in the here and now.[50] Simply living in a liberated way came to be understood as contributing to a feminist revolution, now seen both as the longest revolution but also as something which cannot be actively planned. This cultural feminism, which celebrates

Table 2
Operational Codes Compared

The Political Culture of English Canadian Radical Liberalism	The Political Culture of u.s. Radical Feminism
A commitment to the ordinary political process	A rejection of the ordinary political process/rejection of politics in favour of changes in consciousness
Pro-statism, a belief in the efficacy of state actions, especially of the welfare state	Anti-statism, a belief in the absolute sovereignty of the individual vs. the state and institutions
Pro-active, believing that change is possible	Briefly pro-active; mainly politically quietist, believing change needed to be total and of individual consciousness
Dialogue with those who differ may be useful	Dialogue with those who differ is not useful – splinter or separate
Helping, others, in terms of service, is a valid contribution to change	Assisting others in relation to self-help and aiding the victims of male violence is useful

the differences in the fragment women have created, involves a political quietism completely consistent with the cultural radicalism of the New Left and understandable for women facing the enormous power of the u.s. imperial state.

To summarize, the political culture of u.s. radical feminism was based on a radical alienation from the institutions of u.s. government and society and the belief that only total change would achieve the goal of the absolute sovereignty of the individual living in a harmonious community. While some believed in the efficacy of political action, many radical feminists thought that such action was futile. Rejecting reform and "normal" politics, they directed activity to consciousness-raising, "grass-roots" action, and the building of a counterculture. If we compare this orientation with the political culture inherited by the English Canadian movement, we find a striking "lack of fit," as illustrated in table 2.

The final aspect of these operational codes that we need to explore involves the ideas of how political processes ought to occur within feminist groups. Radical feminists were not alone in rejecting the hierarchy, leadership elitism, and procedural manipulations which characterized the politics of New Left and Old Left groups alike. The dream of an authentic politics within small homogeneous groups kept alive norms of participatory democracy. Since the purpose of consciousness-raising groups was each women's discovery of herself as a woman through a change of consciousness, voting and majority rule were seen as alien structures. In rule-by-consensus (decision-making without voting), "the goal is to achieve a decision that everyone in the group can live with, even though it may not be everyone's first choice." Clearly, such harmony is desirable in an affinity group. As Donna Hawhurst and Sue Morrow further explain, "the major advantage of consensus over majority vote is that no one becomes committed by the others to a decision she cannot live with comfortably."[51] What is less clear is the value of the consensus process in instrumental groups. The principle of absolute individual sovereignty, however, is seen as crucial to solidarity where groups are unable to survive conflicts. Also linked to these ideas of feminist process was a rejection of formal leadership and of bureaucracy (meaning paid staff).

These ideas about political processes *internal* to feminist groups have a saliency which continues to have significant influence in Canadian and American feminist politics. While radical feminist ideas about politics in general, derived from the u.s. context, had relatively little impact on the pan-Canadian movement, radical feminist ideas about political process within feminist groups have been the challenge to which other strains of feminism have had to respond.[52]

CANADIAN INFLUENCES ON CANADIAN FEMINISM

Why were English-Canadian women less influenced by the general ideas about politics represented by u.s. radical feminism? While I believe the answer is complex and still not entirely clear, I have argued that the transmission of the political culture of radical liberalism from the old generations of feminists to their daughters and granddaughters in the 1960s forms an important part of the explanation. I will look at several of the sites of activity where intergenerational communication about feminism took place. The first is the Women's Peace Movement and especially the Voice of Women. The second is that of indigenous leftist or socialist feminism, which operated at least from the 1920s in women's caucuses of the ccf, culminating in the women's caucuses of the Waffle formed in the ndp in 1969.[53] The third locale of activity was Quebec, where the long suffrage fight and the Quiet Revolution involved interactions among cohorts of feminists who shaped the contemporary Quebec movement and altered the basis of possible co-operation between the anglophone and francophone movements.

In Canada integrative (or liberal) feminism and transformative (radical and socialist) feminisms exist as much as tendencies within individuals and groups as they do as separate wings or organizational strains. The individual Canadian consciousness is most often the site where our conflicts between individualism and community are played out. But it also is played out in social movements. Radical feminism, with its commitment to the absolute sovereignty of the individual, has been seen by some as an alien or even imperialist force with its convenient notions of global sisterhood. Some U.S. women who moved north found Canadian women frustratingly different and, they assumed, far less radical. Canadian women's visions of what is radical, however, had been influenced by other forces.

The Women's Peace Movement and The Voice of Women

The 1950s and early 1960s were active years for Canadian women, despite the relative success of the media in luring wartime working women back into their homes. The concern which motivated old feminists to resume activity and which mobilized young new feminists was the fear of nuclear war. In 1950, on International Women's Day, women's organizations, unions and ethnic groups joined together to form a national women's organization – the Congress of Canadian Women. Mrs Rae Luckock, one of the first two woman legislators in Ontario, was elected president, and the congress passed a Charter of Rights for Canadian Women. The charter's feminism was clear: "We women of Canada assert that all human rights are women's rights." The charter's leftism was also clear-cut with its "Right to livelihood, equal pay, opportunities, seniority rights, no discrimination for marital status." Reproductive issues were conceptualized as "the Right to Motherhood unhampered by lack of economic security, lack of hospital care and shelter, nurseries, hot meals."[54] And a central part of the charter was "the Right to Peace." Canadian Women for Peace Action was a founding member of the congress.

The very week the congress was founded, Ontario passed the first equal pay legislation in Canada. In 1954, a group of influential women's groups including the YWCA, the National Council of Women, the National Federation of Business and Professional Women, and the Federation of University Women lobbied successfully for the establishment of a Women's Bureau in the federal Department of Labour.[55] And, throughout the 1950s, local groups like the Women Electors of Toronto undertook educative and political campaigns.[56] The main arena in which old and new feminists interacted was in the Voice of

Women (VOW), founded in Toronto in 1960 and "dedicated to crusading against the possibility of nuclear war." Appealing directly to women, VOW presented a more "respectable" image than some of the earlier anti-war groups. Its leaders were described as "prominent" or as "wife of the well-known."[57] This aura of respectability won the VOW access to decision-makers. Many of its members were also highly respected for feminist work. Thérèse Casgrain, who led the suffrage fight in Quebec, founded the VOW's Quebec chapter and led a four hundred-member delegation to Ottawa in 1961. Casgrain, a founder of the Fédération des femmes du Québec in 1966 and a key figure of continuity between the old and the new feminists, believed that "the women's liberation movement is not only feminist in inspiration, it is also humanist ... The challenge which we, both men and women, must meet is that of living for a peaceful revolution."[58]

Casgrain's interaction with her anglophone colleagues did much to establish in the VOW a dream of creating a bilingual and bicultural organization in which women of both language groups could feel at home. Two VOW members, Solange Chaput-Rolland and Gwethalyn Graham, while on a Peace Train, began a dialogue on French-English relations which resulted in their book *Dear Enemy*, which explored difference in a uniquely Canadian way. Certainly, without these and other relationships within VOW, the co-operation between anglophone and francophone feminists in campaigning for the Royal Commission and establishing NAC would not have been possible.

The activities of the VOW overlapped and interacted with those of the Women's Liberation Movement. But the VOW became increasingly nationalist and critical of U.S. policies in areas that went far beyond the conflict in Vietnam.[59] The VOW, eager for made-in-Canada defence and foreign policies, saw national independence as the key to Canada's role in achieving peace. Many VOW families gave shelter and support to "draft dodgers" and their partners, but the relationship was not always easy. Kay Macpherson and Meg Sears described the conference organized in 1971 to support Indochinese women as especially difficult: "Canadian women, almost swamped by the avalanche of 'American imperialism of the left' as it seemed, felt a new awareness of the need to establish their own national identity, while still acknowledging their bond with women everywhere."[60] Muriel Duckworth describes the role of VOW in bringing together U.S. Black women and Indochinese women at the Vancouver Conference: "These [U.S. Black] women were claiming the Vietnamese women as their sisters and we white women had to accept the social bond they felt."[61] Duckworth's Halifax chapter of VOW was very active in addressing the issues of the oppression of Nova Scotia's indigenous Black community, which dates back to the seventeenth century.

In terms of the transmission of values, the VOW was a crucial link between generations of feminists. Its members "made the discovery that they could be agents of change in the world and this changed them."[62] They were also learning to become agents of change on their own behalf as women and not just on behalf of others. From 1961 the VOW was actively engaged in the campaign to legalize birth control and, in 1970, when the new feminist Abortion Caravan from Vancouver to Toronto imitated the technique of the VOW Peace Train, many old "Voicers" lent support.

The contemporary women's movements in both Canadas benefited from having had access to a bridging generation. In Quebec, the lateness of suffrage meant that women like Casgrain were available. In English Canada, where suffrage arrived early, the first-wave generation was gone, but the VOW generation effectively transmitted the values learned by the first wave. As I will show, however, the existence of socialist feminism in the Anglo-Canadian left provided intergenerational continuity and the transmission of experience from Old Left feminists to indigenous New Left feminists.

Left Feminism in English Canada

Canada has displayed movements and parties of the Left different from those in Europe or the U.S. The institutionalized left involved both a Communist Party and a social democratic/socialist CCF/NDP (Co-operative Commonwealth Federation/New Democratic Party). The latter was as much influenced by the social gospel and Christian socialism as it was by rationalist Fabianism or determinist Marxism. And, while it shared little with the hyphenated socialist-feminists of the last two decades, there was also a strong indigenous tradition of feminists who were also socialists in the decades prior to the 1960s. Joan Sangster, Linda Kealey, and others have explored in detail the history of this involvement.[63] In this discussion, I will simply touch on two moments in which the forces of continuity between generations of feminists in Canada can also be seen.

In the English-Canadian world view, God is invoked as frequently by the Left as by the Right. For many Canadian feminists motivated by first-wave ideas of service, this social gospel tradition meant that involvement in left-wing causes was a respectable outlet for concern. The intense anti-communism of the CCF/NDP, however, made it deeply suspicious of semi-autonomous groups, including what we would now call women's caucuses. Two such groups were the Toronto CCF Women's Joint Committee of the late 1930s and the Waffle of the late 1960s.

John Manley's account of CCF women's efforts to create an autonomous but allied organization effectively demonstrates the conflict which existed between traditionalists and feminists within the non-communist left. Elizabeth Morton of the Women's Guild of the Amalgamated Carpenters of Canada believed that "a thinking woman ... is a dangerous thing to the ruling class."[64] Her position and that of colleagues Rose Henderson and Jean Laing was strongly in contrast to the ideas of Winnipeg's Beatrice Brigden, a traditionalist who believed that "the CCF ... is firmly anchored to the most important social and economic institution, the home and the family." The Toronto CCF Women's Joint Committee (WJC) lasted as an autonomous women's organization for only a few months in 1936 because of the CCF's almost paranoid worry that any separate structure was a portal through which communists would enter to delegitimize its status as indigenous, non-Marxist, and peaceful. Those women involved in both socialist and feminist causes throughout the decade – Laing, for example – resisted attempts by the communist-led Industrial Union of Needle Trades Workers to take control in the 1934 Eaton's strike. In other cases, however, she was willing to join coalition groups led by the Communist Party, as in the case of the Toronto Unemployed Single Women's Association. The WJC attempted to mobilize women and to increase their skills and confidence through a women-centred group. Rose Henderson, like Virginia Woolf, explicitly associated fascism with anti-feminism, linking developments in Europe with her estimates of three million European and a hundred thousand North American women burnt at the stake as witches. The WJC's increasing interest in the East York Parents' Clinic, established in 1936 to provide birth control, was reported in Elizabeth Morton's statement to a WJC meeting as "well received by the women, but not ... by the men"[65]

Clearly, these women accepted the value of local, direct action and coalitions to attain feminist goals and of voicing explicitly feminist analysis. The intense commitment of the CCF to democracy and anti-communism led its leaders to emphasize electoral methods almost exclusively. The first woman MP, Agnes McPhail, for example, stated that "we believe that, in the democratic form of government we have in Canada, the ballot is the only weapon we need to bring about [the] transformation we have in mind."[66] The WJC women did not share her view, but, when push came to shove and the party commanded, the experiment in an autonomous women's group succumbed to the basic belief in the ordinary political process. Laing, Henderson, and Morton were expelled with others because of their involvement in coalition groups other than wjc. The remaining members vigorously defended their departed leaders. Eventually, the Provincial Council allowed them to return, but by then the wjc had folded.

This 1930s drama prefigures the events surrounding women and Waffle women in the NDP in the 1960s. The continuity is important because on the surface the Waffle's "Women's Lib" looks like a u.s. import. The post-war renewal of the Left in Canada was focused primarily in the Waffle group that developed within the NDP in the late 1960s. Its adherents rejected the New Left label, seeing the New Left as u.s. imperialism of the Left.[67] Basically, it challenged the party's long-standing view that socialism could be attained exclusively through parliamentary and electoral activity. A 1969 statement of the Kingston NDP, titled "Extra-Parliamentary Activity," began: "BE IT RESOLVED that it has become clear to Socialists that the traditional social democratic belief that a capitalist society could be transformed into a socialist society solely by legislative enactments after the achievement of parliamentary power is invalid."[68] In this resolution, the weakness of Liberal Pierre Trudeau's concept of participatory democracy was outlined and "a strategy of building community socialism" endorsed. This included three priorities – labour organizing, neighbourhood organizing, and research work on the nature of Canadian society. The absence of any reference to women's issues and the centrality of nationalism to the Waffle initiatives are striking. The September-October 1969 issue of the *New Democrat* also focused on the topic of Canadianizing unions, in which the "Americanized" nature of two-thirds of Canada's labour movement was deplored along with its effect of fragmenting the Canadian movement. The "Watkins Manifesto" in the same issue was headlined "Socialists are the only ones left to fight American colonialism".[69]

A panel titled "Women's Liberation" appeared on the agenda for the National Waffle Conference in 1970.[70] In the resolutions booklet, entitled "For a Socialist Ontario in an Independent Socialist Canada," prepared for the 1970 Ontario NDP Convention, there is a section titled "The Liberation of Women." It asserts that "the oppression of women can only be overcome through women working together" and "that the liberation of women must be a vital part of the struggle for socialism in Canada." Twenty-four detailed resolutions called for state and party action on reproductive rights, education, child custody, sexist stereotypes in advertising, day-care, part-time work, and maternity leave, and called for the government to "pay a houseworker's allowance to the man or woman who performs household duties while his or her spouse is working outside the home."[71]

Desmond Morton, a University of Toronto historian, put the case for the party mainstream in his critique of what he called the Waffle's "Bonnie and Clyde Style of Socialism" in an address to the Steel-workers Political Conference in 1971: "The paradox of the Waffle is that, under the guise of a strident nationalism, the group is almost totally ignorant of the roots of the Canadian left, its traditions and its circumstances." He continued: "In the name of Canadian inde-pendence, the Waffle has turned out to be the most massive Ameri-canizing force in the history of our movement, working flat out to impose the language and the tactics which have left American socialism a shattered, almost wholly irrelevant force." Morton con-cludes: "There is hardly a single, solitary Waffle idea *from Women's Lib* to the slogans about Yankee imperialism, which have not been imported holus bolus from the United States."[72]

Morton's assertion that the Waffle version of "Women's Lib" is purely a u.s. import requires scrutiny. Although the language of oppression and liberation in the statement's preamble reflects u.s. Maoist-influenced anal₋ ₊s, the pro-statist demands of the resolutions look to welfare-state provision of services for women. The demands for reforms in trade unions, parties, and other institutions were also consistent with Canadian socialist feminist traditions. The Saskatch-ewan/Manitoba Waffle Resolutions on Women do not bear even the language of oppression/liberation. Rather they addressed "the problem of women," while demanding reproductive rights, an end to sex stereotyping, access to education, and child care. Further, strong demands on the party itself for the equitable participation of women and for child care at NDP functions were included.[73]

The party's position on "the problem of women" was presented in the *New Democrat* by the Women's Policy Review Sub-Committee (the predecessor to the current Participation of Women Committee [POW]). The committee included future Canadian Labour Congress president Shirley Carr, Waffler Krista Maeots, Kay Sigurjonsson, and Michele Landsberg. This Special Report on Women's Policy argued that an NDP policy "must go beyond feminist platforms" in two respects. First, "it will concentrate on improving the position of women less in relation to men than in relation to society as a whole." Second, "it will not concern itself directly with the validity of traditional sex roles or try to interfere with any of the delicate mechanisms of strength and weakness in personal relationships ... For those who need assis-tance to escape from roles they find inhibiting or crippling, the NDP must propose enabling legislation."[74] Equity "on the job," child care, and non-sexist education were the three areas stressed in the special report. At the 1971 Federal Convention, an NDP Women's Liberation Caucus appeared and focused demands on parity for women within the NDP. "Women's Lib people," both Waffle and non-Waffle side by side, fought a reaction against such structural changes.[75]

Waffle women went through a process of reaction against the chauvinism of their New Left male colleagues and honed their consciousness as feminists in the process. The Waffle, however, responded positively, providing an arena for the development of an analysis and programs which integrated socialism and feminism in a new way. Most Waffle men joined their womenfolk in exploring internal structural change. The operational code of these women, with their acceptance of the state, the party, and the ordinary political process, was similar to that of their predecessors in the CCF who also believed in extra-parliamentary action. By the mid-1970s some of the women involved had left the party with their Waffle menfolk. Some, like Jean Burgess, worked with the continuing Waffle organization. Burgess, whose statement "Power is not Electoral" appeared in 1974, saw the Saskatchewan Waffle as "a Marxist socialist organization" rejecting violence but "committed to extra-parliamentary work as the key to both feminist and socialist change."[76] Women who remained within the NDP joined with vow "old feminists," such as Kay Macpherson and Muriel Duckworth, and with union feminists, such as Shirley Carr and Grace Hartman, to achieve most of the policy goals and structural changes within the party sought by the Waffle and women.

Was Morton correct in seeing the Waffle's "Women's Lib" as a U.S. import? Certainly the *language* used derived most immediately from the U.S. New Left/radical feminist context. Waffle women outside of Ontario, however, used the more familiar language of rights and discrimination. In terms of the style of politics, then, the Waffle women bore much in common with their 1930s predecessors. They did not reject the ordinary political process or set it in opposition to their strategy of community socialism. As their resolutions made apparent, they wished to do both. The deep suspicion of the CCF/NDP about extra-party coalitions, about gender struggle promoted parallel to class struggle, and about extra-parliamentary actions proved to be a stumbling block for both generations of Canadian socialist feminists.

CONCLUSIONS

This preliminary exploration of the forces for continuity in Canadian feminism suggests that our general political culture has exerted considerable force. Despite an important counter-current, the dominant mode of political discourse involves a commitment to the ordinary political process, a belief in the efficacy of state action, and a positive view of the state as a utility of value for women. This has focused women's movements on building co-operative political structures to interact with states and on retaining a tension between autonomy and integration. The movements' service orientation and willingness to depend on the state for financial support also moderates their stance.

From the perspective of a Marlene Dixon, the Canadian women's movement was slow, non-militant, and probably co-opted. But that movement has achieved many significant gains for women. It shares less with the u.s. movement than many interpreters suggest. The very fact of its need to sustain links, however fragile, among groups of considerable difference – traditional and modern, French and English, and in all political parties – requires an operational code directed to ordinary political efficacy rather than to transformative theory or political quietism. It remains to be seen if the challenge raised by the new waves of women being mobilized, especially women of colour and immigrant women, can be met, since many of them find the code's norms unfamiliar. Finally, the relationships of the women's movement with the Native women's movement remain a failure of tragic proportions. It may well be that attempts to create coalitions spanning the multiple cleavages now facing the movement will fail. But Canada's general political culture is growing in its understanding of diversity, and our women's movements remain dynamic spurs to that growth.

4 The Women's Movement in the United States in the 1960s

SARA M. EVANS

Participation in conferences is a complex experience for many of us, a complicated exercise in engaged scholarship, where we walk into a room and confront ghosts of ourselves. At the conference from which this book originated, for example, I met Jo Freeman and Margrit Eichler, both prominent social scientists. But I first knew Jo as a founder of the first women's liberation group in the United States, a group I joined in 1967 about a month after it began. And I met Margrit in 1968 in a consciousness-raising group, and later a child-care co-operative, in North Carolina where we both were graduate students. It is a strange and wonderful thing to be a historian of events which you have also lived.

For this essay, I propose to discuss the women's movement in the United States in the 1960s by describing the broader context of the post–Second World War era, the gradual repoliticization of u.s. women, and the several waves of activism which resulted in the re-emergence of a feminist movement. At several points, this analysis suggests fascinating comparisons with the history of the Canadian women's movement.

Some of the structural characteristics of the post-war era were similar in the u.s. and Canada. It was a period of economic boom fuelled by the cold war. That boom drew women into the labour force in very large numbers, particularly older and married women.[1] Education also boomed as larger numbers of families could afford to send children to college. The numbers for women certainly lagged behind those for men, particularly in the u.s., because the GI Bill

made post-secondary education available to huge numbers of veterans. Nevertheless, larger and larger numbers of women, in fact,
did enter institutions of higher education.

The late 1940s and the 1950s were also an era of political repression.
In the United States, McCarthyism crushed many of the progressive
movements which had been active throughout the period of the 1930s
and the war. Simultaneously, and not unrelated to political repression, domestic ideology gained a new kind of cultural force. Historian
Elaine May uses the metaphor of "containment" for both cold war
foreign policy (containing communism around the globe with threats
of nuclear destruction) and ideas we associate with the ideology Betty
Friedan later labelled the "feminine mystique."[2] In a nuclear world,
the family was a symbol of safety and security. It also "contained"
the dangers of female sexuality in a post-Freudian world, given a
dramatically growing female participation in the labour force and the
threat of homosexuality. Indeed, domestic ideology was in many ways
about denying such changes. Feminism, then, was a response to this
deep contradiction.

Feminism did not emerge as a totally new phenomenon in the
1960s, however. Despite the ahistorical illusions of many younger
feminists, the earlier women's movement in the United States had
not completely disappeared. Through the 1940s and 1950s it
remained relatively depoliticized, marginalized, and invisible on the
political scene, but nonetheless there. The National Woman's Party
was a remnant of aging women who had fought for the Equal Rights
Amendment since 1923.[3] Their primary opponent for decades was
the League of Women Voters, which had equally strong roots in the
fight for women's suffrage. A number of other organizations also
sustained ongoing concerns about women's issues in the 1950s, most
notably the Women's Bureau in the Department of Labor, the YWCA,
whose student branch sponsored numerous programs on issues of
gender and equality, and the Women's Department of the United
Auto Workers.

Several things came together in the late 1950s to repoliticize women
as a group and raise the issue of gender in American society. One
was the clash between changing labour force participation of women
and a mystifying domestic ideology that denied its reality. Another
had to do with the community activism of women reaching a new
level of intensity in the 1950s. Middle-class women moved into sub-
urbs and began to organize them, running their school systems,
building community centres, and getting a powerful political education along the way. They understood all of these activities, of

course, as an extension of domestic responsibilities, and therefore did not initially perceive their political import.

In African-American communities, however, women's activism had always necessarily been highly politicized. For example, the Montgomery bus boycott owed its success to a Black women's political organization, parallel to the all-white League of Women Voters. As soon as Rosa Parks was arrested, a united Black community went into action, printing and distributing thousands of leaflets to every bus stop in the city of Montgomery. As a result of their strategic planning and capacity for action, the entire African-American community stayed off the buses.

Finally, there was a breakdown in the cold war consensus. Containment no longer worked to describe the world, at home or abroad. Third World nations emerged from colonialism to declare their unwillingness to pay allegiance to either side of the cold war. The civil rights movement in Montgomery, Little Rock, and then Greensboro demonstrated that racial tensions and differences could no longer be denied. And when the United States resumed nuclear testing, the moribund peace movement found a new voice with which to challenge the "better dead than red" rhetoric of the cold war.

The result of all of these changes, in my view, was three phases of women's activism in the 1960s, all of which weave together and pull apart in new ways by the 1970s. The first step was a brief repoliticization of domesticity, extending the tradition that traces back to the Woman's Christian Temperance Union (wctu) and even further back to the movement to abolish slavery. The form of this first phase was a group called Women's Strike for Peace. The second step was renewed activism among professional women resulting in the founding of the National Organization for Women (now). Finally, the emergence of the women's liberation movement out of the civil rights movement and the New Left represented the third phase.

WOMEN'S STRIKE FOR PEACE AND THE REPOLITICIZATION OF DOMESTICITY

The combined themes of the decline of the cold war and a newly politicized domesticity appear in sharp relief in the story of the attempt by the House Un-American Activities Committee (huac) to investigate Women's Strike for Peace (wsp) in 1962. During the McCarthy era, huac had become accustomed to using Red-baiting techniques to intimidate, terrify, and publicly humiliate any individual or group it chose to investigate. But the congressmen met their match in the ladies of the wsp. The hearing room was packed with women dressed to a t, many of them carrying babies. With the hubbub of babies in the background, the audience presented flowers to each woman called to testify and applauded wildly whenever she refused to incriminate herself by taking the Fifth Amendment. When the chair ruled applause out of order, they stood in unison. By the end, the hearing was a shambles and the press had a field day. The intimidating power of huac would never be the same.[4]

The women of wsp were suburban housewives. Some of the organizers had been active in the Progressive Party in 1948. They had a history of political activism, but most of them, in fact, had bought into domesticity during the 1950s. In their domestic roles, however, they became involved in Parent-Teacher Associations (pta), Girl Scouts, churches, charitable fund-raisers, and volunteer-supported neighbourhood recreation centres. They did not necessarily understand this work as political. Rather, they were doing what their families and communities needed to make their lives better, but in the process they honed their political skills.

When a small group initiated Women's Strike for Peace, their intention was to raise what they called "mothers' issues," like the radioactive contamination of milk resulting from open-air nuclear testing, which sent radioactive clouds across the United States. After Chernobyl, we can imagine what that fear was like. They sent out a call for women to go on a one-day strike for peace on 1 November 1961, just as a radioactive cloud from a Russian test floated across the country. Word of this strike spread through female networks in ptas, the League of Women Voters, peace organizations, and personal contacts. An estimated fifty thousand women left their jobs and kitchens that day to lobby government officials to "End the Arms Race – Not the Human Race." Within the year they organized groups in sixty communities. Most activists were white, middle-class, and educated. Sixty-one per cent did not work outside the home. Intellectual and civic-minded, these middle-aged women had been liberals and radicals in the 1940s and then had withdrawn into domesticity in the 1950s. They found themselves impelled back into politics by growing fears for their children's futures as well as by the courageous examples of civil rights activists in the south.

Women's rights as such were not on their agenda, except that they emphasized the right of housewives to be perceived as citizens. Dagmar Wilson, one of the founders, spoke of her awareness that "the housewife was a down-graded person" and set out to show "that this was an important role and that it was time we were heard."[5]

A second form of politicized domesticity flourished in the southern civil rights movement, where Black women known as "the Mamas" were key leaders in every community. Their activism, however, was interpreted largely in racial terms. It inspired other challenges to the status quo but did not articulate a gender-based critique.

Women's Strike for Peace enjoyed a momentary triumph, but the politicized domesticity which shaped its success could not provide the political base for a broader women's movement in the 1960s as it had in the nineteenth century. For too many the home was conceptualized as a "closed off cloister unconcerned with what goes on outside," and, while the actual boundaries between public and private were fuzzy, political life that involves citizens, as opposed to politicians, had lost a distinctive, vibrant dynamic of its own. Working-class and lower-class housewives had a far more restrictive definition of domesticity than their middle-class counterparts, along with far less self-confidence about their own achievements.[6] Furthermore, very large numbers of women were working in the paid labour force and had not figured out how to incorporate that work into their identities. A broad-based women's movement would have to address these dilemmas as well.

NOW AND THE POLITICIZATION OF PROFESSIONAL WOMEN

The origins of the National Organization for Women lie in networks of professional women. The story usually begins – and here we have an interesting parallel with Canada – with the President's Commission on the Status of Women appointed by President John F. Kennedy in 1961. Esther Peterson, a long-time labour educator and lobbyist, persuaded Kennedy to appoint the commission, which Eleanor Roosevelt chaired.[7]

Membership on the commission, its staff, and seven technical committees was drawn from labour unions, women's organizations, and governmental agencies. Not surprisingly, a strong majority of the commission opposed the Equal Rights Amendment (ERA). But they strove for a position that would be less divisive than in the past. Declaring in their report that "equality of rights under the law for all persons, male or female, is so basic to democracy ... that it must be reflected in the fundamental law of the land," they argued that this was already achieved under the Fifth and Fourteenth Amendments to the constitution. Therefore they could conclude that a constitutional amendment was not needed "now." The only member of the commission who supported the ERA, feminist lawyer Marguerite Rawalt, insisted on the insertion of the word "now" to leave the door open for change, if the Supreme Court failed to accept their interpretation.[8]

The commission's report was issued in 1963. For comparative purposes, it is important to note the impact of timing, since 1963 was a very different moment from 1970, when the Canadian report appeared. The U.S. report documented in great detail continuing discrimination in employment, disparities in pay between women and men, the lack of social services such as child care, and the legal inequality of women. The first consequence of the report was a presidential order requiring that the civil service system hire without regard to sex. It also provided crucial documentation for advocates of the Equal Pay Act which passed in 1963. For the first time it was illegal to pay women differently for performing the same work as men.

The commission itself activated a network of professional women whose concerns had been growing dramatically in the previous decade. Through its various working committees and research projects, it attracted women who had been active in their professions as well as in their communities. And the existence of a presidential commission stimulated the creation of commissions on the status of women in virtually every state, multiplying its impact at the local level. No longer bifurcated around the issue of the ERA, these environments fostered creative thinking about women's status among professional women (including educators, lawyers, and union leaders). Many of them were stunned by their findings. They had not previously interpreted their personal experiences of discrimination as part of a broader pattern. By documenting the depth and pervasiveness of discrimination and the hardships that accompanied women's double burdens in the home and the labour force, they gave quantified validation to problems they themselves had experienced and observed in more individual ways.

Betty Friedan published *The Feminine Mystique* the same year the commission issued its report.[9] Blaming educators, advertisers, Freudian psychologists, and functionalist sociologists for forcing women out of public life and into a passive and infantalizing domesticity, Friedan advocated meaningful work outside the home as the solution to "the problem that has no name." She was unprepared for the deluge of mail which her book inspired. Women by the thousands, from all over the United States, wrote to thank her for naming their unhappiness and to tell her their own painful stories.[10]

All of this set the stage for debate on the 1964 Civil Rights Act. Howard Smith, an elderly senator from Virginia, encouraged by constituents in the National Woman's Party, suggested that the prohibition in Title VII against discrimination in employment on the basis of race, creed, and national origin should also include "sex." As a long-time supporter of the ERA, he offered the amendment seriously, but as an ardent segregationist he probably also hoped it would help to kill the bill.[11] While their colleagues chuckled at the very idea of including sex in a civil rights bill, Congresswoman Martha Griffiths and Senator Margaret Chase Smith set to work to pass the amendment which made Title VII the strongest legal tool yet available to women.

Once the Civil Rights Act passed, the newly created Equal Employment Opportunity Commission (EEOC) found itself flooded with women's grievances. But most people, including the EEOC, still considered the inclusion of sex a bit of a joke. The *New York Times* referred to it as the "bunny law." What would happen, the editors worried, if a man applied to a Playboy Club for a position as a bunny? Could he charge discrimination if the owners refused to hire him?[12]

The creation of NOW emerged from this confluence of factors: the lack of enforcement of Title VII; the self-organization and increased strategic clarity of women who had worked on commissions on the status of women at state and federal levels; and the growing awareness that there was no organized representative of women's interests positioned to lobby for enforcement. The story is a familiar one today. When the organizers of the Third National Conference of State Commissions on the Status of Women refused to entertain resolutions, those most concerned were galvanized into independent action. Friedan recalled that they "cornered a large table at the luncheon, so that we could start organizing before we had to rush for planes. We all chipped in $5.00, began to discuss names. I dreamed up N.O.W. on the spur of the moment." Thus the National Organization for Women, NOW, was born with a clear statement of purpose: "To take action to bring women into full participation in the mainstream of American society now, assuming all the privileges and responsibilities thereof in truly equal partnership with men."[13]

NOW articulated the clear dilemmas of professional women for whom continuing discrimination violated deeply held convictions about their rights to equal treatment and for whom traditional attitudes about family roles were obsolete. "It is no longer either necessary or possible," they argued in their founding statement, "for women to devote the greater part of their lives to child-rearing."[14]

NOW represented in some ways a modernized version of the Seneca Falls Declaration of 1848 by reclaiming for women the republican ideals of equal participation and individual rights. But its organizers were skilled at lobbying, not movement building. For the first year, organizational mailings went out from the offices of the United Auto Workers' (UAW) Women's Department, while local chapters were slow to develop. Activities targeted the enforcement of federal anti-discrimination laws.

With some successes in the first year, several lawsuits pending, no organized local base, and an increasingly diverse membership, the NOW national conference in 1968 encountered serious disagreements. Endorsement of the ERA meant that UAW women, for example, had to withdraw. Within their union they were working for change, but until it changed its position, which it did two years later, they could no longer participate or offer office and staff support. The issue of abortion precipitated another split as lawyers who wanted to focus on legal and economic issues left to found the Women's Equity Action League (WEAL).

The founders of NOW understood that women were seriously disadvantaged in the American political and legal system, but they presumed a model of political activity which emphasized the direct relation between the individual and the state, very much as the late suffrage movement had done. Its focus on rights and individuals, abstracted from communal relations, did not speak to large numbers of women, and the bonds of sisterhood remained unarticulated and depoliticized, in contrast to Women's Strike for Peace which had built its political identity on womanhood. NOW wanted to be an organization "for" women, not "of" women.

WOMEN'S LIBERATION

Most American women were caught in a series of dilemmas which did not mesh with any culturally available identity rather than the clear-cut dilemmas of the professional woman. They were trapped in the mystifying complexities of a popular culture that simultaneously endorsed individual opportunity and the feminine mystique, a gender-segregated economy that drew women into low-paid, low-status jobs, and a child-centred family premised on the full-time services of a wife and mother. They could not abstract issues of rights from the underlying questions of identity. The third phase of women's activism in the 1960s addressed these issues with the powerful organizing tool of the consciousness-raising group. Such groups offered women a place to begin to unravel all that, to pull it apart, look at it, and start to figure it out.

There is no need here to retell the story of the origins of the women's liberation movement, the radical wing of "second wave" feminism.[15] It grew out of the experiences of younger women who in terms of education and class background were very similar to the women who founded NOW. Because of their age, however, they were shaped in a different way by direct participation in the civil rights movement and the student New Left. Children of the post-war middle class, many of them also children of radical activists from the 1930s, they found within the social movements of the 1960s both a set of radically egalitarian ideas and an experience of participatory democracy which allowed them to challenge received cultural definitions of femininity. The movement was for them a free space in which they could experience themselves as leaders, develop political and public skills, know themselves as courageous, and begin to question what womanhood was all about.

The founders of the women's liberation movement shared their generation's intense search for community and discovered there the power of sisterhood. As a result they challenged the definitions of politics more fundamentally than women had done since the days of the WCTU and definitions of gender more radically than anyone had since the Greenwich Village feminists of the 1910s.[16] With their declaration that "the personal is political," they repoliticized the bonds among women and rediscovered the ground for political action.

THE SECOND WAVE INTO THE 1970S

These three waves, distinct as they were, built on, amplified, and changed each other in the decade of the 1970s. Women's liberation, for example, had an enormous impact on NOW as well as other women's organizations focused on using traditional channels of political activism. Radical women were never as separate as they imagined. Their methods further transformed long-standing women's groups such as the League of Women Voters, Girl Scouts, the YWCA, and church organizations. Denomination after denomination underwent enormous battles over the ordination of women – an issue of power, position, and equal opportunity, such as members of NOW would be likely to raise – as well as the use of inclusive language – a concern about consciousness and cultural change more typical of radical feminism. Subsequent radical feminist re-evaluations of motherhood and emphasis on a uniquely female perspective (especially linked to motherhood), whether in art or psychology, echoed with a new feminist twist the perspectives articulated by Women's Strike for Peace.[17]

Two stories illustrate some of the linkages, the weaving together of strands, that began even as these dimensions of feminism emerged. Del Martin, one of the founders of the Daughters of Bilitis (DOB), a lesbian group, became an early activist in NOW. DOB had made some slight and controversial shifts in the mid-1960s towards a more militant stance but remained a tiny organization, still distant from the growing lesbian culture that flourished in urban bars. Feminism added a dynamic and stressful dimension. Activists debated whether their primary loyalties lay with the homophile movement, where many experienced sexist treatment from gay male activists, or the new feminist movement where they painfully discovered the homophobic prejudices of other feminists. With feminism, however, they had a powerful analytic tool for examining their own social realities, as well as an experience of solidarity and community – sisterhood – which provided a kind of "psychic space" that allowed many women to claim their identity as lesbians.[18] The explosive emergence of Gay Liberation in 1969 further fuelled this process and, by the 1970s, lesbian feminism emerged as a key perspective and source of challenge within women's groups across the political spectrum.

In Washington, DC, Arvonne Fraser, a long-time activist in the Democratic Party who worked in her husband's congressional office and managed his campaigns, invited about twenty women to her home in 1969 to talk about the new women's movement. She had tried to join NOW, but her letter had been returned. Later she found the Washington chapter but thought they were politically naive. Yet the women's liberation groups seemed too young and too radical. So she decided to organize her own group. At the first meeting women decided not to introduce themselves through relationships with men (though many were related to or on the staff of prominent men). They said they would be a discussion group, not a consciousness-raising group. "Many of us realized later," according to Fraser, "that the main difference between the two was in name only." Out of that group came key insider networks that in the 1970s carried out major legislative advances for women, such as Congressional passage of the ERA, and landmark legislation providing equity in education, sports, and employment. Fraser herself went on to become a national officer in WEAL and increasingly active in international women's networks. She tells the story of "the unknown group" with an ironic recognition that few at the time would have imagined that the insider network behind all that legislation was a consciousness-raising group.[19]

CONCLUSION

By the late 1960s, feminist challenges were in the headlines, and opposition to the war in Vietnam had toppled a president. Inflation aroused anxiety that the boom might be ending. Race riots and a divisive war abroad destroyed the optimism of the early 1960s. Both cold war verities and their cousin, the feminine mystique, were under serious stress. Indeed, Women's Strike for Peace, so effective at the beginning of the decade, found itself accused of being reactionary. Younger radical women pointed out that WSP still played on traditional roles of wife and mother, activities in which women's identities remained derivative and dependent.

In January 1968, women in the peace movement mobilized thousands to march in Washington in opposition to the war in Vietnam. They called their march the Jeanette Rankin Brigade, to honour the first woman in Congress and the only congressperson to vote against American entry into both World Wars. A small contingent at the march called a separate meeting of women interested in struggling for their own liberation. Among themselves there was immediate division over ideological issues: were men the enemy or was it "the system"? Should women continue participation in the male-dominated Left or should they break away and work only with other women?

For the moment these angry young women seemed a rude and irritating interruption of the mass movement of women in the mould of Women's Strike for Peace. In fact, they were the core of the burgeoning new women's liberation movement, which by 1970 had eclipsed and apparently rendered obsolete agitation based on women's traditional roles. In declaring that "the personal is political," they introduced a radical challenge to the cultural definitions of male and female. Yet with youthful ingratitude, they failed to recognize the debt they owed previous generations, as well as the complex power of women's traditional identities and associations. That failure also prevented them from understanding the long-run import of a movement that could spread both inside and outside established institutions, bringing consciousness-raising not only to alternative institutions but to Congress, churches, and Girl Scouts as well.

5 The Origins of the Women's Movement in Quebec*

MICHELINE DUMONT

Almost everyone is aware that Quebec is an enigma for most Canadians. Although I am certain that I will not be able to resolve this problem in this essay, after a few introductory remarks, I would like to comment more extensively on the experience of Quebec women.

THE HISTORICITY OF FEMINISM

The rise of feminism seems to have occurred in waves. The familiar concepts of "first wave" and "second wave" can be found in almost any book on feminism. It has been assumed that the first wave occurred at the end of the nineteenth century and faded after women were given the right to vote around 1925, and that the contemporary women's movement constitutes the second wave. I have even encountered the term "renaissance" used for the second wave. In this view, the time between the two waves could be called the "Middle Ages." The term Middle Ages may be appropriate for the Depression and the war years; however, it is an expression borrowed from traditional historiography and does not help us to situate our own history.

History has made much use of dates and facts. Dates probably help us to understand political and economic history: however, the history of women is another matter. Here the trends have been set; the different stages are considered as "early" or as "late" (Quebec, of course was "late"!). One can also speak of pre- or post-something.

---

* Translation by Carol Cochrane.

France, at the moment, is being swamped by, in my opinion, a terrible concept called "l'après-féminisme." It sounds very much like "l'après-guerre." This insistence on time, on chronology, and on succession does not help to explain what has been taking place. Perhaps the official view of time is masculine; perhaps women's time is different: it is not known.

Historical time is a complex reality, which is one reason why I so much appreciated Karen Offen's recent article in *Signs*.[1] She proposes a working definition of feminism which includes the two distinct modes of historical argument or discourse used by women in defence of women's emancipation from male domination in Western societies. She distinguishes between two basic tendencies that she calls "relational feminism" and "individualist feminism." Her definition applies as much to the feminist ideas and claims of the nineteenth century as to those of our own day. Furthermore, this definition is formulated and illustrated in a comparative European-American framework, thus broadening its significance. Finally, Offen directs her study as much towards ideas as towards the experience and the needs of women. In other words, she takes into consideration the collective consciousness of women and finds therein the basis for new political action: "The relational mode of approaching women's emancipation, by honoring women's own interpretations of 'difference' in its manifold complexity, may hold the key to overcoming contemporary resistance to feminism."[2]

Moreover, feminism cannot be considered just another "reformist," "political," or "social" movement, to be studied like any other such movement. We should try to understand it and not try to make it fit into the old, borrowed framework of the social sciences. After all, feminism challenges everything. We must ask ourselves why we are so concerned with chronologies, synchronism, origins, consequences, successions, and so forth.

In 1960, Sara Evans has written, "there were signs of change on many levels, though no one at the time could have put pieces together to find a pattern."[3] I think she was right and that this reflects reality. The present is so full of many possibilities that we cannot see what is happening. Historians take pride in putting reality in order by emphasizing only the important "facts." (I must confess that I have done just that on many an occasion.)

Sometimes, however, historical truth is disorderly. "Historical evidence consists of words arbitrarily imposed to make time into chronology, to turn the unchartered chaos of reality into a simple story complete with a beginning, a middle and an end."[4] History is a discourse on reality. This truth has been known for a long time.

Thomas Hobbes wrote that the vision of the future was only a supposition produced by the memory of the past. Commenting on this statement, the British historian Edward Carr said in 1980 that "Our vision of the future influences our conception of the past." I prefer the latter point of view. Because I see a different future, I try to discover new ways of exploring the past.

Feminists have learned that changing the laws is a difficult task. The dates when they have succeeded are well known. However, compared to changing attitudes and mentalities, revising the laws is an easy task. Not a single date can be found for that kind of change. That is why, in the history of women and, especially, in the history of feminism, we must concentrate on changing mentalities and developing awareness.

Without women's awareness, feminism would be just another movement. Yet we must realize that we know very little about women's awareness. Facts are important and I suppose dates are too, but feminism is something altogether different. It functions on the third level of *durée*, according to Fernand Braudel's perspective, where changes are slow.[5] It is more concerned with cultural and ideological changes than with legislative changes. If we do not succeed in understanding how these changes occur and how to bring them about, feminism will vanish, like so many other movements.

LOOKING AT ORIGINS

The purpose of the essays in this section of the book is to compare the intellectual origins of the contemporary feminist movement in the United States and in Canada. Sara Evans, who has written about the American experience in *Born for Liberty* (1989), deals exclusively with the 1960s yet establishes important links with the preceding era. She offers a description of the pieces of the puzzle which prepared the way for the emergence of the contemporary feminist movement: the civil rights movement, the trap of the feminine mystique, the development of continuing education, the success of contraception, cold war issues, the peace movement (especially among mothers), youth culture, the economic vulnerability of women, new alliances between old groups, and so on. The diversity of these phenomena demonstrates the complexity of what was to become the reformist wing of the feminist movement. Evans also lists the signs of "new" simultaneously emerging currents: the challenging of homemaking and the female nature, the generation gap, draft issues, the ideas of the American Left, the ambiguity of counterculture for women, the experience of sexual abuse, sexual inequality among young activists, and so on. She completes the picture by directing our attention to the complex power of women's traditional identities and associations.

I would have preferred that Evans offer further explanation of the changing boundaries between the public and private sectors when the two trends met at the end of the 1960s. I also wanted to learn more about the traditional women's associations, since, with their 2,520,000 members in 1980, they formed the real base of the feminist movement. I do, however, appreciate how Evans has successfully incorporated the trends of the Black and Chicano women's movements into the general pattern of the emergence of feminism. Her view of American feminism allows us to free ourselves from the already fixed chronological grid found in historiography. This is very exciting and makes one realize the complexity of reality.

Jill Vickers's essay on Canadian feminism attempts to include the facts about the "cas québécois" in her analysis. Although she succeeds in covering the global perspective, she is not able to fit Quebec completely into any of her three themes. She states that Canadian political culture has exerted a considerable influence on the feminist movement. For Canadian feminists, it is acceptable to achieve change through state action. Although this also applies to the Quebec movement, the approach of Quebec women is mostly pragmatic. She also points out the frequent disagreements within umbrella groups over basic orientation and specific issues. Is Quebec's position in "national" groups just a manifestation of that old bugaboo of politics, "regionalism," as she has said? Quebec's stand is a nationalist stand, but, clearly, the rest of Canada does not understand this. From her viewpoint, the women's movement in Canada certainly reflects the major trends of Canadian politics on the Quebec question.

In their writings on the feminist movement, Canadian specialists either forget the Quebec scene altogether, present distorted views, or honestly state that they will not discuss Quebec.[6] However, the Quebec movement is *just* as important as the Canadian movement and is important *for* the Canadian movement.

In the second part of her essay, Vickers explains the ideas of the women's liberation movement (WLM) and radical feminism. She offers an excellent and illuminating comparison of the political culture of Canadian radical liberalism and the political culture of U.S. radical feminism. I am struck, however, by the fact that the vocabulary used in identifying the different tendencies and splits is not appropriate for the situation in Quebec. The distinctions exclude the discussions by theorists, who came mainly from France, that took place in Quebec. Mostly, however, I am not certain that the theoretical explanations and distinctions are helpful in understanding what has happened. Actually, we have met with the very same difficulty in trying to explain the tendencies and splits of the Quebec movement.

In the early 1980s, Les Editions du Remue Ménage undertook the publishing of several feminist magazines of the 1970s, in particular *Québécoises Deboutte!* (1972–74), *Les Têtes de Pioche* (1976–79), and all the major texts of the "radical" movement.[7] These publications reported important verbatim discussions among the militants of the time, who were trying in vain to understand their splits and divisions. But these discussions and subtle analyses do not help us answer the most important questions of all: why were some of the issues raised by these small groups able to obtain public attention and support at certain times and rejected at others?[8] These are the real questions we must ask ourselves in order to understand the feminist movement. Thousands of women say, "I am no feminist, but ... " Why? We must learn about *their* motives, not about *our* interpretations.

In the third part of her essay, Vickers explores the ideas of feminist culture, especially as they are expressed in the Voix des femmes and in the New Democratic Party's Waffle. This examination completely ignores the Quebec phenomenon, where feminism has been both nourished and opposed by the nationalist movement. The slogan "No women's liberation without Quebec liberation. No Quebec liberation without women's liberation" is at the heart of Quebec feminism. Furthermore, Quebec feminists maintained stormy relations with extreme leftist movements.[9] I now wish to consider the period between 1940 and 1960, which seems to be more illuminating for the understanding of Quebec feminism.

THE QUEBEC ENIGMA

When the Women's Rights League met in Montreal for its annual meeting on 30 May 1940, the main topic on the agenda was the recent achievement of women's suffrage. After a struggle of more than fifteen years, an important chapter was closed. Yet the minutes of that meeting contain this terse comment: "Our full work has barely begun!" The handful of militants present (there were only twenty-seven) had no illusions about what the real meaning of their victory was and the objectives that lay ahead of them. Feminism is often thought to have become lethargic at that point; it was not that simple.

Perhaps the period between 1940 and 1960 represents a key stage for understanding what was to happen in Quebec after 1960. Indeed, at that time, Thérèse Casgrain was no longer isolated as was the

Women's Rights League in 1940. She was backed by hundreds of women in the Voix des femmes. This transformation must be explained, which is why it is important to look at a few forgotten events from those two decades.

As the Collectif Clio has tried to show in *Women of Quebec: A History*, the upheaval caused by industrialization produced for women a series of contradictions between their daily lives and the discourse about their femininity and their domestic lives.[10] In this event, the women of Quebec were neither apart nor late in coming; they are full participants in the situation of the majority of women of the Western world. These conflicts were aggravated by the Second World War, which upset the delicate balance between the forces of the past and the forces of change. Once again, women had to save the nation. They were asked to give up their role as mothers and were sent to work in munitions factories. The war over, they were again needed in the home. Their withdrawal from the work force was only temporary, however, because the new economic order set up after the war required more massive and prolonged participation by women in the work force. An impasse had been reached: women were needed in the home to ensure reproduction and were also required in just about all economic sectors.

This impasse explains the individual and collective actions of women between 1940 and 1960. This era was not politically blank for women. Militant feminism was certainly silent; however, women's social and political involvement was changing with that of the rest of society. When feminism resurfaced after 1965, it certainly did not come into being by spontaneous generation.

Two concepts are frequently put forward to explain and situate Quebec feminism: its lateness in appearing, in comparison to Canadian feminism, and its close, often privileged, ties with Catholicism and nationalism. Its lateness seems all too evident: in English Canada, civil rights for married women were changed in 1872; in Quebec, it was 1964. Canadian women received the right to vote in 1918; Quebec women waited until 1940 for the right to vote at the provincial level. Canadian women gained access to universities shortly after 1850; Quebec women, in 1907. The first feminist movements were organized in Canada around 1880; in Quebec, in 1907.

This concept of tardiness, however, has obscured too many analyses and explanations. Most of all, it confirms the traditional and masculine habit of defining historicity, that of punctuating stages of development with dates and events. The tools of the "new history" will enable us to look at reality in a different way. It is time to analyse what was really taking place for those women who were entering into modernity, secretly we might say, because the collective Quebec myth obliterated all objective gathering of data about reality.

Obviously, the grip of the Catholic church on Quebec society for many generations led most analysts to highlight this clerical influence to explain the Quebec difference. This is very clear in works which are polarized by the structural turning point of the secularization of society at the time of the Quiet Revolution, even though the present trend of Quebec historiography seeks the roots of the Quiet Revolution in preceding decades. This explanation is used even more frequently in writings from English Canada, which are quick to use the "priest-ridden society" concept to explain the Quebec difference. It was no surprise to find this note written by Sylvia B. Bashevkin to explain why she does not treat Quebec in her work *Toeing the Lines: Women and Party Politics in English Canada*: "Therefore the background to suffrage in Quebec suggests a distinctive political history as well as a disparate set of attitudes and participation behaviour which are best served by a separate study. In fact, if incorporated within a comparative framework, the political history of women in Quebec might be included most appropriately in a study of France, Italy, and other Catholic cultures."[11]

Yet it seems to me that this method cannot explain why Quebec had more women deputies than any other provincial legislature in 1989, or why Quebecers elected 50 per cent of the female members of the House of Commons in 1984 and 33 per cent in 1988; nor can it explain why Quebec feminism seems so effective to Belgian and French observers.

I sometimes think that Quebec feminism suffers from another kind of double exclusion, both in Canada and in Quebec. On the one hand, the dates and structures of the history of Quebec women do not coincide with the dates and structures of English-Canadian women. Thus they mar the nice charts that could be made. Recent studies in political science and sociology demonstrate this by simply ignoring the existence of Quebec feminism or by presenting an incomplete picture of it. On the other hand, writings about Quebec, by either French- or English-speaking people, have such a difficult time in explaining the data about the Quebec problem within Canada that they do not wish to take the trouble to introduce theories on the reality of women. Often feminism is even presented as a shoot from some foreign root badly planted in Quebec soil. One looks in vain for paragraphs on women or feminism in studies of the Quiet Revolution or Quebec nationalism.

This situation most likely explains why all the studies on the reappearance of Canadian feminism in the middle of the 1960s attribute such slight importance to the role played by the Quebec movements and their leaders or offer such stereotyped interpretations of them. No one would have such an absurd idea as to think that Quebec could have exerted a certain leadership in the rise of this movement around 1965. The vitality of Quebec feminism since the 1970s is certainly well known; it has never really been explained. We need to consider the period between 1940 and 1960 to learn about the resurgence of Quebec feminism.

THE 1940S AND 1950S

I would like to emphasize the importance of a few aspects of the history of Quebec women during the twenty-five years preceding the creation of the Royal Commission on the Status of Women in Canada in 1967. It seems that the arrival of women's suffrage somewhat worried Quebec's religious leaders. At the beginning of the 1940s, all of Quebec society was organized in a myriad of denominational movements with multiple objectives: religious, social, labour or cultural. The organizational structure was diocesan, and clerical control was evident at all levels of the hierarchy.[12] Few organizations avoided the control of the Catholic church. One of the few, les Cercles des Fermières, was established in 1915, under the sponsorship of the Ministry of Agriculture.[13] In 1944, this association included more than forty-nine thousand women in twenty-three federations, which corresponded to the agricultural regions and thus remained outside the diocesan structure. But some feared that "the rural women, organized circles dependent on the State, might be pressured by a hard-pressed government or by unscrupulous politicians in order to influence their votes unduly."[14]

It was at this point, in the beginning of 1945, that the assembly of bishops issued a directive to encourage these women to leave the government organization and to join a newly created movement called the Union catholique des Fermières (Catholic Union of Farm Women), the female equivalent of the Union catholique des Cultivateurs (Catholic Union of Farmers). The reaction of women was revealing. Some 20 per cent complied with the episcopal directives, while others, contrary to all expectations, resisted the various means of persuasion. The farm women spoke with their respective bishops, asking in vain for reasons why they should leave the association. They declared that the bishops did not have the authority to intervene in the economic domain.[15]

This official disobedience was certainly a surprise. In the fifteen years which followed, the "Cercles des Fermières" continued to operate without the church's official support and were subject to fairly skilful criticism from the local clergy in a quarrelsome atmosphere which prolonged the dissension. This first disregard for clerical power was even more interesting in that it happened within a group of women normally considered to be one of the most conservative in Quebec. The dissidence of the "Cercles des Fermières" was exclusively political, because their official line was characterized by a traditional ideology and their practices centred mainly around arts and crafts.[16] Nevertheless, a network of 657 circles in 1950 was significant. Furthermore, at the end of the 1960s, the majority of this association of so-called "Fermières" were women from urban areas, farm women accounting for only 15 per cent.

Meanwhile, the Union catholique des Fermières developed a new specialty in the practice of study groups. Their publications and meetings centred around certain topics. Clerical influence was dominant in the choice of these issues; however, at the end of the 1950s, feminine discourse changed this tone. The themes studied became more and more concrete, more and more related to the social transformations occurring in Quebec, closer and closer to the everyday lives of women. Subjects such as contraception, money, the fulfilment of women, problems of the rural family, and work were discussed. It was by means of this association that a collective feminine consciousness developed in Quebec between 1950 and 1965. Its traditional tone may have been misleading: in fact, this socially progressive commitment by women, through study groups, must have played a decisive role in the changing of Quebec society. The remarkable thing was that the women affected by this evolution were not restricted to a closed circle, characteristic of pre-1940 feminist groups, but more than thirty thousand members were in touch with this association. Less developed than the "Cercles des Fermières," this religious association numbered no less than three hundred circles in 1950. Suddenly, women had opinions and expressed them publicly. This should not be overlooked.

Beginning in 1963 two women's associations, directed by the church, gradually came together to form the AFEAS (Association féminine d'éducation et d'action sociale) in 1966. This injected new life into a whole well-rooted tradition of social commitment. Under the impetus of dynamic and astute women to obtain subsidies for projects to benefit ordinary women, the AFEAS became a true public platform for social and political action. At that time, discussions about women's work still gave rise to harsh remarks about the illegitimacy of salaried work for women. One of the leaders, Azilda Marchand, was one of the first to declare that such discussions were without foundation, since all women worked. What was more important was to look at the problems linked with the productive and free work they did, be it in the home or in the family business. Long before today's feminists, Marchand denounced the invisible character of women's work.

This important collective evolution, which extended from 1941 to 1966, contributed to the formation of a colossal network of women motivated by all political aspects of community activities and by questions which interested women. As we shall see, this network became an important basis for the feminist debates in the 1970s and 1980s. However, this evolution was not the only one to occur. There were also discussions about education for girls and about women working for pay.

For many centuries, male discourse on the education of girls, combined with the denunciation of their presence in the work force after 1850, was unequivocal.[17] There is no reason here to resurrect this analysis, which is at the core of the contradictions which affect the lives of women. In this respect, Quebec was no exception; it has distinguished itself perhaps by the particular tones of the ideas put forward during the twentieth century, while elsewhere "feminist conquests" ensured a minimum number of positions for women in certain universities and in certain professions.

A recent study has demonstrated that the discussion of education for girls in Quebec was a permanent and important topic in collective discourse, even though it has never appeared in studies or bibliographies on Quebec ideologies.[18] Women have been, indeed, expected to ensure the collective Quebec difference when faced with the Anglo-Saxon environment. In this respect, there has been an interesting evolution. Discussion on the subject went from exalting the natural function of the woman before 1920, to becoming "anti-feminist" between 1920 and 1940 by opposing "hoyden girls" to "real women," and, after 1940, under the aegis of Monsignor Albert Tessier, to becoming triumphalist and passionate.[19] Mona-Josée Gagnon has written a searing analysis of masculine writings from the period between 1940 and 1970.[20]

However, the ideas put forward by women during that same period were left unexamined. For the most part, it was nuns and a few professional women who often spoke out in defence of education for girls. It would be possible to put together a surprising collection of careful, sometimes ambivalent, and sometimes even radical texts on the education and work of women. At the end of the 1950s, there was a lively, ongoing dispute in the newspapers about schooling for girls. A psychologist, Monique Béchard, argued brilliantly in favour of instruction for girls and denounced the fallacious reasoning of partisans of domestic education.[21] In 1954 the Superiors of some dozen religious congregations presented a memoir to the Tremblay Commission in defence of a classical education for young girls.[22] In 1958 a nun appeared before a commission responsible for legislating secondary education: "We do not have to ask ourselves," she wrote, "if a woman should or should not work. Woman's work is a fact. It is even a right; a woman's dignity depends on it … There is even an injustice in depriving a woman of her right to work, just as it is a social injustice to force a mother to work outside the home as a labourer, at very long and hard tasks. It is unjust to keep a woman from exercising a profession, allowing her only jobs which require a minimum of education, which pay the least and which command the least influence."[23] In 1962, close to fifteen women's groups – in particular, the Association of Women University Graduates – presented their briefs to the Commission Board of Inquiry into Education, which reflected a thorough, articulate study on the education of girls.

The expression of these ideas was not unusual. They were echoed in student newspapers of the time, and Quebec girls often had the opportunity to hear them, especially from their teachers who were nuns.[24] These teachers offered them an absolutely exceptional model of professional life. Danielle Juteau has well shown the great ambiguity of the models proposed by nuns for the girls, which were often in contradiction to their own childless and celibate status.[25] In *Taking the Veil*, Marta Danylewycz has in fact shown the extent to which the vocation of being a nun represented a professional option for women: "Protected by their vocation, women thus pursued a life-long career, exerted influence and, on occasion, had access to public affairs."[26] Nuns were those who developed many of the professional avenues open mainly to women, such as teaching, social services, nursing, medical technology, and domestic sciences. There were other study programs developed by lay persons, which included dietetics, translation, library science, and physiotherapy.[27]

The great number of religious vocations until 1964, the study of school personnel, and tendencies in women's work have shown that women had started their social revolution long before the Parent Report.[28] The latter only reinforced tendencies already well in place. Of course, most Quebec women continued to choose marriage. After all, at the time, the feminine mystique was prevalent. However, women in the minority who chose to do something else, or tried to combine marriage with a career, received a lot of coverage in the media.

From the middle of the 1950s, a great number of Quebec women involved in various areas of public, professional, and media life formed the ABCs of what was to become the message of a new feminism. They read *Le Deuxième Sexe* by Simone de Beauvoir, which offered a fascinating theoretical framework.[29] Their ideas were published in so-called feminine magazines, which thus initiated the first significant turnaround, on radio and television shows, in "intellectual" periodicals, where they were regular and full collaborators, and in the many associations which solicited their services, such as parent associations, the Mouvement laïc de langue française, various movements of Catholic action, unions, and nationalist movements.[30]

A good example of the ideas at that time can be found in a special section of *Le Devoir* published for the St-Jean-Baptiste Day celebrations in 1961. The theme chosen for this series of articles was "A Tribute to the French-Canadian Woman."[31] In these articles, the diagnosis was clear: women were at an impasse. "Yesterday's Woman Is Dead" was the title of one article, which could well summarize the whole series: "Can it surprise anyone that the woman who wants to break with a certain tradition, because she feels the urgency of it is facing a dilemma which breeds a certain uneasiness? ... Two solutions are possible: give up or fight." "We demand courses in feminine psychology which are not falsified by the same old stories that dilute the woman." "To be a woman is neither a profession nor a social status." "It is up to today's young woman, more lucid, less romantic, to break from the infernal cycle." "We must take charge of our problems (take our problems in hand) and categorically refuse to let ourselves be divided into so-called feminine circles." "Today's young girl has discovered that liberty and equality do not exist." "Confronted with a career and marriage, the young French-Canadian woman has many problems and troubling preoccupations." "I wonder if French-Canadian women are as happy in their homes as we would suppose. Equality is very difficult for us." "What is important is that the woman feels that she has worth, that she feels materially independent." "Enough time has passed for the wind to tear the silken banners of yesterday's suffragettes ... A rational feminism has replaced a narrow assertive feminism which, although not without merit, had, however, inadequate views and objectives." "We must wait for the woman of tomorrow."[32]

These quotations are too brief to summarize the analysis on the situation of women presented in this issue of *Le Devoir*. And who were the women who spoke out? Judith Jasmin, Andréanne Lafond, Michelle Mailhot, Thérèse Casgrain, Jeanne Sauvé, Solange Chaput-Rolland, Thérèse Gouin-Décarie, Fernande Saint-Martin, Adèle

Lauzon, Renée Geoffroy, Michelle Asselin-Mailhot, women who spoke out regularly, especially on "Bonjour Madame" on television and on "Femina" on radio, programs which all housewives watched and listened to just as regularly. The framework for the analysis of neo-feminism was already established, and the main demands were identified. The housewife's prison was emphasized because, more and more, the housewives had unused professional skills. When Thérèse Casgrain started a Quebec chapter of la Voix des femmes, she had no difficulty in recruiting militants.[33]

The period between 1940 and 1965 was rich in various movements which constituted the basic foundation of women in public affairs. In this context, the relationship of women to official politics, and especially to the different political parties, seemed particularly tenuous. Also, it is difficult to verify as certain whether women's obtaining the right to vote constituted an "important date" for the women of that generation. Unfortunately, no scientific study exists on voting behaviour in Quebec before 1960, making it difficult to examine this question accurately. However, a series of observations can be made. In the provincial political arena, Quebec brought to power Maurice Duplessis's Union Nationale four times between 1944 and 1960. If the women of Quebec were grateful to the Liberal party, which gave them their right to vote, this certainly was not evident in the electoral results of the following two decades. Furthermore, Quebec's first scientific voting survey, carried out in the fall of 1959, demonstrated that 63 per cent of women voters favored the Union Nationale and 34 per cent the Liberals.[34]

At the federal level, Quebec women likely voted against the referendum concerning the military draft proposed by the Liberal party in 1942. One can only guess at their motives. Quebec women contributed to bringing the Conservatives to power in 1958; yet, once again, the facts about their choice at the polls are not known. Possibly, many supported Réal Caouette's Créditistes in counties where this third party presented candidates. Published studies on the Créditiste phenomenon in Quebec mention nothing of the "gender gap" or give little importance to the variable of gender.[35]

Finally, the great champion of the right to vote, Thérèse Casgrain, officially broke with the Liberal party at the beginning of the 1950s and became the Quebec leader of the Co-operative Commonwealth Federation (CCF).[36] For Quebec women in the 1950s and 1960s, she was more closely associated with the Quebec Left than she was with her fight for the right to vote, which was seen at the time as an amusing anomaly.

It seems to me that the political and voting behaviour of Quebec women is a rather difficult phenomenon to analyse. In the present state of knowledge, it can be said that if the tendencies observed during the 1960s and 1970s denote a preference by women for the Liberal party, one cannot attribute it, as does Sylvia Bashevkin, to the fact that it was the Liberal party which accorded women the right to vote.[37] The fact is that Quebec women never fought collectively for that right; rather, the general evolution they went through after 1940 better explains their behaviour. If they supported the Liberal party after 1965, then the reasons for their choice must be sought elsewhere.

The great number of different, even contradictory, studies on the participation of Quebec women in politics should put us on our guard. Between the popular adage "A woman should not cancel out her husband's vote" and the studies which illustrate the major changes experienced by Quebec women between 1965 and 1979,[38] one must realize that traditional political science is still powerless to introduce perspectives suggested by feminist analysis.[39] This is especially true for the period between 1940 and 1965.

Thus, as Monique Bégin has well illustrated in her essay in this volume, during the short period marking the emergence of contemporary women as a movement in Canada, Quebec women played the central role because it was the symmetry and the channels of communication between the two linguistic groups which ensured the success of the operation to establish the Royal Commission. Besides, the ideas and demands resulting from its *Report on the Status of Women in Canada* (1970) benefited from, among other things, the very dense networks of Cercles des Fermières and Cercles de l'AFEAS, and from the groups affiliated with the Fédération des femmes du Québec, to encourage public discussion of the report.

In 1971, the question of women became as important a question in Quebec as that of Quebec nationalism. And since Quebec nationalism changed drastically after 1960, the relationship of nationalism with feminism can no longer be examined in the same way as at the turn of the century, at the time of the Fédération nationale Saint-Jean-Baptiste.

THOUGHTS ON THE QUIET REVOLUTION AND NATIONALISM

These preceding observations enable me to propose new ideas on the Quiet Revolution and on the relationship between nationalism and feminism. The turning point of 1960 is so omnipresent in studies on Quebec that it seems to be a boringly obvious detail. In an article which became a classic in the theory of the history of women, Joan Kelly emphasizes a three-part methodology to make women on a par with men as subjects of history.[40] She suggests, among other things, the re-evaluation of periodization, the introduction of the category of gender into all analyses, and the re-examination of social change in comparison with the experience of women.

The coinciding of the rise of feminism with the Quiet Revolution has led most observers to link the two phenomena and to conclude that the feminist movement of the 1960s was just one manifestation, among many others, of Quebec's abrupt entry into the modern world. Since the Quiet Revolution was an important date in the "progress of Quebec," it is, therefore, logical that it be the same for women. All the elements are there to support the theory: bill 16 which transformed the legal status of married women in 1964; universal, free access to secondary and collegiate education; the development of new professions; the decrease in the birth rate; the secularization of society; the increase in the life span; the massive entry of women into the work force. After all, did Quebec women not have the example of the American, French, and English-Canadian women to encourage them?

The reorganization of feminism in 1965 did not occur spontaneously. The processes of changing mentalities were working slowly, as much with the "ordinary" women in traditional women's associations as with the more educated women aware of the impossible dead-ends that society offered to them. This new mentality expressed itself clearly and categorically during the mid-1950s. Moreover, structural changes, which were only accelerated and confirmed by legislation after 1960, were already taking place.

There is more. The examination of a few connected phenomena, usually hidden, even justifies a new look at certain aspects of the Quiet Revolution. In the fields of education, social services, and hospital care, women held a great number of positions of authority, from which they were gradually excluded after 1960. In primary and secondary public education alone, the statistics speak for themselves: women held 59 per cent of the positions of authority in public primary and secondary education in 1960; they held no more than 25 per cent in 1985. At the collegiate level, the process of masculinization was even more outrageous. In fact, in education, secularization also meant masculinization. The same process occurred in hospitals. After the hospital insurance law of 1962, women were progressively eliminated from the administrative positions that they had held.[41]

In the 1960s the so-called women's professions, avenues which had opened up during the 1940s and 1950s, gradually became hierarchical and bureaucratic. University programs were separated from collegiate-level programs. This facilitated the building of a hierarchy, a process which happened with social work, physiotherapy, dietetics, and library science. Certainly, these phenomena were not peculiar to Quebec; they occurred gradually from the start of the twentieth century throughout the English-speaking world. In Quebec, the Quiet Revolution facilitated this process. And women, who for three hundred years had administered hospitals, schools, colleges, hospices, social services, and libraries, became the favourite targets of the new class of administrators.

A few years after the Quiet Revolution, women were completely excluded from the positions of responsibility that they had held, replaced by young, presumably competent administrators, usually male. Through secularization, "desexing," and becoming more hierarchical, these professions became ladders for the advancement of male careers. As long as it was invisible, anonymous, and, especially, free, feminine competency was very well tolerated. It seems that it was not acceptable when it was matched with an administrator's salary.

The secularization of Quebec society is often used to explain these transformations in managerial positions. However, secularization is not to be blamed, because the members or ex-members of religious congregations kept their responsibilities and authority in the new organizational structures. It was the women who were eliminated. Although these phenomena are just starting to be scientifically documented, their gradual discovery has certainly fed the feminist awareness of many women.

There is still more. Quebec society then took another turn: towards coeducation. As the analyses of the Parent Report well illustrated, "a movement of segregation of the sexes existed [in our school system] for which we see no justification." It is well known that the English-speaking world opted for co-education at the end of the nineteenth century. Certainly, it was applied unevenly, but mostly in a most progressive manner. In 1960 Quebec was an anachronism with its duplicate education system where not only the institutions but the study programs as well were distinct.

Thus the rapid adoption of coeducation after 1965 coincided with the democratization of the school system. This coincidence had unforeseen and contradictory effects on the personal orientation and determination of young women. The determination of older women could have been affected positively by their passage into an exclusively female system of education before 1970. Theories on the history of the education of girls have led to a questioning, after several years, of the myth of the positive character of coeducation.[42]

If I were to add that all this happened very quickly, almost overnight, and at the same time as the so-called sexual revolution, one would see that it produced effects that have not yet been examined. In the rest of North America, adolescents were familiar with mixed school classes. It seems impossible to change a system abruptly without affecting the whole society. All of a sudden, women were confronted simultaneously with the opening up of society and the subtle modes of systemic discrimination. We can hypothesize that this gave them additional reasons for mobilizing when feminism spread like wildfire in the 1970s.

Let us not forget, however, that all these transformations were contemporaneous with the rise of Quebec nationalism after 1960. Whatever its face, Quebec nationalism passed through most political options, and it is wrong to associate it with any one party in particular. As well, in Quebec there are many ways to be a federalist. In fact, Quebec reality inspires all social movements, and it would be surprising if it were not so with the whole gamut of feminist positions.[43] This explains the many close relationships between nationalism and feminism, mainly in "revolutionary" groups. *Le Manifeste des femmes québécoises* of 1971 appeared alongside the *Manifeste du Front de libération du Québec* (FLQ) of 1970. As elsewhere in the world, the movement for national emancipation meant specific aspirations for women.[44] In the autumn of 1970, while all of Canada was divided over the application of the War Measures Act in the province, Quebec women who found themselves in prison found additional reasons to become more radical. As elsewhere in the world, feminism was feeding upon movements of social and political protest that were fermenting in Quebec after 1970.

It is clear that the 1960s and 1970s were a complex time for women, a time of both advance and setback, and certainly different from the rest of Canada. Joan Kelly is right; it is not possible to examine this period without taking into consideration the reality of women. When different studies are carried out, it is easier to understand the specificity of Quebec feminism. The term "distinct" could be used to describe it.

It was not by chance that Monique Bégin, Jeanne Sauvé, and Albanie Morin were elected to the House of Commons in 1972. It was not by chance that the Parti Québécois was the first party to adopt a specific policy on women. It was not by chance that its committees on the status of women collapsed after 1978, when women realized that their priorities would never become those of that political option. It was not by chance that the report published by the Council for the Status of Women in Quebec on the overall policy on the condition of women was called *Pour les Québécoises: Egalité et Indépendance* (*For Quebec Women: Equality and Independence*).[45] It was not by chance that at the time of the referendum in 1980, fourteen thousand women from the No camp gathered at the Montreal Forum, whereas, two weeks later, fifteen thousand from the Yes camp gathered at the Complexe Desjardins.[46] Despite solicitation from both camps, studies on the specificity of the vote of women have shown the irrelevance of analyses based on the sexual variable in the referendum campaign.[47]

It is not by chance that Quebec has so many female members of Parliament. The thirteen Quebec women elected to the House of Commons in 1984 were not elected by accident, as stated in the English-language press. Ten of them were re-elected in 1989 along with three newcomers.

The truth is that feminism in Quebec was stimulated and nurtured by the powerful nationalist movement which swept Quebec between 1963 and 1990. Whether opponents or partisans of sovereignty, the women of Quebec knew how to combine causes and, in this way, shaped a feminism different from that in the rest of Canada. In the painful discussions around the debate on the ratification of the constitution in 1981, the women of Quebec did not betray the cause of women; they did not put the Quebec cause before women's cause. They simply defined what seemed indispensable for them to remain both feminists and Quebecers.

PART TWO

The Development and Interactions of the Women's Movement in Canada and the United States since the 1960s

THE ESSAYS IN THIS SECTION BEGIN TO MOVE CHRONOLOGI-
cally beyond the early years of the resurgent feminist movement,
beyond an analysis of the originating influences, to examine the
workings of the women's movement after it had reached fuller
maturity. The constitutional amendment process in Canada and the
United States is the primary focus here, with writers attempting to
evaluate the role of the feminist movement in constitutional reform,
the obstacles and resistance presented to feminist demands, and the
relative effectiveness of feminist activism on constitutional questions.

Naomi Black's essay provides an explicitly comparative focus, in
which she contrasts the activities of the American-based National
Organization of Women to obtain ratification of the Equal Rights
Amendment, and the efforts of the Toronto-based "Ad Hoc Committee" to secure the entrenchment of women's equality rights in the
Canadian Charter of Rights and Freedoms. She undertakes the difficult and complex task of attempting to explain the differing levels
of resistance presented by anti-feminist forces in the two countries,
and the reasons behind the American failure and Canadian success
on the constitutional front.

Micheline de Sève builds upon Black's preliminary discussions
about the dissension of Quebec feminists from the constitutional
agenda of the larger Canadian women's movement. Noting the cultural divide between the French-speaking and English-speaking
parts of the movement, she notes that the two rarely read the same
books or journals and are informed by totally different media. De
Sève points out that English-Canadian feminists struggled for the
inclusion of women within the charter, seemingly oblivious to the
fact that Quebec women would not participate because their province
was estranged from the entire repatriation process.

These essays provide a framework from which to begin to understand the differing structures and environments surrounding the
contemporary feminist movements in the United States, Canada, and
Quebec.

6 Ripples in the Second Wave: Comparing the Contemporary Women's Movement in Canada and the United States

NAOMI BLACK

Men and women shall have equal rights throughout the United States and every place subject to its jurisdiction.
(Proposed "Lucretia Mott Amendment," Seneca Falls, New York, 1923)

All people are equal under the law and there shall be no discrimination because of race, creed, sex, social status or family origin.
(Article 14, New Constitution, Japan, 1947)

Equality of rights under the law shall not be denied or abridged by the United States or by any State on account of sex.
(Equal Rights Amendment, approved by the Congress of the United States, March, 1972)

(1) Every individual is equal before and under the law and has the right to equal protection and equal benefit of the law without discrimination and, in particular, without discrimination based on race, national or ethnic origin, colour, religion, sex, age or mental or physical disability.
(2) Subsection (1) does not preclude any law, program or activity that has as its object the amelioration of conditions of disadvantaged individuals or groups including those that are disadvantaged because of race, national or ethnic origin, colour, religion, sex, age or mental or physical disability.
(Section 15, Canadian Charter of Rights and Freedoms, April 1982)

Notwithstanding anything in this Charter, the rights and freedoms referred to in it are guaranteed equally to male and female persons.
(Section 28, Canadian Charter of Rights and Freedoms, April 1982)

Like most features of Canada's social and political life, the Canadian women's movement has its most salient relationships with the United States. Influenced by that country, Canada has tended to define itself in contrast and opposition to its neighbour. From the United States' perspective as well, shared history as well as geographical and cultural closeness make Canadian-American comparisons both logical and illuminating. Yet, surprisingly, no one has yet seriously attempted to compare the contemporary women's movements of the United States and Canada. We may begin this task by looking at two superficially similar campaigns during which women's groups attempted to obtain approval of constitutional guarantees of women's equality: the feminist activities in support of the American Equal Rights Amendment and those supporting the equality provisions of the Canadian Charter of Rights and Freedoms.

There is a long, largely unexplored history of contact between the Canadian and the American women's movements, known to us mainly through anecdotes. American examples, visitors, and emigrants have exerted considerable influence. Even today, second-wave feminists such as Betty Friedan and Gloria Steinem continue the tradition of visiting lecturers that goes back to Lucy Stone in Toronto in 1855. On that occasion Mary Ann Shadd (Cary), the editor of the *Provincial Freeman*, reported that even in Toronto, "with the strong attachment to antiquated notions respecting woman and her sphere, so prevalent," Stone was "listened to patiently, applauded abundantly, and patronized extensively." Shadd herself was a notable example of the movement of feminists back and forth across the border.[1]

In general, such fragmentary evidence as we have suggests that Canadian feminists have on occasion accepted American precedents, while insisting on Canadian distinctiveness. Canadian consciousness of the border never prevented Canadian feminists from looking to the south for training or inspiration. Emily Howard Stowe and Jenny Trout, Canada's first two women doctors, obtained in the United States the medical degrees refused them at home, and Letitia Youmans started the Canadian Woman's Christian Temperance Union when she returned from the conference that founded the United States branch.[2]

At the beginning of the second wave, as feminism moved once more into the media, American influence increased. So too did Canadian sensitivity. In 1963 the feminist editor of the largest mass-market Canadian women's magazine, *Chatelaine*, rejected an offer to serialize *The Feminine Mystique*. Doris Anderson felt that her journal had already published most of the book's substance and was "far more advanced and 'radical' than any of the large US magazines."[3] Three years later Anderson was publicizing a Committee for Equality that wanted – and eventually got – a Royal Commission on the Status of Women modelled on the American Presidential Commission on the Status of Women.

By the late 1960s the North American women's liberation movement was beginning on a continental scale, in part as an outgrowth of the student radicalism that had retraced the route of the underground railway to Canada. When there were five women's liberation groups in North America, one of them was in Toronto.[4] But soon Canadian women who were student activists agreed with their male compan- ions in opposing American dominance, within the student movement as elsewhere. The women then called upon Canadian traditions in order to reject the chauvinism of those same men. For instance, when the members of Toronto Women's Liberation first considered secession from the Toronto New Left Committee, they declared: "We are going to be the typers of letters and distributors of leaflets (hewers of wood and drawers of water) no longer."[5] Their rhetoric had a specifically Canadian resonance, as did the modelling of the 1970 Abortion Caravan on the "On to Ottawa" trek of the Great Depression.[6] In Quebec, the situation was even more clear cut. Amer- ican feminists provided the catalyst for the first women's liberation group but they were soon expelled; their anglophone presence was incompatible with Quebec's nationalist emphasis on French culture and language.

The history represented by these accounts justifies examination of differences among two national women's movements so closely con- nected and yet clearly distinctive. The goal is, eventually, to cast some light on the relative effectiveness of the two movements, focusing on their impact as political actors.

As scholars finally begin to direct attention to the changes in the status and activities of women, an explanation of progress in the cause of women has emerged among feminist and non-feminist ana- lysts alike. What could be called the "ripples in the wave" theory derives all the landmarks of the women's movement from mainstream ones. It begins something like this: Mary Wollstonecraft, who started modern feminism, represents the Rousseauian revolt as it applies to women. It continues: 1848 was a year of social upheavals producing the Communist Manifesto and the Seneca Falls Convention and Dec- laration. The vote was part of reforms processed in the political renewal after the First or Second World War. The Canadian (or the American) women's movement of our time is just a ripple in the second wave of feminism, which in turn is best understood as part of the student and other revolts most conspicuous in 1968.

In general, the history and analysis of feminism as an organized entity tend to refer to models of social movements, with an emphasis on the adjective "social." The marginality of women's activities is sustained by discussing them separately from what is regarded as normal politics. In this way conventional analysts of politics implicitly disparage the degree of agency and of political involvement of women activists. Such dismissive analyses represent androcentrism at its most obvious. In them, the contest for public resources is defined as an activity with which women are unconcerned and in relation to which they are assumed to be incompetent. Women's organizations are seen as something outside of politics, possibly dependent on it, but in no way interacting with it. The role of the women's movement as a political actor is accordingly minimized, for its membership, by definition, excludes it from struggles for power. It is not surprising that a large amount of what is now identified as the study of "women in politics" consists of rationalizations for the absence of women from politics.[7]

Even feminist activists themselves are likely to explain women's political success in ways that downplay the effort involved. "There is one thing mightier than kings or armies, congresses or political parties," said Carrie Chapman Catt in 1917, "the power of an idea whose time has come."[8] As the triumphant leader of the last phase of fifty-two years of struggle, Catt knew very well that more than the passage of time and the power of ideas had enfranchised American women. And if the time was ripe for the idea of women's vote in the United States and Britain after the First World War, why not in France and Italy?

Or let us shift to the present day, and the attempts at equal rights amendments in constitutions, to wonder why the time was ripe in Canada in 1982 and not in the United States at the same time? And why was an equal rights provision possible in Japan thirty-five years earlier? Surely the indigenous women's movements must be given some credit for the successes. In Japan, for instance, suffrage pioneers played a significant role in the campaigns encouraging women's political activism after they were enfranchised by the Occupation. It seems unlikely that the well-established if little-known Japanese women's movement had no share in the earlier American decision that the democratization of Japan required an increase in the political influence of Japanese women.[9]

Among academic analysts, feminists are becoming aware of the way in which women's political activities are discounted. However, they also, by their own discussions, continue to minimize the potential political role of women's groups. Those "equity" feminists who adapt existing ideologies to include women share the tendency of those ideologies to exclude women's group activities from politics.[10] If discrimination or oppression is seen as the key characteristic of women's situation, then women and women's organizations are identified as remote from the normal interactions of power. The remedy, according to such assimilationist analyses, is to incorporate women into a predefined political structure. Then and only then will they become political.

Thus, equity feminists in the American equal rights tradition argue that women have been denied their entitlement as citizens while being prevented from acquiring the education and economic capacities that would give them an independent chance to seek influence. The Equal Rights Amendment (ERA) represents an attempt at remedy, with its goal of preventing differential treatment of women, which is seen as disadvantageous. In the context of such an analysis, women's groups have only the most tenuous claim to be political. Until the ERA is achieved, women's groups are useful – but only as a temporary sheltered workshop.

Similarly, for a Gramscian (equity) feminist the notion of gender is combined with the notion of class so that "hegemonic and counter-hegemonic blocs and the ideological cement that holds them together are always at least doubly constituted by class and gender politics."[11] Women's organizations then become valuable resources, but only as part of "alternative sources of political power and social reproduction" along with factory councils, trade unions, and political parties.[12] Subsumed into pre-existing theory, the women's movement finds itself used instrumentally to serve a predetermined political analysis, either ignored or manipulated in the service of a predefined, male-dominated cause. Women cannot have any separate group interest in relation to politics for they have no distinctive identity; they are merely one more minority or one more source of counter-hegemonic resistance.[13]

Even "social" feminists – those who base their analysis on goals related to women's differentiated experience and values – have been reluctant to articulate the relationship of their organizational efforts to normal politics. Basing their analysis on the uniqueness and the private basis of women's experience, they may be inclined to accept with pride the designation of social rather than political. Social feminist practitioners deplore the manipulativeness and lack of vision of politics as it exists; they may consequently disclaim any intention to wield power as men have defined and exercised it. Yet how except through politics could they make effective those goals and preferences, which they identify as those of women in contrast to men?[14] The equality clauses of the Canadian charter reflect the complexity of such feminists' suggested remedies for women's disadvantages: inclusion of women in public life has to be accompanied by an attempt to alter structures as well as participants.

By now we should be ready to question the usefulness of denying the political nature of the women's movement, however defined and analysed. It is understandable that conventional analysts find it reassuring to diminish the role of organized feminism by defining out of existence its relationships with other political institutions. Feminist scholars may well want to borrow legitimacy from existing analyses. This may even be effective tactically if feminist activists minimize their need for influence and concern for power. Yet strategy needs a basis in reality and so does scholarly analysis.

This discussion will therefore start with the recognition that women's movements are related to the mainstream political system. More, I shall insist that women's movements themselves are in fact political, since they seek to influence public policy and the structure of public life. For each national or other political unit, it should be possible to consider influences on feminism that are particular to that unit. We can then proceed to analyse feminist activities and particularly their successes or failures in relation to the other political forces.[15]

On the basis of such research we can develop generalizations about how women's movements most effectively operate in relation to supportive – or should we say relatively less unsupportive? – political environments. We can also, as here, use such analyses to characterize and contrast the women's movements of different countries.

In this instance we encounter the hazards of comparative research, and particularly of comparative research on different national women's movements. The most serious problem is the definition or delineation of the women's movements that are to be compared.[16] Mary Fainsod Katzenstein and Carol McClurg Mueller have recently edited a collection of studies of what they identify as the women's movements of the United States and Western Europe. Their introduction directs attention to "the multiple networks through which feminist consciousness and activism is promoted." They list consciousness-raising groups, task forces, collectives, women's caucuses, women's centres, women's studies programs, and feminist publishing houses, all of which must be included in a comprehensive notion of the "women's movement." Katzenstein and Mueller identify all such elements of the movement as political; their goal is "to trace the complicated web that links feminist organizations to other *political institutions*."[17] Any of the groups involved could be used as the focus of analysis of the women's movement.

The individual investigator has to select the point in the process, the sector of the web, on which he or she wishes to concentrate. In the process, certain segments of the network are likely to be identified as being "the" movement. Nor is this present study exempt from such hazards. As a political scientist, I ascribe great value to policy change; as an activist, I have pursued this goal. Yet, at the same time, as a political scientist I fear excessive concentration on the state, given what we know about the lack of autonomy and also the lack of representativeness of the state. And as a feminist, I distrust acceptance of the male-developed and male-centred political process customarily presented as authoritative. Yet study of the women's movement as political actor is likely to direct attention towards those parts of the government that have authority for legislative or bureaucratic change and, accordingly, in the direction of those women's groups that take initiatives towards and interact with those sectors of the government.

In addition, a focus on political change is likely to direct attention to the national level of both political pressure and policy. As the largest-scale and most professionalized arena of attempts at change, national politics may be the least characteristic sector of the women's movements of each country. In a movement which both prides itself in and suffers from its diversity and its localness of scale and project, the grand public campaigns are atypical. Yet such campaigns are the easiest to study. Is it reasonable to hope that they demonstrate, if writ over-simply large, significant features of the national movement?

Further problems appear as a result of adopting as subject matter the constitutional reform campaigns I have suggested. It is all too easy to present on behalf of "the movement" a perception that reflects only that part of the movement which historically supported the measure under consideration. These two cases encourage the analyst to disregard subnational differences and other tensions within the women's movement. For Canada, this is an issue that can refer to the important Quebec women's movement only through an explanation of its non-participation. For the United States, the history of the ERA implies that historical disagreements among feminists were transcended in the period of contemporary support of the amendment. Such problems can be countered, though incompletely, by deliberate effort. But a secondary analysis like this one is dependent on earlier studies which made no such effort at inclusiveness.

In addition, we should note that these campaigns were not necessarily the most important carried on by the respective movements. Certainly activity of the sort that produces, for instance, a women's health centre or a local protest against pornography is likely to be disregarded. A case can without difficulty be made for the greater potential significance of efforts related to pay and working conditions, including those related to child care, or to responses to violence against women, or to issues related to reproduction.

The constitutional campaigns did, however, acquire a considerable symbolic significance; the ERA has had that effect for the American women's movement since the interwar period (though initially with conflicting interpretations), and the charter has retroactively been developed into a source of pride and solidarity among federalist feminists in Canada. Attention to these issues may therefore be given some justification as based on the perceptions of the women involved. And for the analyst seeking something concrete to ground analysis, the constitutional cases have the immeasurably valuable characteristic of having repeatedly been recounted, so that a comparative analysis is now possible.

At this point we need a reminder of the comparative history of the equal rights clauses of the American and Canadian constitutions.[18]

First, let us look briefly at the Equal Rights Amendment, two of whose texts are given on the first page of this article. This constitutional amendment was formulated in the midst of a period in which courts persistently found women to be legally unequal to men; not until 1971 did the Supreme Court overrule its 1894 decision that limited the notion of legal persons to males.[19] Canadians, whose own Persons' Case was decided in 1929, should take note. Pride of authorship of the first ERA in 1923 goes to Alice Paul, who also gets major credit for keeping it alive when it lacked much support from either the public or organized feminists; in fact, during the interwar period, the women's movement in the United States was debilitated by the active resistance to the ERA by almost all women's groups except the National Woman's Party and, after 1937, the National Federation of Business and Professional Women's Clubs. This period can be dated from 1923 to the early 1950s, by which time active feminist opposition to the ERA ceased to be significant. Once it was established that protective legislation for all workers could resist legal challenge, the active women's groups moved into increasingly unified support of the ERA, which finally managed to get out of Congress in March 1972.

The remaining history of the ERA can be summed up briefly. On an aggregate basis, public opinion polls indicated majority support. But after a wave of quick, easy ratifications, the process stalled at the state level, leaving the amendment three short of the necessary thirty-eight state ratifications; a voted extension, again time-limited, was not adequate to produce any additional approvals. During the period of attempts at ratification, the whole range of women's organizations became publicly committed and deeply involved, with the National Organization for Women (NOW) as the most conspicuous. A considerable range of anti-ERA activity, with strong right-wing links, also emerged; Phyllis Schlafly's Stop ERA was the most obvious, and commentators agree that it was highly effective. The ERA seems at present a dead issue, and the women's movement has turned to assessing the reasons for its failure along with an attempt at seeing the results of the struggle for ratification.

We should note that an increasing number of feminist analysts view the ERA itself as unnecessary in legal terms, given the legislation and judicial interpretations of the 1970s and 1980s.[20] Equality under the law now seems an accepted principle, and more activist affirmative versions can be inferred from legislation such as Title VII of the Civil Rights Act. The problem here, of course, is the possibility of the impact of a more conservative series of relevant interpretations by an increasingly conservative Supreme Court. The American feminist reliance on Congress and accompanying distrust of judicial intervention should be noted in the context of Canadian feminists' efforts to insert into their constitution a principle of judicial review.

The politics of the ERA must, it seems, be looked at in the context of two major elements in American constitutionalism: judicial review (and therefore judicial policy-determination) and states' rights (particularly as this issue applies to constitutional amendment). The United States constitution has, as an intrinsic and defining section, a Bill of Rights backed up by a Supreme Court entitled, since the case of *Marbury* v. *Madison* (1803), to review on grounds of constitutionality any laws brought to it under the appropriate procedures. This means that the rights listed in the Bill of Rights, and any added to the constitution by amendment, can be used as a basis of voiding enactments of legislative bodies, including state legislatures. It is understandable that amending the American constitution is very difficult, requiring exceptional majorities of two-thirds in both houses of Congress to introduce amendments and fortifying this requirement by adding to it the need for subsequent consent from legislatures of three-quarters of the states. Joan Hoff-Wilson sums up the conditions for successful amendment: there must be a pre-existing consensus at the state level and a sense of national necessity.[21] She also points out what all commentators insist upon: that constitutional amendments necessarily confront states' rights. The difficulty of the process initially hampered the attempt at ratification.

In stark contrast are the standing and history of the relevant clauses of the Canadian constitution, which date only from the decade of the 1980s. Here the context is federal-provincial relations, only weakly analogous to states-rights struggles in the United States, and affected additionally by the issue of relations between Quebec and anglophone Canada.

Prior to 1982 the Canadian "constitution" consisted of an enactment of the British Parliament, the British North America Act of 1867, amplified by its incorporation of Britain's own "unwritten" constitution of legal entitlements as well as an accumulation of British and Canadian statutes, legal judgments, and accepted practices or conventions. It included neither a bill of rights nor a tradition of judicial review of law on other than procedural grounds. A so-called Bill of Rights, passed in Canada in 1960, dealt only with equal treatment under the law and soon showed itself ineffective in dealing with women's disadvantages. Specifically, as a series of notorious cases demonstrated in the 1970s, the Bill of Rights left unscathed legal discrimination against aboriginal women, farm wives (and by implication all married women), and women in the paid labour force.[22]

At the beginning of the 1980s the question of a formal constitution for Canada became a major issue in Canadian politics. In 1980 Quebec defeated a referendum for independence talks (partly because of women's votes for federalism). During the referendum, the federal government promised redress of Quebec's persistent grievances about the structure of confederation; after the defeat, it was accordingly pressed for a reformulated and "patriated" constitution. The constitution proposed by the federal government included a Charter of Rights and Freedoms entailing, for the first time, a formal judicial review of law in terms of basic principles. The federal women's organizations generally reacted with enthusiasm to the suggestion that women's rights to equality might be enshrined in fundamental law. Individual legislative or administrative acts could then be challenged directly and possibly ruled unacceptable. At the same time, however, civil liberties organizations in Canada demonstrated continuing distrust of judicial interference with legislative enactments, even, sometimes especially, when basic rights were at issue. And Quebec feminists, committed to the province's own struggle for greater autonomy, also feared any supersession of the province's own progressive Charter of Human Rights and Freedoms.

For federally committed feminists, who were mainly though not entirely anglophone, the 1980–81 campaign for women's rights in the Constitution became a landmark similar to the Persons' Case of 1929, an icon of feminist effectiveness.[23] According to Penney Kome, a feminist journalist, "A political earthquake occurred in Canada in 1981, dramatically changing the foundation for government policy making."[24] In a first stage, the lobbying efforts of women's groups produced modification of a proposed equal rights clause so that it would include the concerns raised by the failures of the Canadian Bill of Rights. In January 1981 the minister of justice announced in response that section 15 of the charter was now to read: "Every individual is equal before and under the law and has the right to equal protection of the law and equal benefit of the law." This seemingly clumsy formulation attempted to ensure, not just that laws were equally enforced, but also that they would have no discriminatory provisions and no discriminatory impact.

Then, with considerable publicity, a national conference on women and the constitution scheduled for February 1981 by the National Advisory Council on the Status of Women was cancelled in response to government pressure. A small Toronto-centred group of feminists acted as an Ad Hoc Committee to hold the conference as originally scheduled. They surprised themselves and many others by holding in February 1981, without government funding, a successful three-day meeting of some thirteen hundred women from across Canada. Again, publicity was considerable.

At its 1981 annual general meeting, the National Action Committee on the Status of Women (NAC), Canada's mainstream umbrella group of women's organizations, which had previously been divided in its views about the charter, voted to support the Ad Hoc Conference's resolutions, including the final call for the resignation of the minister responsible for the status of women and a public investigation of the federal Advisory Council on the Status of Women. The Fédération des femmes du Québec, the feminist umbrella group, left the meeting and NAC as it had earlier threatened: among other reasons, Quebec had not given approval to the patriated constitution. Then, in April, after continued lobbying by members of the Ad Hoc Committee, section 15's guarantees of equality were backed up by section 28, which stated that "Notwithstanding anything in this Charter, the rights and freedoms referred to in it are guaranteed equally to male and female persons."

That fall, a federal-provincial conference bypassed Quebec to work out an "override" arrangement that would allow provinces to pass special, limited-term legislation in any area "notwithstanding" any guarantees in the charter. So little importance was attached to the special provision of section 28 that it was not even discussed, and only several days later was it clear that the override applied to that section also. The Ad Hoc Committee once more served as a rallying point and, together with the help of provincial groups, including the Advisory Councils on the Status of Women, and a public pressure campaign of telegrams and phone calls, finally persuaded the provincial premiers to exempt section 28 from the override. Many Canadian feminists were jubilant, inclined to crow that Canadian women had achieved what the Americans could not.

This enthusiasm should be moderated by the reminder that this feminist version of this series of events is by no means the only one possible. Most accounts of the process give only the scantiest mention of the role of women. For instance, Jean Chrétien, justice minister at the time and centrally responsible for the negotiations, has no reference whatsoever in his memoirs to the women's constitutional conference, and not a word about the development of sections 15 and 28. He does refer in passing to the abandonment of the women's guarantee (by the insertion of the override clause), attributing it to the actions of a single provincial premier who favoured "the authority of the legislative assembly." He then notes with some amusement the way in which the women of Canada brought the premier of Saskatchewan to heel.[25] It is the only time Chrétien mentions the role of women in his detailed account of the constitutional negotiations. Aboriginal peoples are far more prominent, and indeed Premier Allan Blakeney was able to block the women's guarantee only because he negotiated support for this position from two other premiers who opposed enshrining aboriginal rights. And for Quebec feminists, of course, the exclusion of Quebec from the final constitutional settlement completely overshadowed the entire issue of the charter amendments.[26]

In practice, the ensuing litigation under the Charter of Rights has operated much as the ERA was expected to: removing those legal distinctions between men and women that were initially designed as protections for women, including provisions establishing offences such as statutory rape.[27] However, the charter has also provided the basis for voiding Canada's rather restrictive abortion legislation and, in anticipation of the coming into effect of the equality provisions (delayed three years for that purpose), a good deal of federal and provincial legislation was brought into conformity with it. Of particular relevance to feminists, the discriminatory provisions of the Indian Act were repealed and, recently, women have been officially given access to all combat jobs in the armed forces. This is more than the ERA would have done, of course (the legislative will of Congress being determinative according to most authorities).

An oversimplified summary of the two constitutional campaigns might say that the ERA was defeated by subnational resistance while Canadian feminists managed to undo such a defeat. In both cases, relations between federal units were key. However, in the case of the ERA, questions related to the situation of women were incorporated into a public debate, so that opposition to the ERA on states' rights grounds was reinforced (and given legitimation) by anxiety about the changing roles and status of women. These concerns were certainly defensive and frightened, in many cases reflecting conservative ideologies. But much of the opposition, especially from women and women's groups, also reflected a vision of women's culture and specificity to which American feminist activists have been relatively unresponsive.

By contrast, in the Canadian case, resistance to enshrining gender equality certainly took similar forms – the more recent rise of the anti-feminist group REAL Women is one piece of evidence – but pro-family rhetoric seems to have had less impact on public life. One reason may be the fact that the mainstream women's movement in Canada has historically been relatively responsive to a feminism based on women's specificity. In general, in Canada opposition to an equality clause (and to exemption to the override) remained almost purely instrumental. Those Canadians opposed to a judicially reviewable bill of rights objected to provisions relating to women but no more than to any other provisions of a judicially reviewable bill of rights. Within the women's movement, civil libertarians were torn between their commitment to women's rights and their distrust of the courts; as an organization, NAC was immobilized by such conflicts for much of the constitutional campaign. For their part, provincial leaders were indifferent to the actual consequences for women of any constitutional reform, but alert to any for federal-provincial relations.

We can see other differences in the struggles. For instance, the mere duration of the ERA battle along with its prolongation from the relatively activist 1970s into the more conservative 1980s permitted anti-feminists to mobilize against the ERA and to fortify the bias towards inaction, while the Canadian struggle was brief and took place when potential opposition groups of women were not yet sufficiently institutionalized to be effective. Or we can delineate similarities, such as the failure of either amending process to become a partisan issue. In both countries the limited and instrumental view taken of the issues by all political parties helped further to disillusion women with partisan politics, while also strengthening the existing women's groups (we may note that here they replicated the experience of the first wave).

But this does not give us the promised contrast of the two women's movements. I shall conclude with a preliminary outline of what these two campaigns show about the movements as they attempted to cope with the vagaries of two rather different federal systems.

The most obvious differences between the Canadian and American women's movements, as studied here, seem to be structural (and again we must remember that the subjects selected incline the analyst to a focus on structure rather than on process). In Canada, a movement that is provincially fragmented but strongly federalist, to the extent that it has a national presence at all, was able to mobilize small-scale but effective elite pressure for an issue where executives could move without consulting their legislatures. I see no evidence that it became, as some claim, an effective lobbyist. The feminist elite was able to demonstrate sufficient public support to imply future trouble, but without mobilizing a new or even a very large constituency. The movement is not unified but it is widespread and has strong local bases, including elite contacts. The umbrella/coalition structure so characteristic of Canadian organizations enables a national group to call on a wide range of other sympathizers – on the necessary local basis. Radical supporters, included but not incorporated, did not surface as a liability. We can guess that a longer-drawn-out struggle would have produced schism, with the more radical components the first to go. Certainly this campaign exacerbated the ongoing tensions between anglopohones, mostly federalists, and francophones.

In the u.s. stronger national organizations exist, and they are not coalitions. They maintain strength, like the u.s. political parties, by assimilating the viewpoints of competitors. This means, however, that in a long campaign they may come to be identified by the characteristics of the least popular contributors to the group position. At the best, their campaigns will be guided by the decisions (and ideology) of the national group in a way that is not possible in Canada. In the ERA case, which had to be fought at a state level, national guidelines were unlikely to fit. But for a truly national campaign, if there was one, the machinery would be excellent, especially for a quick effort. A quick state-level effort might well, however, have been even less successful than the long-drawn-out agony of the ERA; I doubt (on virtually no evidence, admittedly)[28] whether subnational pressures like those which succeeded in exempting women's rights from the charter override could have been effectively mobilized in the U.S.

In Canada, national coalitions can hang together over time but are unable to be effective lobbyists at that level; their coalition structure makes it virtually impossible for them to mobilize resources or even agreement to the necessary degree. The Ad Hoc Committee on the charter was, after all, self-appointed and unsupported by any organizational decisions about appropriate response to the charter proposals. Such inability to exert effective pressure at the federal level is usually relatively unimportant because, given federal structures in Canada, the necessary campaigns are rarely national or cross-provincial.[29] They can well be independently handled by local groups of varying stripes, many of them combined though not assimilated into federal networks. NAC should perhaps look more carefully at its role as co-ordinator or, even more, communication network among locally based and loosely confederated sectors of the women's movement.

There is a further long list of other possible comparisons, even if we look only at the constitutional campaigns. They include such potentially significant differences as those related to funding, the involvement of men in the campaigns and organizations, relationships between NAC and NOW respectively and the longer-established women's groups, the role of unions, and regional and cultural splits including, most importantly, the very serious implications of Quebec's political and constitutional position. The conflict entailed in the competing claims of two women's movements in Canada which see themselves as "national" has been muted in the accounts of the women's movement's involvement in the constitutional struggles, mainly because the dissidence of Quebec's feminists has been casually subsumed under the non-co-operation of Quebec writ large. And the present account is not entirely innocent of such an analysis.

Such a discussion – dismissal? – of Quebec feminism is another version of "ripples in the stream." The anglophone feminists in Canada, who are currently grappling with the need for a "politics of difference" based on class and race, impoverish themselves both analytically and practically by ignoring the relevance of nationalism and its version of group identity. What feminists did not do in Quebec is as relevant to the understanding of the Canadian women's movement as what feminists did in fact do in the rest of the country.

Similarly, it is essential to include in discussion of the ERA the analysis of the absence or presence, success or failure, of each group oriented towards state ratification. The geography of the ERA battle makes it clear that it is not just that a given state was south or north, progressive or reactionary, that explained why ratification occurred. The politics of the women's movement – the active involvement of women's groups – mattered. For, even if the various women's groups of the two countries did not really produce Penney Kome's earthquake, surely we can agree that in the struggles discussed here they showed themselves to be far more than mere ripples.

7 The Perspectives of Quebec Feminists

MICHELINE DE SÈVE

Comparing the contemporary women's movement in Canada and the United States, Naomi Black laments the lack of awareness of United States feminists in relation to the Canadian women's movement. But what about the two solitudes in our one and only country? Black herself does not find the "cultural split" between the French and English fractions of our movement important enough to justify more than a few side remarks, reproducing the same attitude she condemns, nevertheless, in the case of feminists living in a far bigger country, our neighbours but not our compatriots. So, I have to try in a few pages, by way of an addendum or "comatization" as Mary O'Brien would say, to tell you how it feels to live feminism in Quebec now and to still be a Canadian, at least administratively speaking.

A first misunderstanding is related to what it means to be a Francophone from Quebec when most Francophones that English Canadians know are from outside Quebec. They have to master English. Living in places like Toronto or London, Ontario, Francophones cannot manage without speaking English. They are bilingual by definition and, as such, pertain to the same culture as you do. They enter in the global frame of multiculturalism where English is a common referent to all. Such is not the case in Quebec, where 85 per cent of Canadian Francophones live in a mostly French context. It means about 75 per cent of Francophones in Quebec, even with university degrees, do not speak English very well. For example, English is my third language. Statistics Canada (in a study made public 28 June 1989) found that less than 30 per cent of "Québécois" believe themselves to speak English, while 5 per cent of Anglophones from other provinces say they speak French.

So the language problem makes it almost impossible to grasp the reality of both parts of the Canadian feminist movement, because the difficulty that Naomi Black and other English-Canadian feminists have in understanding what is taking place in Quebec works both ways. We do not read the same books or journals, we do not listen to the same media, we do not stress the same events, since we live in totally different contexts and deal with distinct priorities or set of circumstances. I want to explain the surprises I encountered in reading the essay by Naomi Black, although she is one of the best-informed specialists in the field. I realized what it meant for her to speak of the most important topics of interaction between what she presented as the Canadian movement and the regional Quebec movement. She remained blind to the bi-national character of the women's movement in Canada, following the line of multiculturalist analysis, where pluralism always has its limits in the common reference to the English national standard.

Monique Bégin has described the channels of communication which linked francophone and anglophone Canadian women in the 1960s. At the time there were decent channels, but now I suspect that they are almost blocked. My intent is not to create more blockage but to try to explain why this tremendous gap exists between both cultural components of the Canadian women's movement.

When I was a young girl, my mother would tell me that if you want to know who your real friends are, they are the ones who tell you the truth. Perhaps it would be wise to warn you that I intend to be quite friendly in this commentary. I will take two topics for consideration: the Yvettes' movement in Quebec around the referendum of 1980 on sovereignty-association, which Naomi Black presented orally at the London conference, forgetting the association part of the proposal. And the second topic, another major issue: the debate over the federal Charter of Rights and Freedoms.

Reading the conference version of Naomi Black's essay, I was astonished to realize the importance that the Yvettes' rally had had in the representation of our history outside Quebec. A partisan political episode became an epitome of the women's movement in our part of the country. It was as if a Québécoise ignored everything in the English-Canadian movement except the importance of REAL Women. I then read other essays by anglophone feminist authors so as not to generalize too quickly. In *Feminist Organizing for Change: The Contemporary Women's Movement in Canada*, the editors had exactly three entries in the index for Quebec, and each time it said that they did not speak for Quebec since, as they honestly state, "our experiences are within the anglophone women's movement, and that is what this book is about."[1] Well, if such is the case, why not use this subtitle: *The Contemporary Women's Movement in English Canada*? Then I found in Penney Kome's *The Taking of Twenty-Eight: Women Challenge the Constitution* and in her *Women of Influence*, that: "Quebec as usual, presents a special case."[2] So special that the Yvettes are also very much there as the sole event worth mentioning for the account of the referendum in relation to feminism in Quebec.

The Yvettes were a large gathering of women for the No side during the debate on the Quebec provincial referendum in 1980. The Liberal party organized the meeting. It was quite striking for the English-Canadian feminist movement to see that there were fourteen thousand women rallying in the Montreal Forum speaking for the No side. It comforted the English-Canadian women's movement to think that feminists in Quebec, as elsewhere in the country, were federalists. Such famous names as Thérèse Casgrain and Monique Bégin were present on stage to support the credibility of this version of the event. However, seen from Quebec, the event was much more ambiguous. As Renée Dandurand and Evelyne Tardy have documented, the press presented the rally not as a No to the referendum but as a No to the feminist minister responsible for the status of women, Lise Payette.[3] In a partisan Parti Québécois rally, Payette had accused the wife of the leader of the opposition in Quebec, the Liberal leader of the campaign for the No, of being an Yvette. "Yvette" had been a character in school books for children: a sweet, obedient little girl, whose brother Guy was an aggressive, "normal" little boy. In her presentation, Payette said she herself, like all women, was raised as an Yvette and encouraged women to lose their fear and take the risk of voting Yes to the referendum. But she committed a blunder in responding to questions when she claimed that Claude Ryan, the leader of the opposition, was married to an Yvette.

This was the beginning of a parallel campaign to say No to Lise Payette as having not only attacked a respectable woman, Madeleine Ryan, but insulted every housewife in Quebec. The Liberal party invited women to say No to Lise Payette and ... No to the referendum. The Liberals played on the way women at home felt scorned by being identified with little Yvette washing the dishes, while her brother Guy trained to become a sports champion. To vote No was a way of saying that women at home were proud of their work, even if feminists called them Yvettes.

At the rally of the Yvettes, the women on the podium who were feminists and for the No side in the referendum succeeded in not allowing the REAL Women aspect to be stressed in their discussions, so the rally was not anti-feminist. Of course, all francophone feminists rushed as well to deny the media view that the rally had a "quality of backlash against the pronouncements of militant feminists."[4]

What is interesting is that the English-Canadian presentation of this ambiguous event fails to report that it was followed by another rally ten days later, at Place Desjardins, for the fortieth anniversary of women's right to vote in Quebec, with fifteen thousand women chanting Yes to the referendum, including other feminists as famous as Madeleine Parent, side by side with Lise Payette and the "Comité des Québecoises pour le Oui."

Thus feminists were not all on one side. In fact, they were very cautious because of the divisive character of so dramatic an issue. The official feminist organizations, like the Fédération des femmes du Québec (FFQ), which had fifty thousand members at the time, and the Association féminine d'éducation et d'action sociale (AFEAS), with thirty-five thousand members, stayed neutral, letting every woman decide for herself between the Yes and No sides in the referendum. The truth is that females were, like males, equally split. In this context, it is disturbing to know that English-Canadian feminists were so eager to defend their own federalist convictions that they sent letters of support to the No forces during the referendum campaign.[5]

You can see, I hope, how painful it is even now to raise this topic: it is absolutely shocking that English-Canadian feminist scholars stated that Quebec feminists as a group were for the No option, while this is far from clear for anybody familiar with Quebec politics. This is a very important point, because it reveals a deep misunderstanding of the structure of the Quebec feminist movement and how we are all involved in the political definition of who we are as women, as Quebecers, as political scientists, or whatever, in search of a global project of society. Leftists and reformists, liberals and radicals, can be found among Quebec feminists, although I do not think there are very many women on the rightist part of the political spectrum at present. Why do English-Canadian feminists exhibit such misunderstandings?

Of course, there is literature available in French, but, in terms of books available in English, the story ends quickly. The volume written by the Clio Collective, *Quebec Women: A History*, ended in 1979.[6] For the contemporary period, one should consult *La Vie en rose*, a monthly feminist magazine covering a wide range of issues, published from 1979 to 1987. Its fifteen thousand copies were widely read and circulated during all these years without attracting the attention of English-Canadian feminists. Since 1987, *La Gazette des femmes* offers an overall view of what is happening in the Quebec women's movement. Neither source is usually even mentioned in listings of feminist journals in our so-called national accounts, although *La Vie en rose* was especially important in reflecting most of the debates that were taking place in the Quebec feminist movement for almost a decade.

Another aspect of the problem is that when authors present the relationship between the Canadian and Quebec feminist movements as a national and a local (regional) movement, they miss the fact that Canada is still a largely bi-national country. The fact is that more and more French-Canadian culture has its centre in the homeland of the Francophones for all of Canada, which is Quebec and not Ottawa. How can you react as a feminist from Quebec when you find you are totally ignored in lists which correctly recognize as national associations the Indian Rights for Indian Women or the Black Women's Congress of Canada, but systematically ignore the Association des femmes autochtones or the Fédération des femmes du Québec and other French-Canadian umbrella groups? The national character of these associations arises from their overall cultural identity, in spite of a territorial regionalization which reflects nothing but the historical erosion of French Canada outside the provincial constituency of Quebec. More often that not, if you are fortunate in reading national feminist authors, you will find a footnote saying that the Fédération des femmes du Québec was created in 1966, without any further comments.

There is sometimes another mention of the Fédération around the famous charter debate to state that the Fédération did not participate in the glorious fight to insert section 28 in the Charter of Rights and Freedoms.[7] Nowhere is it explained why Quebec feminists would not involve themselves in an event which ignored the estrangement of Quebec from the repatriation of the Canadian Constitution. Women from Quebec are portrayed as having deserted from a most important feminist constitutional battle simply because they supported one of their own, Lucie Pépin, instead of joining the protest movement closing ranks behind Doris Anderson after her dramatic resignation as head of the Canadian Advisory Council on the Status of Women. By the way, Lucie Pépin was a member of the Fédération at the time, but she was not an active member of any committee or a member of the executive, so perhaps the case is not so clear. The truth is that the claim for a specific amendment to the Constitution could not be approved by Quebec feminists, since the Constitution itself was not recognized as legitimate by our own democratic institutions in Quebec, women and men united. This was an English-Canadian issue which Quebec-identified feminists could not address without strong reservations.

Furthermore, the issue was complicated by English Canadians' silence with respect to the lawfulness of the Quebec Charter of Human Rights and Freedoms. Feminists from Quebec had just obtained recognition of affirmative action programs in this provincial charter. It was not clear at the time if the Canadian equality proposal would be as strong as our own charter on this matter. This is never treated in the English-Canadian version of the "betrayal" of feminists from Quebec in the so-called national battle to enshrine equality of the sexes in the federal Constitution. English-Canadian feminists were justly proud of gaining the kind of protection of their rights that their American sisters had failed to obtain with the rejection of the Equal Rights Amendment. But they totally discarded the idea that there could be another side to the national coin. In such a context, every objection from Quebec women is discarded as Quebec nationalism, as if being federalist was not another form of nationalism, asserting a monolithic conception of Canadian unity based on the dominion of English Canada neither more nor less suited as such to one's feminist convictions. Nationalism, as a collective instrument to forge cultural links, is no more exterior to feminism in Quebec than federalism is in the rest of Canada.

The problem is that there is still no discussion between two equally important factions which each express a distinct national standpoint in a feminist setting. One is presented as treacherous, emotional, or locally oriented, while the other pretends to represent a pure feminist position devoid of all petty partisan considerations. The gap is so great between the French and English components of our bi-cultural country that even feminists have not succeeded in breaking down our "two solitudes." As Barbara Roberts stated in her most accurate account of the discrepancies between feminist groups on the ill-fated Meech Lake Accord, we awoke on "two shores of the same lake."[8] At least it would be progress to acknowledge that such is the case and to stop pretending that there is unanimity in a movement where pluralism should feed a lively debate between feminists eager to understand and respect each others' differences.

The pressing issue for Quebec feminists is to claim the status of "national association" for the Fédération des femmes du Québec. Democracy even inside feminism requires self-representation. We cannot accept being considered as one more regional chapter when our cultural identity is at stake. Until now, we have remained in the National Action Committee (NAC) because we considered this channel of communication between the two parts of the Canadian women's movement to be most important. Recently, however, the Fédération des femmes du Québec decided not to renew its membership in NAC. We would hope that you would agree with our stand for full recognition of our national identity as "Québécoises". The point is that federal subsidies should accompany this kind of cultural recognition, whereas the Secretariat of State is reluctant to recognize as national any association which is already represented by the National Action Committee. How can we stay in NAC if this means losing our right to state for ourselves, in our own voice, our specific cultural identity?

The point I want to make is that nationalism does not move Quebec women away from feminism any more than your feelings as Canadians prevent you from networking with feminists from other countries. We learn from our dialogue with women from all territories. Canada has a special blessing as a multicultural and a multinational country. Feminism, which did so much to inscribe pluralism in our global vision of politics and quest for personal identity, should be better prepared to cope with such a range of structural differences.

English-Canadian feminists should not discard nationalism as unfeminist in the case of Quebec, because nationalism cannot be ignored as a crucial dimension of the Quebec feminist movement. It is part of our identity and an important form of self-assertion, just as it is for a Black woman to define herself as Afro-American or a Native woman to become a member of the Assembly of First Nations. All are ways for a feminist living under Canadian rule to claim full recognition of her own specific voice inside the women's movement. There could be many more interchanges between all of us, and it is sad to reflect that this is not yet occurring.

The reduction of Canadian women's history to English-Canadian women's history is not acceptable. Feminist methodologies have taught us that only women could really trace our story. Following this line of thinking, to say something about the story of women in Quebec demands much more reliance on interviews and immersion in a distinct setting. What about more direct collaborations between researchers from both cultural environments? What about a little more equilibrium in the sharing of subsidies and the matching of really representative research teams to stop equating national studies or projects with Anglo-Canadian hegemony on federal institutions?

PART THREE

The Interrelationship of Academic and Activist Feminism

THE THREE ESSAYS IN THIS SECTION MOVE TO EXAMINE THE American and Canadian women's movements at a point which is indisputably well into the current wave of revitalization. They describe how feminists have changed the landscape of academic studies, through demands for the inclusion of women in research agendas and by reworking course curriculum and teaching methodology. They consider the linkages and tensions between the newly established feminist academics and the community activists. They begin to delve into the difficult questions of how feminism can accommodate the multiple experiences of women of diverse races, classes, disabilities, and sexual orientations.

Margrit Eichler notes that the field of academic women's studies emerged in Canada at about the same time as the most recent wave of feminism and probes the connection behind the chronological complementarity. She documents the off-campus, extra-curricular connections between women's-studies feminists and community-based organizations, concluding that there is a high degree of interdependency, and tension, between academic feminism and the activist community.

Jean O'Barr describes the phenomenal growth and institutionalization of women's studies programs on American campuses. She identifies the progression which has taken place, from the initial creation of discrete courses on women's issues, to the implementation of women's studies programs supported by a network of feminist academic journals. O'Barr documents the incipient integration of feminist materials into the mainstream curriculum as a new phase, which has begun just as feminist scholarship is poised on the brink of yet another cataclysmic shift away from the undifferentiated concept of women ("totalizing feminism") and into a recognition of multifaceted, shifting, potentially contradictory feminist ideologies.

Lorraine Greaves raises fundamentally important questions about the structural divisions within the feminist movement. She queries whether feminists who possess privileged positions within our discriminatory society – by virtue of class, race, able bodies, or sexual orientation – recognize their imbalanced positions of power and will act to diminish these inequalities. Greaves predicts that the ability of feminists to comprehend the complexities of women as a group "will be the key to developing not only a mature women's movement, but one that ... visibly survives."

These essays document the victories achieved by the feminist movement in securing an established place within the academy. They also pinpoint some of the challenges facing this wave of organized feminism, outlining the demands for greater representativeness and participation within feminist activity and thought.

8 Not Always an Easy Alliance: The Relationship between Women's Studies and the Women's Movement in Canada

MARGRIT EICHLER

INTRODUCTION

Interviewer: How would you describe the general relationship between feminist studies and the women's movement?
Professor: Hmmm. Well. Not always an easy alliance, I guess.

It is part of our conventional wisdom that women's studies have emerged "out of the women's movement," not just in Canada, but in other countries as well.[1] Usually, this causal connection is stated in the form of an obvious fact that does not require further consideration. A second assumption is that of an ongoing relationship, in which women's studies is seen as the educational arm of the women's movement, or as Robyn Rowland says "if we are not – why the hell aren't we?"[2]

Given these two assumptions, it seems astonishing that there is, to the best of my knowledge, not a single empirical study that has actually examined (rather than postulated) the relationship between the two. This seems important both for the sake of understanding the women's movement and for interpreting women's studies. Examining this relationship provides another, possibly unique, opportunity. Women's/feminist studies represent a major shift in thinking that can be considered paradigmatic.[3] This change is related to a major social movement. An examination of the connection between the two while the process is still going on may capture some of the complexities experienced by people involved in a scientific revolution connected to a social movement.

There are many ways in which the relationship could be explored. At the very least, questions could be asked about the relationship of academic feminists to the women's movement, the association of feminist activists with women's studies, and the institutional linkages (or lack thereof) between the movement and women's studies. This essay will address some aspects of the first question only, using data from a large-scale study of Canadian women's studies/feminist professors.[4]

The Canadian Women's Studies Project has collected a large amount of information on professors who have taught women's/feminist studies at Canadian universities that give at least a bachelor's degree.[5] The study involved four phases: first, writing to all universities and colleges and obtaining official information on their offerings in women's/feminist studies; second, identifying and surveying all professors who had taught at least one course in the area at the university level. Eight hundred and ninety-two of our respondents declared themselves as eligible and returned a completed questionnaire. This represents, in our estimation, a response rate of more than 80 per cent of the total eligible population. In the third phase, a randomly selected sample of 100 of the 780 women as well as 87 of the 112 men in our population were interviewed, via telephone, in a more qualitative, open-ended manner on substantive issues. These respondents are representative of our total population of professors. Phase four involved telephone interviews with the authors/ thinkers who had been named as the most influential by the entire population about their thoughts concerning women's/feminist studies. The study is described in more detail elsewhere.[6]

This essay draws on two of the four data sources: some of the information from phase two and the qualitative interviews with the women only from phase three. The text considers women only, because men are obviously in a different relation to the women's movement than are women. (The issue of men in women's studies is addressed in a separate publication.)[7] There are at least two central sets of questions: one concerning the nature of personal involvement of professors who teach women's/feminist studies and the other their view of the relationship between the movement and women's studies in general. I shall look at both of these issues.

THE INVOLVEMENT OF WOMEN'S STUDIES PROFESSORS IN THE WOMEN'S MOVEMENT

Are women's/feminist studies professors involved in women's movement activities? To the degree that there is a connection, what came first for them? Were they first involved in the women's movement and subsequently in teaching women's/feminist studies,[8] or did they begin by teaching, which led them to an involvement in women's movement activities? What are the effects on their teaching of being more or less (or not at all) involved in movement activities? In our mail-out questionnaire, we asked several questions which address these issues. We asked respondents whether prior to teaching women's/feminist studies they had worked with others involved with women's concerns.[9] Of all our female respondents, we found that 407 or 52.2 per cent indicate a prior involvement with a women's group.

Looking at their motivations for teaching their first women's studies course, we found that 519 or 67.9 per cent stated that political motivations aimed at improving the position of women was one of the factors motivating them to start teaching in this area. Out of a total of twelve possible answers, this ranked as the third most important one, after interest in the subject area and the desire to develop the area of women's studies. In addition, 175 women or 22.8 per cent indicated that a woman's consciousness-raising (CR) group was another reason. The relevance of such a CR group was not dependent on when people first started teaching such courses.[10] More than half, then, were involved in a women's group before they taught their first course, and more than two-thirds started teaching in the area for reasons that included the political concern of improving the situation of women.

Turning to women's involvement since they started teaching women's/feminist studies, we found that 490 women, or 62.8 per cent, had been active in a women's group.[11] When asked whether they had ever been members or held co-ordinating positions in a women's group, 637 or 82.7 per cent indicated they had been members of a women's group, and just more than half of all the women (51.5 per cent) had held co-ordinating positions in a women's group.[12] Finally, when asked whether they identified themselves as feminists, 90.9 per cent (697) of the women identified themselves as such, 5.2 per cent (40) said that they were not feminists but were concerned about women's issues, 0.1 per cent (one person) said she was neither a feminist nor concerned about women's issues, and 3.8 per cent (29 people) defined themselves in other terms.[13]

By using various indicators together, we created a Women's Movement Involvement Index.[14] The results are summarized in table 3. As we can see, only a small percentage (6.9 per cent) have participated in none of the six activities that indicate some relationship with the movement outside the academic setting. By contrast, 66.4 per cent indicate that they have been involved in three to six, and the

Table 3
Degree of Involvement in Women's Movement Activities

No. of Activities	n	%
0	54	6.9
1	83	10.6
2	125	16.0
3	149	19.1
4	158	20.3
5	160	20.5
6	51	6.5
	780	100.00

$\alpha = .65$

Table 4
Centrality of Interest for First and Most Recent Course

	Most Recent Course					
	Primary	Major Secondary	Minor Secondary	Marginal	None	Total
First Course						
Primary	183	35	4	2	0	224
Major secondary	155	165	10	2	0	332
Minor secondary	40	50	37	4	0	131
Marginal	8	12	3	5	0	28
None	1	1	0	0	2	4
Total	387	263	54	13	2	719

Missing Observations: 61
Kendall's Tau-b .397

remaining 26.6 per cent indicate that they have been involved in one or two such activities.

One question that seems relevant in this context is whether the degree of involvement in women's movement activities affects our respondents' teaching. We asked two questions: How central were women's/feminist studies to their entire work at the time they taught their first course, as well as at present, and how did they see their teaching experience – positively or negatively?[15]

Turning first to the issue of centrality of interest, for the majority of these professors, women's studies are their primary or major secondary interest. The proportion rises from 78.1 per cent (594 people) to 90.4 per cent (651 people) from the first course to the most recent course in the area.[16] When we compare the centrality of interest

Table 5
Centrality of Women's Studies Interests by Movement Involvement

	Number of Women's Movement Involvements						
Interest	*0*	*1*	*2*	*3*	*4*	*5 or 6*	*Total*
Primary	13	27	57	66	83	141	387
Major secondary	21	35	43	61	55	49	264
Minor secondary	9	7	12	12	7	7	54
Marginal	6	2	2	2	0	1	13
None	0	0	1	0	1	0	2
Total	49	71	115	141	146	198	720

Missing Observations: 60

for the first and most recent courses, it is remarkable to what degree the interest increases from the first to the most recent course, as seen in table 4. While there are 57 professors (7.9 per cent) whose interest decreased between their first and most recent course, there are 270 (37.5 per cent) whose interest increased – a proportion of almost 1:5.[17]

If we correlate the centrality of interest at the time of the most recent course with involvement in women's movement activities, we find that a high degree of participation in the women's movement corresponds to a greater centrality of interest in women's studies in the academic setting, as seen in table 5.

There are only 49 women (6.8 per cent) among our respondents who have no involvement in the women's movement. Of these, 34 or 4.7 per cent identify women's/feminist studies as their primary or major secondary interest. In other words, it is unlikely that a female professor teaches women's/feminist studies courses without having any personal participation in the women's movement. If we look only at those 387 professors who declare that women's/feminist studies are their primary academic interest, the percentages shift. Thirteen or 3.3 per cent have no involvement in the women's movement, 84 or 21.7 per cent have low participation (one or two instances), and 290 or 74.9 per cent have a high involvement (three or more instances). It seems that involvement in the women's movement correlates positively with the centrality of interest in women's/feminist studies in terms of the total work of these female professors.

Turning to the quality of the teaching experience, we see a similar image emerging. The majority of professors obviously enjoy teaching such courses and identify the experience as very positive: 447 or 59 per cent for the first course and 461 or 60.8 per cent for the most

Table 6
Quality of Teaching Experience for First and Most Recent Course

	Most Recent Course					
Experience	Very Pos.	S.W.Pos.	V. Mixed	S.W.Neg.	Very Neg.	Total
First Course						
Very positive	339	51	16	8	2	416
Somewhat positive	92	115	3	3	0	213
Very mixed	16	17	20	0	0	53
Somewhat negative	12	11	1	6	0	30
Very negative	1	1	0	0	1	3
Total	460	195	40	17	3	715

Missing Observations: 65
Kendall's Tau-b .39

Table 7
Quality of Teaching Experience by Movement Involvement

	Number of Women's Movement Involvements						
Experience	0	1	2	3	4	5 or 6	Total
Very positive	35	6	63	88	90	139	461
Somewhat positive	9	20	38	41	34	53	195
Very mixed	2	3	9	7	11	8	40
Somewhat negative	3	2	2	4	3	3	17
Very negative	0	0	0	0	2	1	3
Total	49	71	112	140	140	204	716

Missing Observations: 64

recent course. By comparing the quality of the teaching experience of the first and most recent course, we find that 84 or 11.7 per cent experienced a deterioration in the quality of the teaching experience, while 149 or 20.8 per cent experienced an increase in the positive quality of the teaching experience (see table 6).

Considering the mixed chronology we noticed before, in which some professors were active in the women's movement before they started teaching women's/feminist studies, while others first started teaching and subsequently became active in the movement, we are obviously not dealing with a one-way causal relationship but with an interactive, mutually reinforcing process. If we cross-tabulate the quality of the teaching experience of their most recent course with their women's movement involvement, we find that the likelihood of having a very positive teaching experience is markedly higher if there is a higher (three or more) participation in women's movement activities than if there is none or a low (one to two) involvement in movement activities (see table 7).

Only 7.6 per cent of the professors who find the teaching experience very positive have no involvement in women's studies activities, 23.6 per cent have a low participation, and 68.8 per cent of those who find the experience very positive have a high involvement. Once more, it appears that involvement in the women's movement and enjoying teaching women's studies/feminist courses are positively related.

So far, we have used data from phase two of the study, drawing on the answers of all women in our population to a series of questions we asked in the mail-out questionnaire. With such an instrument, one is always constrained as to the depth with which one can pursue any question. In order to capture some of the variety and subtleties of the experience of these women, we asked a random sample of one hundred of the women open-ended questions on some of the same topics we examined for the entire population. In one of these questions, which is relevant here, we asked respondents how they first became involved in their area of work, using the term they themselves had supplied to describe this area. Interviewers then probed for further details.[18]

This question generated longer responses than any other we asked. Most people shared a large portion of their life histories in response. The following is not a complete analysis of the responses, since there is a vast richness that deserves to be carefully considered. Here I am only concerned to draw out those aspects which deal with the relationship between women's studies and the women's movement.

The sense one gets when reading people's accounts of their first involvement in women's studies is that, for the vast majority of them, women's studies and the women's movement are, indeed, inextricably linked in their own lives. How this linkage is structured, however, varies. About two-thirds[19] of the respondents indicate that their first involvement was through some group activity, for as one of them said, "I came to recognize that one could not be feminist in solitude, that feminism implied the need for a group."

Such group activity included involvement with general movement groups as well as with groups located within the academic context. The list of local, regional, and national groups that are mentioned is long and includes, among others, the Feminist Party of Canada, consciousness-raising groups, involvement in the first Morgentaler campaign, affirmative action committees, an abortion information centre, the Royal Commission on the Status of Women, the Canadian

Research Institute for the Advancement of Women, the National Action Committee on the Status of Women, the Canadian Abortion Rights Action League, Women Against Violence Against Women, the Voice of Women, Women and the Law Association, and shelters for homeless women. The groups located within the academic context include, among others, student groups, the Radical Philosophy Association, Society for Women and Philosophy, the Women's Studies Students' Association, study groups, the Canadian Women's History Group, the Corrective Collective, etc.

For many of these women the involvement was an all-encompassing one. As one woman says: "It's very difficult to talk about this in a fairly discrete, piece-by-piece way, because my whole social life, my whole personal life, my whole academic life was centred around feminist issues and struggles to come to grips with the world." About one-third of the respondents indicate that teaching was, in fact, their first involvement.[20] Many of them acknowledge an intellectual debt to the women's movement. One historian, for instance, recounts: "I do credit the feminist movement very much because they started in the late sixties and early seventies raising questions that got me thinking ... Since I couldn't find the answers (no one had the answers) I thought well, maybe I'd better start doing the research myself. So it was, I think, a strong impetus from feminists who, I don't think, always got their history straight, but they were asking the right questions." This same professor says about her lack of political involvement outside the university setting: "We've got a good network of women scholars at [her university]. We have developed an academic women's association. We have developed a program for sexual harassment, things like that. So it's been primarily institutional. I've not aligned myself with any particular women's organization. I send money to the various funds to soothe my conscience."

A literature professor, who has not been politically involved, says about it: "The politics, I'm interested, I always keep an ear open on what is happening in the political arena, but because of the limited time I cannot get involved yet, but in the future I will." What is remarkable is the feeling that comes through that if academic feminists are not involved in politics, they should be, which expresses itself in the need to excuse oneself if one does not engage in political action beyond the university. Other academic feminists do become active in various women's organizations, once they have started dealing with the issues in their teaching and often as well in their research.

Beginning to teach women's/feminist courses was, for some professors, the end result of a lengthy, slow, and gradual process, with no clear single incident that moved them in this direction. As a philosophy professor states: "It's been a gradual process like with everybody. I've identified myself as a feminist as long as I can remember hearing the word." Many others, however, cite some concrete incident – attending a conference, a workshop, an invitation to write an article for a book, to give a lecture, or to participate in a group effort to develop a women's studies program – that provided the stimulus to start teaching in the area. Some professors were invited to give a women's studies course. Some named individuals who set them on this course: a teacher or thesis supervisor (both males and females were named in this role), family members (such as one's mother, grandmother, or father), colleagues, friends, and others.

A very strong theme that recurs again and again is the importance of personal experience. It exemplifies the applicability of the feminist slogan "The Personal Is Political" to feminist academics. There is a strong desire to create a match between one's personal life, views, philosophy, experiences, and one's professional activities, "realizing that the things that happen in my life outside academics have to relate, that there can't be a gulf between what you do as an academic and the rest of your life." This need can be stimulated in more than one manner. Some professors recount examples of discrimination that they themselves experienced and that changed their views about how the world worked, turning them towards integrating these insights in their teachings. A professor in media and communication studies cites her own personal experience: "When I got divorced, I couldn't get a credit rating; although I had had credit ratings, for ten or fifteen years, as a married woman, then I couldn't get one." For others, injustice done to other women but witnessed by them had the same effect: "One was a woman raped on campus. The president referred to it as an alleged rape and that really brought to people's attention [to the fact] that things were not secure for women on campus, the lighting, the key control, and so on."

Yet another group only went back to university because women's studies had already emerged and they saw this as an opportunity to study issues which they had determined to be important prior to ever deciding to return to study or teach. As one of them said: "I was a feminist and then went back to university, for just that reason."

The result of combining academic with political activity is both exhausting and exhilarating. As one education professor stated:

In some ways, I feel my life is totally fragmented, and at the same time, I feel that my life is totally connected. I think it's fragmented in the sense that

I am doing so many different things with so many different organizations and groups, and my paid employment, and my volunteer work, and so on, that sometimes I feel like I am run ragged, that I'm extraordinarily tired.

But on the other hand, when I do have time to be self-reflective, and look at what I'm doing, I can see the ways in which all of the pieces are, in fact, connected, and in many senses, my analysis of women's education has been enriched by all my experiences. My experience on the [national women's group] executive has been an extraordinarily rewarding experience for me, in terms of my intellectual development and my sense of power over what I know, in the development of my knowledge, and my understanding of how the world works.

Having looked at some of the ways in which women professors are involved in movement activities and having found that the degree of interaction is, indeed, very high, we can now turn to our last question: how do professors who teach women's/feminist studies courses themselves view the relationship between women's studies and the women's movement?

THE RELATIONSHIP BETWEEN WOMEN'S STUDIES AND THE WOMEN'S MOVEMENT AS SEEN BY FEMALE WOMEN'S STUDIES PROFESSORS

Beyond looking at the professors' personal involvement in the women's movement, it is important to examine their perception of the relationship between women's/feminist studies and the women's movement. This is, after all, the group which will produce most of our theoretical writing about feminist scholarship and the feminist movement. What they have to say of the relationship is, therefore, of interest not only at the level of personal perceptions but also as an indication of the manner in which those who collectively define the relationship through research and publications approach it.[21]

We asked our respondents how they would describe the general relationship between women's studies and the women's movement. Of the one hundred respondents, there was only one who denied that there is a relationship of great import. This respondent simply said "I do not see that they are necessarily connected." All others either stressed or assumed as given the importance of the link between the two. How the relationship is described in detail varies, of course, and is the topic of the following pages. But the overarching theme is that the relationship between the two is acknowledged – by 99 per cent of our respondents – as a crucial one. Moreover, although there was considerable evidence of strain between the two, the vast majority of respondents expressed in some form their regret at this and suggested that it was desirable to maintain the link between women's studies and the women's movement, which was generally seen as vital.

Looking, then, at the specifics, there is virtually unanimous agreement that "There wouldn't be women's studies without the women's movement." Some people comment on the mechanics of this process: because the women's movement starts from the assumption of the oppression of women, this generated an enormous demand for examining ways to overcome this oppression, and this in turn was the motive power behind the establishment of women's studies. Others highlight the role of students in getting the first courses established. In several instances, the first courses were, in fact, taught by students. As we know from other parts of our research, 7.6 per cent of our respondents were themselves students when they taught their first course.[22] But even where this was not the case, the fact that there was (and continues to be) student demand for these types of courses is a necessary precondition for the emergence and continued existence of women's studies as an academic specialization: "We, within the institution, would not survive, we would not continue, if there wasn't political pressure from outside. If there weren't the interest expressed by these feminist students then, and the university didn't realize that these were the ones who were filling these huge classes and bringing in their tuition fees, then the powers that be, who don't want it to happen, wouldn't let it happen." Others mention specifically support from community groups in trying to set up the first women's studies courses. On this matter, then, there is clear agreement: women's studies owe their existence to the women's movement.

Once in existence, the relationship evolved, and at present it is not seen as a simple one by most professors. "Rocky," "precarious," "tenuous but critical," "Familial? Genetically related? … hit-and-miss … " were some of the terms used to describe it. "Somewhat confused, somewhat contradictory, and sort of generally friendly but uncertain" was the way one professor put it. The overall situation is best captured by the term "dialectical relationship," which several people used to describe its nature.

The women's movement and women's studies are seen as inextricably linked, mutually interdependent, mutually nurturing, symbiotic, "very intertwined," inseparable, "hand in hand. Sometimes, the one is ahead of the other and pulls the other along." However, the overlap is partial, not complete. "In some ways they connect and in other ways they do not." Moreover, the links are personal, not institutional: "It is more a linkage of individuals than a specific connection between teaching courses and the movement as such." Academics are friends with non-academic activists, sit on some of the same committees, meet in organizations such as NAC, CRIAW and others: "I find the same people in both places [women's studies and the women's movement], but then, that's because they are my friends."

The nature of the relationship is seen to vary with the locality. Several people draw explicit comparisons between large cities and small towns, others simply express their own local conditions and see their own experience as typical for all women's studies teachers. In either case, with one notable exception that I shall consider in a moment, a consensus emerges that in smaller communities, particularly in the Maritimes and Newfoundland, the connection between the women's movement and women's studies is considerably closer than in larger cities. For instance, a woman from Newfoundland says: "Some people, maybe, are not available to the women's movement, but here, I would say that in general, women's studies profs are very available ... There's almost always one of us on the steering committee of the women's centre ... We do things at the local Advisory Council, or provincial Advisory Council. One of us [name] has been responsible for getting CRIAW going here as a local group. ... We don't look at ourselves as ivory tower people." Another respondent conveyed a similar image: "Academics play a very prominent role in the women's movement ... It's hard to find women out there in my community, which is rural Nova Scotia, with some kind of feminist consciousness who didn't get it from a university." The sentiment is echoed by someone from PEI, who says that there is a "very close connection, certainly on the Island, because we are such a small community."

Smallness in size is, however, not always an advantage. Where there is an active core of people in a small community, they tend to work together out of necessity as much as choice. If such co-operation is difficult, for whatever idiosyncratic reasons, there is little opportunity to go elsewhere. As one woman states: "I'm so isolated here in the north. We have a women's centre ... but the contact between the women's centre, and the university['s] ... women's studies program, has been for the last few years minimal ... I did my damnedest to try and tie the two together, but I don't think it's happening." Similarly, a woman from rural Quebec complains about the fact that there are so few feminists, and they are utterly overburdened.

The image of a close relationship, in which academic feminists meet and interact in a multiplicity of ways with local feminist activists, is not the picture that emerges from larger urban centres. Explanations for this are located on both sides of the equation.

On the part of the professors, this "fracturing" includes at least two different aspects: first, what may be politically the most important issues need not be theoretically the most interesting ones. As one professor states: "Women's scholarship, feminist scholarship, has developed its own agenda and is asking questions about the future and all kinds of other ... issues that the women's movement, which is more political, is not. And the women's movement is still being forced to confront issues that are not very interesting, at all, theoretically, but may be important." This can still be seen as a case of "the one pulling the other"; some issues emerge from women's studies proper, others out of the daily political struggle. The second perspective does not present the issue as one of exploring new avenues but more as one of political laziness – the lure of simply thinking without necessarily translating one's thoughts into political action: "In the bigger centres there is – and has been for some years – a real problem with the temptation ... just to go on and do your own little quiet academic thing to your friends and not actually get out and do political work."

Many respondents noted such disengagement of women's studies professors from political action, but, when we look at the actual behaviour, this seems to be more a self-critical evaluation that collectively the academics should be more politically involved than a reflection of a true disengagement, and the culprit seems to be lack of energy and time rather than lack of willingness. As a woman from Saskatchewan says: "People find themselves spread thin, sort of having joined six different committees or different organizations." Another woman says: "There is a strong sense among women's studies people that they would like to have closer linkages with women and the general community and the women's movement in general and that there simply isn't energy enough to stretch oneself to be as active as one would like to be ... everyone feels they would like to do more, but simply, the energy required to get a women's studies program going, and to keep it going, is not such that it leaves a lot of extra time."

Besides personal limitations in time and energy, there are also structural barriers which impede a closer co-operation of women's studies people with women outside of academia:

The academic institutions are letting them [women] down, to a large extent. I don't think that we have as yet, within the teaching and administrative levels of the institutions, the critical mass where we've been able to make enough changes to make the learning experience what it should be, and to make the publishing style what it should be in order to be more accessible to women outside academia ... Most of us are also still too cautious, you know, too concerned about being booted out ourselves if we do something a little too radical. And so we're not being radical enough, I don't think.

While mutual interdependence is generally acknowledged, there is also a pervasive theme that communications are often difficult, even if they are vital. There is fair evidence of mutual distrust and of mutual ignorance that makes it difficult to establish and maintain the close interconnection that the vast majority of professors see as desirable: "There is a ... certain amount of suspicion that might border on hostility from both ... sides." People talk about "reciprocal ignorance" and distrust. One says: "I have felt that mistrust, that somehow if you are not on the barricades you are lost to the cause. On the other hand, I think scholars often talk to each other and not to the outside community." The distrust may even take the form of disdain: "Sometimes I've heard academics refer to activists – not that academics aren't – as ruffians or scruffy ... But I do both ... I find that I have one foot on either side and sometimes I do the splits." One respondent summed up the situation as follows: "There are elements of the non-academic women's movement that are very alienated from academics, and there are elements in women's studies that are so elitist, that they won't give their sisters out in the street much credence."

Academics complain about a certain anti-intellectualism among movement activists that academic feminists experience as a put-down. They also comment on the state of the women's movement. "I do not know where the movement is," says one woman, and another adds: "With the fragmenting and the location of the women's movement increasingly in specific groups, the relationship has been less continuous and program-to-program ... it's been more individual and ad hoc." Another professor makes careful qualifications for both sides of the equation. She specifies:

If you define the women's movement as essentially liberal and reformist, then I would think that women's studies would be seen as absolutely central in producing an educated core of people ... to work within that structure. If you take a very left-wing radical position ... about the women's movement, then, again depending upon the particular program, any other particular program could be seen as virtually reactionary, class-biased, racist, given the structure of universities at present, and as having been co-opted by patriarchal institutions. So, I think it probably depends ... both on how you're defining the women's movement, and the particular nature of the women's studies program that you're looking at.

Nevertheless, the clear consensus is that women's studies would not have come into existence without the women's movement, and that they remain dependent on an ongoing women's movement to provide the political pressure that ensures administrative support – even if grudgingly given – as well as the student population that fills the courses.[23]

On the other side, the women's movement is likewise identified as a clear recipient of benefits. Women's studies provide the data that allow activists to carry on the struggle, they have resources that they make available to women's movement activists: "The more we can do to really research, study and publish … the … more chance the women's movement has to survive because it's going to be working from a solid base of knowledge and not … from bias, prejudice, bigotry, which we're just as prone to as anyone else."

Where is the relationship going? It depends on whom you listen to. There are academics who speak about the "growing intersection between feminist theory … and the women's movement," while others nostalgically hark back to the days in which there was a greater overlap between academic and non-academic activities, deploring that today there is none: "In the early days, they were very close … I think it has gone, drifted apart."[24] If each activity is seen in the context of the other, it is apparent that respondents speak from their own personal experiences, which they generalize to "the" movement and women's studies in general, when they say, for instance, that the relationship is "improving," or "one of increasing separation," that they are "quite connected" or "quite distant," without being aware that the experiences of others may be diametrically opposed to their own.

CONCLUSION

In this essay, we have learned about the relationship between women's studies and the women's movement through the personal experiences of women's/feminist studies professors and their reflections on the general state of affairs between the two. What emerges is a complex picture of historical interwovenness between women's/feminist studies and the movement, which is reflected in the personal lives of the professors we interviewed.

The connection is seen as vital by virtually everyone and also as quite challenging. Difficulties are seen to come from three sides:

academics who are too shut up in their ivory towers, movement activists who fail to understand the demands put on these professors and who may be anti-intellectual in their own orientation, and structural barriers within the university system that make an ongoing interchange between women's studies programs and the movement difficult. As a consequence, relations are of a personal rather than institutional nature. The personal links are also ambivalent: they are "tremendously important ... the life blood," but they also impose demands which sometimes seem almost impossible to combine: "I do the splits."

In spite of the difficulties, the vast majority of academics endorse the links, while fully recognizing the problems. It is particularly interesting that while at least half and possibly more of the professors had links with the women's movement *before* they started to teach courses in women's/feminist studies, there is also a very sizeable minority – around one-third or more – who became active in the women's movement as a consequence of having started to teach such courses. The two-way relationship, then, about which professors talk, truly is a two-way relationship not only for individuals but also for the political and the educational arms of the women's movement as collective entities – in spite of the lack of institutional linkages.

Furthermore, our data reveal that a closer connection, at the individual level, with the women's movement seems to strengthen one's involvement in women's/feminist studies. Professors who have higher rather than lower or no involvement in the movement are more likely to have made women's/feminist studies their central area of interest and are more likely to find teaching courses in the area a very positive experience.

The common wisdom of a close connection between women's studies and the women's movement, then, is correct. It is not just a historical link – although that is universally acknowledged – but an ongoing, difficult, frustrating, demanding, vital, and genuinely two-way connection.

9 Exclusions and the Process of Empowerment: The Case for Feminist Scholarship

JEAN F. O'BARR

INTRODUCTION

Surveying the evolution and characteristics of feminist scholarship and linking that body of work to the larger political task of feminism are clearly impossible tasks, certainly for a single individual and definitely within a limited scope. Confronting the task of organizing my essay, I realized that I would be clearest starting autobiographically, then outlining what I see to be the current patterns in feminist scholarship.

While it is obvious that one individual's experience is just that and that *Signs*, as a journal, is one among many, I think that my own travels in feminist scholarship are representative of the roads that have been available to many of us as scholars and that the particular journal I edit is one of the better road maps we have.[1] I am here particularly interested in the contributions of feminist scholarship to feminism when that scholarship is not directed towards investigating the contemporary social movement. I am also drawn to provide a general survey, reflective of my experience at *Signs*, rather than engaging in Canadian-American comparisons.

Women have long sought access to education, tried to gain entry into academic institutions, and fought to be physically present in the places where knowledge was created and distributed. Sisters tried to take places beside brothers when tutors set up schoolrooms at home. Daughters followed teacher fathers into schoolrooms as exceptions to their sex. Persistent women sought individual exceptions to the unwritten norms that women could not study in new institutions. Groups of women challenged formal rules of exclusion, arguing that women could and should learn, for themselves and their contributions to the polity. Indeed, they frequently set up their own institutions. By the 1900s, after centuries of debate about women's capacity and need for formal instruction – always debating questions about what kind? for what end? – women gained the right, through petition, institutional rule changes, and financial support, to education. But the right, as we shall see, was a right limited to claiming or creating a place, not a right to determine much about what happened once that place was occupied.

AUTOBIOGRAPHY: EXCLUDING WOMEN AS LEARNERS

My entry into feminist scholarship came in 1971, four years before *Signs* published its first issue. I had received a Ph.D. in political science two years earlier and had been teaching African politics. I do not remember saying a word about women in a classroom, or mentioning them in the articles I wrote. I do remember being very involved in discussions about the beginnings of the women's movement, and the occasional book was making its way to my desk. I read Elizabeth Janeway's *Man's World, Woman's Place* and Kate Millett's *Sexual Politics*.[2] Although history and literature were clearly foreign territory to me, I immediately became a multidisciplinary junkie.

In 1971 I took a position as the director of continuing education at Duke University. I was to counsel women re-entering the university to complete baccalaureate degrees or to prepare for graduate and professional schools. I was also to set up a series of non-credit, liberal arts courses for adult learners that would further both their professional and personal goals. I had talked to fewer than a dozen returning women in the first week when it became clear to me that they were asking for something the academy did not offer: equal access to its degree programs on terms that matched their life circumstances and a course of study that linked their past experiences to their current studies and future plans.

I spent the next decade in a political struggle to make the American academy where I worked responsive to the needs of adult women:

• we argued about how to evaluate older women for entrance. Did they have to take standardized entrance examinations?
• we argued about how many of the rules made for eighteen-year-olds living in dormitories they had to follow. Must they go full time?

- we argued about the kinds of research projects they wanted to undertake. Was the women's movement a legitimate subject of study?
- we argued about how to combine courses into a program of study they valued. Could their volunteer experience be used in their course work for credentialling purposes?

At the time, the task seemed straightforward enough – with sufficient patience and wisdom on my part and theirs, the academy would respond to this new resource, the adult learner, and change its rules of access. In retrospect, I see that the adult women returning to school were posing a much larger challenge. They were not asking simply to be let in. They were asking the institution to change its ways. And all the while – just to be on the safe side, in case the institution proved too slow – they were also trying to make themselves seem enough like men that they could pass. But it never quite worked. They could never change themselves enough, in large enough numbers, to leave the institutions they entered unaffected.

Three recent scholarly evaluations of this process in the American context give rich testimony to the political struggles of women seeking access to knowledge. The *Signs* reader called *Reconstructing the Academy: Women's Education and Women's Studies*, which I edited along with Elizabeth Minnich and Rachel Rosenfeld, investigates the common theme that links women's nineteenth-century struggle to enter institutions of higher education with their current efforts to acquire knowledge about themselves in the classroom.[3] The shape of higher education in the future, now that women are the majority of students, is taken up in *Educating the Majority: Women Challenge Tradition in Higher Education*, edited by Carol Pearson and her colleagues for the American Council on Education.[4] Asking how institutions must transform themselves to meet the educational needs of women students, they explore the diversity among women, the way women shape their learning environments, the need to reconceptualize the ways we think and teach, ending by outlining the transformations that institutions, not women as individuals, need to make in the twenty-first century. *Women and Academe: Progress and Prospects*, edited by Mariam Chamberlain for the Russell Sage Foundation, provides an update to Alice Rossi's classic study, tracing the phenomenal growth and institutionalization of women's studies programs, the notable gains of women in non-traditional fields, the emergence of campus women's centres and research institutes, and the increasing presence of minority and returning women.[5]

Now why did these women I counselled, whose history is now recorded by scholars, want knowledge? Women want knowledge because they understand that it is fundamental to the larger goal of equity, however defined. Knowledge is, of course, the necessary but not sufficient basis for the task that women face. Knowledge means women will participate with men in society and culture. Knowledge means that women will understand why they have been excluded. And knowledge will tell women how their foremothers dealt with these issues, what the risks and possibilities are, what might work this time around.

While I was working with these women on an individual and daily basis, talking with the few women on the university faculty and reading the beginnings of a new literature, I found my own classes changing. I found myself talking about African women. It is one of the better-kept secrets of American higher education that research and scholarship are driven not by abstract, disconnected, isolated thought, but by the very real questions we debate in our daily lives and that we introduce in classrooms and debate with our students. As I thought about the women I was counselling in the morning, in my afternoon classes I started investigating the situation of African women.

I had actually noticed women in Tanzania in 1967 and 1968, while researching local party structures. I had noticed that they were elected officials in some areas and not in others. I had recorded the stories of their successful tax riots during the colonial era. I went back to that data, fuelled with the women's personal questions and supported by parallel questions in other fields and asked some new questions myself. Those concerns led in 1975 to my offering the first course in an American university on gender and politics in the Third World. That year was the beginning of the International Decade of Women, launched in Mexico City. And 1975 was the year *Signs* began publishing. While I did not place my first pieces there, I certainly was beginning to write about what I taught and saw in the larger community. And, clearly, so were others.

The rest, we might say, is our history. Hundreds of the women who had entered the academy in the late 1960s and early 1970s were turning their scholarly interests to the subjects that had come to them primarily through their political involvement in the women's movement.

I need to add one more piece to this autobiographical account. During this same time period, I had joined with my colleagues to team-teach an introductory women's studies course. Like its sister courses across the country, it had all the characteristics of a marginal endeavour. We taught it as an overload, without pay. We let everyone in, hoping to build support. We worked without teaching assistants and relied extensively on guest lectures and films. But we did it. And we did it for many years until we saw that we needed a full-fledged women's studies program rather than a single course to relieve student pressure.

Teaching the survey course fuelled my by now well-established bad habits of being as interested in the study of women and gender systems in other disciplines as in my own. Soon a clear view of the terrain emerged. The traditional disciplines were very poor maps to women's experiences, expressions, expectations. The subjects important to understanding women's oppressions as well as their agency crossed disciplinary lines. We had to understand their work and its culture system, not economics alone. We had to examine their family lives, not analyse them in aggregate patterns or on the couch alone. We had to ask about their sexual experiences and not only from a biological perspective. We had to examine their relationships with other women, whether similar or different, rather than confining ourselves to men's views of women's relationships to men. We had to look at their spiritual and artistic selves, relying on direct observation rather than the commentary of religious leaders or mainstream cultural critics. My habits apparently were not peculiar. The first issue of *Signs*, composed of fourteen articles, drew authors from twelve different disciplines, and each wrote from the perspective of more than her own field.

WOMEN'S STUDIES: OVERCOMING THE EXCLUSION OF WOMEN AS SUBJECTS

I have chronicled briefly my travels as a scholar through the 1970s, drawing some parallels to the developments of the journal along the way. I have suggested that the challenges posed by women already in the academy, particularly returning women, combined with the research and teaching activities of the faculty, particularly the women faculty, to create a new body of scholarship that we now call feminist and that is a critical part of the feminist enterprise. The scholarship and the individuals and institutions producing it were in a synergistic relationship, informing and encouraging each other. Just as our foremothers had fought physical exclusion, we have rebelled against intellectual exclusion.

Women's studies is often called the academic branch of the women's movement. It began in the late 1960s when political movements posed questions universities could not answer. Do women have a history worth investigating? What do we know about debates on women's condition? Have women in the past attempted to improve their situations? Are women in other countries and cultures also treated as second-class citizens? How are the Victorian mother, her immigrant laundress, and her single aunt similar, or are they different? Was the apostle Paul right in saying that women were always silent in churches and synagogues? The questions were straightforward enough, but it turned out that those who researched and taught in various disciplines did not know the answers.

As scholars – women and men – tackled the questions that arose outside the academy, their activities in classrooms, at conferences, and through journals and books took three forms. (1) They needed to add new information to the information that already existed. In the field of literature, for example, scholars began to recover the wealth of material written by women in the nineteenth century and earlier that had not thus far been studied in the twentieth century. Most of us easily recognize the names of Hawthorne, Melville, and Poe but get lost if asked to name three female authors who wrote before 1900. Male authors come readily to mind; female ones do not. Why? (2) They needed to correct existing ideas. In the field of psychology, for instance, researchers showed that there are multiple ways to reason and to reach decisions. While both men and women engage in moral reasoning, they tend to use different criteria of value, have different goals, and interpret the context of situations differently. Understanding gender differences in thinking and knowing is important, for it validates alternate approaches to reasoning. (3) They needed to rethink a number of their basic assumptions and theories in view of this new and corrected information. To use a familiar example, historians came to understand that the record of the past was more than a series of military and economic events carried out by men in public places. It is also constituted by the stories of individual women and men negotiating their way through the life cycle and attempting to integrate their familial and civic concerns. History moved from being a list of battles to a more in-depth look at societal patterns and the choices women and men have made as they lived their lives and constructed their environments.

How, you might be asking at this point, was all this done? Feminist scholarship as an academic activity is about twenty years old. In that time it has moved through three interrelated and overlapping phases. The first phase was the simple creation of courses that looked at the changing condition of women, usually white American women. At the same time scholars were beginning to undertake extensive research into topics within their disciplines, putting forth the basic information we now take for granted. I stress courses before publications because, by and large, I believe that feminist research arose from the demands made by students and in classes rather than from abstract contemplations.

The second phase followed quickly on the first, although in different ways on different campuses. While courses were offered for the first time in the late 1960s, programs first appeared in the early to mid-1970s. Groups of scholars interested in the new scholarship on women got together and lobbied university administrations for support staff and directors to co-ordinate their curricular efforts, to advise students who wanted to do more than take a single course, and to make the presence of women's studies felt on the campus more generally. Programs legitimized scholarly endeavours by providing research seminars, publishing work, and generally articulating the growing coherence of feminist inquiry. By the end of the 1970s, there was a professional association of people in women's studies, several scholarly journals promoted the new scholarship on women, and foundations were funding colleges to promote women's studies.

By the late 1970s, with courses on women and programs in women's studies existing on approximately half of America's campuses, a third phase of activity evolved. The scholars "doing women's studies" wanted to get their colleagues to include the new scholarship in all courses. Thus began the efforts that are known as *mainstreaming* – curriculum balancing, integration, or transformation projects. To date, some one hundred campuses have formally worked to bring feminist scholarship into the full range of courses. The ways in which this is done vary, and the problems scholars encounter in convincing colleagues to take a new look at old thoughts are numerous. The title of a new book, a report on one curriculum integration project at the University of Arizona, sums it up. The book is entitled *Changing Our Minds* and records the experiences of male and female faculty encountering women's studies over a three-year period.[6]

In the beginning feminist scholarship was corrective. It insisted on adding women's voices where none had been before. It soon became a full-scale enterprise of its own as women became the centre of inquiry. And more recently it has become an even more fundamental epistemological endeavour. Peggy McIntosh first identified the stages in the evolution of feminist scholarship, stages she saw in her work on curriculum integration.[7] She points out that most of the knowledge as we had received it until as recently as two decades ago was womanless. Books, courses, theories proceeded with no mention of women. If women were mentioned, they had to be exceptions, notable for how unlike other women they were. If women as a group attracted scholarly attention, they were seen as problems and anomalies, the set of individuals who did not fit the universal, read male, patterns. At later stages women became the focus of attention, but often in isolation. Thus we do women's history, women's literature, women's music, women in politics, but rarely do we do more than implicitly compare male and female. The final goal towards which McIntosh urges us is a concentration on women, the patterns in women's thoughts and activities, and the gender systems of which they are a part. While any individual, any course, any women's studies program, any publication might be placed at any of these stages – and the placement will vary with time and topics – it is accurate to say that feminist scholarship at twenty is well into investigations at the fifth stage. What are women's experiences? How do they compare to those of other women and to men? What can we say about how they shaped and are shaped by social and cultural contexts, by institutions and ideologies?

What ideas are central to all of these activities, no matter which campus one is discussing or which particular book or article? While each person in women's studies has her or his own list, the following points constitute the core of mine. This list comes from a seminar my colleagues and I last conducted several years ago.

We held a series of lunches between our provost, our college dean, and our graduate dean and the scholars on the Women's Studies Advisory Board. The board had found itself stuck in policy negotiations with the administration. While the latter uttered encouraging sounds, they failed to put resources and conviction behind those sounds. In one session with the college dean, I suggested we table our requests and simply sit together over the course of the summer several times and see if we, as feminist scholars, could explain what we did and why it represented such important intellectual shifts. In turn, the administrators were to do assigned reading in feminism and try to learn as students a field outside their own. Before we got to specific research on gender and the origins of the state and research on discrimination, we began with a summary of central ideas.

First is the basic distinction between sex and gender. The vast majority of individuals are biologically male or female, with biological sex linked to the presence or absence of certain physical characteristics. Beyond this biological distinction, culture, ethnicity, class, region, and many other factors interact to shape a person's gender. We often describe this process of socializing biological beings into gendered beings as the social and cultural construction of gender. That is, each one of us is shaped by the subtle interplay of her or his environment as well as her or his anatomy. Moreover, each society understands what it means to be men and women in the terms of its own sex/gender system.

Second, not only are we as individuals socially constructed, so is our knowledge of ourselves and our culture. The realities of women's lives differ substantially from how those lives are remembered and valued in the formal systems of knowledge that constitute the curricula of schools, colleges, and universities. As higher education became more common in the nineteenth century and burgeoned into a major industry in the twentieth, what we know and how we know it has become increasingly standardized. In the process of organizing knowledge, women's experiences have usually been entirely left out or, at best, marginalized. Contemporary feminist scholars spend a great deal of time explaining this mass amnesia and, at the same time, reconstructing the realities of women's lives.

Third, women are simultaneously both powerful and powerless. In some areas, individual women and groups of women command considerable resources and exercise great control over their environments. Jokes about domineering mothers-in-law and groups of subversive women planning revolutions over lunch tables implicitly acknowledge women's power. However, at the same time, these women or groups of women are subject to forces they cannot change and are constrained by practices and ideas of the society at large they barely know. Hence, one in four American women is likely to be sexually harassed, abused, or raped; women make only sixty-two cents to a man's dollar; and only 5 per cent of the highest decision-making positions in politics, business, and the arts are occupied by women.

Today's feminist scholars approach women's studies from a variety of backgrounds, and only the very youngest have had formal training. We have all had to relearn much. It has been, in the words of the poet Adrienne Rich, "a dialectic between change and continuity that is painful but deeply instructive and energizing."[8] Today's generation of students is being trained in the midst of a debate about what constitutes the liberal arts. They begin with an advantage over their predecessors, for they know that the very foundations of what an education should be are a question for debate. Still, they are disadvantaged by the uncertainty, controversy, and a lack of history. They do not yet have the luxury of being taught the history of feminism, social movements, and theories. Reconstructing knowledge is a large and ongoing project, at the heart of feminist scholarship.

FEMINIST THEORY: CHALLENGING
EXCLUSIONS FROM THE PRODUCTION
OF KNOWLEDGE

We at *Signs* have recently compiled a new theory anthology entitled
Feminist Theory in Practice and Process.[9] I have a keen sense of what it
is that we are seeing happen in feminist scholarship and I want to
use the second half of this essay to explore those evolving patterns
with you. Marilyn Frye, in *The Politics of Reality: Essays in Feminist
Theory*, wrote that "the measure of the success of the theory is just
how much sense it makes of what did not make sense before."[10] I
want to argue that feminist theory has been making a great deal of
sense and that its new developments promise to unravel still more
complex issues in understanding exclusion and subordination.
Having placed ourselves in the academy and succeeded in putting
forward our agenda for learning, we feminist scholars are now in
the process of complicating knowledge.

What follows is a sketch of some of the transdisciplinary frameworks that feminist theory is working with in an attempt to create a
place for the study of women in the academy. We at *Signs* sense a
moment of transition, a shift in our scholarship, from the necessarily
continuing work of examining the categories and constructs that
confine us towards a more self-reflective re-education of ourselves. It
is not that the angry theory of the 1970s has been supplanted. The
anger remains just as the reasons for it remain. Nor have we found
a single construct or explanation to define our experiences. Rather
we see a series of changes in our record of our experiences.

Perhaps the greatest change we see in u.s. feminist scholarship is
a shift away from an undifferentiated concept of women. The perspectives of Black women, in particular, confirm Sandra Harding's
observation that "once essential and universal man dissolves, so does
his hidden companion, woman."[11] This means that just as one of the
first acts in the development of feminist theory was to reject the
standpoint and experiences of white men as normative, so too, one
of the first acts in developing Black feminist theory has been to reject
the perspectives of white women as normative, focusing instead on
the concrete everyday experiences of Black women as the basis for
theory-making.

At the same time, there is a new complexity in feminist thinking
about the subjectivity of the individual woman. This development
has reintroduced the first person into feminist scholarship. The first
makers of feminist theory wrote directly out of their own experiences,
searching for the patterns in those experiences by reaching out to
others. Then for a decade or more feminist theory adopted the formal

language of the academy and experimented with using discourses that distanced the individual. We hear and read a new emphasis on the self. As one *Signs* editorial put it recently, "We are our own subject matter as, and because, women or Woman is our subject matter. We live and think and write within the gender constructs about which we think and on which we work. The narrative 'I' of the woman may break the subject/object dichotomy that distinguishes the individual from the general."[12]

A third aspect of the developments we see in feminist theory is the emergence of the concept of a multiple, shifting, and often self-contradictory identity. Deborah King, looking at the multiple exclusions experienced by Black women, argues that we can only understand the position of Black women by abandoning the totalizing analytic constructs of race, class, and gender and replacing them with an understanding of Black women as independent subjects who practice a multiple consciousness and maintain a multifaceted ideological stance.[13] Her formulation says that we do not simply "raise consciousness" but rather constantly juggle our various social and psychological identities as we make decisions about the strength and direction of our resistance to multiple oppressions.

All of this means that we are required to assume less and question more about our own theory-making. Our critique of totalizing systems in the male tradition, with their worship of rationality and that circular, academic, analytical thinking, has taught us to be deeply suspicious of totalizing feminisms as well. The notion of a single feminist theory, or even the possibility in the near future that many strands in feminist theory will be woven into a single fabric, seems distant to us. Rather, we are, as Elizabeth Young-Bruehl suggested, engaged in a conversation, "a constant interconnecting of all sorts of representations of our experiences as we hear ourselves and others reflexively interpret ourselves in and through novel conjunctions and conversational moments."[14]

Let me hasten to add that these developments, involving women as a collective concept and seeing the multiplicity of the individual woman's subjectivity, have little in common with the academic nouveau. Rather, they affirm the insight of the editors of the previous theory reader from *Signs*, *Feminist Theory: A Critique of Ideology*, who maintained that women's experience, "in one sense ungraspable but also a human construct," should be the direct focus of feminist theory.[15] Feminists seem to have adopted a notion of theory that rejects the discourse of elite empowerment, formulating instead an understanding of theory as a process, a constellation of ideas reconfigured and reconfiguring within a myriad of feminist practices.

We find ourselves complicating the idea of gender. The insight that the behaviours that marked masculinity and femininity are socially constructed was a fundamental contribution of feminist theory, as I argued before. It was an essential step in resisting the exclusion of women from knowledge production. Yet now we see that gender relations as experienced by any individual are not fixed and immutable but part of a larger category of social relations, positioned in time, place, and political/economic contexts.

We find ourselves thinking about consciousness-raising in new ways. Consciousness-raising is the process that mediates between our inner and outer worlds. Yet we have come to understand that it is not only a state of being but a strategy, as Linda Alcoff says that it is, a departure point for political action.[16] Gender relations as we now understand them include a sense of growth that has no fixed end.

We find ourselves engaging contradictions rather than seeking only to resolve them. We see the energy that can be released by looking directly at what seems diametrically opposed. We see the need to include what was so often discarded, that is, we understand the very focus on women to be a contradiction of and challenge to knowledge itself.

We find ourselves transforming our experiences through the literary and/or autobiographical representations for women's words. There is a renewed determination to end the distortions that have so shaped women's lives and their relations with one another. As Celie says in Alice Walker's *The Color Purple*, "I felt sorry for mama. Trying to believe his story kilt her."[17] Transforming experience is the way that those who were excluded attempt to take their marginal status and make it a positive experience, to unmarginalize it, to refuse to be silenced and instead document and represent both the marginalization and the survival.

We find ourselves self-consciously naming the politics of theory. We find ourselves not only reconsidering the experiences of women that have heretofore escaped attention. Naming the politics of theory is a way of thinking about how processes of exclusion can undermine/discourage trying to build a framework at the theoretical level. That is, disciplinary boundaries tend to interrupt/question multidisciplinary, transdisciplinary work, because disciplinary experts have vested interests in "specialized knowledge" defined in traditional ways with specific vocabularies. We find ourselves investigating what informs those experiences and how those experiences are used by us and by others to give meaning to our lives.

Surveying the myriad feminist activities that surround us at *Signs*, we see an emphasis on our prefigurative practices and the ways they inform our construction of human knowledge. We see ourselves structuring an understanding of the patterns of women's lives through theories that reject totalities and embrace temporalities as enriching and empowering opportunities for new insights. We cannot argue away the daily realities of the radical inequalities that are based on sexual preference, race, class, culture, region, or religion (it is a long list), generated and perpetuated by and for the hegemonic power of white male privilege. We can be sure that our ability to effect social transformation will be doubted, by ourselves and by others. But we see in the outpouring of writings and teachings a collective affirmation of an intention to proceed with feminist pattern making that is undaunted – indeed that is energized by twenty years of effort.

CONCLUSION

Having given a brief outline of what I see to be the major developments in current feminist scholarship, I want to return in closing to one more autobiographical story. For the past few years I have been teaching a graduate seminar in the history of feminist thought. In that seminar I take some fifteen students from as many departments through a trip to the past. We do not look at current questions and theory – indeed, we barely look at the second wave of feminism. Instead we go back, far back, to Hildegard von Bingen, to Christine de Pizan, to Mary Astell and Aphra Behn, to Harriet Martineau and Anna Howard Shaw and Matilda Joslyn Gage, to Virginia Woolf, Mary Bead, Simone de Beauvoir, and Margaret Mead. We do not assume that concern by and about women began with suffrage and industrialization. Why? To establish an intellectual heritage for ourselves, to analyse how women have been thinking about themselves, and to look through their answers for our own. In other classes students get the latest in feminist theory, methodology, pedagogy. In this class we focus on empowerment, on demonstrating to the students – of whatever age – who are no longer excluded and are now in the academy, and whose studies include the contemporary constructions of womanhood, that there is a third road to be travelled. We cannot exclude our past, just as we cannot be excluded from the places where knowledge is produced or from using our own minds to generate knowledge. We must know where we have been in order to know where we are going. Let me end with a quote from Adrienne Rich:

Suppose we were to ask ourselves simply: What does a woman need to know to become a self-conscious, self-defining human being? Doesn't she need a knowledge of her own history, of her much politicized female body, of the creative genius of women in the past – the skills and crafts and techniques and visions possessed by women in other times and cultures, and how they have been rendered anonymous, censored, interrupted, devalued? Doesn't she, as one of that majority who are still denied equal rights as citizens, enslaved as sexual prey, unpaid or underpaid as workers, withheld from her own power – doesn't she need an analysis of her condition, a knowledge of the women thinkers of the past who have reflected on it, a knowledge, too, of women's world-wide individual rebellions and organized movements against economic and social injustice, and how these have been fragmented and silenced?

Doesn't she need to know how seemingly natural states of being, like heterosexuality, like motherhood, have been enforced and institutionalized to deprive her of power? Without such education, women have lived and continue to live in ignorance of our collective context, vulnerable to the projections of men's fantasies about us as they appear in art, in literature, in the sciences, in the media, in the so-called humanistic studies. I suggest that not anatomy, but enforced ignorance, has been a crucial key to our powerlessness.[18]

Rich eloquently names the problem. Feminist scholarship is one way in which that ignorance is going to come to an end.

10 What *Is* the Interrelationship between Academic and Activist Feminism?

LORRAINE GREAVES

It is a daunting task to comment on the interrelationship between academic and activist feminism. The tensions between these elements of the women's movement, as described by Margrit Eichler's respondents, have likely been either observed or experienced by all women. So to introduce a moment of lightness, but a realistic one nonetheless, I want to say that more than one observer has said that the major difference between academic and activist feminists is that the former have access to photocopiers and the latter do not. As well as being a division, this difference may often account for the great deal of interaction that we do in fact have.

Margrit Eichler and Jean O'Barr take very different approaches to shedding some light on the relationship between academic and activist feminism. Eichler comprehensively surveys the academics teaching women's studies in Canadian universities, seeking their perceptions of their relationship to the women's movement and measuring their "direct involvement in the women's movement" in Canada. In contrast, Jean O'Barr traces the evolution of feminist scholarship in the United States over the last twenty years, using both her own experience and an astute analysis derived in part from her position as an editor of *Signs*.

Both of these essays constitute very interesting, albeit very different, contributions to one side of this important debate. For many women, categories and roles overlap constantly, allowing us to safely conclude that certainly some, and quite possibly many, feminist academics are also activists. On the other hand, while one can say some feminist activists are also academics, one cannot say that many or or most feminist activists are such. In other words, activist feminists constitute a larger group than academic feminists. Thus, if a non-academic feminist activist had been asked to address this issue and had commentators from Quebec and the United States been invited to participate, we would be hearing a somewhat more complete debate.

In offering my comments, I will include my impressions of a fragment of the other half of the debate as well as offer some critique and some questions that may elaborate the debate further. As a faculty member at a community college, I am not, at least by university faculty, regarded as an academic. In a less elite context, however, I am an academic, based on the access I have, compared to most women (and men), to speaking publicly, discussing ideas and research, and publishing opportunities. Indeed, in the Ontario college system, the purpose of the community colleges explicitly does not include the carrying out of research but stresses teaching and, secondarily, community development and involvement.

Although we teach women's studies in the community colleges, we do not, officially, do research, feminist or otherwise. And when some research is done by feminists in the colleges, it is usually very applied and without institutional support or approval. It is in this context then that I have, for over fifteen years, participated as an activist in both the grass-roots and political arms of the women's movement in Canada, and in addition, done some applied, woman-focused research. In short, I speak from the margins of academia as it is currently defined, but from a privileged part of the Canadian anglophone activist movement.

Even though I speak from this relatively privileged position as a feminist securely employed in a college, I often feel a great distance from "academic feminism." Most of the women in the women's movement as I know it clearly and continuously feel this distance. As Margrit Eichler points out, this is no easy alliance. Part of this distance stems from the inaccessibility of the work of academic feminists. By this I mean not just whether or not the words get out, but what kind of words they are. Are they big words, and if so, why? Are they words that are working on many presumptions of prior knowledge and, if so, are those presumptions explained? Are the words set up in ways that invite only argument, imply answers, or draw limits to women's involvement? Or, are the words set up in ways that encourage spiralling discussion and what I call the "freeing of speech" among women?

Further, are the words representing ideas that are relevant to activist feminists, and are those words placed where activists will ever read them? Do these words ever turn into multiple forms of communications such as video or audio tape, theatre, music, dance, Braille, film, or pamphlet that are accessible to more women, whatever their language or location? And finally, do the ideas that academic feminists develop have their roots in the movement? Some of these questions have been addressed by both Margrit Eichler and Jean O'Barr. Much of what they both report is, in fact, encouraging to me. But some major ground has not been covered in their essays, or in fact by the form of this volume itself. The ground uncovered by asking this question is indeed a central concern of feminism at the moment.

The questions are: What is the women's movement, what is activist feminism, what is academic feminism, and what operational definitions do we use to discover the interrelationship between these groups?

The question of defining the women's movement is quite possibly a trap. The analysis that Jean O'Barr applies so well to feminist theorizing also applies, I think, to feminist activism. Let me paraphrase her words and apply them to feminist activism. The notion of a single feminist movement is elusive and unlikely, but the multiplicity of individual women's experience, and the resulting complexity of the ideas of feminist activism, lead us away from a notion of a single women's movement. Totalizing feminisms, as Jean O'Barr puts it, are out, and the engaging of contradictions is in.

I am very glad to hear and read this. Many feminist activists have come to this conclusion in a different way. The current debates about accessibility, representativeness, and inclusiveness are, in short, about defining the complexity of the women's movement. Many activists have found themselves not recognized by white mainstream feminism, or perhaps worse, recognized in ways that deny them their complexity and thereby their essence. Growing past the need for the security of a "totalizing feminism," whether that is in theory or practice, and growing comfortable with the contradictions and the complexity of women as a group, and then the women's movement, allows us to more freely acknowledge and understand the different experiences of many women. This, in my view, will be the key to developing not only a mature women's movement, but one that in fact visibly survives.

It is also the key to its strength and vitality and its attractiveness to younger women. Without such maturity in the activist movement, the "paradigmatic shift" in knowledge to which Margrit Eichler refers and the encouraging shifts in feminist scholarship to which Jean O'Barr makes reference will not be maintained or supported very easily or for very long.

Having said this, I still believe we need an operational definition of the "women's movement." After reflecting on both of these essays I have a sense of what we might mean when we say this, and I am able to make certain assumptions, but I need more. I do not propose this need with an eye to coming up with a restrictive definition, but rather to take responsibility for the fact that we do give meaning to a term that we rarely bother to define. And who are we? Predominantly white, apparently heterosexual, usually educated, articulate, verbal women. I think if we bothered to define our terms, we would be thrust directly into the actual challenges facing our movement today, whether we are activists or academics, or on the margins.

In Margrit Eichler's essay, the respondents' involvement in the women's movement is measured by asking whether the academic had ever had a membership in a women's organization and, if so, if they had ever held an organizing position in one of these organizations. But what is a women's organization? Most women's organizations are, in fact, not explicitly or necessarily feminist. Does this render them and the professors' participation in them more useful to our research, or less? And even if the majority of the respondents in this study were members of feminist organizations, does that mean that they were, in fact, in touch with the movement? Not necessarily.

Similar gaps in the definition of the sites of feminist scholarship exist in both essays. Both authors situate feminist scholarship solely in the universities. In Canada, at least, considerable women's studies activity has taken place in the colleges. In Jean O'Barr's essay, the reconstruction of knowledge is central to her description and analysis of feminist scholarship, as it should be, but the site of such reconstruction is much larger than the university.

This raises an equally important need for another working definition: what is academic feminism? In some discussions I have had on this question, women have included such criteria as writing in refereed journals, teaching in universities, or publishing books. These criteria may be sufficient, but are they necessary, to qualify particular women as feminist academics? I implicitly reject that these criteria are both necessary and sufficient.

When I sent the pamphlet for the 1989 conference at the University of Western Ontario to a friend who is an activist and a Black woman, she called me to ask one question. What contemporary women's movement did the conference think it was representing? The question was rhetorical and somewhat derisive, and the implication was that it was not her contemporary women's movement. And she was right, it is not. Another friend, a white woman working with immigrant women, upon hearing that I intended to address the relationship between academic and activist feminism asked: "You mean there is a relationship?" This comment was only half in jest.

These comments illustrate the size and importance of the task: to acknowledge our apparent need to control not only the definition of feminism, but of woman, to examine our various ideological bases for this, and to *drop our collective defensiveness* about hearing criticism or facing the complexity of both women and ideas. Is this too much to ask? Do we feel undervalued because our hard work is not, apparently, enough, or correct? As many of Margrit Eichler's respondents report, and as many of us probably feel, we do not have the energy to do more. But of course, what we do with our energy is a political choice.

Measuring our effectiveness by assessing what we produce in a certain time span is not an adequate answer to the women who criticize the exclusiveness or the incompleteness of the women's movement. Yet we often assess the costs of inclusiveness as opposed to the benefits. But if we are truly interested in the participation of all women in both the building of feminist theory and the building of the feminist movement, there ought to be no choice. This was well put by the DisAbled Women's Network of Canada (DAWN) in a well-circulated newsletter some years ago. After admonishing the women's movement for its inaccessibility and dismissing, among others, the economic arguments against accessibility, DAWN stated explicitly that "being disabled is not cost-effective." Well, inclusiveness in general demands that we give up some old notions of operating and adopt, in the name of women and for the sake of the women's movement, some new ways of operating. They may not be as "efficient," but they will be more authentic.

There are increasingly insistent challenges within the women's movement for representativeness and full participation in the defining of feminist activity and thought. These challenges are being mirrored in many other social movements, political parties, and institutions as well. Much as these challenges are a source of excitement to me, there have been points when my own presumptions about work, women, and feminism have been challenged.

For some years, I worked with various disabled women in committee settings. First, a woman in a wheelchair, where physical barriers were the question. We all adjusted. Second, a woman who was deaf, where my whole conception of language and communication was shifted. I thought I managed very well and I learned a lot about disability. And some of us learned to lessen our pace. But it was when the suggestion was made to integrate a woman with an intellectual disability into the committee that I wondered how we would all cope. She would not understand us, I thought. How would we function? How could she adequately represent disabled women, I asked myself? I tell you this story because, as academics or activists, or at least as verbal, intelligent, idea-mongering women, we rarely care to really think about what it means to include all women in the making of our movement.

There is no doubt that one of the issues most often forgotten by all of us with access to words, ideas, and places to print them is that we are a privileged class. Not only is education, particularly higher education, still very much a privilege of the few, but so is training. Further, intellectual capability – our actual ability to think and reason – is in itself something we rarely consider, in either promoting our movement, or our ideas.

This large oversight can cause those of us engaged in the enterprise of academia, teaching, research, or writing to adapt to the institutions we are a part of, instead of remembering to constantly ask them to adapt to us. The battles that we engage in from these positions of privilege, whether with each other or with institutions, can become less and less relevant to the ordinary woman. We must constantly ask the ordinary woman, particularly the ordinary activist woman, what we should be doing. Failing to do this not only renders us irrelevant, but more important, incomplete. Only by staying in touch with less privileged women's lives, dreams, and ideas will we be enabled to use our access to the academy and the movement effectively and responsibly and for the benefit of women.

Both of these essays caused me to see the parallel challenges in both the feminist academy and in feminist activism. Jean O'Barr's title, "Exclusions and the Process of Empowerment: The Case for Feminist Scholarship," would apply equally well to an analysis of the activist movement. These efforts have provoked me into considering the additional questions, beyond the relationship between activist feminism and academic feminism, that have formed the content of my commentary.

I want to close by posing a challenge to our entire movement, whether we call ourselves activists, academics, or both. When we are criticized for being racist, elitist, classist, ablebodyist, heterosexist, exclusive, rigid, arrogant, or anything else … why don't we act in a way to resolve these criticisms as we ask men and the patriarchy to react to us? We ask for mandatory affirmative action, but do we ever offer our places and access to resources to those women excluded from this enterprise of feminism? The questions are rhetorical, the answers are obvious. Should we ever be able to drop our collective defensiveness and do this, our movement will be richer, more exciting, and truly revolutionary.

PART FOUR

Racism and the Women's Movement

THE THREE ESSAYS IN THIS SECTION SCRUTINIZE THE WRIT-
ings and activities of the feminist movements in Canada and the
United States for evidence of sensitivity to racism. It is their collective
conclusion that racism remains well ensconced within the contemporary women's movement and that the ability of feminists to confront their own racism will be one of the quintessential challenges
facing late twentieth-century feminism.

Mariana Valverde locates herself as a "mostly white, or off-white
feminist" (a non-Anglo-Saxon immigrant to Canada, in government
parlance a member of an "ethnocultural minority"). She describes the
challenge ahead as "becoming conscious of the whiteness of white
feminism." She stresses the need to reconceptualize our own history
and reminds us that Canadian feminist heroines of the past (citing
Nellie McClung) were racist. Valverde takes issue with the tendency
of historians to explain (and condone) such behaviour as "an unfortunate external blot due to the racism of the time." She claims that
racism is not externally caused but integral to mainstream Anglo-
Saxon feminism.

Arun Mukherjee identifies herself as a "non-white Canadian feminist" and addresses the "crisis of legitimation" that racially conscious
demands have begun to posit for mainstream American feminist
theory. She remarks upon the invisibility of Black women and other
women of colour in most women's studies courses, and the reluctance
of most academic feminists to critique white feminist theorists on
racism. She recounts the painful splitting of the second-wave wom-
en's movement along racial lines and queries whether this represents
the tragic repetition of American history in the making.

Glenda Simms, a Black woman, speaks from her position as the
first woman of colour to serve as chair of the Canadian Advisory
Council on the Status of Women. She outlines the dramatic shifts in
racial composition that recent immigration patterns have brought for
Canada. She reminds Canadians that slavery, segregation, and racism
had long-standing historical roots in Canada as well as in the United
States. Simms challenges the Canadian feminist movement to recognize its complicity in the role of "Miss Anne," the white woman
in the "big house." She demands that the women's movement integrate the perspectives of women of colour and aboriginal women
into feminist activity without delay.

As a group, these essays hold Canadian and American feminism
up to race-sensitive scrutiny and find it distinctly wanting.

11 Racism and Anti-Racism in Feminist Teaching and Research

MARIANA VALVERDE

There is no doubt that racism is the major issue of the women's movement as the 1990s begin. Third-World women and women of colour in developed countries have been making their voices heard for some time in specifically feminist contexts, but few white feminists really listened, much less contemplated giving up some space and some power. While white feminists as a whole are probably still not interested in giving up our newly acquired and still fragile institutional power (power to control women's organizations, to define feminism, to represent women vis-à-vis the state, and so on), women of colour and Third World women have made it clear that they are in the women's movement to stay. As a result, it is becoming increasingly difficult for white feminists to act as if they are unaware of their own race privilege.

The type of presentation that would be most appropriate in this primarily white feminist volume would be a critique of the Canadian women's movement, in both its activist and its academic currents, by a Canadian woman of colour, followed by a similar presentation by a feminist of colour from the u.s. In fact, I considered not contributing, since I did not want to falsely claim the position of speaking for, or even about, women of colour. I think that, because of my ethnic origin, there may be some ambiguity about my position vis-à-vis race and ethnicity. Although I am a non-Anglo-Saxon immigrant and thus a part of what government jargon calls the "ethnocultural minorities," I am for almost all purposes white, although of course in the u.s. I might be considered Hispanic and hence a woman of colour. This ambiguity certainly demonstrates that race, like gender, is socially constructed in different ways in different countries; but I do not want to take opportunistic advantage of this ambiguity in order to avoid considering my inherent responsibilities as a mostly white, or off-white, feminist.

I wish to address these responsibilities, since there is some value in white women taking time and energy to reflect on race and racism, whether or not women of colour are present.

From women of colour I have learned that racism is an integrally feminist issue, not just a human rights issue that feminists support from the outside, a view which presupposes a white standpoint. One way of implementing what I have learned is to change the content of the women's studies courses that I have been teaching for five years. Although I am by no means happy with my courses now, I have begun to alter what I teach and have thought a great deal about how to avoid tokenism. One way to make women's studies less ethnocentric is obviously to include a lot more material from Third-World feminists throughout the course, not only in a ghettoized section. I do not claim to have done this yet, but I have at least started the process. Fortunately, a great deal of material by Third-World women and women of colour is available in English, so that the bulk of the work lies in reading a considerable amount of relatively unfamiliar material, ordering books for the library, and changing lectures and course outlines. Of course, this process sounds simpler than it is, considering that many of us change jobs and courses every year and are at the overworked bottom of the academic hierarchy: but being very junior, or being overworked, is not a valid excuse for continuing to teach in an ethnocentric fashion – inertia too is political.

There is, however, a second and rather more difficult task facing those interested in transforming the women's studies curriculum. This involves continuing to teach materials concerning white and/or middle-class women but from a new perspective. We cannot simply add Third-World materials to an inherently ethnocentric curriculum: we have to begin to teach "old" subjects, such as the history of suffrage or the legal issues around abortion and reproductive technology, through new categories. I call this becoming conscious of the whiteness of white feminism. Few women of colour are going to spend the majority of their research time on such tasks as writing biographies of Nellie McClung; it is the responsibility of white feminists to reconceptualize our own history, to reconceptualize feminism itself, through an awareness that being outspoken and even radical on feminist issues has not meant historically, and does not now mean, that racism is either non-existent, or (as white feminists often claim), the racism of x or y white feminist is an unfortunate external blot due to "the racism of the time." The racism of white feminism is neither externally caused nor accidental: it is integral to what the mainstream Anglo-Saxon tradition has called "feminism."[1]

To give one concrete example of how my awareness of the whiteness of white feminism is forcing me to critique my own work, let me present a quick, thumbnail analysis of "the sex debates" from what I hope is an anti-racist perspective. The example is relevant, given the poor effort I made in my 1985 book on sexuality to take racism seriously as it relates to sexuality.[2] Incidentally, this self-critical perspective led me to write a new preface to the book, which I was hoping would be included in the French and German translations. Curiously enough the publishers, both feminist small presses, chose not to include it, one publisher saying that it gave too negative an image of a book which, after all, they were trying to sell. It would seem that there is not much incentive for white feminists to critique our earlier work, although I am hopeful that reprints of both the Canadian and the u.s. editions will include the new preface.

Publishing politics aside, let me summarize this new preface in case it never sees the light of day. That race and ethnicity are integral to our sense of ourselves and others as sexual beings has been amply demonstrated by women of colour, who have argued that gender is not a sufficient concept to theorize sexuality. Women of colour have also pointed out that, just as gender is present everywhere and not only where women happen to walk, so too race is a fundamental social structure exerting determining force even where only white people are present. Taking this into account, how does my earlier view of the "sex debates" change?

Part of our sense of being embodied sexual beings is rooted in our sense (however unconscious or silent) of being white. And what is involved in that? I think that part of our sense of being white has little content other than that contained in that awful word "civilized." "We" are civilized, our parents and teachers told us, which meant not only that we ate with forks and knives rather than with chopsticks or fingers, but also that we exercised what is known as "self-control" over our bodies. As though our bodies were our property rather than our selves. "We" are civilized, it was said: and it did not need to be said that the grammar of that phrase presupposes that nameless others are not civilized. These nameless or named others were envisaged as having no control over their instincts (and again, the idea of self-control presupposed the questionable philosophical axiom that the self is external to the body and its desires). The named and nameless others (the "savages" of Tarzan movies, the Africans of

National Geographic specials, the Red Indians of Westerns, the "fanatical" Arabs of recent newscasts) have no sense of right and wrong because they are simply not civilized, not fully rational. They therefore have no "shame," an interesting word which I suspect is a good indicator of a white standpoint when used in relation to the body. The Eurocentric anxiety about shame and propriety reveals, I think, a common Eurocentric perspective among white feminists, who are otherwise at daggers drawn when discussing sexual politics.

The feminists described in my book as sexual pessimists are, I think, informed not only by a particular view of gender relations in the late twentieth century, but also by a certain culturally specific view of the body and its desires. In both Christian and secular Western systems of thought, there has been a long quest for "purity" – and sexual purity was always connected to, and defined partly in terms of, racial purity. Mary Daly's most recent book, *Pure Lust*, is an example of sexual pessimism: and it is not coincidental that she mobilizes the concept of purity to give some content to the quest for a post-patriarchal female sexuality.[3] It is also not coincidental that she speaks fondly of a "Race" (capital R) of women, never reflecting on the hopelessly racist connotations of such a term, particularly as used by a white woman who is a citizen of the United States. The view of female sexuality as "purer" than that of men's, a view found among Anglo-Saxon feminists now as well as a hundred years ago, is ethnocentric through and through.

But if one side of the sex debates has mobilized ethnocentric and racist concepts of purity for feminist purposes, this does not absolve the other side. The "pro-sex" feminists (Gayle Rubin in the u.s., for instance) rely on a different but equally ethnocentric tradition in their conceptualization of sexual desire, namely psychoanalysis.[4] In its radical and/or feminist varieties, psychoanalysis promotes a toleration of the irrational and an acceptance of the diversity of sexual desire: it is still, however, grounded in a sense of sexual desire as inherently anti-social (as Freud eloquently argued in *Civilization and Its Discontents* [1930]). The great Western opposition between reason and passion, civilization versus the libido, which is in any case of questionable utility for feminist purposes, is worse than useless – is positively harmful – in trying to develop a perspective on sexuality that is both anti-racist and feminist. The work of some neo-Freudians who have been influential among feminists (most notably Wilhelm Reich and Herbert Marcuse) can be perceived as radical in so far as it questions social mechanisms of repression; but it is, from another perspective, a very unradical revival of the Romantic nostalgia for "pre-civilized" times in which "noble savages," unburdened by super-egos, frolicked with one another without guilt. This nostalgia is simply the flip side of the racist coin of "civilization," as African and Asian scholars are demonstrating in their critiques of European anthropology.[5]

While the advocates of female sexual purity appear, from an anti-racist feminist perspective, as imprisoned in Western concepts of the body and its desires, the advocates of sexual emancipation for women can also be seen as racially conservative, in so far as they often assume an ethnocentric European view of sexuality as an inner individual identity of an anti-social character.[6]

The sex debates of the early and mid-1980s, then, can be re-visioned from an anti-racist perspective as debates between different white perspectives on sexuality and gender. This is not to say that no women of colour contributed to the debates or have strong opinions on such issues as censorship or pornography. It is simply to point out that the main lines of the debate were drawn by white feminists within the boundaries of an ethnocentric white feminism which, from an anti-racist perspective, is not as fragmented as it appeared. Eurocentrism provided an underlying unity.

In conclusion, then, it was rather presumptuous to engage in debates which claimed to be about "female sexuality" – as though female sexuality was not racially determined and divided; as though gender was the only problematic term. In future debates about sexuality, rather than proceed immediately to "take sides," we will have to question whether the two sides really do cover the whole spectrum or whether they are in fact a small and rather ethnocentric part of the spectrum. In other words, in this as in many other areas of feminist inquiry, we have to start over again from the beginning. Only that, I think, will entitle us to call ourselves radicals.

12 A House Divided: Women of Colour and American Feminist Theory

ARUN MUKHERJEE

Although groups of women who identify themselves variously as women of colour, Native women, Third-World women, African American women, and Black women have consistently attacked the theoretical constructions generated by the various brands of (white) Anglo-American and (white) French feminist theory as imperialist, racist, Eurocentric, and exclusionary, the crisis of legitimation their critiques have caused regarding mainstream feminism is beginning to be felt only now.[1] There are many indications of this development. While major reformulations of mainstream feminist theories that take into account the contradictions pointed out in the theoretical work of women of colour are few and far between, at least lip-service to the need to include race as a variable is becoming quite noticeable.[2]

At the moment, however, not all white feminists seem to be aware of this crisis of legitimation. The majority of them continue to write about "women's oppression," "representation of women," "sexual difference," "gendered subjectivity," etc. as though they had never heard of the objections raised by women of colour that these terms mask an exclusionary attention to middle-class white women under their unitary veneer. It is ironic that although postmodern "feminisms" have proclaimed "plurality" and "difference" as the new modes of feminist analysis, what Catharine Stimpson has called "herterogeneity,"[3] the difference between their self-image as promoters of plurality and difference and the image seen by their detractors can be gauged by the fact that the latter see the various Anglo-American and French feminisms as one monolith and have given it a parodic name: the White Women's Movement.[4]

This name suggests that the divisions are primarily along racial lines. It is the women of colour, predominantly, who are charging middle-class white women with having played an exclusionary politics in the structures of the women's movement, such as executive bodies, the media of communication, and women's studies departments in universities. These exclusions, they say, are also evident in the theories produced by these exclusionary groups. It is suggested that many white feminists have appropriated the category "women" to speak only about middle-class white women's experience. Hurtful as the exclusions through absences and silencing are, the critics say that even more hurtful are the overtly racist attitudes and their theoretical expressions, as these further exacerbate the oppression women of colour face in a racist, sexist, and capitalist society.[5]

This splitting of the second-wave women's movement along racial lines, one hopes, is not another tragic repetition of American history. One hopes that this time around, instead of playing the "separate but equal" game, we can take stock of the past, calmly assess its mistakes, and begin to build for a more promising future. It is by no means an easy task. As historic creatures, we are deeply implicated in the day-to-day strifes within the feminist enclaves that are themselves embattled in a social structure that is deeply racist, sexist, and classist. Such conditions of existence make dialogue extremely difficult, if not impossible.

I speak as a non-white Canadian feminist who is deeply implicated in these disputes and divisions along racial lines. I have personally experienced the gamut of emotions described in feminist writings on racism: guilt, denial, and hostility on the part of many white women, anger, frustration, and a sense of just cause on the part of women of colour, and jubilation and glee among people who would like to see feminism discredited at all costs. I want to say that it is not easy to formulate words when one is hedged by such contexts and considerations. How to make sure that one does not sound accusatory and hostile? How to make sure that one's valid points will be heard and taken note of, as well as invalid or questionable assumptions pointed out, in a critical but friendly manner? How to make sure that one's personal grievances against racist structures and racist individuals will not surface in one's discourse? I assure you it is no easy task. However, to not even try, despite repeated failures, is defeatist. We must try to articulate our disagreements if we wish to go beyond this impasse, if we wish to save this "house divided against itself."

Perhaps we should begin with a charge that is the easiest to substantiate: the invisibility of women of colour in most women's studies courses. The first time I read the following words in bell hooks's *Ain't I a Woman*, they had an electric effect on me:

The hierarchical pattern of race and sex relationships already established in American society merely took a different form under "feminism": ... the form of women's studies programs being established with all-white faculty teaching literature almost exclusively by white women about white women and frequently from racist perspectives; the form of white women writing books that purport to be about the experience of American women when in fact they concentrate solely on the experience of white women; and finally the form of endless argument and debate as to whether or not racism was a feminist issue.[6]

I was, at this time, teaching a women's studies course and, although I had included the usual couple of books by Black women novelists and poets (my course, like most other women's studies courses being given at my university, was predominantly composed of white women's writings), I was having difficulty interpreting them in terms of the major theoretical assumptions of feminist theories that both I and my students were familiar with. Works like Toni Morrison's *Sula* and Alice Walker's *Meridian* refused to fit into feminist theories that only talked about gender oppression, for they represented a world where Black women suffered the multiple oppressions of race, class, and gender, in that order of severity. These works created a personal theoretical crisis for me because, when juxtaposed against the rest of the course offerings, they brought out the whiteness of white women's writing, a fact that had remained occluded for me and my students because of the unitary language used by the white feminist theorists we were using. We were forced to acknowledge, when we read *Sula* and *Meridian*, half-way into the course, that the white women's theories that we had used as our overarching frameworks did not deal with the oppressive force of racism in the lives of women and men of colour, and the race and class privilege of white women in a racist and classist society.[7]

I also realized that my notions of American literature were racist, not so much because I had consciously thought racist thoughts as because I had never questioned why I had been taught only the texts written by white American men and women. In fact, I had never noticed the fact of their uniform whiteness as something unusual. It was a painful discovery to realize that my formalist training had hidden from me the racist criteria of selection applied at graduate school. An even more painful discovery was that feminist literary theory, through its exclusionary canon-building and theoretical practices, was being equally racist while it presented itself as a revolutionary gesture against androcentric canons and theories.

When some of these same feminist theorists defended their exclusionary works on the basis that they could not include areas they had no "experience" with, they came out looking only more racist. I will never forget what Alice Walker said about Patricia Meyer Spacks's *The Female Imagination*: "Spacks never lived in nineteenth-century Yorkshire, so why theorize about the Brontës?"[8]

While I thoroughly understand that one is limited in one's research by one's education and one's analytical tools, a very liberatory gesture on the part of feminists like Spacks and Elaine Showalter would have been to acknowledge the absence of non-white women writers' texts in their books by, on the one hand, commencing their analysis with a thorough indictment of the racist educational system that had kept them in the dark about the artistic achievements of non-white men and women and, on the other, acknowledging the white-middle-class social location of the writers they chose to emphasize. That gesture, had it been made, would have freed the minds of the next generation of scholars from the shackles of racism. It would have made them see how racism deprived even the best-read Americans of the richness of a truly American heritage.

However, not only was that gesture never made, the racism of several nineteenth-century women's texts was never questioned.[9] It was a great disappointment for me to realize that the work of feminist critics like Patricia Meyer Spacks, Ellen Moers, Elaine Showalter, and Sandra M. Gilbert and Susan Gubar follows exclusionary criteria of selection on the one hand, and, on the other, totally ignores the racist aspects of the texts of their chosen authors.[10]

Critical writings of women like bell hooks, Alice Walker, Barbara Smith, and Hazel Carby have made me think about the racist implications of dominant feminist paradigms.[11] The treacherousness of the privileged feminist concept of "experience" should have become glaringly clear after Walker's brilliant critique. However, it continues to be privileged and misused.[12]

Hazel Carby, in her work on Harriet Jacobs's *Incidents in the Life of a Slave Girl, Written by Herself* (1860), has shown how the rhetoric of sisterhood used by white feminist critics in writing about this text takes us away from those areas of the text that speak about the cruelty of the slave mistresses and their indictment by the female slave narrator. Instead, the critic looking for sisterhood focuses on the possibility of sisterhood across race and class lines, thus totally obliterating the complicity of white women in the system of slavery.[13]

Such theorization constantly stresses that "Women's hands were clean."[14] It is men, so the logic goes, who are responsible for the sins of patriarchy, racism, imperialism, capitalism, war, and gynephobia. This is, of course, the line openly taken by radical feminists. But a reader may be forgiven for assuming that such messages also come through in feminist theorists who only talk about the "oppression" experienced by writers like Charlotte Brontë, Rebecca Harding Davis, and Charlotte Perkins Gilman and never whisper a word about the racism and classism of these same women.

It deeply disturbs me to read critical theory that, on the one hand, remains silent about the hard-core racism of writers like Charlotte Perkins Gilman and, on the other, celebrates the so-called liberatory feminism of their texts. It also disturbs me equally deeply to read feminist history that only celebrates and "rediscovers" white "foremothers," and does not take into consideration their collusion with the racist and imperialist forces of the time.[15]

While the uncritical celebration of racist texts and racist feminists of the past is disturbing in itself, even more disturbing is the unconscious racism and xenophobia present in the discourses of some modern feminists themselves. Kate Millett's *Sexual Politics* (1978), whose canonical status is affirmed by the publisher's blurb proclaiming it as "the feminist classic" on the cover of the latest paperback edition, is full of passages denigrating the humanity of nonwhite people of the non-Western world. The following extract, describing the "men's house of Melanesia," vies with the racism expressed in texts like Joseph Conrad's *Heart of Darkness*:

The men's house of Melanesia fulfill [sic] a variety of purposes and are both armory and the site of masculine ritual initiation ceremony. Their atmosphere is not very remote from that of military institutions in the modern world: they reek of physical exertion, violence, the aura of the kill, and the throb of homosexual sentiment. They are the scenes of scarification, headhunting celebrations, and boasting sessions.[16]

Millett's book is full of false information about the cultural practices of non-Western areas of the world. It often uses phrases like "the primitive world," "oriental priesthood," and "oriental behavior." And sentences like the following leave no doubt in the reader's mind that Millett's definition of "women" excludes women of colour: "In modern capitalist societies women also function as a reserve labor force ..."

In this role American women have replaced immigrant labor and now compete with racial minorities."[17]

A sceptical reader may feel like asking, after reading such passages, why sexism in men should be so strongly rebuked but not racism in women? Why is sexism considered worse than racism? For those who suffer from multiple oppressions of race, gender, class, and sexual orientation, the kind of analysis which creates such oppositions as "women and Blacks," "women and minorities," "women and the colonized people," is a bitter mockery.[18]

The lack of desire on the part of the women's movement and its theorists to deal with racism as a theoretical issue was the reason so many women of colour either never joined or, if they did, left soon after to form their own alliances. Angela Davis has said that the assumption on the part of the late 1960s' feminists that Black women were not feminists because they were involved in the civil rights movement made many Black women, including herself, "completely dissociate ourselves from this women's movement."[19]

The writings, speeches, and manifestos of non-white women's alliances of the 1970s and early 1980s persistently demanded a feminist theory that would integrate race as an important analytical category.[20] However, as we read the books and articles by women of colour, it becomes painfully obvious that instead of theoretical progress, what we get are accusations and counter-accusations among white and non-white feminists. The following passage from Audre Lorde's speech to the National Women's Studies Association Conference in June 1981 is a good example: "When women of colour speak out of the anger that laces so many of our contacts with white women, we are often told that we are 'creating a mood of hopelessness,' 'preventing white women from getting past guilt,' or 'standing in the way of trusting communication and action.'"[21]

bell hooks says that when white women discuss racism, they tend to personalize it by talking about "changing attitudes rather than addressing racism in a historical and political context."[22] That is, racism is talked about in the good old consciousness-raising sessions style where one self-flagellates in public. That, however, is no substitute for a systematic analysis of racism as a system which is a set of economic, cultural, and political arrangements. However, it appears that the consciousness-raising session is still the predominant feminist mode of talking about racism.

Gail Pheterson's "Alliances between Women: Overcoming Internalized Oppression and Internalized Domination," originally published in *Signs* in autumn 1986 and now a part of its 1988 anthology of selected essays called *Reconstructing the Academy: Women's Education and Women's Studies,* describes three extended consciousness-raising sessions on racism, anti-Semitism, and heterosexism that went on for five months as part of a psychology project. Although the footnotes do mention a few books on these subjects, the focus of the paper remains on reporting the "feelings and experiences" of participants. Once again, we hear of the "anger" of the women of colour and "guilt and fear" expressed by the white women. We are told that the participants' lives "changed significantly" as a result of the session. However, we are not told what theoretical insights the participants obtained from the workshops. We are told of the "deep shock" a white woman received when she "realized the racial bias in every aspect of her life." But we are not told about how the participants will "include an emphasis on anti-racist work." Judging from the information provided in the paper, it appears that their anti-racist work will involve setting up more consciousness-raising workshops.[23]

When feminist theory about gender is no longer produced or written about in the form of workshop reports, what makes this style appropriate for writing about race and racism? Secondly, why were the participants in Pheterson's workshop given no works by Black women theorists? Did she not know them herself or had she made a personal decision against using them because she thought them to be of no particular merit?

In a recent article, hooks complained about Black women's work being suppressed through silence in the form of lack of reviews and citations by peers.[24] One could give numerous examples of this curious phenomenon, but its latest manifestation is Toril Moi's prestigious postmodern feminist literary theory book which justifies saying "nothing" about "black or lesbian (or Black-lesbian) feminist criticism in America" because *"in so far as textual theory is concerned* there is no discernible difference" between this criticism and "the rest of Anglo-American feminist criticism."[25] I interpret this persistent denial of the importance of theoretical work by women of colour as a form of institutionalized racism. Personally, I judge the recent work in feminist theory by its scheme of inclusions and exclusions. For example, when I do not see any references to non-white theorists in the index, I make a personal decision about the nature of such a work. The writer of such a work, however well known she may be, instantly loses her credibility with me when she excludes the voices and concerns of women of colour from her work.

While one way of silencing the voices of women of colour is not to read or cite their works, another is to exclude them from decision-making positions. The same 1988 *Signs* anthology includes a paper written collectively by four women of colour. "The Cost of Exclusionary

Practices in Women's Studies" was first published in *Signs* in winter 1986 as a "Viewpoint" article and discusses how institutional structures such as hiring practices of universities, hierarchalization of the institutions of learning, funding procedures, networking, and the composition of editorial boards of important journals marginalize working-class women and women of colour. Their findings suggest that the latter are effectively shut out from jobs at the prestigious universities and from editorial boards of prestigious journals, *Signs* included. The result is, they say, that "the current organization of the academy perpetuates the production and distribution of knowledge that is both Anglo and middle-class centered."[26]

Interesting as this paper is, its discourse is victimized by the exclusionary nature of feminist theory which it critiques, like so many other papers and books by women of colour. My essay, similarly, is caught in the same double bind. It, too, cannot go beyond the binary opposition between, on the one hand, racist and exclusionary discourse of those in power and, on the other, its critique by those who feel oppressed and excluded by it. In Audre Lorde's words, "This gives rise to a historical amnesia that keeps us working to invent the wheel every time we have to go to the store for bread."[27]

This state of affairs can only be described as an impasse. If there is a sizeable body of feminist theory created by women of colour, and white women continue to write and talk about women as though this theory did not exist, then there is a crisis of legitimation which might indeed destroy the house called feminist theory. Because women of colour may not want to invent the wheel every time they put pen to paper, a time may come when they may feel compelled to dissociate themselves completely.

If such an eventuality is to be avoided, white women in positions of power will need to act as well as rethink. For example, they may want to begin affirmative action hiring of women of colour in the women's studies programs, both to make them look inclusionary and to diversify their offerings. They may want to think about formulating anti-racist guidelines for feminist journals. They may want to think about why major works by women of colour are not properly reviewed in feminist journals, if and when they are reviewed at all. They may find it useful to invite letters to the editor where readers may critique published articles in terms of racist assumptions, exclusionary practices, anti-racist feminist goals, etc. They may also think about theoretical engagements with racism and invite papers on the topic to explore how it undergirds different disciplines in the academy.

I am, of course, assuming that, at this juncture in the history of second wave feminism, racism can be seen as a very important feminist issue. I am assuming that we have gone beyond the point where we need to convince people about something as simple and commonsensical as that. The daily realities of my life as an academic at a Canadian university, which hires few non-white women and which teaches predominantly from Eurocentric perspectives, like most other Canadian universities, militate against that assumption. My encounters with some of my past and present women's studies colleagues and the courses they teach also militate against that assumption.

However, I also feel encouraged by colleagues who understand the problem and are actively working for anti-racist hiring practices and anti-racist curriculum. I feel encouraged by the anti-racist conscious-ness of many of my students who speak out against racist practices wherever they find them. I feel encouraged by the anti-racist theory being generated by white women like Elizabeth Spelman. And, finally, I feel encouraged and empowered by myriads of voices of women of colour who are rejecting the imperialist, racist, and Euro-centric designs of many Western discourses.

As a woman of colour, I no longer believe in studying, or teaching, women's texts that are racist, sexist, and classist unless their racism, sexism, and classism are brought under the microscope. For example, I can no longer read about Virginia Woolf's "ordinary woman" with a straight face:

The extraordinary woman depends on the ordinary woman. It is only when we know what were the conditions of the average woman's life – the number of her children, whether she had money of her own, if she had a room to herself, whether she had help in bringing up her family, if she had servants, whether part of the housework was her task – it is only when we can measure the way of life and the experience of life made possible to the ordinary woman that we can account for the success or failure of the extraordinary woman as writer.[28]

Many of my students, both white and non-white, have commented on how hard it is for them to "sympathize" with such "ordinary women." They and I no longer believe that the voices of white middle-class women speak and theorize for all women. Nor do we believe that all women are equally oppressed by a monolithic system called patriarchy. We believe, on the other hand, that a truly feminist theory must consider the interrelatedness of gender, race, and class oppressions and the privilege of skin colour that accrues to white women in racist societies. We believe that a truly feminist theory must construct women's studies courses that introduce students to a diversity of voices. We believe that a truly feminist theory must not cast all men in the role of oppressors of all women but must distinguish between victims and victimizers and concede that non-white men lack the power to oppress white women. We believe that a truly feminist theory must critique racism and reverse sexism perpetrated by self-styled feminists of past and present.

These are political demands, not outbursts of anger. It is time women in power started talking about political imperatives and goals and time tables. For our patience runs out and will not hold too long. It is our hope that "the house divided" will not only survive but will some day be "the house united," a house united against racial, sexual, and class injustices. But, only time will tell.

13 Beyond the White Veil

GLENDA SIMMS

Mariana Valverde is in the fortunate position of choosing her racial identity. She has said that she is Hispanic in America and white in Canada. I, on the other hand, am Black in America, Black in Canada and Black wherever I am. I cannot change this identity, even if I wanted to. Arun Mukherjee speaks very eloquently on the perspective of Black women in the United States. Mariana Valverde also spoke about exclusion, the fact that white feminists, no matter what happens, continue business as usual because they find it so impossible to change.

My argument is that feminists will have to change, because Canadian society is changing in significant ways. John Samuels, who worked with the Department of Secretary of State, wrote in 1988 that recent Canadian immigration patterns will affect the way in which all of us experience this country now and in the future. He produced some statistics on this vision of the Canada that we need to plan for. Samuels pointed out that most of the immigrants in the 1980s came from Asia, and that immigration from Africa, South America, and the Caribbean has risen dramatically in the same period. In fact, during the years 1981 to 1986 the country of birth of 63.5 per cent of immigrants to Canada was a Third-World country.[1]

Whether we like it or not, the Canada of the future will not be a Canada of middle-aged white men and women. It will be a Canada of women and men of varying colours, cultures, and perspectives. We have no choice in this; therefore, we will have to change our attitudes to each other. We need to prepare this country for future generations, for our daughters and granddaughters. We need to prepare them in the same way that my mother and grandmothers prepared me to deal with the issues with which I am dealing today.

You should further understand that I cannot split myself into an academic activist or an activist academic. I have to be both at the same time because I was prepared to be both. My mother once told me to "go to school and learn very well, because you will not be cleaning any white woman's floors."

My great-grandmother also told me: "You have to try to change the course of history." This lesson is clearly demonstrated in a story she told me when I was still a little girl. Being rather precocious, I wondered aloud why there was so much injustice and difference between how the white people and the Black people experienced life in Jamaican society. My great-grandmother delighted in her ability to wash the white shirts of the white doctor in the community. Once I inquired of her: "Why do the white people have so much money?" She responded with the following story: "A long time ago, when the good Lord made human beings" (my great-grandmother had very little formal education) "God really liked Black people and he wanted to give them a break in life. In order to do this he provided two bags of things and called forth the white man and the Black man. He gave the Black man the first choice of the bags." According to my great-grandmother, one of the bags had all the working tools, the pickaxes and shovels. The other bag had feathers. In exercising his choice the Black man checked both bags and thought, "I am going to pick the heaviest one because it must have the best goodies." In so doing, he chose the pickaxes and the shovels. That was my great-grandmother's explanation of the injustices. I have no idea of whether she believed this story or not, but in my child's mind I decided that I did not want any Black man to make choices for me. I guess that is when I became a feminist.

In coming to terms with my adult perspective on feminism, I need to describe what is real about women's experiences. In Canadian society, it has been demonstrated that the two most oppressed groups of women are Black women and aboriginal women. This is not to say that other women are not oppressed; however, as I struggle at the grass roots with immigrant and visible minorities, with Black women and with mainstream women, there is an obvious hierarchy of the oppressed. Until women understand this hierarchy, we will not be liberated from all our unique forms of oppression.

Black feminism, as it is articulated in the literature and practised in the Black communities in Canada, captures the nature of the struggle of all women of colour, while it reflects the day-to-day experiences of women of diverse backgrounds, cultures, and age ranges.

In Michele Wallace's words, women "have no choice but to fight the world. Black women must fight the world because they struggle daily against the racist, sexist, classist power of white men, against the racist, classist power of white women, and against the sexist power of powerless Black men."[2] It is therefore no wonder that Wallace asserts that being a Black woman means frequent spells of impotent, self-consuming rage. The recognition of the triple oppression of race, class, and sex has been reflected in the works of all Black women activists and in those whose lives have been celebrated and recorded in the history books and in contemporary writings – women like Sojourner Truth, Harriet Tubman, Audre Lorde, Angela Davis, bell hooks, Alice Walker, Carrie Best, and Marlene Nourbese Philip, to name but a few. There are also many thousands of others whose leadership in their communities went either unnoticed or unrecorded. Therefore, the ideas about racism that are being raised today are not new. These are the ideas that have been constructed by the experiences of generations of Black women in both the United States of America and in Canada.

In our attempt to address the issue of feminism and racism, we need to recognize that contemporary contradictions have their historical roots in the life experiences of both Black women and white women in the slave societies of North America. I refer to North America, because Canadians pride themselves on being polite racists, a cut above their American counterparts. Every time one tries to discuss racism and slavery, the typical Canadian response is: "That happened in the United States." The record needs to be set straight. We need to acknowledge that slavery has existed in Canada. Our foremothers were oppressed in this country. They slaved and they were also segregated in parts of Nova Scotia. In addition to this they broke many frontiers in southwestern Ontario, in the Amber Valley in Alberta, in Maidstore in Saskatchewan, and in other early Black communities in Canada. It is in some of these communities that Black women were most dehumanized and oppressed, and it was in slave society that the concept of white privilege gave white women a degree of power over both Black men and Black women.

hooks, Davis, Giddings, and many of the foremost writers in the United States have discussed in detail the unique ways in which sexism and racism magnified the sufferings and oppression of Black women under slavery. hooks argues that some of the practices that set the stage for the total oppression of Black women included the curtailing of interracial relationships between white women and Black men, the masculinization of Black women through field work (a role that was not performed by white women), the harsh beatings of Black women by both white men and white women, and the wholesale sexual exploitation of Black women of all ages. In other words, these were the earliest periods of rape of our foremothers, done at the time when there were no transition houses. The peculiar institution of slavery reveals most starkly the conflict between the privileges gained by white women within a patriarchal and capitalistic society and the powerlessness of Black women in the same society.

One might argue that privilege is an inappropriate concept in this context, since white women were merely part of the slave masters' property as well. Logical as such arguments might be, the reality of social arrangements, then, were such that white women were prized property. The shift away from the traditional image of white women as sinful and sexual to that of white women as virtuous ladies occurred at the same time as the mass sexual exploitation of enslaved Black women. bell hooks states: "as American white men idealized white womanhood, they sexually assaulted and brutalized black womanhood."[3] hooks's discussion dramatizes an emotional field of Black and white women. She conjures up the image of the privileged white woman looking passively at the plight of the oppressed Black woman as she is brutally tortured. Of course, passivity does not imply complicity. However, hooks posits that the white woman must not be seen as an unwilling victim of this particular period in history. She states: "While white women rarely physically assaulted Black male slaves, they tortured and persecuted Black females. Their alliance with white men on the common ground of racism, enabled them to ignore the anti-woman impulse that also motivated attacks on Black women."

In popular parlance we can extrapolate that "Miss Anne" was in the big house but she knew that her man was in the slave quarters with a Black woman. Did she see this woman as her rival, or did she believe that her man needed to find some lesser species on which to release his powerful sexual energy? Was this out of regard for her or was this in disregard of the slave woman?

Several theories explain the torture of Black women by white women as a result of the distortion of power relationships and the historical practice of pitting woman against woman in sexual competition for a male. Heleieth Saffioti, who wrote about Brazil, produced a different analysis of this phenomenon.[4] She tried to make the white woman the real victim of slave society. Inherent in her analysis is the idea that this situation was not all bad, because the mulatto offspring of the liaison between the white man and the Black woman became the focus of dynamic tensions in modern Brazil. In fact, in her analysis she posits that it was obvious that white women were indeed burdened. She argues that they had to oversee all these slave women and supervise their work and, on top of all this, they had to put up with all the kids that their husbands were producing. The juxtaposition of Saffioti and hooks's points of view demonstrates what has to be seen as a very real difference in perspectives, especially when the concepts of racism and sexism are separated in feminist analysis of women's life.

Of course, the issue is not the denial of the universal oppression of all women in both slave society and contemporary society. The theme is that not all women are equally oppressed or oppressed equally. Therefore, the nature of oppression experienced by different women becomes part of the psychological baggage that they take into their daily lives. Dionne Brand, a Toronto writer, makes the case for us. She says that feminists should strive to understand the linkages between socialization and what she defines as "racist, sexist, common sense." She argues that just as slave women were expected to satisfy the slave master's sexual whims, so today in Canada the white male employer may feel that he has the right to sexual relationships with the Black woman who has not been able to escape from his kitchen or his factory, or who must still be nanny to his children. Brand also moves beyond this question of sexual exploitation of individual Black women by particular white men to discuss how the state tries to control and distort the sexuality of Black and other working-class women. She also discusses women on welfare who cannot have a man in their homes, because if you are a woman on welfare you are not supposed to have a sexual life.[5]

It is important for Black and white feminists to understand their responses to each other as an outcome of the accumulation of experiences which are rooted in a very intense and emotionally charged historical reality. Understanding this history will propel women to plan the future in ways that do not replicate the negative outcomes of the past.

"Miss Anne" is the personification of the white woman's predisposition to women of colour. Miss Anne resides in our psyche. She is rooted in history. She sits in the big house. She is both mistress and victim. She embodies all of our contradictions. She needs to liberate her soul. She is heard and seen through the voices of women of colour. In racial terms, she is the white woman. In heterosexist terms, she is the homophobic sister.

We can understand "Miss Anne" through the voice of Rachel, who came to Canada as an exchange student from the Gambia. She spent ten months in Winnipeg. When I interviewed her, she said:

I understand my meaning to my host through the comments that she made about the Canadian Native. I can remember accompanying her to a bingo, and she remarked about the number of Natives in the hall. I asked her to tell me how I can identify a Native. She mumbled something about their hair – the inability of their hair to curl even if they cut it. I sometimes wonder what she was trying to say. I was not naive. I needed some kind of marker to identify who is Native and who is white, since these distinctions were obviously important to social relationships in the city of Winnipeg.

In Africa, the distinction between Native and white is stark. This is a distinction not only of skin colour but of social distance. Back home in Gambia, there are no egalitarian bingo halls. Is a bingo hall occupied by whites and Natives a sign of a progressive society or is it part of the charade that satisfies my host's conscience? I detected an attitude that was subtly condescending. My host needed to distinguish herself from the Native women. Her point of reference was the hair. (Hair became the metaphor for social and racial barriers to the feminist vision.)

I am a twentieth-century African woman, born and bred in a continent that has been raped and pillaged by colonialism, neo-colonialism, and imperialism. A continent that has by and large bought into the Western capitalist camp. A continent that has aped the best and the worst aspects of Western thought and lifestyle. As such, I am an African woman who has had no choice but to understand the Western world. Imagine my state of mind when I came to Canada and met people who expected me to be stupid, primitive and totally devoid of any knowledge of technology, mass society, and consumerism. How can I explain my host's anger on the occasion when I touched her VCR or her consternation at the fact that I not only knew about the use of refrigerators and freezers, but that I owned one of each back home? Was she angry because I rendered her useless? Inadvertently, I robbed her of the multiple role of teacher, missionary, benefactor, and goddess. Why did she find it so hard to be just a woman, a sister, a comrade, and a friend?

I came, not to see gadgets; I came, not to be startled by bright lights; I came, not to tread the corridors of department stores or to stare in wonder at the aisles of food cages. I came to find human values, to make friends, to participate and to share. I was rendered helpless. I became angry.

In trying to state my case, I will close with the words of Maxine Tynes, a Black Nova Scotian educator and poet, a woman whose ancestors came here four hundred years ago, but whose people still remain part of the Canadian underclass. Maxine writes: "Women are always looking into mirrors, looking for a mirror to look into or thinking about, regretting, sighing over or not quite believing what they are seeing in the mirror. We are looking at ourselves, looking for ourselves, searching, always searching in mirrors for people of colour. For Black people, for this Black woman in particular, the search is the same but different. We are constantly looking for who we are. So many of the signals have been lost, historically and culturally, along the way."[6]

PART FIVE

Violence against Women

AT THIS POINT IN OUR COLLECTION OF ESSAYS, WE MOVE into a discussion of a series of discrete issues that have preoccupied the current wave of the women's movements in Canada and the United States. Violence against women is the focus in this section, and, most particularly, the pervasiveness of sexual assault. Many would argue that it was the springing up of community-based rape crisis centres and battered women's shelters out of the first conscious-ness-raising groups in the United States and Canada that heralded the coming of age of the contemporary women's movement. Violence against women quickly assumed a special place in the feminist anal-ysis of the costs borne by women within a patriarchal system. Strat-egists for change devoted extensive efforts to defining the problem from the perspective of women, and to designing agendas for reform.

Catharine MacKinnon is well placed to comment on the feminist movement's response to sexual assault, having been active in both academic and activist circles in the United States and Canada. She concludes that contemporary feminism has distinguished itself in the extent of its attempts to intervene in sexual violence, particularly through legal reform. She describes and critiques the feminist cam-paign to redefine "rape" as a more gender-neutral "sexual assault," a campaign which achieved success on both sides of the border. MacKinnon objects that sex is "deeply understood and experienced as gendered" and suggests that the reforms have not delivered much in the way of real change. Instead she calls for a redefinition of rape as "sex forced by aggression, threat, or authority."

Patricia Monture-OKanee takes issue with the feminist record on violence against women from an even more fundamental position. Her essay provides a perspective which views current feminist cat-egorization of issues as artificial, even irrelevant to First Nations women. The violence of racism which surrounds First Nations com-munities transcends categories which subdivide issues and classify violence as merely "against women." "Racism is not just violence against women," she asserts. Monture challenges the predominantly white women's movement to ensure that First Nations and other women from distinct racial groups be provided the opportunity to participate in setting the definitions under which the discourse on violence against women operates.

These essays represent a critique of the work of the contemporary women's movements in Canada and the United States on issues of violence against women, and provide a provocative commentary on one of the issues which has become central to the work of the current wave of feminism.

14 Feminist Approaches to Sexual Assault in Canada and the United States: A Brief Retrospective

CATHARINE A. MACKINNON

Even alone, women find ways to resist sexual violation. Organized women's movements, in varying vocabularies, have also opposed abuse through sex as essential to women's freedom. These struggles leave a trace only when they surface, are noticed, and recorded. Such recognition is rare. A distinctive feature of the contemporary women's movement is its focus on making sexual abuse visible. As a result, for the first time in history, we are beginning to have real information on the extent, interconnectedness, and etiology of the problem. Contemporary feminism has also distinguished itself in the extent of its attempts to intervene in sexual violence, including through law.

Confining myself to the example of rape, I want to assess the information that we have, the approaches we have taken, and the legal interventions we have made. As I see it, a distinction between sex and violence, and an accompanying gender-neutrality, has infused the approaches taken to legal change to date. We are now in a position to reassess these concepts through their practical consequences and, in light of feminist insights, to go further.

The information on sexual abuse uncovered by the women's movement has revealed its epidemic proportions. Feminism has further theorized that sexual abuse is endemic to male dominance. In other words, sexual abuse has been found not only to happen a lot but to be structural in the social inequality between women and men.

The new information, which has supported new analysis of the relations between the sexes as well as of the law of sexual assault, includes both direct reports of survivors and Diana Russell's epic study of 930 San Francisco households, using a sample carefully randomized for race, language, and other social variables.[1] Partial replications in Canada have produced startlingly similar numbers. Acknowledging that the United States is one of the most violent countries in the world, statistical differences between the u.s. and Canada, at least so far as current information suggests, may not be so substantial in this area.

In Russell's study, 47 per cent of all women report being victims of rape or attempted rape at least once in their lives. Thirty-eight per cent of girls report being sexually abused or molested before they reach the age of majority. Black, Hispanic, and Asian women and girls are abused more often, on the average. The sexual abuse of Native children in residential schools in Canada is a similar situation of intensified exploitation of subordinated groups. The report on this abuse has yet to be released, but estimates by the people who compiled the data are that half to all Native children removed from their nations by white society were sexually abused, producing what some have called a lost generation of Native people. Here, sexual assault is a form of cultural genocide.

The approach the women's movement has taken to sexual abuse began with telling the truth: women did not want to be raped. This became translated as: rape is violence not sex.[2] Perhaps it was argued this way because to say sex had meant to presume desire and because rape had long been exonerated as a form of sex. Whenever anyone thought an account looked like sex or felt like sex – including to the perpetrator or the trier of fact – it was implicitly considered to be sex and found not to be rape.

I have tried being agnostic about the value loadings of the terms sex and violence and just listened to the meanings they code. Violence is a word we use for things we oppose. Sex is a word that we use for something we value. Violence is a word we use when the pain of what is done is real to us. Sex is a word we use when what we think is happening is pleasure. Violence is a word we use when we recognize degradation. Sex is a word we use when we think what is happening is elevating, natural, or chosen. Violence is a word of moral disapprobation. Sex is a word of moral approval. In other words, this discourse is structured as an analytic melodrama. When you want the audience to hiss, you say violence; when you want the audience to cheer, you say sex.

In this world, it made some strategic sense to call rape violence, not sex.[3] Women wanted it disapproved, not even tentatively exonerated. The gender-neutrality of the term also seemed a benefit. You cut off a man's arm. It hurts. He bleeds. Society disapproves. Law

188 Catharine A. MacKinnon

acts. Therefore, maybe, if you cut off a women's arm, her pain and her blood will be disapproved and acted against as well. The point is to conceive rape as being as much like something that can be done to men, something men do to men as men, as possible. Maybe the moral disapprobation will extend from men to women – a big improvement.

Unlike violence, sex is difficult to sell as gender-neutral. Sex is deeply understood and experienced as gendered. The conventional definition of sex in heterosexuality is nothing if not gendered. This remains true, for example, even for gay men and lesbians, whose sexuality is not ungendered, merely same-gendered.

Under the rubric of rape as violence not sex, feminists promoted a gender-neutral rape law. The idea was to detach rape from sex, and thus, it was hoped, from women. Since rape was defined by distinction from sex, the line between them needed to be moved to encompass more of women's experiences of violation by naming them as women felt them. Violent, not sexual; forced, not consensual.

Feminists hoped to change the gendered reality of rape by altering the ways the law authoritatively wrote it back onto society. Everyone knows that it is women who are raped and that they are raped by men. Feminists hoped to remove the mark of rape from women and also to recognize rapes in which men are the victims.

Pursuing these views, law in the u.s. and Canada made a substantial number of changes. In Canada, Parliament makes a single federal criminal law; in the United States, criminal law is made state by state. Some call the u.s. system a laboratory of experimentation, others a chaos of inconsistency, but whatever you call the federal system, there is a lot of it, and a lot of variation in it. These changes can, however, be broadly summarized.

What was done to rape law in the name of the women's movement began with changing the definition of the crime from rape to sexual assault.[4] This was a move to make the law of sexual violence a part of the law of assault rather than a special law of sex. I think there was a subtheme of gender-neutrality as well. Women were socially marked for rape. Detaching rape from women by calling it sexual assault seemed to communicate that it could happen to anybody – a full citizen, a real human being, a man. If it is put into the same category as things that happen to men, maybe some of the seriousness with which male injuries are regarded will rub off.

Other changes inspired by the gender-neutral ideal were the elimination or erosion of the penetration requirement and the lack of exclusive focus on the penis. Digital penetration or penetration by objects, always part of women's experience of rape by men, became a part of the law once it tried to imagine how a woman would rape a man. The search for ejaculate – corroboration through semen – was also eroded or eliminated, to envision rape as less like sex and more like violence. The move was away from intercourse, the model for which was penile intromission followed by thrusting to orgasm, and towards attack, the model for which was mugging.

The law's victim went from woman to person and the perpetrator was no longer necessarily a man. The law went from rape as intercourse without consent and against her will by a man with a woman not his wife, to sexual assault as forced sex without consent.

Not a small change was permitting rape in marriage to be recognized as a crime, a change achieved by statute in Canada and to varying degrees in some u.s. jurisdictions.[5] The notion had been that what happened between a man and his wife was sex no matter how much force was involved. A famous aphorism attributed to a legislator who opposed recognizing rape in marriage said it all: "If you can't rape your wife, who can you rape?" If you cannot have sex with your wife on your terms, who can you have it with? Recognizing marital rape as a crime moved it out of the category of sex into the category of violence, and the answer to his question became no one.

Keeping women's sexual history out of sexual assault trials under most circumstances was another expression of the attempt to distinguish violence from sex in the rape context. This change was based on the view that rape is not continuous with a woman's prior sex life but is, rather, an assault. To consider sexual history relevant to assault is to suggest that assault is part of sex. Say you are walking down the street and somebody jumps you and takes your money. The law does not assume you were a walking philanthropist, nor do the police inquire how many times this has happened to you, or whether you contributed to United Charities last week. Excluding sexual history from sexual assault trials detaches the act of assault from the experience of sex. The way it was before, if you ever had sex, your credibility in charging rape was shot for life. I call this the "when you're fucked, you're fucked" rule. All you have to do is have sex, ever, and no one will ever believe you again. At least formally, this has been undermined.[6]

The exclusion of sexual reputation evidence has a similar logic. A woman's sexual reputation became no longer relevant to whether or not a man raped her. To see rape as assault makes irrelevant what anyone thinks a woman might have previously done, or had done to her, sexually. Other changes such as removing the unique corroboration requirements some jurisdictions placed on rape, and its special short statute of limitations, are also consistent with the feminist approach. The old idea was that women fabricate rape reports, lie about sex they want, and the longer they take to report, the more likely it is that they will make up a story. If it takes the victim of mugging two days to recover before reporting, the mugging is not typically disbelieved, nor does anyone tell the victim she still has her money. The special jury instructions that rape is uniquely easy to charge and uniquely difficult to disprove have also been removed.

We do not know what these legal changes have accomplished ideologically. We do know that in reality conviction rates have not risen significantly. None of these changes has significantly affected our ability to convict rapists. Nor has the incidence of rape decreased – it has increased. It may be a bit much to attribute the failure to reduce the incidence of rape to particular law reforms, but what is this exercise about? Rape reporting rose somewhat, in some places. But, even adopting feminist legal initiatives, the effectiveness of government's response to rape has not increased.

Did we miss something? Did we leave something out? When we asked whether rape is sex or violence, did we accept a distinction that does not exist? Were we perhaps too involved in rebutting men's misconceptions, too distracted by their categories, too enmeshed in their values, too reactive to their agenda, even too trapped by their reality, to say what rape really was? Because they said it was sex, therefore above question, did we have to say it was violence not sex, in order to question it? If rape is sex as well as violence, might that not indict sex instead of, or as well as, exonerate rape? If rape is violence, not sex, why don't perpetrators just beat women up? If rape really is gender-neutral, why don't women do it to almost half of men?

We might consider that the distinction between sex and violence is a false one. We have actually known this for a very long time, which is why we called rape sexual violence, sexual assault, sexual abuse. The experience of both the victim and the perpetrator is that this form of assault is sexualized – not just an assault that is done through sexual means, but an assault that is itself a sexual experience, in which the violence is part of the sex. To analyse rape this way also reintroduces a critique of gender, a gender that is not gender-neutral, a critique of the meaning of sexuality in the context of the inequality between women and men. In gender inequality, women are unequal to men, not the other way around. Once the problem is not gender-neutral, the solution is not either. We need to look at what rape is to women, what rape is to men, to unpack the non-gender-neutrality of its reality.

This makes it possible to analyse rape as sexual sadism, as an expression of misogyny. Violence is included, as sex. If rape is

situated in the context of gender inequality, in a hierarchy of dominance and subordination that is continuous with women's experiences of both intercourse and battering, sex and violence are
interpenetrated, not wholly distinct, experiences. For battering men,
for example, battering may be an act of sex. Often it replaces sex. It
has cycles like sex. It can be experienced sexually. Many experiences
of force, violation, and non-consensual intercourse under conditions
of gender inequality eroticize dominance and subordination, sometimes for the victims as well as for the perpetrators. This does not
mean that women want to be raped. It means that rape, including its
violence, can be sex: sexually violating to its victims and potentiating
and pleasurable to its perpetrators.

The point is that violence is sex when it is practised as sex, when
it is experienced as sex. Although it was productive to point out the
violent elements in rape, we did not need to distinguish violence
from sex to do it. Perhaps we thought we needed to because violence
is not something one consents to, and to suggest that one consents
to violence is generally recognized as "blaming the victim."

If rape is analysed in a context of gender inequality, consent
emerges as its real issue, but not in its usual abstract way. Consent
distinguished rape from sex. While the women's movement raised
the issue of consent, and some important matters of proof that go to
it were changed, the fact that women have no credibility when we
say we did not consent to sex was not frontally targeted. Sex is
regarded as consensual, rape non-consensual. (Note that mutuality
is not the standard.) One problem is that often women do not like,
want, or consent to sex even when no overt force is present. Is that
rape or not? Legally it is not, and the analysis of rape as violence not
sex did not change that but reinforced it.

If concepts of consent in the law of rape are placed on a continuum,
statutory rape is on one end, marital rape is on the other.[7] Statutory
rape assumes that children cannot, or do not meaningfully, consent to
"intergenerational sex." No matter how much it looks like sex, sex
between adults and children is regarded by law as violent – that is,
consent is irrelevant. It is rape. The prototypical victim is the virgin,
the madonna, the daughter. Its eroticism is "violate the pure." At the
other end of the continuum is marital rape and the rape of prostitutes,
the first impossible *de jure*, the second impossible *de facto*. No matter
how much violence there is, non-consent is irrelevant. It is sex. The
prototypical victim, regarded as a non-victim, is the whore (who can
be used by all men with impunity), and the wife (who can be used by
one man with impunity). Its eroticism is "wallow in filth." The poles of
consent in the law of rape correspond to two poles of male eroticism
defined by the virgin/daughter and whore/wife stereotypes for women.

The law of forcible rape, it is my argument, is interpreted and applied in parallel terms. A woman who is victimized by forcible rape is seen as raped under law to the extent she corresponds to the statutory rape paradigm. Her chances diminish to the extent she corresponds to the marital rape paradigm. Women are placed in these spheres of consent according to stereotypical characteristics. These concepts mark out spheres of access for men to women in the world. They tell men which women they can have sexual access to and what will, in theory, be done about it. In fact, neither construct does anything significant about rape. The virginal prohibition, by making it taboo to violate the pure, helps eroticize the powerlessness of young girls, targeting them more than protecting them.

The way this law works is that it does not work. Until we redefine the crime of rape itself, we tinker without going to the heart of the problem. To say, as the rape law does, that rape is intercourse with force and without consent is to adopt the sadomasochistic view of sex as the definition of rape. It says women consent to forced sex. It says women enjoy being violated. So women constantly have to disprove we consented to sex with force. This definition of sex, the sex of eroticized hierarchy of dominance and subordination, is the definition of sex the rape law is predicated upon.

I suggest we define rape as sex forced by physical aggression, threat, or authority, as a crime of sexual inequality. Leave non-consent out.[8] The *mens rea*, if there must be one, can go to force. If the defendant then wishes to prove that we consented, let him try. The woman proves the man forced sex on her. The man can then try to prove she consented. In many cases, what passes for consent is despair, terror, lack of life options, and a gamble to save one's life. The more a woman resembles a dead body, the more she consents, in this model. When her lack of response is presented by the survivor to negate her consent, she is often not believed; when it is presented by the perpetrator as supporting her consent, he may not be.

Force should be redefined to take age, race or ethnicity, disability, and other inequalities into account. What counts as force should comprehend being five years old, being Black, being Native, being an immigrant or a refugee, being the victim of one's employer or caretaker or a police officer. Those dimensions of social life heighten a woman's vulnerability to unwanted sexual access and diminish her sexual credibility in challenging it. As it is now, the law in effect defines these forms of heightened vulnerability as consent, attaches them to women, and then virtually anything can be done to us.

Since rape is an institution of social inequality, perhaps taking systematic inequalities into account in the rape law would make the difference that has eluded our attempts to stop it so far.

15 The Violence We Women Do: A First Nations View

PATRICIA A. MONTURE-OKANEE*

This topic "violence against women," it mystifies me. I am not mystified because I do not understand the meaning of violence. I know what rape is. I know what assault is. I know what pornography is. I know what sexual abuse is. I know what these things are vis-à-vis First Nations and First Nations women all too painfully well. I understand the theory and the real life experience. But, I also understand what racism is. I know the result of racism is violence. The violence of racism often echoes in a silenced world. What I do not understand is violence in its definitions as merely "against women." Racism is not just violence against women. I am going to tell you a story while trying to explain my dissatisfaction with the definitions feminism has accepted. It is a rather long story about who I am.

My story includes what I heard at the 1989 conference at the University of Western Ontario. Catharine MacKinnon's essay, for example, contains many definitions and a lot of talk about consent.[1] I am going to try to discuss these two themes, definition and consent. Also, we have heard much questioning and talking at the conference about a debate between academics and activists. I thought, "I wonder if I am an academic yet?" Then, I thought, "Well, I wonder if I am an activist?" And then I thought, "Oh well, maybe I am a feminist?"

* This paper was originally given in the way of my people, by oratory not by prepared text. This text was later constructed from the recorded transcript of my oral presentation. The content of the original text has been protected by using footnotes to insert new material of any length.

I still do not have answers to those questions. I do not find those three definitions – academic, activist, feminist – helpful to me. What I do know is who I am.

I am a Mohawk woman. I am a citizen of the Haudenosaunee Confederacy (the Six Nations Iroquois Confederacy).[2] I am one woman. That's who I am. I do not represent all First Nations women or even all Mohawk women. My woman's identity comes from the fact that I am a member of that Confederacy, that I am a member of the Mohawk nation. You cannot ask me to speak as a woman because I cannot speak as just a woman. That is not the voice that I have been given. Gender does not transcend race. The voice that I have been given is the voice of a Mohawk woman and if you must talk to me about women, somewhere along the line you must talk about race.[3] You, as women (academics, activists and/or feminists), must talk about race if you continue to commit yourself to the commonality of all women. It is out of my race that my identity as a woman develops. I cannot and will not separate the two. They are insepa-rable. I cannot separate the two because you need to ignore race, because it challenges and confronts your theories and construction of the world. That is essentially one of the problems I have with the construction, "violence against women." It is the initial problem that I have with that concept. I cannot stand up here and just be a woman for you. I cannot stand up here, therefore, and just be a feminist for you. I cannot and will not do it. I do not know how to do it. And it hurts me (and that hurt is violence) that you keep asking me to silence my race under my gender. Silencing me is the hurt which is violence.

At the conference I inwardly cheered loudly at Arun Mukherjee's statement: "Please see these as a list of political demands, not as outbursts of anger."[4] I, too, am so very tired of being called angry, of having somebody else (and in this case another woman, usually a "white" woman) define my feelings. I am not angry, I am actually a very kind and gentle woman. Whenever you call me angry, and that is frequent, it hurts. Labelling me as angry is one way in which you silence me. I do not understand why you believe you can define how I feel.

This whole idea of double discrimination, that is race and gender, just does not work. I mean look at me, I do not separate that way. My race and my gender are all in one package. My race does not come apart from my woman. There is not a little piece of me I can put up here for you to say, "OK, this is the woman talking now." I need to know where all of that thinking came from – that I come apart.[5] I do not understand where all this separationist thinking arises. We separate ourselves from ourselves all the time on lines of race, on lines of class, on lines of gender, on lines of sexuality. Once it is understood that I do not come apart, the entire discussion of discrimination as "double" must be understood to fail. I cannot trace the discrimination I live to one source – race or gender. It is better described as "discrimination within discrimination."[6] It is complex and certainly not linear.

Another thing that I need people to understand is that First Nations people are not homogeneous – the experience of a Cree woman, the experience of a Mohawk woman, the experience of a Haida woman, and the experience of a Mi'kmaq[7] woman are not the same. We are distinct nations with distinct experiences. We have separate ways. You cannot have one First Nations woman up here and then say "Oh, gee! Now I understand how all First Nations women feel and think." Our experiences are different. And so will the solutions be different among First Nations people because the situations we face are different. Some of us no longer live on reserves. And even if we do, the solutions still vary. The sizes of the reserves are different. The economic resources available on reserves differ. So there is not one problem, and there is not one solution.[8] I tie all of that to this separationist thinking that has been adopted.

We are now back to why I cannot and will not write about "violence against women." Why I cannot jump into that "little box" you created to deal with my life in a way which you defined because you found it convenient. Next I want to talk about education. Again this is another jump into the "little box" phenomenon. When I hear the definition of a university as "a place for the creation and dissemination of knowledge," I think about all the other ways one can and does learn things that are not validated in this society, particularly in universities.[9] That has a specific reference for First Nations people. If you put your hand over your heart, what do you feel? You have a spirit. You do not just have a mind. Your spirit knows things. Go out and sit under a tree in the bush somewhere. I do not mean in a city park, I mean in a bush somewhere and learn who is out of balance. It is not the trees. It is not all the things that grow (they too have spirit). It is not the animals. It is not the winged ones – the insects or the birds. They all remember their original instructions. It is us, people, who have forgotten those things and that balance.

In ten years of being at university, I have not spent one single day in any of those institutions where I was dealt with as a complete person. I was merely a mind. No one wanted to address my spirit, or my emotions, or my sexuality. We have to look at the definition of what is knowledge – the way we learn things – if we are going to address First Nations concerns. Some of the wisest people that I know, some of the best teachers – my true teachers, my real teachers – have never spent a day in university in their entire life. I feel so sad for non–First Nations peoples because you do not have access to those things or to those teachers. Because the definitions you picked up and maintain shut the door on those people's brown, wise faces. You invalidate their experience. And their experience is the wisdom of entire nations. Those Elders and Traditional Teachers are our "Ph.Ds."

I learned at law school that I had two responsibilities. I did not learn this because of legal study, but because law school was a process of silence and exclusion. By agreeing to go to law school I picked up the responsibility of learning the Canadian legal system. I said I was going to learn about that and I did. I learned about constitutional law, criminal law, human rights, contracts, property law, about all of those legal things. But as a Haudenosaunee woman, I also have the responsibility to teach my son, and the men, and my nieces, and my nephews, and my sisters, and all the little ones. I also had to go back and continue to learn about medicines, about my spirit, about those sacred things, so I could live them and teach them. So I had these two responsibilities. What I learned at law school was that nobody else recognized that those "second" responsibilities validly existed for me. Nobody else recognized the fact primarily because of their white privilege. They never understood that they too had more to do than learn the law.[10] They must recognize their obligation to start to learn about the First People who were put here on Turtle Island [North America]. Property law is perhaps the best example I have of the point I am trying to make. I sat for eight months, quietly. We did not mention First Nations once. We talked about land in this country, about my Mother, about Turtle Island for eight months, and not once did we mention First Nations people! This fact is still one which I do not understand. Yet it is still happening in some law schools today.[11]

What needs to be understood is who has done the defining. It has not been First Nations.[12] Many of us do not accept this great lie any longer. We understand the solution lies in our inalienable right to define ourselves, our nations, our government, and in protecting the natural laws the Creator gave us. Nor has the restructuring of law and government on Turtle Island to conform to European norms been achieved with the expressed or implied consent and/or assistance of First Nations.[13] Enforced European definitions and the willingness to overlook the absolute failure to gain First Nations consent and participation are the two historical preconditions to the construction of Canadian law and government, which leads to the situation I experienced with property law (and, of course, elsewhere in the law).

Enforced European definitions and the willingness to ignore consent brings us back again to responsibilities. Think about responsibilities and understand what your responsibilities are. And maybe after we have thought about responsibilities alone and together, we can have a conversation on the specifics of "violence against women." But then again, maybe if we talked about responsibilities instead of rights, we would not need to have the same kind of conversation about "violence against women." When you come from a philosophy that is responsibilities-oriented, as opposed to rights-oriented, the community and not just individuals are important.[14] Rights is "me, me, me! I want!" What a right is about is "I have this thing and you cannot take it away from me. It is mine!" But responsibility is about connections. You can only have a responsibility in relation to someone else. You cannot have a responsibility all by itself. Maybe it is a responsibility to nature – to the moon, to the earth, to the water. It is a responsibility to you, to a man, to a grandparent. Responsibilities, unlike rights, are not done in isolation. Belief in an individual or group-rights philosophy (that is, rights which are not collective) is the precondition for most of the rights battles brought forward for resolution within the legal system. Rights will be balanced and the winner will triumph over the loser. As far as I am concerned, a right which can be trammeled by another is not much of a right at all. It is merely a privilege. I do not believe the same problem is inevitable in a system which focuses on responsibilities. It seems to me that with rights philosophy we just continue separating and separating. This preoccupation with separation breeds violence.

Having discussed definition and consent, we need to return to a discussion of the themes of violence, racism, and silence. The process of racially controlled definitions and the overlooking of consent creates silence and perpetuates racism. The result is violence.

Look to my whole experience in this country. Think about this country, and what this land is to me. All other people, all non–First Nations people in this country, come from some place else. Theoretically, you all have a home to go to.[15] But this is my only home. I cannot go back ten, or twenty, or thirty or forty generations and say I came from someplace else. This land is all I have. This is the only chance I have. The continual denial of our experience at every corner, at every turn, from education at residential schools through to universities, is violence. The denial of my experience batters me from all directions. Because others have the power to define my existence, experience, and even my feelings, I am left with no place to stand and validly construct my reality. That is the violence of silence.

I am sure you already know some of the statistics that follow, but some are not often bandied about: 1.9 per cent of Registered Indian people have a university degree, compared to 10 per cent of the general population.[16] Just over 20 per cent of First Nations people have any post-secondary school education at all, yet 40 per cent of the non–First Nations population have post-secondary education.[17] Just think about that.

There has just been a big crisis about "Indian Education" policy.[18] There were young people from our nations fasting in Ottawa for thirty-six days. I think they went that long before they stopped their fast.[19] The women's movement says to me – the Mohawk woman – you are anti-feminist. But when those young people, those young leaders, were in Ottawa fasting and willing to give up their lives, I did not see any "white feminists" in the group of seventy Indian people who were arrested at the Department of Indian Affairs. When the police arrested that group of people, they said, "We'll take the women last and we'll release them first." Do you think they did that? One of my friends was the last woman to be released at six o'clock in the morning. She was also the last person to get released.[20] I did not see any white feminists there and I want to know why. You want me to be there for you. I want to know why you are never there for me.[21] Do not ask me to run and catch up with you because I am not running. I do not see what it is that you have for me to catch. But, I do wish you would come stand beside me. I do wish you would make the effort to fulfil that dual responsibility that you also have. Only then will we stop doing violence to each other.

With respect to criminal justice, the Canadian Human Rights Commission has recently said that it is more likely for a First Nations person growing up in this country to go to prison than to university.[22] Now that is an education! Pretend you are a First Nations woman growing up in Saskatchewan, sixteen years old. By the time you reach twenty-five, you will have 131 times the chance of going to prison than a non–First Nations woman.[23] Note that is a non–First Nations woman, not a white woman.

Women's "consent" in specific circumstances of a crime, such as rape, is not as fundamental or basic as the issue of non-consent to the entire legal system. The entire criminal justice system, the entire legal system in this country, were never consented to by First Nations. Yet you put the weight of that whole system on our backs. Because of the over-representation of First Nations people in prisons,

if the rape laws are made harsher, or if capital punishment is legalized, disproportionately more First Nations men will be serving the
sentences for those rape convictions. I also suspect that First Nations
women will disproportionately be the victims of rape, not necessarily
by First Nations male perpetrators.

I do not believe for a minute that First Nations men are more
violent than non–First Nations men. I do not believe that they are
more often rapists than non–First Nations men. I do not believe that
First Nations women are "better" victims. I cannot participate in a
system like that. And I cannot fix it by myself. I choose not to fix it,
as it is not my system. My concerns about consent reach the heart
of the Canadian legal system. It is a system of force and coercion.[24]
The concerns of the feminist movement go to the specific application
of consent in the factual situation of rape. First Nations apprehensions must be seen by other than First Nations as fundamentally
bringing the totality of legal relations into ill repute, not just one
situation.

The Ontario Native Women's Association recently completed the
final draft of a report on family violence.[25] We found that the incidence of abuse for First Nations women in Ontario is eight times the
national average. Eight out of ten First Nations women currently
living in this province are survivors of either child sexual abuse,
incest, rape, or a battering relationship. It gets worse, because when
I rack my brain and think about all the First Nations women I know,
I can think of only one who is not a survivor of child sexual abuse,
rape, a battering relationship, or incest. Most women I know are
survivors of more than one of those kinds of abuse.

There is a lot of destruction going on in our lives, and abuse of
women is just the tip of the iceberg. The mistreatment that First
Nations women confront is not only continuous – it is inescapable. I
believe such experience across women as a group to be unique to
First Nations women (and perhaps our sisters of colour). I do not
believe the continuity of the abuse or its inescapableness are attributes
of abuse confronted by white women. Yet, white women are the
ones who have had the power to set the definitions under which the
discourse on violence against women operates. Their violence is not
the total violence that is just now being exposed as the experience
of First Nations women.

The next essential step is that First Nations and other women from
distinct racial groups must be provided room to speak and the power
to define. We are capable speakers and do not need someone else to
speak for us. All too often when others speak for us, they use our
harsh reality to support their positions. That only reinforces "power

over" dynamics, which I believe to be the true source of the difficulty.[26]

In closing I want to share this with you. First Nations women are strong. There is a Hopi prophecy that says:

> A Nation is not conquered
> Until the hearts
> of its women
> are on the ground.

The woman is central in the First Nations philosophy, because we are the ones who bring forth life. That is why we are respected. That is the gift – the great gift of life – that was given to us by the Creator.[27] That is why it is not finished until the women's hearts are on the ground. My heart is not on the ground. Nya-weh![28]

PART SIX

Women and the Economy

THE SECOND AREA CHOSEN FOR PROFILE IS WOMEN AND THE economy, an area of undeniable importance for feminist analysts and activists in both Canada and the United States. Economic issues have been a focus of feminist attention in North America since the nineteenth century, and the current wave of feminism has inherited some of the historically prominent matters such as wage disparity and access to a diversity of occupations. The contemporary women's movement has also begun to address some new economic issues, such as pay equity and affirmative action. These essays examine the barriers to women's full participation in the paid labour force and feminist struggles to overcome these impediments.

Marianne Ferber's essay documents the rising participation rates of women in the formal labour force in the United States, the increasingly high educational attainments of women, and the changes in the marital and family structures which have stimulated female interest in the waged labour market. She notes the stubborn continuity in patterns of occupational segregation and gendered differentials in earnings. Ferber claims that current u.s. laws stipulating equal pay for equal work and affirmative action initiatives have offered little substantive improvement for most women. She speculates that comparable worth and pay equity laws will prove more promising, but expresses concern about any possibility for significant gains in the face of powerful right-wing forces currently prominent in the United States.

Marjorie Cohen provides a cautiously more optimistic assessment of the Canadian situation. While the economic subordination of women is no less obvious in Canada than the United States, Cohen argues that the organized women's movement has moved to confront economic issues more effectively than their American counterparts. She credits the leadership of the National Action Committee on the Status of Women with recognizing the structural nature of women's oppression and seeking to intervene on a broad range of economic policy issues, from the formulation of the budget to trade policy and deregulation. Cohen admits that feminist intervention in the 1988 Canadian federal election against the Mulroney government's free trade platform failed. But she argues that the feminist movement emerged collectively stronger and more committed to claiming recognition of its interests in the general structuring of the Canadian economy.

Marjorie Heins's essay builds upon Marianne Ferber's effort, exploring in more detail the impact of affirmative action programs in the United States, particularly in the legal forum. Scrutinizing u.s. Supreme Court rulings on the constitutionality of affirmative action employment programs, Heins criticizes the lack of receptivity towards remedial programs designed to redress historical and continuing race and sex discrimination in the work-place. At the same time, she embraces the potential for radical redefinitions of merit inherent in effective affirmative action policies, claiming that such programs are a part of the necessary process of "changing narrow or inherently biased views of female excellence."

These essays confront some of the historically intractable problems experienced by women in the paid labour force in Canada and the United States. They recognize the homogeneity of the structural barriers to economic equality in the two countries, as well as the distinctive cultural factors which have caused the organized feminist movements to diverge, at least in some respects, in their agendas for change.

16 Women and the American Economy

MARIANNE A. FERBER

The "traditional" family, with a husband who goes out into the world to earn a living and to manage the affairs of state, while the wife and mother takes care of the children and tends to hearth and home, making sure it is an attractive, comfortable place for the head of the family to retreat to from his toil and struggles, developed late in human history, was never universal, and proved to be rather short-lived.[1] Prior to the industrial revolution, men and women were both providers who worked hard, at times side by side, taking care of the needs of the household. It was only when paid work increasingly became the norm that the factory and the office became the place for production, home the place for consumption, that the wage earner became the breadwinner, the homemaker the dependent. Though among Blacks, immigrants, and the poor generally this never fully became a reality, as it did among the more affluent, they were likely to view it as the ideal to aspire to.

Thus, by the late nineteenth century, when the relevant data first became available, we find that among the population fourteen years and older, about 85 per cent of men, but only 18 per cent of women were in the labour force. Further, a large proportion of the latter were young unmarried women and widows. True, many of those excluded women nonetheless contributed to income, doing seasonal work, taking piece-work home, taking in boarders, or being unpaid family workers, but just as this was not acknowledged in the official statistics, so it was often not acknowledged within the family,

Table 8
Labour Force Participation of Men and Women Sixteen Years and Older, 1890–1987[1]

	Percent of Men in the Labour Force	Percent of Women in the Labour Force
1890	84.3	18.2
1900	85.7	20.0
1920	84.6	22.7
1930	82.1	23.6
1940	82.5	27.9
1950	86.8	33.9
1960	84.0	37.8
1970	80.6	43.4
1980	77.9	51.6
1987	76.6	56.1

Sources: 1890–1980 Blau and Ferber (1986); 1987 u.s. Department of Labor, Employment and Earnings, August 1988.
1. Prior to 1950 based on population 14 years and over.

except perhaps as the wife helping out temporarily or adding pin money.

The most striking feature of the years since then, however, is that during every decade the labour force participation of women, and especially wives, increased. Meanwhile, the participation rate for men declined since 1950 (see table 8), as young men stayed in school longer and older men retired earlier.[2] Thus, the traditional family no sooner came into its own than it started becoming obsolete, fundamentally because the value of women's work in the labour market rose, while the need for them at home became less urgent.

From the beginnings of industrialization in the early nineteenth century, it was obvious that women were capable of doing much of the work in the new factories, for it often required endurance and dexterity more than physical strength or long training. The same was true later of many of the clerical and service jobs. Hence the women, moving to towns and cities with their husbands, who increasingly abandoned rural areas, often had no difficulty finding employment. At the same time, more and more of the goods and services that used to be produced in the household came to be available for purchase in the market. It was possible for a growing number of women to attain a higher standard of living for themselves and their families by contributing their wages rather than by being full-time homemakers, so long as they were willing to break out of the traditional mould. This was especially so as additional education raised women's potential earnings, and as new and enticing products, desired by most people, required a good deal of money to buy.

Urbanization also brought about other changes, beyond taking away the wife's opportunity to grow vegetables, raise chickens, and participate in some of the work required on the farm. Children were similarly deprived of the possibility of being productive and became an economic liability for a far longer period of time, all the more so after child labour laws were introduced in the early twentieth century. Further, raising them was more expensive with greater costs for rent, food, and education. Not surprisingly, families became smaller, further reducing the requirements for the mother's time at home. Meanwhile, life expectancy was rising, so that women lived far beyond the age when they had young children.

These changes took place gradually over a long period of time. At times they were inhibited or speeded up by particular developments. During the depression of the 1930s, the view gained currency that so long as there were not enough jobs for men, women should not take away those that were available. During the Second World War, on the other hand, when there was an acute labour shortage, women were encouraged to work outside the home as a matter of patriotic duty. It has been noted that when the men came back, young people made up for lost time in starting families, and female labour force participation declined for a few years. But that was not the end of the story. This was the first generation of wives who returned to the labour market in substantial numbers when their children began to grow up, consistent with the interpretation that, having got a taste of independence and their own paycheque, they were no longer satisfied to spend the rest of their lives at home.

It was also after the Second World War that the veterans who went back to school on the GI Bill did not want to finish before getting married, and employed wives supported many of the couples. This further served to legitimize woman's role as wage earner, especially when it was for the good of her family.

So far we have emphasized economic changes, and their impact on women's behaviour and attitudes. It would, however, be a mistake to fail to recognize that women themselves were active participants in this process. They did not merely find that they could earn more because they were better educated. They obtained more education because they planned to seek employment. They did not merely have more time because fertility had declined. They had fewer children in order to be able to spend more time in the labour market. Not only did their own tastes for market work change, as suggested above, but there is evidence that husbands' preferences tended to adjust to wives' work status.[3] The extent to which women worked for pay increased because families were less stable, but breakups became more likely because women were more capable of supporting themselves. Last but not least, the feminist movement during the early part of this century, and even more so that which began in the 1960s, helped to bring about substantial changes, influencing women, men, and the legal environment.

Thus, it is not surprising that the labour force participation rate of women between ages twenty-four and fifty is today in excess of 70 per cent, or that it is expected to continue to increase, though, as is true for their male counterparts, young women are entering the labour market later, and older women are leaving it earlier.[4] More surprising, perhaps, is the fact that women's economic status in other respects has changed far less. Occupational segregation has declined only modestly, and the earnings gap between males and females remains large.[5] Equally important, men's participation in household work lags far behind women's participation in market work.

Occupational segregation appears to have been substantial and relatively stable for the first half of the twentieth century. During this period, the proportion of women that would have needed to change jobs to duplicate the male distribution fluctuated only between 66 and 68 per cent.[6] After 1960 this ratio went down somewhat, and in the 1970s it fell by almost 7 per cent.[7] In the 1980s, however, segregation again declined more slowly, mainly because some previously male occupations that had become integrated were turning female as more women entered.[8] It remains to be seen what will happen in the future, but meanwhile the index of segregation even by the most optimistic estimates remains about 57 per cent.

We would not, of course, want to leave the impression that in a world of entirely equal access men and women would necessarily have the same occupational distribution. It is entirely possible that, to a greater or lesser extent, capabilities, talents, and tastes differ, on the average, between the two sexes. It is, however, entirely unlikely that there would not generally be a considerable overlap, and that the widespread sex-typing of occupations is caused entirely by such inherent differences between women and men. The fact that a good many occupations are predominantly male in some countries and female in others provides support for this view. Table 9 shows to what extent the distribution of workers in the u.s. differs by race, as well as by sex, even when the seven major and very broad categories are used instead of individual occupations. (Table 10 gives a more detailed breakdown by race and ethnicity.) Table 11 shows the percent of workers in each category who are female in the u.s., and, for comparison, the highest and lowest percentages of women among other countries that provide this information.

Table 9

Occupational Distribution of Black and White Men and Women, September 1988 (percentages)

	White		Black	
	Men	Women	Men	Women
Executive, administrative, managerial	14.5	11.4	6.2	6.9
Professional specialty	11.7	15.1	6.5	10.1
Technical and related support	2.8	3.3	1.9	3.7
Sales	11.8	13.5	5.1	8.6
Administrative support, incl. clerical	5.3	28.6	8.7	26.5
Private household service	a	1.5	0.1	2.9
Service, except private household	8.3	14.8	17.1	25.3
Farming, forestry and fishing	5.0	1.3	3.2	0.5
Precision production, craft, repair	20.8	2.3	14.5	2.0
Machine operators, assemblers, inspectors	7.2	5.9	11.3	9.7
Transportation, material moving	6.6	0.8	12.5	1.4
Handlers, equipment cleaners, helpers, labourers	5.8	1.6	12.2	2.4

Sources: u.s. Department of Labor, Employment and Earnings, Oct. 1988.
a Less than 0.05 per cent.

To the extent that there is occupational segregation based, at least in significant part, on arbitrary sex-typing, the question arises why this is a matter of concern. One reason is that reduced efficiency will result when individuals do not enter occupations best suited to their particular characteristics, but rather those considered suitable for their sex. A second reason for concern is that occupational segregation appears to be a factor in perpetuating the wage gap. One careful study found that more than one-third of the earnings differential is associated with differences in the distribution of women and men among 479 occupations.[9] Beyond these economic considerations there is also the likelihood that such segregation reinforces the notion that there are fundamental differences between men and women.

The earnings gap, though it has been declining, remains substantial. Annual earnings of full-time, year-round women workers, as compared to those of men, which fluctuated around 60 per cent for a long time, had risen to 69 per cent by 1989, but this ratio appears to be far lower than in such countries as Australia, Denmark, Norway, and Sweden, where the ratio of women's to men's hourly earnings in manufacturing is in excess of 80 per cent or higher, and the u.s. ratio is also somewhat lower than in many other advanced industrialized countries.[10] (One notable exception is Japan.) Furthermore a forecast by authors who hail recent changes as "the largest and swiftest gain in this century," and who expect the skills and experience of women

Table 10
Occupational Distribution of Men and Women by Race and Ethnicity, 1980 (percentages)

	White		Black		American Indian, Eskimo and Aleut		Asian and Pacific Islanders		Spanish Origin	
	Men	*Women*	*Men*	*Women*	*Men*	*Women*	*Men*	*Women*	*Men*	*Women*
Executive, administrative, managerial	13.5	8.0	5.6	4.8	7.6	6.7	13.4	7.7	6.7	5.0
Professional specialty	11.4	14.9	5.8	11.8	6.7	11.4	20.4	16.6	5.4	7.8
Technical and related support	3.1	3.2	1.9	3.3	2.4	3.1	6.3	4.8	2.0	2.2
Sales	9.5	11.3	3.8	5.9	4.4	7.7	7.3	8.7	5.5	8.6
Administrative support, incl. clerical	6.5	32.6	9.1	25.7	5.6	27.4	8.9	26.5	7.0	27.6
Service, except private household	7.5	14.6	15.7	23.5	11.5	23.0	13.2	15.4	12.3	17.3
Private household service	0.03	0.7	0.2	4.7	0.06	1.2	0.1	0.9	0.007	2.2
Farming, forestry, and fishing	4.1	0.8	3.3	0.5	5.8	1.2	3.3	0.9	6.6	2.2
Precision production, craft, repair	22.1	2.4	15.9	2.4	24.9	3.4	12.9	3.6	21.2	4.0
Operators, fabricators and labourers	21.3	11.5	38.6	17.3	31.0	15.0	14.2	14.7	38.1	23.0

Source: U.S. Bureau of the Census, 1980 Census.

Table 11
Percentage of Workers Who Are Women, by Major Occupational Category

Occupational Category	U.S. (1984)	Highest	Lowest
Executive, administrative, and managerial	33.7	Canada (1982) 29.2	United Arab Emirates (1975) 0.7
Professional, technical, and kindred	48.3	Venezuela (1981) 55.1	Bangladesh (1974) 5.9
Sales workers	49.4	El Salvador (1980) 70.9	United Arab Emirates (1975) 0.8
Farming, forestry, and fishing	14.1	Korea (1981) 37.5	United Arab Emirates (1975) 0.1
Administrative support, including clerical	80.1	U.S. (1981) 80.6	Bangladesh (1974) 1.1
Service occupations	60.9	Norway (1981) 77.6	United Arab Emirates (1975) 6.2
Precision production, craft, and repair, operators, fabricators, and labourers	18.8	Japan (1981) 48.2	Bangladesh (1974) 0.2

Source: U.S.: U.S. Department of Labor, Bureau of Labor Statistics, *Employment and Earnings*, Dec. 1984. Other countries: calculated from data in International Labour Office, *Yearbook of Labour Statistics*, various years.

to increase sharply from now on, predict a ratio of only 74 per cent by the year 2000.[11] This raises the question what could be done to improve upon this record.

It has long been recognized that equal pay for equal work legislation, now in force for over twenty-five years, has had little, if any, effect. There is rather convincing evidence that the same is true for affirmative action.[12] For some time now, the alternative that has received most attention is equal pay for work of comparable worth, more recently also termed "pay equity." In the u.s. this remains a controversial, emotionally charged subject, enthusiastically supported by many feminists, bitterly attacked by conservatives and many mainstream economists. It made no progress at the federal level during the Reagan years (1980–88), nor is there any reason to be sanguine about its prospects under the present administration of George Bush, especially with increasingly conservative courts. On the other hand, more than half of the states have introduced some comparable-worth laws, at least for state employees, and a number of other states, as well as a large number of local governments, are seriously considering the introduction of similar legislation. Unions also have shown some interest in this subject and have, in some cases, introduced pay equity considerations in their bargaining agreements.

Opponents of comparable worth have not only pointed to the imperfections of evaluation schemes, but have variously argued that "Economy-wide pay scales based on comparable worth principles ... would bring us to a planned economy, with all the distortions that would likely occur";[13] that paying for work on the basis of job evaluation is as flawed as assigning a higher price to milk than to cognac because it would receive higher ratings in terms of a hedonic index;[14] that raising wages for women will lead to a reduction in demand for their labour;[15] and, finally, that the policy will not have enough impact to make it worth while.[16]

Proponents, on the other hand, point out that allocation of resources would be more efficient if wages were not distorted by discrimination;[17] that in large establishments employees, after they have been hired for entry-level jobs, are generally deployed in accordance with established rules and procedures, rather than in direct competition with workers from the outside labour market;[18] that the demand for the labour of women is very inelastic, especially in the public sector;[19] that market conditions are taken into account when the "policy-capturing approach" is used;[20] and that the mean earnings in female-dominated occupations might be expected to rise from

57 per cent of those in male-dominated occupations to between 70 and 86 per cent, depending on the precise methods used.[21]

Rather than attempt to evaluate the merit of these conflicting claims, it will be more useful to examine what happened in Australia when a policy essentially tantamount to comparable worth was introduced in 1969. The outcomes, as summarized by Robert Gregory and Vivian Ho, were as follows: (1) By 1977 the wage gap had narrowed from 63 per cent to 82 per cent, while that in the u.s. remained at 60 per cent. (2) During this period the human capital endowments of women relative to men were comparable in the two countries. (3) Over the preceding decade and a half the changes in employment, unemployment, and labour force participation of women relative to men had been similar in both countries, and similar to past trends in each.[22] It would be difficult to find more convincing evidence that comparable worth can be very effective and that unfavourable side-effects, if any, are likely to be minimal.[23] It is not, however, likely to convince those whose minds are made up, and who will not permit themselves to be distracted by facts. Nor is it likely to influence determined advocates of the free market, who may be expected to continue to oppose all government interference as a matter of principle. The evidence of the recent past suggests that such views will remain politically powerful in the u.s.

It would be a mistake, however, to end on this negative note. We have already seen that women's labour force participation continues to grow rapidly. Occupational integration is making some progress, especially among the educated, as shown by the burgeoning enrolment of women in non-traditional college majors and professional schools. The earnings gap has at least begun to narrow somewhat. To these developments must be added that, at long last, there is even evidence that men are taking a somewhat larger share of household responsibilities.

Such data as were available generally showed that, up to the late 1970s, husbands did very little housework, whether or not the wife was in the labour market. Some more recent studies, however, show that husbands of employed women tend to spend more time on child care,[24] and that husbands in general spend about one hour more per week on domestic chores, while the opposite is true of wives.[25] These developments have broader implications, to the extent that it has been women's household responsibilities that have reduced their labour force attachment and inhibited their careers. Instead of the old vicious circle, when specialization of women in the household was justified because men had a relative advantage in the labour market, and women's lower wages were justified because they specialized in housework, we are now seeing the beginning, albeit a slow and tentative one, of a benign circle, when improved conditions in the labour market justify more equal sharing in the household, which in turn will enable women to continue to improve their position in the labour market.

17 The Canadian Women's Movement and Its Efforts to Influence the Canadian Economy

MARJORIE GRIFFIN COHEN

The issues of the women's movement in Canada in some respects have not changed. The problems which were highlighted in the 1970 *Report of the Royal Commission on the Status of Women* are still with us.[1] This report documented women's inequality in Canada under the law and in the work-force. It showed that women were poor because we did not have equal access to jobs, equal pay for the work we performed, or adequate public child care, and that we were treated unfairly in property and tax legislation. The most important result of this document was that it enabled women's groups to bring to public consciousness the discrimination women faced, a discrimination that was blatant and widespread. The government was forced to recognize that women had not been sufficiently heard and that something should be done about this.

Government's initial reaction was to attempt to subsume all major action on women's issues at the federal level under the government itself. At the historic "Strategy for Change" conference which inaugurated the National Action Committee on the Status of Women (NAC), one of the major issues was whether this group should support the creation of a government body on women or organize an independent national women's organization.[2] Although a collective voice for the women's movement was certainly not yet strong, the government saw the wisdom of containing this movement by direct control. Fortunately, women at this conference thought otherwise, and NAC became an independent organization. Nevertheless, throughout its history it has been largely funded by the federal government: this fact certainly has had mixed blessings for the organization and, at this point in its history, is presenting particularly alarming consequences.

At the federal level, work was immediately begun to eliminate overt sexism in federal legislation. By 1975 Marc Lalonde, the minister responsible for the status of women, reported in his department's publication celebrating International Women's Year that discrimination against women had been eliminated from Canadian legislation. This, of course, was a joke to activists in the women's movement. While the words of the legislation might have been gender-neutral, its effect certainly was not.

The early efforts of the women's movement focused to a considerable extent on economic issues. Most notable were the efforts to highlight the wage gap between men and women who worked for pay, which led to a major campaign for "equal pay for work of equal value." This was a difficult concept to communicate to the public and to the government, but partial recognition of the principle was achieved when the words were included in the federal Human Rights Act of 1977.[3] The issue of property rights for women was another consuming matter of the 1970s, when the case of an Alberta farm woman highlighted the unequal treatment of women under the law. Of course, most economic issues were not fought at the federal level but by women within their own community. The most dramatic were specific fights for women at the work-place – at the banks, at Bell Canada, in factories. Women's attempts to organize were fought hard by employers, but the positive result of the 1970s was the increasing involvement of the women's movement in an effort to achieve recognition of women's right for decent wages and working conditions.

For most of the issues of the 1970s there was not a clear distinction between economic issues and other equality issues. The case of Native rights for Native women was a good example of this. The women's movement became involved in this issue (supporting the Native women who had been excluded from their bands because they had married white men) as an equality rights issue, but it quickly became an economic issue as well, the implications of which could not be ignored.

Deciding which issues to pursue and which to ignore created considerable tension within NAC in the 1970s. While it is clear even from the beginning that almost every problem in society was a women's issue, there was a feeling that the organization should confine itself to those which could strictly be defined as "women's issues." This became most evident in the debate about federal wage and price controls in the mid-1970s. Many of us argued that women would be most damaged by this measure primarily because it would prevent women from trying to close the gap between male and female wages. We wanted a strong statement against this from the women's movement. This did not occur and, while the reason may have been that many women in the organization had close ties to the party in power, the argument was won on the grounds that we would lose credibility if we became just one other organization speaking on a wide range of issues; we should confine ourselves to what was obviously and directly of concern to women because no one else was doing this. A similar argument was used when attempts were made to link NAC with the peace movement.

The early attempts of the national women's movement on economic issues tended to focus on women's right to make choices. The publication of Gail Cook's book *Opportunities for Choice* (1976) stressed this theme, which seemed appropriate to many at the time.[4] We were to fight not the system but how we were treated within it. While there were conflicts with those in power in the federal government, these were fairly minimal. The overriding objective was to influence power – to exert influence behind the scenes, while at the same time claiming tremendous support for our position from the women's movement in general. This, in many respects, was a "subdued feminism." I do not mean to imply that feminism in Canada was at this time without fire and fight, but at the federal level we were not much of a threat to the government. (And this is probably why they continued to increase our funding.) At other levels, much was going on: Henry Morgentaler went to jail for performing abortions, and women's groups were actively defying the government on this issue; Grace Hartman went to jail to defend women's right to strike at hospitals; and women's groups across the country were organizing to provide services for women and were in open conflict with powerful forces in their communities and work-places.

The focus on economic issues has changed perceptibly for the women's movement since the 1970s. By the 1980s government and employers had accepted women's intervention in issues like equal pay, maternity leave, and the movement of women out of traditional occupations. They also accepted our right to speak on day care, reproductive choice, pornography – anything that could be seen as a women's issue. But more and more women realized that the crucial issue would be the extent to which women could have a role in economic decision-making. Having "opportunities for choice" was no longer the crucial point; being able to determine what the choices would be constituted the real fight for women in Canada. Women began to make the connection that ultimately all of the issues we were fighting for are related to the way the society is constructed. We recognized that economic decision-making by government and business affects how successful we can be in just about every area of our lives. More and more the realization took hold that, although we can fight for years and years for such legislation as equal pay for work of equal value – and ultimately may make gains in this area – it is a small victory if a government economic policy (such as the current obsession with international competitiveness) means that fewer people will be employed. Equal pay laws do not help much if you do not have a job.

Initially, women's attempts to discuss broad economic policy issues were ignored. From the perspective of government and business, women and economics do not mix well. Our demands are seen as "take-aways" – not contributions. What we want is perceived as a drain on the economy: full and equal employment, equality in decision-making, economic security, better social services, a safe world. These demands are considered unrealistic in the hard world of economics. It is not that our demands are considered totally unreasonable, but they just do not mesh with hard-time economics. What women have had to say has been treated as a discussion of welfare policy, not economic policy.

When feminists talk about economics it makes government and business nervous because we tend to focus on the irrationality of what is going on. We emphasize goals and objectives and are critical of choices which have been made, choices which have been damaging to people. Never before in the history of human existence has there been as much food produced in the world as now. Yet people starve to death in some parts of the globe while vast quantities of food rot in warehouses in North America and Europe. We see this as irrational.

We know that in Canada there is considerable poverty and that this poverty is increasing, in spite of the fact that Canada is a rich nation with abundant resources. We know that there is a need for better social services and a need for people to provide them, yet our unemployment rate is huge. We see this waste of labour as irrational. We are downright hostile to government programs which are directed towards supporting the war industry, rather than towards meeting real human needs. Most important, we are critical of the priorities which have been established and feel that our leaders have lost sight of the goal of a more just and equitable society. When we began to talk about economic issues like the budget, trade policy, privatization, deregulation, and the general structure of the Canadian economy, we were going too far. These were not women's issues:

women were not "experts" and therefore our criticism had little credibility. But one of the very positive results of the massive women's movement in the past twenty years had been the rejection of "credentialism" – the belief that you cannot talk about something unless you have a piece of paper which says you can. Women's confidence in challenging the experts has grown as we questioned their wisdom on health care, education, and child care.

In the field of economics our challenge had initially been confined to explanations of why we were paid less than men. We were told it was because we were less productive than men. We did not choose the right jobs, we did not get ourselves trained properly, and we had bad work habits: we preferred to work part-time, we regularly dropped out of the labour force, and because of our commitment to home and hearth, we did not take our work as seriously as men did. (Of course, this was all couched in proper academic language – we did not accumulate sufficient "human capital.") Women intuitively rejected these expert pronouncements. What we were told defied common sense. We knew that someone must be profiting from paying women lower wages and confining us to a rather narrow range of occupations. We challenged the experts. We fought the collective, subconscious belief that it was the natural order of things for women's work to be narrowly confined and to be valued less than that done by men. And, although we certainly still have a long way to go in this regard, we have made headway in making people view women's work differently.

In the 1980s and early 1990s, the economic conditions for women are much the same as those we faced in the 1970s, some of which were outlined by the Royal Commission on the Status of Women. Women's work is still occupationally segregated; women's wages are still much less than men's; women still do most of the work in the home; public child care is still woefully insufficient; poverty is still overwhelmingly a women's lot; and Native women, immigrant women, and women of colour still face particularly gruesome obstacles in their lives – barriers based on racism which are distinct from those all women face.

The issues did not change, but our analysis of what is wrong began to shift. We no longer focused our briefs to government in a way which would show how "rational" a more just society would be or how it could be in the economic interest of employers to reduce discrimination. There is no economic argument which will convince employers that they will be better off paying women one-third more than they do now. They know better and so do we. We continue to fight for the kinds of things we have focused on previously, but we have broadened our scope and have entered the general debate on macro-economic issues. The logic of the situation has demanded this: we could not ignore the larger agenda of economic restructuring and the government's designs for Canada, since they would affect virtually every issue on women's agenda for action.

The change in focus in the 1980s, at least at the federal level of the feminist movement's confrontation with the state, is a result of a great many changes, but four of them are quite distinct. First of all, there has been a greater awareness in the women's movement altogether of the structural nature of women's oppression, the recognition that it is not simply the sexist nature of individual employers or legislators which is responsible for women's position in society. Secondly, the dramatic economic downturn in the early 1980s highlighted the structural problems with the economy itself, something which no groups interested in economic and social change could ignore. But there were also changes which affected the nature of the women's movement at the national level and had an impact on NAC's ability to focus on broad economic issues. The first is that after 1984 the Liberals were no longer in power, so the Liberals on the NAC executive were no longer placed in a defensive position about government economic policy. NAC is an extremely broad-based feminist organization with a membership of about six hundred women's groups, including those from political parties as divergent as the Progressive Conservatives and the Communist party. However, Conservative women were very rarely elected to the executive. With the Conservative party in government no one was protective of their own party interests. The second major change to affect NAC directly was in the composition of its executive body. The 1980s saw the organization expand considerably to include representatives from all regions of the country, but there was also increasing membership on the executive from more left-oriented women, trade unionists, and women from minority groups. The greater representativeness on the executive meant more sympathy for action which was critical of existing structures.

The move towards dealing with broader economic issues initially focused on the tremendous social upheaval which occurred in the depression period of the early 1980s. Unemployment rates were the highest they had been since the depression of the 1930s. In 1983 and 1984 the official figures indicated that unemployment rose to over 20 per cent in Newfoundland and hovered between 13 and 15 per cent in other Atlantic provinces, British Columbia, and Quebec. Even Ontario, which traditionally does much better than other provinces, had unemployment rates over 10 per cent.[5] At the same time, interest rates rose to 23 per cent. The government's dogged insistence on fighting inflation at a time when international economic pressures were severely damaging the Canadian economy simply compounded the problem. Women were hit particularly hard as their unemployment rates soared and they were forced to take up the slack in social programs.[6] The women's movement joined in the condemnation of government economic policy and called for full employment policies and lower interest rates.

In the early 1980s the Liberal government initiated the Royal Commission on the Economic Union and Development Prospects for Canada. The commissioners travelled the country eliciting presentations from various community and business groups on the state of the economy. The responses were predictable: the popular sector called for greater government direction in the economy to eliminate what were considered the most pressing problems – high unemployment and poor provision of social services.[7] The business community called for greater reliance on the private market mechanism and government intervention in controlling inflation. The report of the commission, which was published in 1985, clearly reflected the views of business.[8] Its major recommendations centred on a greater reliance on the market mechanism, primarily through a free trade agreement with the u.s. It also recommended increased privatization of publicly owned enterprises and drastic changes in social services systems. This report has been the blueprint for government policy since it was produced.

NAC had been alarmed by the previous discussions on free trade that had taken place during the 1984 election, primarily because of the adverse effect free trade was likely to have on the manufacturing industries where immigrant women were concentrated. It held a series of discussions on the impact free trade was likely to have on women, although at this point the overall implications were fairly sketchy. Since the Progressive Conservatives, who had won the 1984 election, had indicated that pursuing a free trade agreement with the u.s. was tantamount to economic and political suicide for Canada, it appeared that the issue would be dropped. However, very strong pressure from the international business interests was successful in gaining Tory support for pursuing this initiative.

NAC had aroused considerable interest in its economic positions by the time the Royal Commission's report was published, primarily through the economic statement prepared by the NAC executive and read by its president at the Economic Summit sponsored by the government in early 1985. This hard-hitting analysis was widely publicized. Earlier efforts of NAC during the 1984 election to obtain a debate on women's issues between the contestants for prime minister were successful and added to the public credibility of the organization. Also, NAC had received considerable attention for its criticism of federal budgets. Altogether, the organization had established itself as credible on economic issues with other popular sector groups.

The response to the report of the Royal Commission (known in Canada as the Macdonald Report) was swift. In its publication *The Macdonald Report and its Implications for Women*, NAC strongly criticized the recommendations related to changes in economic and social programs, arguing that women would be most adversely affected by these changes.[9] This launched a major campaign against the free trade agreement which was taken up by women's groups across the country. Free trade was perceived as a major policy shift on the part of the Canadian government towards a much stronger reliance on international market forces to shape the economic and political direction of the country. It was viewed as being closely related to other government initiatives to privatize crown corporations and aspects of social services and to deregulate transportation and communication systems.

From 1985 to 1988, NAC and other women's groups researched the impact these initiatives would have on women and pursued extensive public education campaigns to communicate this information to women throughout the country. The first issue to receive attention was the attempts by the government to deregulate the telecommunications industry, an attempt which was successfully thwarted for a time. Then the issue of privatization grabbed public attention as the discussion of Air Canada and Canada Post raged. But as the negotiations began with the U.S. on a free trade agreement, this issue became paramount.

The intent of this essay is not to explain why free trade will be so damaging to women and to Canadians in general, but to indicate that it was an issue which could not be ignored by the women's movement because it threatened everything we had worked for in the past.[10] One of the major contributions which the women's movement made to an understanding of the implications of this initiative was not simply what it would mean for women themselves (although this was certainly important), but what it would mean for the services sector altogether. The effect on services had simply not been a feature in the discussion on free trade until the feminist analysis introduced it. Actually, many issues in the free trade debate were ignored until women took them up: the impact on manufacturing industries where women worked; the impact on consumers. As women's groups became more familiar with trade issues, they quickly applied this knowledge to their own area of expertise. Nurses, teachers, public health workers, social workers, farmers, environmentalists, immigrant women's groups, child-care advocates, and women in the peace movement analysed the impact of free trade in these areas.

Women also organized for action. They published pamphlets, presented briefs to provincial, local, and federal governments. They organized rallies, conferences, and demonstrations. They wrote articles for local and national newspapers and were frequently on the airwaves condemning the move towards free trade. They became conversant with obscure international trade law and its language: words like "countervail duty" became a normal part of their language. They also participated in coalitions with other groups to an unprecedented extent.

NAC was instrumental in organizing many of these coalitions on the national and provincial level.[11] The first association of over thirty groups was convened in Toronto by NAC in November 1985, and it was a prominent participant in the national coalition, the Pro-Canada Network, which began in March 1987. While the coalition work was not without difficulties, particularly in the early stages when male-oriented groups attempted to dominate the coalitions, feminist assertiveness prevailed, and, in most (though not all) cases, the coalitions functioned well. One of the most interesting documents to come out of this period of action was the declaration on social and economic policy directions for Canada, *A Time for Social Solidarity*.[12] This was a statement produced jointly by NAC, the Canadian Labour Congress, the Confederation of Canadian Unions, the Confederation des syndicats nationaux, the Canadian Conference of Catholic Bishops, and the United Church of Canada; it was the first time any such joint statement had been attempted. It began a process of analysing the causes of the current socioeconomic crisis and identifying alternative economic and social policy directions.

While initially the government ignored the whole issue of women and free trade, ultimately it became alarmed by the polls which showed that women's opposition to the agreement was enormous and had grown steadily. The "gender gap" on free trade was not a minor issue. By the time of the 1988 election, the government had issued pamphlets explaining why free trade would be good for women, and the minister responsible for the status of women took to the airwaves with the same message. Economists working for the government went to great lengths in public debates to explain that they knew what was really good for us and that the women's movement was very narrow in its understanding of economic issues. Women were not convinced.

The 1988 election was fought on the free trade issue and the anti–free trade forces lost. There were many reasons for this result, not least of which was the massive spending on the part of business to promote free trade during the last two weeks of the election campaign. The implications of free trade began to be felt immediately, including a series of plant closures, mega-mergers, and the granting of bank status to American Express. But the finance minister's first free trade budget in the spring of 1989 was probably the most important indication of changes in the economic and social systems in Canada. Almost all government cutbacks and regressive initiatives are now presented as a necessity in light of our need to make Canadian business competitive in international markets. The budget was an attack on the universality of social programs, the cultural community, regional development programs, public ownership, unemployment insurance, foreign aid, and advocacy groups. NAC, by the way, had its funding cut by 50 per cent between 1989 and 1992.

There have been positive results from the women's movement's attempts to combat macho-economics. We did not win, but we scared them. The drastic reduction in NAC's funding is probably the most flattering evidence of this. We are becoming effective and are a serious threat to the way government and business want to rule this country. We have gained strength by expanding our collective analytical abilities to encompass areas usually the preserve of specialized economists.

The efforts of the women's movement to influence the Canadian economy have raised issues in a new way. But what is especially clear is that the women's movement will have to continue to develop its analysis and action of broad economic issues. We will continue to develop our understanding of why one of the intrinsically richest nations in the world has such deep-seated structural problems and find ways in which these can be solved.

18 Affirmative Action and Women's Rights in the Reign of Chief Justice William Rehnquist

MARJORIE HEINS

I am humbled by the task of addressing the current state of sex discrimination and women's rights law in the United States, not only because of its complexity, but because there are probably as many different views to hold on sex discrimination and women's rights as there are civil rights lawyers – a notoriously contentious bunch – to take them. My account, consequently, will be impressionistic, and naturally will highlight those issues that I find particularly wrenching politically or intriguing intellectually.

This essay will discuss two interlocking subjects: first, affirmative action as a legal concept and a social practice in the United States: how its underlying principles have been misunderstood by large segments of the public and most recently and dramatically by our Supreme Court. Secondly, I will treat the debate over what has come to be abbreviated among feminists in the United States as "sameness" versus "difference." Should the law and the marketplace act in purely gender-neutral fashion, treating women as "similarly situated" to men, even when in reality – whether biological or cultural reality – most of us simply are not? Or should differences be recognized and accommodated in the service of a truer equality and, if so, how do we distinguish between necessary acts in accommodation of differ-ence and what Justice William Brennan of the u.s. Supreme Court dubbed "romantic paternalism," which places women "not on a ped-estal, but in a cage"?[1]

Let me start by defining terms. In the United States, affirmative action means many things to many people. Perhaps most commonly it conjures up quotas that rigidly require the hiring (or admission to colleges or professional schools) of given percentages of women and/ or members of racial or ethnic minority groups. Sometimes a court imposes such quotas as a remedy for proven past discrimination; sometimes they are voluntarily adopted by a university, an employer, a city, state, or town.

On 23 January 1989 the United States Supreme Court, now captained by Chief Justice William Rehnquist, had much to say about racial and ethnic quotas in the construction industry – so-called minority "set asides" – that had been voluntarily adopted by the City of Richmond, Virginia, capital of the Old Confederacy.[2] The court applied what is known in American constitutional law as "strict scrutiny" to Richmond's affirmative action plan, which required that at least 30 per cent of the city's construction subcontractors be minority-owned firms. The plan defined minority to include not only Blacks, who comprise more than half the city of Richmond's population, but Native Americans and "Eskimos" [sic], who are not much in evidence anywhere in Virginia.[3] This failure of the city's preference to correspond to the city's population or, more precisely, to the available population of minority contractors contributed to the Supreme Court's conclusion that the Richmond plan was not justified – not, in the words of the "strict scrutiny" formula, "narrowly tailored to accomplish a compelling state interest."[4] And thus it was unconstitutional.

But, more important, the court insisted that Richmond could not give a numerical preference to minority businesses in an effort to remedy past discrimination, without specifically showing that specific minority groups had been the victims of discrimination in the Richmond construction industry – arguably a superfluous requirement given the painful legacy of Jim Crow laws, strict school segregation, and blatant racial exclusion by trade unions, in the long, not-so-proud history of Dixie.[5] The fact that before the inception of the affirmative action plan only a minuscule percentage of the city's construction business went to minorities was not enough, for the Rehnquist court, to justify the remedial preference.[6]

It may seem odd that the justices of the Supreme Court could not take what lawyers call "judicial notice" of the fact that in the capital of the Old Confederacy the most pernicious forms of race discrimination were pervasive in all aspects of commercial life for at least a century, before which, of course, there were several centuries of slavery. Equally odd – indeed, positively perverse – was the inability of the justices (with the exception of the three dissenters, Thurgood

Marshall, William Brennan, and Harry Blackmun) to appreciate the difference between the hateful, invidious racial discrimination against Black citizens that stains United States history, and remedies designed in some small measure to correct the continuing effects of that past discrimination. As if from an ivory tower, undisturbed by the still-extant realities of racism, Ronald Reagan's first appointee to the court, Sandra Day O'Connor, wrote in the Richmond case that the same rigid "strict scrutiny" must be applied to the city's discrimination against white contractors as the court had developed to test the myriad racial classifications in our benighted culture that stigmatized, oppressed, or excluded Black citizens from political and commercial life. The stubborn unreality of the court's approach was striking. Indeed, I was reminded of Justice Blackmun's dissenting words in a very different Supreme Court case several years before: "there truly is another world 'out there,' the existence of which the Court, I suspect, either chooses to ignore or fears to recognize."[7]

But why digress about a race discrimination case when the topic is sex discrimination? In part because the two are, in legal terms, and especially for purposes of affirmative action, closely related; in part because their differences are instructive. It is an irony peculiar to constitutional law in the United States that because the Supreme Court has not considered sex discrimination to be as egregious as race discrimination – therefore not egregious enough to trigger our "strict scrutiny" test – courts in the post-Richmond era will be able to uphold affirmative action plans for women under a more relaxed "intermediate scrutiny" standard that the court invented some years ago for sex discrimination cases.[8] By contrast, they will have to invalidate affirmative action for minorities using the more demanding strict scrutiny that was developed to combat discrimination against minorities.

It is another irony that Justice O'Connor referred repeatedly in her *Richmond* opinion to a sex discrimination case in justifying her unwillingness to use the more lenient intermediate scrutiny standard in reviewing Richmond's set-aside plan. In the earlier case, the court had said that the mere recitation by government of benign motives does not relieve judges of their duty to scrutinize discrimination carefully.[9] This was a point particularly well taken, given the history of "romantic paternalism" – protective labour laws and such – that has long deprived women of equal opportunities in public life. The argument has considerably less force, however, when applied to Black individuals. Only the most diehard racist would describe the United States' historical treatment of its Black citizens as benevolently paternalistic, even less as romantically so. Racial minorities, unlike white women, face little danger that so-called remedial preferences are likely to oppress them further.

The Richmond decision will have widespread reverberations as cities and counties, states, and towns re-examine their preferential hiring programs. But because goals and quotas are the types of remedies that most frequently make the headlines, the public does not often perceive that affirmative action may have other meanings. Originally, the term derived from federal labour and equal employment opportunity laws that directed courts, after findings of discrimination, to order the guilty parties to take whatever "affirmative action" the judge deemed necessary to remedy the injustices of the past. During Lyndon Johnson's presidency in the 1960s, the executive branch of the u.s. government borrowed the term "affirmative action" from these statutes and court orders and began to require both private companies that contracted with the federal government and institutions, whether public or private, that received federal funds to adopt affirmative action plans that included goals for the hiring of members of minority groups (and sometimes women as well).[10] Those goals, in turn, were to be based on studies of the availability of qualified women or minorities in the particular geographic area.

In attempting to reach the goals, institutions were to take a variety of affirmative steps to open up the hiring process and eliminate racial or sexual stereotyping and old-boy networking in the filling of desirable jobs. Simple requirements, such as advertising and recruitment or the conducting of a search before a university filled a teaching position, were important first steps in opening what had often been a closed process with discriminatory effects on outsiders.

But prohibiting discrimination and opening up the process, even when conscientiously pursued, did not lead to dramatic improvement in the representation of women or members of ethnic minorities in the work-force, particularly in high-echelon, prestigious jobs. As I explain in my recent – and for these purposes aptly named – book, *Cutting the Mustard*, affirmative action should be a process of rethinking the definitions of such amorphous terms as "excellence," "merit," or "qualifications," definitions that somehow, mysteriously, seem to keep women and minorities from capturing and consuming the more desirable pieces of the economic and political pie.[11] Numbers, in this view of affirmative action, whether used as measurements of progress, as formal goals, or even as quotas, are warning lights, signals that something may be wrong with the selection system or the definition of merit that, whether intentionally or not, whether motivated by explicit or subliminal biases, produces skewed and discriminatory results.

I could give many examples of this phenomenon. Some derive from *Cutting the Mustard* itself. I was inspired to write this book in large part because of the fascinating first-hand evidence of discriminatory decision-making at work that I saw while litigating a free speech lawsuit against Boston University's School of Theology. In 1980 and 1981 the university's theology school faculty was embroiled in agonizing political and moral debates over the persistent and overwhelming dominance of white males in tenured faculty and powerful administrative jobs. The student government organization had publicly complained – much to the embarrassment of the dean – that the school's power structure resembled the "theological version of a small-town rotary club." In the previous years the university had rejected a nationally known feminist scholar for an endowed chair in social ethics after a brutal grilling by the university's president, John Silber; the theology school dean later explained to the faculty that the candidate was not considered competent because she was not only a feminist but also a Marxist, who believed that groups, not individuals, were the moving force in history. It would be difficult to find a better example of dubiously value-laden standards of competence or excellence at work.

But this was not all. The dean of the theology school had also recently fired its highest-level female administrator because, as he put it, they did not "dance well" together; some listeners heard sexist assumptions that, as in dancing, women must follow and not lead. The dean told one student on another occasion that he wanted to hire married women because they "knew how to compromise with men." And in yet another incident he wrote to President Silber recommending the hiring of a female historian because she was "not just a woman's woman" – she lacked "those hard edges we expect nowadays."

By the 1980–81 school year, many on the School of Theology's faculty were urging a redefinition of assumptions about excellence that seemed, to say the least, related to the persistent inability of the school to diversify its faculty. Such a "recredentialling" would take account of the school's need for a variety of role models to serve the heterogeneous student body, including feminist scholars, teachers whose expertise was in ministry or pastoral counselling rather than in disgorging reams of erudite scholarly publications, and individuals committed to the "prophetic" or social change brand of ministry for which Boston University's School of Theology had been famous even before the young Martin Luther King, Jr studied there in the early 1950s. Needless to say, perhaps, those in power at Boston University did not respond hospitably to these radical suggestions, and the battle over defining excellence, at that university and elsewhere, goes on.

Another instructive example of credentialling at work was the affirmative action case of *Johnson* v. *Santa Clara Transportation Agency*, decided by the U.S. Supreme Court in 1987.[12] Diane Joyce had been selected as the first female "road dispatcher" in the history of the Santa Clara, California, Transportation Agency. Paul Johnson, who had been one of her competitors for the post, sued, claiming that Joyce was less qualified than he and had got her job by virtue of an affirmative action plan that favoured women and therefore discriminated against him as a male.

The remarkable thing about Mr Johnson's claim was that there was simply not a shred of persuasive evidence that Diane Joyce was one whit less qualified to be a road dispatcher than Paul Johnson. He relied on the fact that he had scored two points higher than Joyce on an oral interview evaluation that was highly subjective and, indeed, was itself permeated with sexism. (One of the interviewers had described Ms Joyce as a "rebel-rousing skirt-wearing person.")[13] The interviewers nevertheless rated Joyce, with Johnson and one other candidate, as fully qualified for the position. At the same time, there was no question that the agency's loosely defined affirmative action plan, which recognized the complete absence of women in many Transportation Agency job categories, including road dispatcher, was a factor in Joyce's selection.

The Supreme Court rejected Paul Johnson's claim of sex discrimination. But, sadly, despite the facts of the Johnson case, the news media almost universally trumpeted the result as allowing the promotion of a "less qualified" woman over a "more qualified" man.[14] Nowhere in the Supreme Court opinion could such an intimation be found; the Fourth Estate was reflecting its own biases and assumptions about affirmative action.[15] Few cases could illustrate more clearly the bitter perils of powerfully loaded and subjectively defined words like "merit" or "qualifications."

I cannot resist offering you one more, particularly vivid, example of the need for redefinitions of merit. This example comes, again, not from my fevered imagination but from a real Supreme Court case, in 1989. Ann Hopkins is an accountant and financial consultant – high-powered, highly competent, conscientious, and talented. Price Waterhouse, one of the most prestigious accounting, tax, and management consulting firms, was considering her application to become a partner in the firm. Although there was no question about Hopkins's professional competency and her abilities as a "rainmaker," her chances were dubious because of opposition by a few powerful partners.

The Supreme Court described the reasons for the opposition as follows:

One partner described her as "macho" ... ; another suggested that she "overcompensated for being a woman" ... ; a third advised her to take "a course at charm school" ... Several partners criticized her use of profanity; in response, one partner suggested that those partners objected to her swearing only "because it[']s a lady using foul language."[16]

The Price Waterhouse partners decided to postpone the decision on Hopkins's candidacy. Hopkins's biggest supporter at the firm, summarizing for her the problems that others had identified, advised her "to walk more femininely, talk more femininely, dress more femininely, wear make-up, have her hair styled, and wear jewelry."[17]

That many of the qualities for which Ann Hopkins was criticized – aggressiveness, macho image, tough talk – are forgiven, if not actually prized, in males, should go without saying. As one woman lawyer I know – the only female senior partner at the largest law firm in Boston – described the attitudinal phenomenon, there is simply a much narrower margin of tolerable behaviour for women than for men, particularly in very competitive professions. A woman cannot be too aggressive or she is deemed masculine and threatening; she alienates male partners whose standards of "excellence" embody, at a fundamental and perhaps even unconscious level, stereotypical assumptions about how women and men should act. But she also cannot be too passive, or she becomes a shrinking violet, unlikely to blossom into a sufficiently revenue-producing flower of the firm. Women must walk a thin tightrope while the line for "similarly situated" males (to use the lingo of American constitutional law) is much wider; they can indulge in a far greater range of personal conduct and style and still be accepted for their professional competency.

Why have I entertained you with these stories of life in the fast lane? Because affirmative action in my definition is part of a necessary process of changing narrow or inherently biased views of female excellence, which artificially depress the numbers of women who might otherwise qualify for jobs ranging from prestigious accounting partnerships to lucrative sinecures as road dispatchers. Examine the definitions of merit. How subjective are they? To what extent do they reflect sexist biases or reward predominantly masculine modes of behaviour? Simpler, objective job qualifications – height or weight requirements for prison guards, for example – have sometimes been invalidated under u.s. equal employment law because they have a discriminatory impact on women and are not demonstrably related to the job. Subjective notions of merit must also be recast in terms that are effectively non-discriminatory in the results they produce.

Let me turn now to a closely related controversy: the debate, as it has been denoted in women's-rights lingo, over "sameness versus difference." In her now-famous book, *In a Different Voice*, Harvard psychologist Carol Gilligan describes observed differences between girls' and boys' modes of solving moral dilemmas and posits that traditional standards for measuring moral judgment have been improperly based on an exclusively male norm.[18] Whatever the reasons for the gender differences that Gilligan observed, and accepting that not all girls and boys, women and men, necessarily conform to the styles she describes, her work illuminates my point about affirmative action as a process of redefining merit. It also raises a related question: if most females are really different from most males in their moral reasoning – not necessarily better and not necessarily worse – then a test that, on its face, seems to treat them both equally may in fact discriminate.

Another example of the conflict arises in the realm of athletics. It is too obvious to require demonstration that if boys and girls competed equally for places on school athletic teams in any age group above about twelve – and, for cultural reasons, probably below twelve as well – boys would overwhelm girls in such dramatic numbers, especially in sports requiring upper-body strength, that only a small handful of girls would have the opportunity for varsity athletic experience. To ensure equal opportunity for females in the field, we must take account of difference. To ignore it would itself be discriminatory. Thus there must be sex-segregated teams and sex-segregated competition.

Yet this does not necessarily mean that the individually exceptional girl who can compete with boys in, for example, soccer or basketball should be relegated to the girls' team. Sameness theory (treat women as if they were similarly situated to men; that is, let the exceptional girl try out for the tougher team) and difference theory (acknowledge and take account of the difference; that is, establish separate girls' teams) both have a place on the equal opportunity roster.

The argument from athletics for the necessity of sex segregation is sometimes extended to defend separate schools for males and females. I am more dubious about this proposition, but it is based in part on the actual experience of educators that young women participate more actively in class and extra-curricular activities when there are no males present to dominate the proceedings, or in the presence of whom females may feel shy or wish not to compete too aggressively. Whether sex-segregated schools are a good idea, whether they promote equal opportunity or simply reinforce stereotypes, or do a little of both at once, is a complicated question that I leave for another day. I raise it here to demonstrate the conflict between sameness and difference approaches to women's rights.

Sometimes it is quite difficult to treat women equally while at the same time accommodating our biological (or culturally induced) differences. The dilemma arose in a case that reached the Supreme Court in 1986 and that drove differing camps of feminist lawyers and theoreticians nearly to a state of war. The case, *California Federal Savings and Loan* v. *Guerra*, involved a California law that required employers to grant any pregnant employee up to four months of disability leave and to hold her job open for her if she returned before the four-month period expired.[19] The California Federal Savings and Loan Company (CalFed, as it came to be known) challenged this state requirement as a violation of the federal equal employment opportunity law, which prohibits any discrimination in employment on the basis of sex or pregnancy. The California law, said the employer, mandated discrimination in favour of pregnant women, thus disadvantaging men who might also need time off because of temporary disabilities. Since in the American constitutional scheme federal law invariably trumps state law where the two conflict, CalFed argued that the state law was unconstitutional and that it, the company, could therefore not be required to restore the complainant to her old job or an equivalent one after her pregnancy/disability leave.

A substantial camp of feminists agreed with CalFed in theory, though arguing that the remedy for California's violation of the federal law was not to invalidate the maternity leave requirement but to extend it to disability leaves generally and therefore to men. The American Civil Liberties Union (ACLU) Women's Rights Project and the National Organization for Women both took this view, despite some discomfort at opposing the female employee in the case. They argued further that the California law, although appearing to help women, actually hurt their job prospects by making them less desirable employees and by perpetuating the stereotypical notion that childbirth was special, unlike other temporary disabilities. Ergo, California was engaging in that oppressive romantic paternalism you have already read about, which, in the guise of helping women, actually puts us not on a pedestal but in a cage.

But CalFed's – and the ACLU's – position had two major defects. First, extending the California law to men and to disability leaves generally would have been a very bold stroke for a court. Such a result was probably far from the intentions of the legislators who passed the law and thus arguably beyond the judicial power to impose. Second – and this was the major argument of the opposing camp of feminists, including the ACLU chapter in Southern California, a frequent rebel from national ACLU policies – treating pregnant women the same as men may be intellectually satisfying but it ignores the reality of economic as well as biological life, especially for women in lower-status jobs. The reality is that without the California statute women would in many instances simply be out of a job if they took off even a relatively brief time to bear a child and recover from delivery and labour. The two ACLU factions clashed angrily on this issue at one national conference I attended, with the Southern Californians accusing those in the Women's Rights Project, headquartered in New York, of that most deadly sin, East Coast intellectual elitism, of elevating theoretical purity above concern for the real economic plight of working women.[20]

Putting aside for a moment the force of the Southern Californians' economic arguments in this instance for "taking account of difference," the simple biological fact is that men and women are not similarly situated for purposes of reproduction. Both can become parents, but only women need to take biological time out to bear the child.

The Supreme Court agreed with the Southern Californians and with many others who opposed the employer's arguments in the CalFed case. The majority opinion by Justice Thurgood Marshall essentially undertook an affirmative action analysis. The California statute was legitimate and consistent with the spirit of Title VII, the federal equal employment law, because it represented an attempt to remedy a disadvantage uniquely suffered by women in the workplace.[21] It was not demeaning; it was not "romantic paternalism." It promoted true job equality. Federal law did not in all circumstances prohibit discrimination in favour of pregnant women.

Affirmative action in favour of women can nevertheless be a dangerous and tricky concept. Often measures that seem to favour women do stereotype us more than they help us economically or politically. The U.S. Supreme Court rejected the remedial affirmative action argument when the female-only admissions policy of a Mississippi state nursing school was challenged under the equal protection clause of the Fourteenth Amendment; our only female justice, who wrote the opinion for the court, opined that maintaining the women-only policy would do more to perpetuate stereotypes of nursing (a notoriously underpaid and undervalued profession) as a women's job than it would to advance women economically.[22]

Yet the u.s. Supreme Court has not always got it right on the sameness/difference issue. In 1987 it upheld a California criminal law that defined statutory rape only in terms of sexual relations with an underage girl.[23] The state defended this gender-based classification on the theory that since only females can become pregnant, the law was properly designed to protect them from this risk. A majority of our high court judges bought this argument even though the relevant legislative history demonstrated that the dominant purpose of the law had not been a concern with the perils of pregnancy but a patriarchal and arguably outmoded obsession with female chastity.

The equal treatment/special treatment debate goes on. There are no easy answers. One resolution posited by feminists is that a rule or practice or law should be presumptively invalid only if, in actual impact, it subordinates or disadvantages women. Thus, ostensibly benign discrimination that really looks like romantic paternalism based on overbroad generalizations would not survive, while measures like California's maternity-leave law or affirmative action programs, whose primary effect is to prod employers to overcome entrenched discriminatory patterns or attitudes, would be approved and encouraged.

The problem, of course, in any case is to distinguish between forms of sex discrimination that demean, degrade, or disempower women from those that simply recognize and honour immutable differences between the sexes. We in the United States cannot as a society even agree what, if any, those immutable gender differences may be, beyond our indisputably contrasting reproductive equipment. It is both the genius and frustration of constitutional law, as it has developed in the United States, that so much of the politically charged task of drawing these difficult distinctions is entrusted to judges. And so, as American civil rights lawyers, even now in the reign of Rehnquist, we doggedly continue trying to persuade our often remote judicial guardians of the "other world out there," the world of both sexism and racism.

PART SEVEN

Reproductive Rights

ISSUES OF REPRODUCTION – THE RIGHT TO CHOOSE TO BEAR, or not to bear, children – have commanded a central preoccupation for feminists active in the most recent wave of the women's movement almost from the outset. The initial demands were for access to abortion, to medically safe birth control, and to voluntary sterilization. Demands to wrest control of the birthing process from an alienating hospital environment and male doctors and to reintroduce midwifery followed. More recently, responding somewhat belatedly to the problems of women of diverse races who have experienced racist interventions designed to limit fertility, feminism has begun to demand freedom from forced sterilization. Confronted with a rapidly developing host of new reproductive technologies designed to combat infertility, the women's movement has also begun to address the potential benefits and dangers posed by an array of fertility-enhancing procedures, controlled by a predominantly male medical establishment.

Christine Overall's essay constitutes a thoughtful pause in the face of the otherwise relentless demands for instant development of feminist strategies and positions on reproductive issues. Working from fundamental principles to evaluate which perspectives offer most to a feminist concept of "reproductive rights," she provides a philosophical framework against which to scrutinize the feminist agenda on reproductive matters.

Patricia Fernández Kelly provides a provocative and original examination of the class dimensions of pro-choice and pro-life ideology and activism around access to abortion, an analysis applicable to both Canada and the United States. Defining herself as inclined to the pro-choice perspective, Fernández Kelly yet provides an eloquent exploration of the inherent rationale underlying the activism of women within the pro-life movement. Her sympathetic treatment of certain aspects of the ideology of the pro-life forces reveals many positive and diverse strains within that movement, some of which will inspire surprised recognition and warm acceptance in feminist circles.

These authors offer refreshingly new approaches to the rapidly evolving debates within the feminist movement on reproductive control. Recounting the historical record from *Roe* v. *Wade* to *Morgentaler*, these essays provide an insightful re-examination of the feminist agenda in the field of reproduction.

19 Feminist Philosophical Reflections on Reproductive Rights in Canada

CHRISTINE OVERALL

I approach the discussion of the women's movement and reproductive rights as a feminist philosopher who has been concerned, over the last eight years, with moral issues and social policy questions pertaining to reproduction and reproductive technology. I am particularly interested in investigating both current ideas and ideologies about reproduction, and the values and goals most relevant to feminist action with respect to reproduction.

In this essay I shall examine the concept of a "reproductive right," a notion which plays a central role in discussions of issues relating to women's reproductive health. While the concept of rights in general does not by any means constitute all that is important in ethical discourse, and the concept of a reproductive right in particular does not exhaust all that is significant in the moral evaluation of reproductive issues, the idea of a reproductive right is, at this point at least, indispensable to a complete discussion of reproductive ethics and social policy.

Barbara Katz Rothman has expressed reservations about the use of the term "reproduction." She argues that we do not literally produce babies or reproduce ourselves.[1] While I agree with this observation, I shall continue to use the phrase "reproductive right" because I specifically want to explore the strengths and the ambiguities of that phrase. In particular, I want to analyse and evaluate the ways in which this notion of reproductive right has been given a unique legal and moral expression within Canadian society during the last two decades, manifesting itself within the struggle for abortion, the debates about midwifery and the place of birth, and the introduction of social practices relating to the new reproductive technologies, such as *in vitro* fertilization.

Originally, the concept of a reproductive right seemed to find a natural home within the abortion debate, but it is now being extended to discussions of new reproductive technologies. What is extraordinary is that the idea of a reproductive right is used not only by feminists, whose priority is promoting women's well-being and ending oppression, but also by non-feminists, whose agenda usually includes preservation of the traditional family, extension of male sexual and reproductive entitlements, and enforcement of a morality whose primary tenet is access to women's bodies. In other words, while the idea of a reproductive right is both useful and central to the advancement of women's reproductive freedom, there are also ways in which it can be and is being used against women's best interests. Feminists need to think well about what we mean when making claims for reproductive rights. For these reasons, then, the idea of a reproductive right is in need of close and careful analysis.

THE RIGHT NOT TO REPRODUCE

In my writings on reproduction I have suggested a number of distinctions between different senses of "reproductive right," and I shall make use of them here.[2] It is necessary, first, to distinguish between the right to reproduce and the right not to reproduce. The two are sometimes unnecessarily conflated as, for example, when Madam Justice Bertha Wilson referred in her Supreme Court decision in the *Morgentaler* case to "[t]he right to reproduce or not to reproduce which is in issue in this case."[3] The right not to reproduce means the entitlement not to be compelled to beget or bear children against one's will. To say that women have a right not to reproduce implies that there is no obligation on women to reproduce. The right not to reproduce is the entitlement not to be compelled to donate gametes (eggs or sperm) or embryos against one's will, and the entitlement not to have to engage in forced reproductive labour. Women do not owe their reproductive products or labour to any person or institution, including male partners or the state.

Compared to the United States, recognition in Canada of the right not to reproduce has been slow to develop. Full exercise of such a right requires, among other protections, access to safe and effective contraception and abortion services. In other words, the moral entitlement to abortion access follows from the broader right not to reproduce. Stipulations introduced into the Criminal Code in 1969 provided for the possibility, under certain carefully specified conditions, of therapeutic exceptions to the general law that procuring a miscarriage on a female person was an indictable offence. According to the then-new section 251 of the code, such a therapeutic abortion had to be performed by a qualified medical practitioner who was not a member of a therapeutic abortion committee, in an accredited or approved hospital, and only after a decision by the hospital's therapeutic abortion committee, consisting of at least three members, each of whom was a qualified medical practitioner, that the continuation of the pregnancy would or would be likely to endanger the life or health of the pregnant woman.

In the ensuing years, the interpretation of, and conformity to, section 251 were subject to extreme variation and outright injustice. In some areas hospitals could not obtain accreditation or approval; in some hospitals there were not sufficient doctors to constitute a therapeutic abortion committee. Hospitals had no legal obligation to set up a therapeutic abortion committee and those that did exist had no obligation to meet. Some hospitals imposed quotas on the numbers of abortions performed or limitations on patient eligibility based on place of residence. Women had no right to appear before the committees to present their case, and interpretation of the phrase "life or health" of the pregnant woman was left entirely in the hands of members of the therapeutic abortion committees. Their interpretations varied enormously from one committee to another, and some even introduced extraneous considerations such as the marital status of the applicant, the consent of the spouse, or the number of previous abortions.[4]

Section 251 of the Criminal Code placed severe constraints on Canadian women's right not to reproduce. In effect, it said that some women – directly, those whose abortion requests were rejected by therapeutic abortion committees and, indirectly, those who had no opportunity to bring their request to an abortion committee – had a legal obligation to procreate; it sentenced them to forced reproductive labour. This, surely, is a major violation of what the Canadian Charter of Rights and Freedoms now refers to as "security of the person." In the words of Supreme Court Judge Jean Beetz in the *Morgentaler* decision, "a pregnant woman's person cannot be said to be secure if, when her life or health is in danger, she is faced with a rule of criminal law which precludes her from obtaining effective and timely medical treatment."[5]

The so-called pro-life movement in Canada and the United States places heavy emphasis upon what is alleged to be the fetus's right to life. But without specifically recognizing such a right and, indeed, without making any direct references at all to the fetus or to its physical condition, section 251, in my view, implicitly attributed to the fetus a right to the use and occupancy of the woman's uterus. The woman's body was simply a container, with various utilities, that the fetus happened to need for nine months. Indeed, fetuses are the only group of entities that have been given entitlement under Canadian law to the medical use of the bodies of adult persons.

Section 251 also helped to perpetuate a right of access to women's reproductive labour which potentially benefited both individual men and the state. In the words of Madam Justice Bertha Wilson, section 251 of the Criminal Code "assert[ed] that the woman's capacity to reproduce is not to be subject to her own control. It is to be subject to the control of the state ... She is truly being treated as a means – a means to an end which she does not desire but over which she has no control."[6]

Fortunately, in January 1988, the Supreme Court removed these Criminal Code impediments to women's access to abortion.[7] No longer is a woman seeking an abortion required to obtain the approval of a therapeutic abortion committee. For, according to the judicial decision, "forcing a woman, by threat of criminal sanction, to carry a foetus to term unless she meets certain criteria unrelated to her own priorities and aspirations, is a profound interference with a woman's body and thus a violation of security of the person."[8]

Nevertheless, the Supreme Court decision has by no means permanently removed a significant danger to women's right not to reproduce. Like women in the United States, Canadian women cannot assume that access to abortion will remain indefinitely protected.[9] In at least three areas there are potential threats to such access.

First, there is a danger that the recent expression of concerns about the reasons for abortion and for abortion-related procedures may lead to renewed limitations on access to abortion. One example is the growing media discussion of the issue of abortion for sex selection.[10] Another example is the demand for regulation of, and limitations on, so-called selective termination of pregnancy. This procedure is performed in cases of multiple pregnancy in order to reduce the number of fetuses in the uterus and usually involves the injection of potassium chloride into the thorax of one or more of the fetuses to stop the heart. The "terminated" fetus is reabsorbed into the woman's body, without further need for surgery.[11] Recent media news reports quote Canadian ethicists and physicians challenging the justification of the procedure and calling for limitations on the number of fetuses to be terminated.[12]

A second reason for concern about potential threats to the right not to reproduce is the persistence of the claim that there is a need for protection of fetal life and alleged fetal rights. In March 1989 the Supreme Court of Canada dismissed Joseph Borowski's argument that section 251 of the Criminal Code contravened the life, security, and equality rights of the fetus, as a "person" protected by sections 7 and 15 of the Charter of Rights and Freedoms. In the absence of a law governing abortion, the court found the appeal to be moot, and stated that the appellant no longer had standing to pursue it. The court added that "in a legislative context any rights of the foetus could be considered or at least balanced against the rights of women guaranteed by s. 7 ... A pronouncement in favour of the appellant's position that a foetus is protected by s. 7 from the date of conception would decide the issue out of its proper context. Doctors and hospitals would be left to speculate as to how to apply such a ruling consistently with a woman's rights under s. 7."[13]

Nevertheless, despite this ruling, the Conservative government used the decision as yet another part of its rationale for reintroducing a law to recriminalize some abortions. Indeed, even the 1988 decision striking down the existing abortion law left open the very real possibility, expressed in the voices of the majority, that legal steps might be taken by the government to protect so-called fetal rights. For example, Madam Justice Wilson stated: "Section 1 of the Charter authorizes reasonable limits to be put upon the woman's right having regard to the fact of the developing foetus within her body." She added:

A developmental view of the foetus ... supports a permissive approach to abortion in the early stages of pregnancy and a restrictive approach in the later stages ... [The woman's] reasons for having an abortion would ... be the proper subject of inquiry at the later stages of her pregnancy when the state's compelling interest in the protection of the foetus would justify it in prescribing conditions. The precise point in the development of the foetus at which the state's interest in its protection becomes "compelling" I leave to the informed judgment of the legislature which is in a position to receive guidance on the subject from all the relevant disciplines. It seems to me, however, that it might fall somewhere in the second trimester.[14]

Similarly, then–Chief Justice Brian Dickson said that "state protection of foetal interests may well be deserving of constitutional recognition under s. 1."[15] And Justice Beetz added:

[A] rule that would require a higher degree of danger to health in the latter months of pregnancy, as opposed to the early months, for an abortion to be lawful, could possibly achieve a proportionality which would be acceptable under s. 1 of the Charter ... Parliament is justified in requiring a reliable, independent and medically sound opinion in order to protect the state interest in the foetus ... [T]here would be a point in time at which the state interest in the foetus would become compelling. From this point in time, Parliament would be entitled to limit abortions to those required for therapeutic reasons and therefore require an independent opinion as to the health exception ... I am of the view that the protection of the foetus is and ... always has been, a valid objective in Canadian criminal law ... I think s. 1 of the Charter authorizes reasonable limits to be put on a woman's right having regard to the state interest in the protection of the foetus.[16]

More recently, it has been claimed that without protection of fetal rights, there is nothing to prevent the occurrence of abortion for purposes of sex selection, harm to fetuses by the use of dangerous drugs and by third-party attacks, and the buying and selling of fetuses and fetal parts.[17] The Law Reform Commission of Canada's Working Paper, *Crimes against the Foetus*, expresses serious concern about dangers to the fetus and proposes a new category of criminal offence, "Foetal Destruction or Harm."[18] Thus the stage is set, potentially, for a continuation of major conflict between women's right not to reproduce and the alleged rights of the fetus. Unfortunately, as the Law Reform Commission's Working Paper makes clear, recognition of fetal rights would almost inevitably mean the judicial recognition, via the recriminalization of abortion, of the fetus's alleged right to occupancy and use of a woman's body, and concomitant limitations on women's autonomy and self-determination.[19]

A third reason for concern about threats to Canadian women's right not to reproduce is the growing use by anti-abortion groups of not only non-violent civil disobedience but also active interference in the operations of abortion clinics.[20] In addition, "pro-life" leaders such as Joseph Borowski have threatened the use of violence in defence of their cause. Says Borowski: "The war goes on. There is no end to this fight, and certainly no compromise. They [pro-choice] are the enemy. It's a war. Our side has one advantage. We pray. They don't ... I'm glad I did not come to Ottawa for the [Morgentaler Supreme Court] decision. I probably would have gone into the court and punched the judges in the nose ... I'm a non-violent man, and I don't believe in violence but if the seven judges or whoever were here right now, I would have great difficulty restraining myself from punching them in the mouth."[21]

In the face of these potential threats to the right not to reproduce, feminist research and activism must insist that there is no need for the recriminalization of abortion, including late abortions. No woman deliberately sets out to kill a highly developed fetus, and abortion is not sought by women for its own sake. Instead, in the words of philosopher Caroline Whitbeck, it is a "grim option."[22]

While abortions late in pregnancy may seem particularly problematic, they are usually requested for one of the following reasons. In some instances it was impossible for the woman to obtain the abortion earlier, because convoluted legal procedures delayed its approval. Cases such as these can be avoided by making very early abortions easily available and accessible. In other instances, a late abortion is sought either because prenatal testing reveals a fetal condition that is or is perceived as being severely disabling or even life-threatening, or because the woman's own life or health is endangered.[23] There is, therefore, insufficient justification for the introduction of legislation to protect the late-term fetus from the pregnant woman, or indeed for any new Criminal Code limitations on abortion.

Moreover, in my view, entitlement to choose how many fetuses to gestate, and of what sort, should be seen as a part of the right not to reproduce. The protection of this choice is essential within a cultural context where mothering gets little social support, persons with disabilities are the subject of bias and stigma, and raising several infants simultaneously is a personal and financial challenge of heroic dimensions. (It is also significant that the upsurge in the incidence of multiple pregnancies has been generated by the administration of fertility drugs and by the use of *in vitro* fertilization and the technology of gamete intrafallopian transfer ["GIFT"].) There is no more reason to set limitations on the numbers or types of fetuses that a woman must be required to gestate than there is to set limits on whether she gestates a given fetus or fetuses. To set limits on the numbers or conditions of fetuses a woman must gestate is to accord those fetuses an unjustified right of occupancy of the woman's uterus.

If protection of the fetus seems to be a worthwhile and neglected social goal, then what is needed is greater protection of the pregnant woman herself. Even, surely, on the basis of the non-feminist and implausible assumption of an adversarial relationship between pregnant woman and fetus, the reinstallation of physicians as body police enforcing fetal rights is unlikely to improve the behaviour of pregnant women towards their fetuses.[24] Furthermore, in order to prevent the commodification of fetuses and fetal parts and other undesirable uses of the fetus, there is no more need to assign personhood or rights to the fetus than there is to assign personhood or rights to blood or body parts. Instead of using that blunt instrument, the criminal law, in a *post hoc* fashion to attempt to manage undesirable reproductive practices, existing regulations governing health care and the utilization of human tissues can be used. And ultimately, of course, it will be necessary to minimize and finally eliminate the powerful underlying conditions of oppression that generate such practices as fetal commodification and fetal sex selection.

THE RIGHT TO REPRODUCE

The right not to reproduce is distinct from the right to reproduce; that is, the right not to reproduce neither implies a right to reproduce nor follows from a right to reproduce. The right to reproduce has two senses, which I have called, perhaps misleadingly, the weak sense and the strong sense. The weak sense of the right to reproduce is the entitlement not to be interfered with in reproduction or prevented from reproducing. It would imply an obligation on the state not to inhibit or limit reproductive liberty, for example, through racist marriage laws, forced sterilization, or coercive birth control programs.[25]

In my view, the right to reproduce, in this sense, is also compromised by restrictions on the place of birth and on birth attendants, and by court-ordered Caesareans. Like the United States, Canada has a history of the gradual medicalization of birth. Midwives have been replaced by physicians, from general practitioners to obstetricians, hospitals have replaced the home, and medical innovations from fetal monitoring, amniotomy, and forceps deliveries to anaesthesia and Caesarean sections have made birthing into a health crisis. Without the genuine freedom to choose home birth, to be attended by midwives, or to avoid obstetrical technology, women's right to reproduce in the weak sense is seriously compromised.

In its strong sense, the right to reproduce would be the right to receive all necessary assistance to reproduce. It would imply entitlement to access to any and all available forms of reproductive products, technologies, and labour, including the gametes of other women and men, the gestational services of women, and the full range of procreative techniques including *in vitro* fertilization (IVF), gamete intrafallopian transfer, uterine lavage, embryo freezing, and sex preselection.

Non-feminist writers such as American legal theorist John A. Robertson defend the right to reproduce in the strong sense by claiming that it is just an extension of the right to reproduce in the weak sense. As he puts it, "the right of the married couple to reproduce noncoitally" and "the right to reproduce noncoitally with the assistance of donors and surrogates" both follow from "constitutional acceptance of a married couple's right to reproduce coitally."[26] (Robertson's heterosexist bias is not much mitigated by his later concession that there is "a very strong argument for unmarried persons, either single or as couples, also having a positive right to reproduce.")[27] Robertson believes that these rights entitle married couples certainly, and possibly single persons, to "create, store, transfer, donate and possibly even manipulate extra-corporeal embryos" and "to contract for eggs, sperm, embryos, or surrogates." They would also, he thinks, justify compelling a contract mother to hand over a child to its purchasers, even against her will.[28]

In addition, American attorney Lori B. Andrews argues that the right to reproduce in the strong sense is probably founded upon the right to marital privacy.[29] Hence, some feminists may want to claim the right to reproduce in the strong sense both because of arguments such as those of Robertson and Andrews, and because of a fear that otherwise access to reproductive technologies, such as IVF, may be treated by the state as a privilege to be gained only through possession of the requisite social criteria, such as being heterosexual and married.

Nevertheless, I have serious doubts about the legitimacy and justification of this right to reproduce. Recognizing it would shift the burden of proof on to those who have moral doubts about the morality of technologies such as IVF and practices such as contract motherhood. For it suggests that a child is somehow owed to each of us, as individuals or as members of a couple, and that it is indefensible for society to fail to provide all possible means for obtaining one. Thus it might be used, as Robertson advocates, to imply an entitlement to hire contract mothers, to obtain other women's eggs, and to make use of donor insemination and uterine lavage of another woman, all in order to maximize the chances of reproducing.[30] In other words, recognition of the right to reproduce in the strong sense would create an active right to access to women's bodies and, in particular, to our reproductive labour and products. For example, it would condone the entitlement to hire a contract mother and force contract mothers to surrender their infants after birth. And it might be used to found a claim to certain kinds of children – for example, children of a desired sex, appearance, or intelligence.

Exercise of the alleged right to reproduce in this strong sense could potentially require violation of some women's right not to reproduce. There is already good evidence, in both the United States and Great Britain, that eggs and ovarian tissue have been taken from some women without either their knowledge or their informed consent.[31] It is not difficult to imagine that recognizing a strong right to reproduce could require either a similar theft of eggs or embryos from some women, if none can be found to offer them willingly, or a commercial inducement to sell these products. It could be used as a basis for requiring fertile people to "donate" gametes and embryos. And even if some people willingly donate gametes, there is no right or entitlement on the part of the infertile that they should do so.

We need to be very clear that the feminist language of reproductive rights is being illegitimately co-opted when it is used to defend an alleged right to become or to hire a contract mother, to buy or to sell eggs, embryos, or babies, or to select or preselect the sex of one's offspring. There can be no genuine entitlement to women's reproductive labour, or to buying or otherwise obtaining human infants. Contract motherhood entails a type of slave trade in infants, and it commits women to a modern form of indentured servitude.

My hope is that Canada will choose neither the legalization of contract motherhood nor the criminalization of contract mothers. We should opt instead to reduce the potential motivation for such contracts by making them unenforceable and by rendering criminal both the operation of contract motherhood agencies and the actions of professionals who participate in surrogacy arrangements. It is important for Canadian social policy to resist the incursion of u.s.-style commercialization of reproduction and reproductive entrepreneurialism, the most likely victims of which would be poor women and women of colour. These are the sorts of issues that should be explored by the current Royal Commission on New Reproductive Technologies. The nine members of this federally mandated commission have been instructed to inquire into and report on "current and potential medical and scientific developments related to new reproductive technologies, considering in particular their social, ethical, health, research, legal and economic implications and the public interest, recommending what policies and safeguards should be applied."[32]

At the same time, there is no necessity for access to procedures such as *in vitro* fertilization to be treated as a privilege to which it is legitimate to erect social barriers that discriminate on arbitrary and unfair grounds – grounds such as marital status, sexual orientation, putative stability or parenting potential, or economic level. While I cannot wholeheartedly support and endorse highly ineffective, costly, painful, and unsuccessful procedures such as IVF, I also cannot endorse the call by some feminists for a total ban on the procedure. State provision and financing of IVF is different from state provision of contract motherhood. Many compelling reasons – primary among them being the sale of babies and the exploitation of women's reproductive labour – militate against state recognition of contract motherhood through legalization or financial support. These two reasons are not present, or not inevitably present, in the case of IVF.

Instead, my view is that, without asserting a strong right to all possible reproductive assistance, we can nevertheless critically examine the artificial barriers, such as marital status, sexual orientation, and ability to pay, that hinder women's fair access to reproductive technologies. We can also provide protections for women entering and participating in infertility treatment programs. This would require making sure that applicants make a genuinely informed choice and consent, in full knowledge of the short- and long-term risks, possible benefits, chances of success and failure, alternative approaches and treatments, and perhaps even the pronatalist social pressures to procreate. If IVF seems to be a valuable medical service (and I think that view is still debatable), then it deserves to be made available, like other medical services, through medicare, as it is now in Ontario. It would also be important to ensure thorough screening for donors of eggs and sperm, to maintain an adequate system of record-keeping to track the long-term effects of IVF on women and their offspring, and to ensure that any women who provide eggs for the program have genuinely chosen to do so. Finally, in the long run, feminists should be thinking about whether it is possible to incorporate high-tech infertility treatments such as IVF into women-centred and women-controlled reproductive health centres.

The approach that I have just sketched avoids both of two perspectives that I believe are undesirable: on the one hand, treating access to reproductive technology as a privilege to be earned through the possession of certain personal, social, sexual, and/or financial characteristics and, on the other hand, a kind of feminist maternalism that seeks in the best interests of women to terminate IVF research and treatment.[33] While many feminists have stressed both the social construction of the desire for motherhood and the dangers and ineffectiveness of *in vitro* fertilization, it is, surely, dangerous for feminists to claim to understand better than infertile women themselves the origins and significance of their desire for children.[34] It is not the role of feminist research and action to protect women from what is interpreted to be their own false consciousness. Instead, we should assume that when women are provided with full information about the possibilities they will be empowered to make reproductive decisions that will genuinely benefit themselves and their children.

CONCLUSION

The themes that have structured the struggle over reproductive rights in Canada are apparently contrasting ones: on the one hand, access to various reproductive services and technologies and, on the other hand, access to the use and exploitation of women's bodies for reproductive purposes.

Nevertheless, the contrast is more apparent than real. The goals of access to reproductive technologies and access to women's bodies come together within conservative discourse on reproduction, discourse which is pro-natalist, pro-family, and pro-traditional roles for women. It is also classist, racist, ableist, and heterosexist. The oppressive nature of this discourse is often disguised by the co-optation of feminist language and concepts. In recent lectures and papers, for example, members of the anti-abortion movement have claimed that there is "sexism" in the pro-choice movement and have depicted the fetus as a member of a maligned minority group.[35] The same voices that want to ban abortion because women engage in sexual intercourse "by choice" also want to compel contract mothers to sell their babies because they enter the contracts "by choice." Meanwhile, non-feminists are proclaiming that new reproductive technologies actually promote women's autonomy and reproductive choice.[36]

But paradoxically, both the non-existence and the existence of certain reproductive "choices" or alternatives can be coercive. While lack of access to contraception or abortion clearly violates reproductive choice by failing to respect the right not to reproduce, conversely the availability of such practices as contract motherhood and the sales of gametes and embryos can potentially violate reproductive choice. For respecting a right to reproduce in the strong sense for some may violate the right not to reproduce of others.

Feminists want to preserve and enhance access to the reproductive services and technologies that benefit women, while preventing further encroachments on access to women's bodies whether by the state or by individuals. The way to do this, I suggest, is by insisting both upon women's right not to reproduce and upon our right to reproduce in the weak sense, and also by developing a critical analysis of the ways in which the right to reproduce in the strong sense is now being exercised.

20 A Chill Wind Blows: Class, Ideology, and the Reproductive Dilemma

M . PATRICIA FERNÁNDEZ KELLY*

INTRODUCTION

This essay stems from my own apprehensions about the polarization of discourses on abortion. Those who share my discomfort include more than men eager to perpetuate power over women and more than fanatics. Ambivalence about the limits of choice and the value of life also extends to millions of individuals, of both sexes, wrestling with integrity over moral alternatives.

As a feminist, and a woman, I value political action that aims at enhancing human life. For the same reason, I believe in the merits of choice, particularly as it refers to the ability of women to bear children. But choice is a necessary, not a sufficient condition for creating a society consistent with feminist aspirations. In the same vein, the adherence to abstract definitions of life ignores the actual conditions that make human existence bearable in the first place.

"Life" and "choice", the words at the centre of the contemporary debate on abortion, are not self-evident realities but disputed terms within a broader political discourse. Their meaning appears obvious only to those who ignore history. Yet words have records that cannot

* I thank Horace Judson and Alejandro Portes for their helpful insights and suggestions. Andrea Portes provided valuable research assistance during the summer of 1989. Only I am responsible for the views expressed in this essay.

be overlooked without treachery and distortion. "Life" and "choice" are no exception.

Many women in the United States view the emphasis on reproductive choice as an abdication of social responsibility, a rejection of commitments to service, home, and children. We have made a habit of dismissing those qualms as an effect of impaired judgment, itself the consequence of patriarchal manipulation. In doing that, we have robbed women – those women – of their dissenting consciousness and reduced it to a product of hegemonic ideology. They are the victims of skulduggery. We are enlightened to know what is best for them.

We discuss pro-life positions as propaganda and present pro-choice stances as devoid of ideological contamination. This does not improve an understanding of the dilemmas raised by abortion. It is not enough to claim that pro-life proponents are seeking to turn back the clock. We require, in addition, a critical examination of our own consciousness. That goal cannot be accomplished without addressing the class roots of pro-life and pro-choice positions.

In this essay I initiate an inquiry into the socioeconomic origins of pro-life and pro-choice discourses. Several obstacles lie in my path. Research on the relationship between class structure and views on abortion is negligible.[1] Given the paucity of empirical data, my analysis must remain preliminary.

Difficulties inherent to the definition of class further complicate the inquiry. Class distinctions are elusive, partly because of their shifting boundaries and partly because, in addition to objective criteria, they are also defined by subjective assessments.[2] Gauging class divisions in the United States is especially difficult, given the historical trajectory of a country that de-emphasizes economic hierarchies and stresses instead a plurality of interest groups vying for political power.[3] There are few commonalities of experience between an African-American sales clerk in Baltimore and a Caucasian software consultant in San Diego. But chances are that both consider themselves as members of the middle class. Definitional constraints notwithstanding, class is not a category we can overlook when analysing the contemporary debate on abortion.

In this essay I focus on economic changes that, for the past two decades, have led to growing income differentials in the United States and to the exclusion of large sectors of the population from meaningful political participation. I propose that these transformations bear a complex relationship with the debate on abortion. Instead of discourses emphasizing economic inequality and political mobilization, the disfranchised have turned to the realm of morality to express class resentments.

From that vantage point, pro-life and pro-choice currents are the expression of separate political coalitions. One reflects the uneasy convergence of reactionary leaders seeking legitimacy and large numbers of people threatened by eroding economic conditions and alienated from feminist currents. In contrast, pro-choice discourses are part of an ideological alliance between professional women and reformist forces addressing the concerns of various interest groups, but reluctant to challenge the underpinnings of the economic system.

In the first section, I provide a comparative critique of the internal rationale of pro-choice and pro-life discourses. This is followed by a sketch of the socioeconomic trends that have paralleled the most recent debate on abortion. The concluding section considers some practical implications of the analysis.

THE CONTEXT

Early in 1989, sixty-five thousand pro-life advocates met in Washington, DC, voicing their conviction that abortion is tantamount to murder. On 6 April, they were countered by more than three hundred thousand pro-choice demonstrators who gathered at the same place, on the occasion of hearings held by the u.s. Supreme Court to consider the case of *Webster* v. *Reproductive Health*, a Missouri law. At stake was women's right to terminate a pregnancy as permitted by the landmark *Roe* v. *Wade* decision of 1973.[4]

On 3 July the Supreme Court, by a small margin, stopped short of abrogating *Roe* v. *Wade*, but affirmed several sections of the Missouri law. In an eighty-one-page document, the court accepted *Webster*'s preamble, that life begins at conception. It also affirmed the right of the states to legislate the conditions under which women seek abortions and reversed the trimester format in the pre-existing law by allowing for medical tests to determine the viability of a fetus after the twenty-third week of pregnancy.

In dissent, Justice Harry Blackmun recorded his fear "for the liberty and equality of the millions of women ... who had come to believe that the Constitution guaranteed [the] right to exercise some control over [their] unique ability to bear children ... [a right] vital to the full participation of women in the economic and political walks of American life." With characteristic eloquence, he added "the women of this nation still retain the liberty to control their destinies but the signs are evident and very ominous, and a chill wind blows."[5]

The decision was greeted with euphoria by pro-life activists, who saw it as a step towards the repudiation of legal abortions, an outcome consistent with the defeat of the Equal Rights Amendment, seven years earlier. News broadcasts over the Fourth of July holiday carried the image of thousands of demonstrators throughout the country in vehement confrontation. Not since the civil rights era had there been such an expression of collective rage.

Where does this sustained burst of energy originate? What are the factors that explain the persistence of the bitter dispute over abortion? Why do so many women take a pro-life position when they have the most to lose through the shrinking of reproductive alternatives? Why do they view feminism with animosity, despite the congruence of that trend with democratic traditions they otherwise value? To answer those questions, it is first necessary to situate the two opposing discourses within the frame of history and to examine their internal logic.

Choice and Its Ambiguities

The most recent debate on abortion, following the *Roe v. Wade* decision of 1973, coincided with the strengthening of the women's movement in the United States. This feminist wave was heterogeneous from the beginning. Nevertheless, its most influential strand was rooted in liberal philosophy and thus stressed individual freedom and equality under the law. Leaders of the women's movement emphasized the proposed Equal Rights Amendment to the Constitution, women's full entrance into the labour force, and reproductive choice as preconditions to expand women's options in the economic, political, and social spheres.[6]

In supporting abortion rights, pro-choice advocates reasoned that biological reproduction has tended to be more onerous for women than men. Motherhood reduces women's capacity for political participation and increases their social and economic vulnerability.[7] Therefore, women should be entitled to ultimate jurisdiction over pregnancy, as they know best when, and under what conditions, they are able – and willing – to bear children. The availability of reproductive alternatives, including abortion, levels sexual disparities by giving women what men have always had: control over their own bodies.

To the extent that feminist thought affirms personal autonomy and full citizenship, it is in harmony with older traditions that brought about the Bill of Rights and the u.s. Constitution. In consonance with liberal philosophy, the women's movement highlighted the superiority of mind over body and the perfectibility of the human condition.[8] Other features also characterized liberal feminism: it was a decidedly secular trend. It questioned and sought to reform "traditional" institutions that subordinate women in the private and public sectors. Finally, the focus of liberal feminism was on patriarchy and only subsequently on the economic system.

The concept of patriarchy, elaborated during the same period that witnessed the ascent of liberal feminism, entailed a critique of the institutions that perpetuate women's subordination: the sexual division of labour, the nuclear family, and organized religion.[9] Observers characterized patriarchy as an independent system of domination anteceding capitalism and consisting of the uneven distribution of economic and political power between men and women. According to this view, women's gradual confinement in the home was consummated, under industrial capitalism, through the alliance of working-class and capitalist men.[10]

Men's appropriation of women's labour, partly achieved through the enactment of protective legislation and the family wage, removed women from the sphere of remunerated work and charged them instead with reproductive tasks. Uplifting women's condition would require the elimination of the sexual division of labour and women's incorporation into the paid employment. That in turn could not be achieved without expanding women's reproductive choices.

The emphasis on patriarchy illuminated the specificity of women's socioeconomic experiences and showed that these are not reducible to those of men. At the same time, the concept failed to clarify historical changes in the content of the sexual division of labour, nor did it allow for variations in the nature and degree of women's subjection.[11] It also underestimated the extent to which women have participated in social actions that seem detrimental to them. That was the case of women's involvement in the struggle for the family wage, at the turn of the century, and the case of women opposing abortion at present.

Finally, the emphasis on patriarchy surmised that men of different class and ethnic backgrounds have equivalent interests in the appropriation of women's sexuality and labour. That assumption was lacking in precision. The patriarchal family, the sexual division of labour, and the home may be viewed as mechanisms to suppress women's socioeconomic progress. But they can also be seen as channels for controlling men, particularly working-class men, by transforming them into "providers" with primary responsibility for the support of women and children.[12] Without the benefit of class analysis, patriarchy became an ahistorical explanation for women's subservience. This was tantamount to denying women's agency in the shaping of history by portraying them as the ever-passive victims of men's machinations.

Reliance on patriarchy as the sole explanation for women's subordination moved the analytical focus away from inequalities shared by people of both sexes, and towards a presumed opposition of fundamental interests between men and women. For the same reason, liberal feminists did not articulate an affirmation of motherhood, marriage, and home with the same vigour that guided their efforts at raising women's status in the public sphere.[13] Housework was portrayed as an inherently devalued form of labour.

This perplexed and offended many women, who saw their homes as the moral fulcrum of society, the place where the injuries of the market-place could be restored, and the site where dignity could be achieved through dedication to children. The debate on abortion eventually captured this growing polarization.

It was not that liberal feminism had failed to address the conditions that would alleviate the oppression of mothers and wives, or that the women's movement was not sympathetic to the concerns of working-class women, immigrant women, and women in racial and ethnic minorities. It was, rather, that liberal feminism drew its first energy, and its language, from the concerns of middle-class Caucasian women for whom marriage, home, and family had translated into isolation, frustrated professional aspirations, and feelings of devalued identity. Betty Friedan captured this phenomenon with clarity in *The Feminine Mystique* (1963). Her analysis referred to experiences that had been moulded since the nineteenth century.

Throughout the nineteenth century the consolidation of industrial capitalism redefined the position of men and women within the larger system of production. The invention of the factory led to greater levels of efficiency in the manufacture and distribution of goods and services but it also created a split between home and work-place. While men populated the public sector, women were confined to the domestic realm.[14] This was reflected in a sexual division of labour by virtue of which women increasingly depended on men for subsistence and public representation.[15]

In addition to expanding cities, rural-urban migration, and a new proletariat, industrial capitalism also brought about the erosion of extended kinship networks, the consequent reduction in the size of households, the lengthening of childhood, and the commodification of reproductive services. As the market overtook many of the tasks previously fulfilled by women, a new concept of housewife emerged, characterized by its focus on consumption and non-remunerated work.

Severe friction between capitalists and workers paralleled the growth of industry in the United States. Class conflict was neutralized during the 1920s and 1930s, partly as a result of the achievements of organized labour and partly as a consequence of concessions made by employers aiming to expand markets.[16] The growth of middle-income sectors during the following decades led to the emergence of new styles of life that circled around monetarized transactions. Consumer power engulfed class identity.[17] The suburban explosion of the 1950s epitomized an American claim to prosperity for all.[18] Class distinctions appeared to fade from the collective consciousness, although they persisted at the foundation of the new society.

This had varying effects on people of either sex. Manhood was gradually equated with the ability to support a family.[19] Breadwinners became, by definition, male. In contrast, frailty, subservience, and a commitment to the domestic sphere defined femininity. Reduced to isolated home environments and responsible for tasks assumed to be devoid of economic value, women in suburban America were besieged by all the afflictions described by Friedan.

Such women did not identify the source of their discontent in the process of capitalist accumulation that had robbed them of meaning as productive social beings. Instead, their anger focused on men, who seemed to have reaped all the rewards: money, status, the excitement of competition. Class identity, already fragmented by the extension of consumerism, was further diluted by gender polarization. Alternatively, men saw themselves oppressed by parasitic women, and women resented men who appeared to be unambiguously powerful and abusive.[20] The concept of patriarchy gave a name to the modern estrangement between the sexes.

The leadership of the women's movement articulated a world view consistent with those perceptions. It assumed that working-class women equally shared the perspectives of relatively affluent, mostly suburban, women. Nevertheless, like many of their forebears, working women, immigrant women, and women in racial and ethnic minorities often saw home and family, with more optimism, as a channel for economic mobility and personal fulfilment. Their hopefulness may have been unjustified in some cases but it was, nonetheless, based on their own historical experience and perceptions.

It was among those women, who saw themselves excluded from the feminist agenda, that distrust and then hostility surfaced.[21] Animosity was fuelled by conservative organizations who appropriated the language of dissent but used it to build constituencies for purposes of their own.[22] Given their ambiguous meaning, "country," "home," "family," and "life" opened new avenues for creating ideological alliances. The unborn child became a condensed symbol of a broader opposition to secular rationalism. Feminism was equated with mainstream ideologies emphasizing individualism, competition, and success in the public sphere. Thus, pro-life currents evolved in response to the opportunism of politicians but also as a reaction to the perceived limitations of the women's movement.

There is irony in this. Feminist thought grew during the 1970s in consonance with the aspirations of the civil rights era. Both trends were informed by a desire for the dissemination of social justice. However, many today perceive the women's movement as an elite current, alien to the concerns of ordinary people. This is a misconception. But unless popular feelings are acknowledged and addressed, the price of conceit will be defeat. The setbacks endured by the campaign for the Equal Rights Amendment in the early 1980s have already illustrated that quandary.[23]

The Other Meanings of Life

While liberal feminism stresses women's individual rights and equality under the law, the organic intellectuals of the pro-life movement emphasize the rights of unborn children. Liberal feminism is distinguished by its secularism. The right-to-life movement is unabashedly religious.[24]

Those who object to abortion believe that the measure of a moral society is the degree to which protection is extended to vulnerable groups. In the same way that the definition of humanity has been expanded to include racially diverse groups, the physically and mentally impaired, and slaves, it must also encompass potential life.[25] According to that view, the rights of adults should stop at the point where they interfere with those of the unborn. Because life begins at conception, abortion is tantamount to murder and, therefore, it should be renounced.[26]

Pro-life advocates argue that women's subordination cannot be resolved by equalizing men and women's reproductive capacities. Allowing women to compete successfully in the labour market by having fewer children exalts selfishness and devalues potential life. Instead, efforts should be geared to creating conditions that uplift motherhood, family, and children. That cannot be accomplished through the legalization of abortion for several reasons.

Abortion allows men to evade responsibility for their role in procreation while at the same time increasing the physical and psychological burden on women. It degrades women by placing them at the mercy of an "abortion industry" built for profit rather than the social good. This process transforms children into commodities subordinated to the personal convenience of both men and women.[27]

Finally, abortion – as well as other reproductive technologies – raises moral questions about all fragile forms of life. If unborn children are disposable, what prevents those who control technology and economic power from eliminating the diseased or the racially different before they are born? With this, pro-life activists are expressing a concern about "throw-away children" in a society that gives priority to expedience, individualism, and the logic of the market.[28] The paradox is that, from this vantage point, the pro-life position contains a vigorous anti-establishment strand.

Pro-life discourses may be conceptualized as an alternative ideology of resistance to the social atomization fuelled by capitalist expansion. They are especially appealing to sectors of the population threatened by declining standards of living and exclusion from the social mainstream. Pro-life organizers and demonstrators, at the grass-roots level, tend to equate their own social and economic devaluation with the degradation of life in general as represented by attacks on unborn children.[29] Therefore, the fight for the embryo symbolizes a broader struggle against the follies of materialism. The vindication of community, home, and mutuality between men and women are part of that contention.

The anti-establishment thrust of pro-life discourses is an important aspect of a complex totality. However, there are two other dimensions that require further analysis. One refers to the internal logic of pro-life positions. The second consists in this: despite their euphonic label, pro-life stances are, in fact, part of a larger political discourse aimed at suppressing sexual expression, particularly among women.[30] Below, I examine each of these two components separately.

The incongruities of pro-life positions have been noted before. They include a fixation with unborn children but meagre empathy for the varying experience of vulnerable adults, particularly women. Those willing to speak for the rights of embryos often endorse the elimination of social programs that make life bearable for the poor. The extension of civic rights to the unborn is a debatable concept from a juridical standpoint.[31] But perhaps the largest logical infraction entails the very adoption of the moment of conception as the beginning of human life. This assertion is flawed for several reasons.

Even from a narrow religious perspective, the moment when life begins has remained contested terrain for most of history. Prior to the mid-nineteenth century, it was not conception but "quickening" – the moment when a woman could feel the fetus move – that was widely regarded as proof that a soul had entered the unborn child.[32] The period that preceded that event – many weeks after impregnation – afforded women considerable discretion in the use of folk remedies to restore the regularity of menstruation. Those cures were not considered abortifacients.

Technological progress, during the nineteenth century, led to the identification of conception as a critical moment in the development of human life. But even more recent advances could push the mark further back. If we accept that life begins at conception, then, why not before? Research in cloning, a new reproductive technology, reveals that every cell contains the genetic code of a whole being. The time is near when the replication of individuals will be a distinct alternative.[33] Does this mean that every bodily cell should be protected as potential life? A reliance on *reductio ad absurdum* exposes the logical fissure in this aspect of the pro-life movement. It also allows for a better understanding of the reasons why conception is central to its broader rationale.

Pro-life advocates are not affirming that all forms of human life are equally defensible. Their position on capital punishment, war, and military expenditures illustrates this point.[34] They are claiming that, to the extent that heterosexual contact entails the possibility of conception, individuals should refrain from intercourse unless they are prepared to meet the consequences. From this vantage point, pregnancy and childbearing are the penalties women pay for their sexual transgressions. These can be atoned in the context of the patriarchal family where, according to Randall Terry, director of Operation Rescue, "you consummate your marriage as often as you like and if you have babies, you have babies."[35] Abortion is inadmissible because it allows women to escape the biological consequences of sexual expression. For the same reasons, radical segments of the pro-life movement object to almost all forms of birth control.[36] By positing an adversarial relationship between women and unborn children, pro-life activists are updating world views that centred on the opposition between good and evil. In this case, women are cast in a villainous role that simplifies the complexities of their experience at the same time that it affirms the need to control them.[37] The irony is that an ideology that propounds compassion conceals, in actuality, a pessimistic view of human nature that obliterates democratic ideals of self-determination.

An analysis of pro-choice and pro-life discourses discloses internal limitations and some potentials. It also suggests a demarcation in terms of class. The following section examines this second aspect in more detail.

THE CHANGING ECONOMY AND IDEOLOGICAL POLARIZATION

The growth of the women's movement paralleled major economic changes characterized by the internationalization of investments and the shift from manufacturing to services and information. Since the early 1960s, advanced technology and cheap transportation made possible the transfer of productive stages from advanced industrial countries to less developed areas of the world. Seeking to retain the advantage in the wake of growing foreign competition, investors moved operations to countries where the cost of labour was low and where labour movements were, for the most part, unobtrusive.[38]

In the United States, capital flight led to economic restructuring. Income inequalities grew during the same period that witnessed epidemics of plant closings and worker dislocation. Membership in labour unions fell from 30 per cent of the labour force in the early 1960s to less than 15 per cent in 1989. Hourly wages stagnated while the service sector expanded. About 70 per cent of all jobs created since the mid-1970s offered yearly earnings of $13,000 or less.[39] The United States moved from being the largest creditor to the largest debtor country in the world.

Various sectors in the United States felt the effects of internationalization differently. The expansion of computer technology, producer services, banking, and finance opened new opportunities for professional and highly skilled groups linked to the global economy. For most professionals, the shift to a service- and information-based society entailed material gains, expanded options, and added status.[40] For working- and some middle-class groups, the same transition represented a deterioration in standards of living and an assault upon the possibility of attaining "the American Dream." Growing income distribution differentials followed internationalization.[41]

Within that setting, symbolic issues acquired prominence. In the largest capitalist nation, most people did not turn to a critique of the system of production to explain economic decline. Instead, they questioned moral fabric. Devoid of historical perspective and propelled by common sense, they focused on a presumed failure of collective character. Diminishing loyalty to country and family, the disappearing work ethic, individualism, and egotism are among the concepts that many Americans use to explain loss of economic power.[42] From whence, the meaning of debates over school prayer, sex education, the family, and flag-burning. From whence, also, the volatility of discourses on abortion.[43]

There is a complex relationship between economic restructuring and perspectives on abortion. Constituencies endorsing pro-life and pro-choice positions are characterized by their internal diversity and, although there is a dearth of research on this subject, there appears to be no direct relationship between either of the two discourses and a particular group. However, pro-life views seem to be especially appealing to large sectors of the population with a weakened economic and political position in North American society.[44] For different reasons, they are also shared by religious leaders and those in self-designated conservative organizations vying for legitimacy.[45]

Pro-choice positions, by contrast, express world views consistent with the goals of intellectuals, professional groups, and liberal organizations. Thus the debate on abortion reflects more than moral concerns over the value of life and the merits of choice; it also mirrors the growing economic polarization in American society. Partly as a result of economic change, class antagonisms have shifted to the realm of morality. The dispute over abortion has become a metaphor for expressing anxieties about social inequality.

There are two intersecting processes at work in that respect. One consists of convergence between pro-life leaders, articulating abstract concepts of morality as a way to consolidate credibility among new constituencies, and people experiencing political and economic losses at the local level. The other process entails a contestation of feminist priorities on the part of the same vulnerable populations. In other words, the appeal of pro-life positions cannot be understood by giving sole attention to the manoeuvres of reactionary political groups. In addition, women's perceptions about the ramification of items at the top of the feminist agenda must be considered.

Changing economic circumstances made problematic the meaning of liberal precepts at the core of the women's movement. At the same time that feminists were espousing women's full participation in the labour force and equal wages for comparable work performed by people of both sexes, the economy was already generating a large number of jobs where women were the preferred workers. These were jobs characterized by low wages and levels of skills, temporary jobs, jobs with diminished benefits, non-unionized jobs. Most women were joining the labour force, moved not by a desire for emancipation but by the need to support families at a time when men's incomes were eroding. In that context, the emphasis on individual choice, personal autonomy, and paid work acquired dubious significance.

Economic restructuring mimicked a conspiracy of reality against theory. Women aspiring to motherhood, and torn by the need to combine domestic work and wage employment, as well as individuals of both sexes losing their economic grip, perceived feminism with ambivalence. Women's work outside the home, and men's diminishing capacity to support families on a single wage, fuelled anxieties about family atomization, the neglect of children, and men's loss of status. The image of women shedding traditional values to succeed on an equal footing with men galvanized those apprehensions. Abortion was perceived not as a precondition to expand women's options, but as the embodiment of self-indulgence.

Anxieties in crescendo at the local level allowed religious leaders and conservative groups to refurbish their own discourses. There is more diversity among the pro-life leadership than is generally acknowledged. Phyllis Schlafly, who led the anti-ERA Campaign, and Randall Terry of Operation Rescue share a commitment to restricted sexual behaviour and the maintenance of gender hierarchies. Both draw freely from a Christian symbolic reserve. Nevertheless, Schlafly stumbled upon the Equal Rights Amendment and abortion as part of her efforts to gain popular support for military programs and personal legitimacy within the Republican Party.[46] She is part of a well-financed network of conservative organizations whose agenda has focused, with deliberation, upon the maintenance of class domination. The pro-life discourse has offered those groups a tool to shift attention away from economic inequality and towards abstract notions of morality.

Terry, by contrast, is a grass-roots organizer whose own trajectory reflects ambivalence extending beyond the issue of abortion. His appeals have been successful to the extent that they echo a yearning for community, the validation of parenthood, and patriarchal relations of reciprocity between men and women. It is among Terry and his followers that the anti-establishment bent of pro-life discourses is most apparent. Without understanding the cleavage within pro-life leadership, we are also unable to apprehend the reason why large numbers of ordinary men and women have adopted positions that appear to be antithetical to their personal interests.

The experience of Sue, a woman I met in a small North American city, illustrates this point. She viewed herself as a feminist when she was a twenty-year-old unwed mother. Twelve years later, she is married and has a newborn baby. She drives a cab because she cannot afford to do otherwise, and hates the job that deprives her of the opportunity to be at home with her children. Her husband works as a mechanic. Their two incomes meet the requirements of a modest life. They have no savings. In answer to my questions, Sue expressed an objection to abortion on demand and leaned towards the pro-life view. She is no longer a feminist. Why? "Well, I don't think feminists are interested in women like me." Sue is not just a casualty of those who are trying to perpetuate oppression on the basis of class and gender. Her position also maintains an embattled relationship with the women's movement. The question is whether the women's movement can articulate a discourse relevant to women like her.

CONCLUSIONS

29 April 1990: Amidst folk music and banners reading "Abortion: The Ultimate Child Abuse," crowds gather at the base of the Washington Monument for a pro-life demonstration. Vice-President Dan Quayle – a politician in search of legitimacy, if there ever was one – addresses over 200,000 people; 135,000 more than those attending a similar event in early 1989. To warm applause, Quayle declares: "Will the American people continue to accept that an unborn child is disposable?" No! Is the resounding answer to the rhetorical question.

The image encapsulates a central point in this essay: throngs of Americans gathering in defence of "life," a concept deceivingly obvious to the majority. A politician eager to improve sagging popularity ratings. A highly polarized ideological climate that prevents the identification, let alone the discussion, of common ground. Who benefits from this state of things?

This essay maintains that pro-choice positions reflect an optimistic view of human nature consistent with democratic ideals. Endorsing reproductive choice is based on the recognition that most women are deserving of trust, that they are responsible individuals who often must opt for less than perfect alternatives after heart-wrenching consideration. Pro-choice views aim at creating a social space for those women.

At the same time, we err in believing that the pro-life movement is but a reflection of reactionary forces bent on maintaining women's subordination. We have been myopic in dismissing qualms surrounding the issue of abortion. Partly as a result, the anti-establishment strand of the pro-life movement has filled the vacuum by capturing those concerns to our unending confusion. But how did we allow those concerns to be spirited away from the feminist agenda in the first place? How can we put them back where they rightly belong?

Answering those questions requires that we critically examine the changing economic foundations of American society. Over the last two decades, industrial restructuring has accentuated class polarization in the United States. The erosion of manufacturing, the decimation of labour unions, and the move of industry to overseas locations have undermined the standards of living of many Americans and changed the terms of the debate over a variety of issues, including abortion. Pro-life positions are part of a broader political discourse that expresses growing class resentments in metaphorical terms.

For the most part, pro-choice discourses have not addressed the changing economic conditions that have confounded the meaning of the liberal agenda as well as the symbolic meaning of abortion rights. What is the significance of choice among undocumented immigrant workers, the spouses of displaced steelworkers, or the inhabitants of regions devastated by the flight of industry? For women in those categories, competition in the labour market – as well as the need to restrict their reproductive capacities – may reflect narrowing, rather than expanding, alternatives. This is a point that has been neglected by analyses exalting the incorporation of women into paid employment – as well as equality under the law – without challenging the underpinnings of the productive system.

Opportunism has characterized the actions of conservative leaders who have appropriated "family," "home," and "life" as part of tactics to gain legitimacy among the politically disfranchised. But they have been successful only to the extent that those terms resonate with vigour at the grass-roots level. The lesson is that motherhood, family, and home matter deeply to women and therefore must be placed at the forefront of the feminist agenda. A refurbished agenda must also make reproductive choice an aspect of a wider array of claims including proper supports for domestic work and child care.

Perhaps, from that vantage point, we would be in a better position to forge an alternative discourse on abortion. That discourse would make a claim on the expansion of choice as well as the enhancement of life. Debating whether life begins at conception or whether fetuses are extension of women's bodies is an exercise in futility, because all decisions in that regard will continue to entail a measure of arbitrariness, uncertainty, and, yes, anguish. Instead, we should inquire about the conditions that make pregnancy and motherhood into a calamity for a large number of women, about the ways in which "the terror of parenthood" can be eliminated, and, finally, about the criteria for erecting a society in which respect for life can truly complement expanding choices.

Equitable treatment under the law is a necessary but not a sufficient condition to create a society consistent with those feminist objectives.

The defence of personal autonomy and individual rights must now expand to include a transformation of the conditions in which women choose. This can only be accomplished by moving away from the characterization of women as a special interest group, and by reframing the question of choice in terms of class, race/ethnicity, and gender.

PART EIGHT

Alternative Visions of a Feminist Future

21 That Which Divides Us; That Which Unites Us

GRETA HOFMANN NEMIROFF

INTRODUCTION

This introduction is neither a disclaimer nor a complaint; rather it is an account of how I organized myself to make the closing remarks with some semblance of coherence at the conference at which the essays in this volume originated, and why I have structured what follows this way. At the conference, I took note of every presentation and of the responses and discussion which followed each offering. The spoken word has different weights and colourations from the written one and, frequently, it was the oral presentation, the response to a comment, the intervention from the floor, which brought the discourse into focus.[1]

While I would like to be able to fulfil my mandate of arriving at "alternative visions of a feminist future," I hope the reader will be satisfied with "alternative glimpses." The themes and subtexts percolating through this conference were all of import to the feminist struggle in Canada, in the United States, and ultimately throughout the world. It is impossible for one person to see in its completeness a "feminist future." For this reason I hope that all wisdom dialectically developed at such conferences will continue to evolve, and that feminist visions of, and strategies for, social transformation will continue to inform the academic discourse of women's studies.

While the main topic of this conference was a retrospective assessment and the articulation of future prospects of the contemporary women's movement in Canada and the United States, there were many subthemes running through the proceedings. Interventions were made from varied sources: individuals, grass-roots organizations, academia, and governmental agencies. In addressing those issues most common to the presenters and respondents, I might inadvertently give less attention to a particular essay or response than is its absolute due. It is my hope that all participants will forgive me, if I have had to sacrifice references to their finer and most delicately calibrated insights in order to give my sense of the whole.

WHOSE CANADA?
WHICH WOMEN'S MOVEMENT?

While it is evident that the subject of this conference, "The Contemporary Women's Movement in Canada and the United States," is important to most Canadian feminists, I do not know how important it is for our American counterparts. The contents of their excellent essays force me to the conclusion of "not very important." While Canadian presenters and commentators made numerous references to American influences on the Canadian women's movements, most of the American presenters concentrated solely on the American situation. This is understandable, since the hegemony under which Canadian women live is primarily formed in response to male power groups south of our shared border. There has been little systemic movement of ideas or ideology southward from Canada, a country whose total population is 10 per cent of our American neighbour's. This asymmetry may be particularly unfortunate for American scholars, who have very little exposure to many of the methodologies developed by Canadian feminist scholars; Canadian feminists often benefit from exposure to American feminist scholarship.

It is not the purpose of this essay to focus on the differing contexts of the experiences and conclusions which divide and unify North American women. Nonetheless, as I listened to the discussions at the conference, I was continually reminded of the asymmetry of our relationship, no matter how much genuine interest our American sisters showed in the Canadian women's movement when we were together. Indeed, Jo Freeman of New York began her elaborate and extemporaneous presentation on the history of the American women's movement with the somewhat complacent remark that she knew "nothing about the Canadian women's movement." Perhaps it was because of this asymmetry that the discussion of the American women's movement was much more dispassionate than that of its Canadian counterpart. Far from home, our differences tend to blur as we absorb the vision others have of us. Much of the intensity at this conference was grounded in intra-Canadian conflicts, confrontations, misunderstandings, and missed opportunities. Indeed, much of the interaction regarding Canada was a reaction to its fragmentation and to the numerous promises which have been betrayed.

One question which nagged at the Canadian presenters was the eternal "What Is Canada?" question: "What Is the Canadian Women's Movement?" We were immersed gently into this preoccupation by an excellent keynote address from Monique Bégin, who introduced herself as "just a person who lived it," a position belied somewhat by the closeness she has had to important events in the histories of Canadian women. She began with a general overview of developments in the Canadian women's movement and provided a candid assessment of the successes and failures of the Royal Commission on the Status of Women. As a person whose own intellectual development regarding women's issues has paralleled the burgeoning of feminist scholarship, Bégin pointed out the important fact that many conceptual tools necessary for a full discussion of women's issues were developed only after the commission had completed its job. Thus, subjects such as violence against women, pornography, health care, and mental health were not addressed within it.

It is instructive to recollect that the attention of early feminist scholarship was not focused on these troublesome subjects. Although books on these issues began to be written in the early 1970s, when community-based groups formed to address rape and other forms of male violence, the Canadian women's movement's first confrontations with patriarchy took place on abortion rights, child care, and work-related issues. Perhaps this was strategic: men of good will would be less likely to be aroused to the guilty defensiveness which often meets the subject of systemic male violence in our society. As one who was there, I recall feminist scholars reluctantly edging our way into the subject of violence against women; it became immeasurably sad and angering as we progressed in our analysis to realize how pervasive misogyny is in our society.

Several Canadian essays offered comparative material on the Canadian and American experiences, although their focus was on Canada. Jill Vickers identified three women's movements in Canada: the federal/English, the French, and the First Nations women. She demonstrated the continuity of women's political action in Canada from the struggle for the vote onwards, through movements of the Left in the 1930s, and the peace movement of the 1950s and 1960s. She has also formulated a theoretical framework for comparing the Canadian and American women's movements on the basis of their relation to the state and their forms of addressing differences.

Naomi Black also covered the Canadian and American women's movements in her essay, "Ripples in the Second Wave: Comparing the Contemporary Women's Movement in Canada and the United States." She attacked a common interpretation of the women's movement which depoliticizes it by situating it as a "ripple" from other movements or from earlier versions of the women's movement. She compared the Canadian and American equal rights movements, characterizing both as struggles against systemic (male) resistance to "enshrining gender equality" in basic human rights guarantees in both countries.

Black's conclusions regarding the efficacy of Canadian feminist coalitions appeared to be in direct opposition to the more optimistic view of Vickers. The Quebec respondents found much to criticize in both presentations. Micheline Dumont of the Collectif Clio considers Vickers's schema inapplicable to Quebec. In a detailed and fascinating sketch of the history of the struggle for women's rights in Quebec, she demonstrated how very different both the history and praxis of feminism are in Quebec and English Canada. Micheline de Sève's response to Naomi Black's essay further reinforced this view. De Sève claimed that most Anglo-Canadians have no idea of what it means to live in Quebec and yet be a Canadian "administratively speaking." To most French Canadians, Canada is not a bi-cultural country, she claims, but a bi-national one. Quebec is the homeland to all Canadian Francophones. Nationalism, she said, "is a crucial dimension" of the Quebec's women's movement, and Quebec's umbrella women's organization, the Fédération des femmes du Québec (FFQ), must be recognized as a national organization in the same way that the National Action Committee on the Status of Women (NAC) already enjoys such recognition. Expressing surprise at the cursory treatment of the Québécois women's movement by Black, she concluded that English-Canadian feminists need a kind of "simultaneous translation" by bilingual Québécoises in order fully to understand the subtleties of the francophone women's movement in Canada.

My own experience as a bilingual Quebec "anglophone" exemplifies so many of the inevitable difficulties and contradictions contained in the words "The Canadian Women's Movement." I sometimes find myself a somewhat unwelcome "Quebecer" in the rest of Canada, because my presence cannot inflate the "participation rate" of "active" Québécoises in a "national" event. Indeed, the very word "national" has different connotations within and outside of Quebec. In Quebec it means Québécois, as in "la question nationale;" the Quebec word for "national" meaning "Canadian" has become "pan-canadien." Within

Quebec I have always been warmly received by my francophone sisters, even though we know that we cannot share nationalist causes with equal fervour, since nationalism of any sort is anathema to me. The latter attitude, on the other hand, makes me a suspicious character among the Brontosauran "protectors" of "anglo-rights." Perhaps that is why Micheline de Sève submitted my candidature as "simultaneous translator."

Both Vickers and Black gave considerable attention to the American women's movement. One key factor which neither essay covered was the effect of population scale on how these respective women's movements developed. While both countries are vast land masses regionally divided, there is perforce a greater multiplicity of means among 250,000,000 than among 25,000,000 people. This is particularly true among women who do not have the resources necessary to communicate an unmediated version of our lives.

Despite the fairly optimistic theorizing and the attitudinal disagreements of white academic women of good will, the message from those presenters who were women of colour, Native women, visible minority women, or working-class women clearly indicated that these factors are extremely divisive in the Canadian women's movement. Glenda Simms reminded us that women of colour are rarely accorded prime time at conferences, being considered even after immigrants, notwithstanding the fact that two-thirds of all immigrants to Canada are from Third World countries and are visible minorities.

One of the most emotional moments of the conference came when Patricia Monture-OKanee responded to Catharine A. MacKinnon's essay on the debate on sexuality and violence in Canada and the United States. Monture-OKanee, a young Mohawk lawyer, gave a short talk explaining why she could not talk to us. She could not speak with the voice of a woman qua woman, she explained, because the "voice I have been given is the voice of a Mohawk woman" whose identity comes from her race. She described how formal education led her into a life of "separation," where she is forced continually to separate her life as a Mohawk woman (with its particular history and responsibilities) from her life as a lawyer responsible to the "white law" which has oppressed her people. "I can't stand up here and just be a woman or feminist for you," she said, "and it hurts me that you keep asking me to do it." Then she left.

The issue of racism was addressed in many essays and contexts, including those dealing with epistemological issues. There is no doubt in my mind that there exists an undefined white feminist hegemony emanating particularly from academic feminists who, after all, are successfully trained double agents operating from the very heart of patriarchal power. While some attention is devoted by white academic feminists to the issues raised by women who consider themselves marginalized, or not at all represented, by the self-defining women's movement in Canada, it is often not much more than the "add colour and stir" variety, a parody of the short shrift accorded women's content in regular university pursuits within the prevailing patriarchal mode.

Roxanna Ng, a participant, commented that "White women must give up ownership of the women's movement and support women of colour." I would have liked to hear a clearer account of what is meant by "ownership." It could mean being spokespersons, having access to better positions or grants, or it could mean that white women should give up all access to the very slim resources available for women's issues in Canada. The question of access to resources, and of the compensatory relinquishing of resources from one beleaguered group to another more beleaguered group, is a very volatile one in the women's movement, as witnessed by the charges and counter-charges of racism that have so preoccupied the Canadian feminist literary scene over the past few years. Few white women will publicly respond to the demand that we "give up our ownership" of the movement, yet I myself do not know what most white progressive women feel under the usual banalities murmured at such moments. I have yet to see a rational and fair public discussion on the subject of "ownership" and the fair sharing of resources between various Canadian and/or Quebec women's groups.

While women of colour, Native women, francophone women in and out of Quebec, immigrant women, lesbians, and working class women – to name a few – each have a discrete agenda in their struggle for self-realization, it is clear to me that all women still have many issues in common, and that collective action is worth struggling for. In her comments, Jacqueline Anderson from Chicago said: "Racism is not my problem; not simply a blot on the good name of America. It's every woman's problem." Canadian feminists cannot smugly allege that all racism is embodied south of the border; nor can we continue to act qua Canadian women without paying strict attention to words such as the ones quoted in the essays of distinguished "minority" feminists. They know where they stand; I hope that "white majority" feminists will develop the courage to examine where we stand and where we are willing to move. I am convinced that Canadian women will remain divided, except as we are attacked by external "enemies," unless we are able to talk frankly of the oppressions which divide us as well as those which unite us.

THE AMERICAN WOMEN'S MOVEMENT

There were several fascinating overviews offered regarding the history and development of the women's movement in the United States. Sara Evans gave a very full and interesting account of the American women's movement of the 1960s. Without so much as a note, Jo Freeman gave an extraordinary, extemporaneous *tour de force* on the Equal Rights Amendment struggle. These presentations did not include comparative data regarding Canada.

However, many of the essays describing the American experience contained theories applicable to the Canadian experience. Jacqueline Anderson's contribution, "Truth, Freedom and Christopher Columbus," focused primarily on the United States. She covered the issues of racism, colonialization, and homophobia in a manner which makes them universally considerable. Marianne Ferber's conclusions regarding women and men in the labour force and the division of household tasks also is generally applicable to Canada, although her statistical base is solely American. Certainly Patricia Fernández Kelly's considerations on the relationship of reproductive ideology and social class is applicable to the Canadian reality as well.

As mentioned above, most Canadian presentations took into account the American reality, thus substantiating their points and enlarging their sources. American presenters did not show the same familiarity with either the Canadian context or our scholarship; nor did they seem to feel the same impulse towards inclusiveness. The character of both Canadian and American feminist scholarship in this respect indicates to me the extent to which the official categories of feminist knowledge are delineated by patriarchal superstructures, in this case the limits imposed by the concept and borders of nation states and notions of power as physical and economic forces. While it may be argued that this is simply the way things are, I do think that feminist scholars must develop an epistemology of inclusion, an imperative to transcend those walls constructed to separate people into arbitrarily designated "interest groups," which may have nothing to do with how women perceive ourselves in this world.

FEMINIST KNOWLEDGE: EPISTEMOLOGICAL TRAPS

Racism

The issue of racism also informed the discourse on knowledge. Numerous presenters referred to the conspicuous absence of women of colour in bibliographies, citations in learned papers and presentations, and in academic departments of women's studies as well as in male-stream disciplines. The ethnocentricity of feminist epistemology was continually revealed. It was striking to hear Patricia Monture-OKanee's description of the violence done to her own beliefs through white education, forcing her into an alienated "double life" of white and Aboriginal truths. She mentioned the ethnocentric assumptions regarding property law as it is taught in law schools; the First Nations notion of the land as a "mother" to whom humans are "responsible" is not on the white establishment's academic agenda. "Do you understand," she asked, "what that has to do with violence? All other people come from someplace else? All have a home to go to? This is all I've got ... the only chance I've got."

Arun Mukherjee elaborated on the issue of racism in scholarship in her essay, "A House Divided: Women of Colour and American Feminist Theory." She discussed the various ways in which women of colour and their concerns have been silenced by white women academics. She moved beyond the obvious visibility of white women in the few decision-making positions in universities and on the boards of journals, to the exclusionary nature of some feminist theory based solely on white women's experience, often excluding citations or other evidence of relevant work by Black scholars. Not only are works by women of colour invisible in most women's studies courses, she argues, but white women's very concept of "experience" is limited to the narrow confines of being white in a sexist, racist, capitalist society. An important issue ignored by white women is their complicity in the system of slavery. The implicit racism and imperialism of various famous white women writers of the past is frequently ignored in the accolades poured upon them by white feminists. Sexism in men is thus implicitly considered worse than racism in women. Mukherjee deplored the treatment of racism as an "emotion" rather than as a convergence of economic and political realities, the contemplation of which should result in theoretical insights. White women must rethink their position, hire Black women for open positions, and formulate anti-racist guidelines along with feminist goals for their publications.

Mariana Valverde, in her essay "Racism and Anti-Racism in Feminist Teaching and Research," also addressed the necessity of white feminists' seeing racism as an integral feminist issue. She acknowledged that this means an enormous task of learning for many women's studies teachers but insisted that "inertia is political" and that the politics of inertia is the politics of privilege. As well as becoming educated in the work of women of colour and "Third-World women," white women's studies teachers must become "conscious of the whiteness of white feminism," and must attempt to reconceptualize idealized feminist figures like Nellie McClung in terms of their racism, rather than simply dismissing their views as the "racism of the time."

It was somewhat frustrating for me to hear only oblique mention of opinions with which I am not familiar. For example, I have never been aware of racism in the few McClung works I have read. I would appreciate some elucidation on this point, as well as a more detailed account of how the history of feminism in Canada has been internally shaped by racist ideology, as Valverde argued. While there is immense importance in her discussion of the definition of sexuality and the values attributed to various forms of sexual expression by white people, it is not clear how racism has been a fundamental factor in the shaping of the Canadian feminist movement. Not even Glenda Simms's excellent discussion of Black women's history, and of the dubious position of "Miss Anne" internalized by a "bunch of middle-aged white middle-class women," pinpoints specifically where or how this racism is actively manifested in feminist scholarship. I think it is essential that a more detailed analysis and explication of these views be undertaken by both white women and women of colour.

The complexity of racism and the dangers of appropriation were well demonstrated when Micheline de Sève asked Glenda Simms if it was easier for her to deal with the Canadian women's movement as a single national movement rather than a bi-national one, or if she shared the view of some Québécoises that they were really the "white Negroes of America" who were forced to "speak white." Simms did not seem to be enthused by this comparison, claiming that the issues facing Black women in Canada must be seen from one national perspective of racism. Lorraine Greaves talked of the need for feminists to challenge ourselves regarding inclusiveness, to ensure mandatory affirmative action within the women's movement. She sees it as an absolute necessity for feminists to address our collective defensiveness when faced with challenges regarding elitism, racism, classism, ablebodyism, heterosexism, or any other "ism" which excludes anyone.

Certainly the issue of exclusion is an important one for white middle class women to face, especially white feminist scholars. The importance of extending our inquiry to an assessment of our own profiteering from racism and classism, however inadvert it may be, cannot be exaggerated. The discussion and the reactions evoked brought to my mind the excellent essay by the feminist philosopher

Marilyn Frye, "On Being White," where she talks of her feelings at understanding the extent to which her entire formation and inter-action with the world have been informed by her "whiteness":

Some of my experience has made me feel trapped and set up so that my actions are caught in a web that connects them inexorably to sources in white privilege and to consequences oppressive to people of color (especially to women of color). Clearly, if one wants to extricate oneself from such a fate or (if the feeling was deceptive) from such a feeling of fatedness, the first rule for the procedure can only be: educate oneself.[2]

Frye concludes that whiteness is much more than pigmentation; it is related to the politics of dominance. Therefore, since whiteness is more than pigmentation, she reasons that one can in fact "disaffiliate" from whiteness in the same way that males sympathetic to feminism can "disaffiliate" from the culture of masculinity. Because white women do live through the exercise of "unwarranted power," no matter how much we consciously shed, we must undertake actions of conscious disloyalty to our very whiteness.[3] Frye suggests one way of achieving this is by refusing to have the children of white men.

In my view there are many other ways in which white feminists can live in actively anti-racist good faith. Our first educational move is to subject ourselves to a personal inventory-taking by which we examine those ways in which we have each gained from race and/or class in our own lives, despite those difficulties we have experienced qua women. Such an analysis should pinpoint where we must con-centrate individually and then systemically in breaking down the racism in that very system which sustains us all, even women of colour. While it is presumptuous for white women to ask women from groups oppressed by racism to behave generously to us, we nonetheless need their help in educating ourselves.

Terms of Definition: Repossessing Knowledge

One of the aspects of this conference which I found most stimulating was its focus on the nature of knowledge and the inappropriateness of many patriarchal terms and ways of organizing knowledge relating to women. One way in which feminist scholarship differs from its masculinist counterpart is in its connection to the women's movement. Margrit Eichler's report on her research on this subject indicates that although it is "not always an easy alliance," it is a strong and healthy one, especially in non-metropolitan regions where feminists are not numerically strong enough to indulge in the luxury of isolated academic feminism.

In tracing her own growing interest and expertise in women's studies since 1971, Jean F. O'Barr outlined a history shared by many feminist scholars of that heady period during the development of women's studies courses, then programs, and then initiatives towards "mainstreaming and balancing all curriculum" developed throughout North America. She traced how limiting and inappropriate the regular male-stream disciplines are for the study of women's experience. She described the "synergistic relationship" which developed between feminist scholars in different disciplines as they set out to reconstruct knowledge, the ongoing project for feminist scholarship. Initially women's studies scholars had to learn and add new information to the existing body of knowledge about women; they also had to review existing information and correct many ideas, and most of all they had to rethink many of their most cherished basic epistemological assumptions. Currently feminist scholarship has developed beyond the "undifferentiated" notion of women, as the interventions on racism in this very conference indicated. Indeed, O'Barr emphasizes that women experience a "multiple, shifting and often self-contradictory identity," and that in order fully to appreciate and understand the complexity of women's experience, we must scrutinize the past.

At the root of O'Barr's discourse is the understanding that feminist scholarship is a potent tool for the empowerment of women. In the discussion period she elaborated on her opinion that feminism must engage in contradiction and respond to it by developing a group of interrelated feminist movements, rather than one monolithic women's movement.

Lorraine Greaves criticized the locus of women's studies scholarship in both Eichler's and O'Barr's essays as too narrowly confined to the elite university environment. For example, there is much women's studies scholarship carried on in community colleges, but this kind of scholarship is often marginalized or dismissed by university researchers as being "too applied." Research is not considered an important part of community college teaching. There is also much community-focused research undertaken by various women's organizations. Greaves identified a problem with the language of academic feminist research: it is too esoteric for many feminists and based on many presumptions of prior knowledge not to be found beyond the confines of the academy.

In order to combat some of this reduction of access to important feminist research, Greaves advocated the "freeing of speech among women" beyond print to other media that are more accessible. On the other hand, Greaves also expressed the view that the entire conference was not sufficiently geared to examining fundamental questions regarding the nature of the feminist movement, feminist activism, and academic feminism. While she did not speculate on the reasons for this omission, I would venture that one reason may be the desire to maintain unity where subject matter can be divisive. On the whole, community college or adult education teachers or community-based researchers did not appear to be represented at this conference. Perhaps their presence would have exhumed some of the contradictory elitism one finds in university-based feminist research. Although Greaves advocated the inclusion of all women in the making of our movement, it was not clear if she thought that all women would be interested in, or able to participate in, active research.

One explanation of the tendency of university-based women to regard the academy as the locus of the most meaningful feminist scholarship may be found in the excellent book by Nadya Aisenberg and Mona Harrington, *Women of Academe: Outsiders in the Sacred Grove*. They suggest that in order to pursue university careers, most women undergo a process of transforming their identities in which there is a "constant skirmishing" between "professional practicalities and intellectual engagement."[4] Women who "make it" in the university environment do so at a greater cost than their male counterparts for whom such career success is deemed "natural." In addition to learning their disciplines and jumping through the appropriate hoops for advancement and tenure, women have to learn the politics and the rules of the game: "to become a professional, for women, is not simply to acquire a marketable skill, but to acquire a dignified empowering identity, frequently for the first time."[5] While university women speak in a different voice from their male colleagues, they also often speak in a different voice from their feminist colleagues in the areas identified by Greaves.

University women face a constant struggle for validation within the academy, where their preoccupations do not fit in with the preconceived canons of their male-defined disciplines. Often the root of their interest is a commitment to social transformation and egalitarianism. It is ironic for feminist scholars in universities sometimes to find themselves situated by non-university feminist scholars where they themselves define some of their male colleagues: as an actively disconfirming and "maternalistic" force. Within the university women are expected to "combine commitment to shared institutional values with loyalty to the critical experience and memories of an outsider."[6] They are also often urged by other academic feminists to take on positions of authority in order to pave the way for other women and for feminist discourse in the academy. Outside the university they are expected to share feminist values with a loyalty to feminist praxis and equality. University-based feminists engaging in community-based activism may be faced with contradictions and divided loyalties which are difficult to reconcile. To add to the burden, they may also be harried, overextended women trying to do three full-time jobs well. Nonetheless, there is a real validity in the critique of university exclusiveness, and it is a critique which must be openly addressed in various forums.

There were many fascinating feminist attacks against the traditional epistemological boundaries set within the academic disciplines. Marjorie Cohen gave an interesting account of how over time the Canadian feminist analysis regarding women's economic oppression began to broaden beyond an exclusive focus on women and poverty, since it became increasingly clear that all aspects of women's oppression are interconnected and "related to the way in which society is constructed." This increasing consciousness of the structural nature of women's oppression helped feminists understand that the theoretical bases of economic decisions affecting Canadian women are not irrefutable truths but simply "macho-economic" theories based on serving the interests of some men. These theories had to be countered through economic analysis made from women's point of view.

The usefulness of a collective feminist analysis become increasingly clear when the free trade negotiations began with the u.s. in the mid-1980s. Canadian feminist organizations analysed and published studies on the impact of this agreement on Canadian women, focusing not only on public assistance programs but on the impact of the "deal" on women's employment and access to better jobs. For this initiative there was a strong connection between feminist researchers and "front-line" feminist groups. Cohen said that although the anti–free trade forces lost that battle, Canadian women have now served notice that we are willing to develop the intellectual tools necessary to counter "macho-economics."

Micheline Dumont offered a fascinating critique of some of the assumptions underlying the conventional conceptual tools used in the study of history. She did not consider the notion of "waves" as in "waves of feminism" to be useful in considering women's history. Women's time is different, she claimed, and the insistence on chronology, clear succession, and synchronization is not applicable. "Sometimes historical truth is disorderly," she said. "The dates when feminists have succeeded are well known. However, compared to changing attitudes and mentalities, revising the laws is an easy task. Not a single date can be found for that kind of change." Women's history is about changing attitudes, although facts are also important, she claimed, illustrating her point with a fascinating thumbnail sketch of the struggle for women's rights in Quebec.

Both Christine Overall and Catharine MacKinnon raised questions about the methodological biases inherent in the discourse on reproductive rights and rape. Overall's thoughtful essay analyses the concept of "reproductive right" in itself, introducing into the discourse such concepts as the "right not to reproduce" and the "entitlement not to have to engage in forced reproductive labour." The naming of these rights, which many women have felt for centuries without having the words to describe them, is an important addition to the language of feminist activism as well as the terminology of feminist scholarship.

Overall is especially effective in her discussion of "fetal rights," where she claims that "fetuses are the only group of entities that have been given entitlement under Canadian law to the medical use of the bodies of adult persons." These definitions are immeasurably important to women in the battle for abortion rights. In retrospect it is fascinating to recall the false sense of security so many of us had about our "enshrined" rights to abortion in May 1989, at the time of this conference, during that wonderful hiatus after the Canadian Supreme Court had struck down previous abortion legislation in January 1988. It was only three months after the conference that the Chantal Daigle case fully revealed to Canadian women how very vulnerable we are to the will of the pregnancy-enforcing lobby.[7] Overall was especially prescient in her warning regarding the co-optation and transformation of feminist language into the language of "reproductive rights" to support lucrative commodification of fetuses for infertile women. By showing us where conservative interests have brought together the unlikely subjects of reproductive technology and abortion rights, Overall in fact foreshadowed much of the discourse surrounding the Daigle case, where the benefits and costs for women were consistently confused with the function of women in dispensing reproductive services to a pro-natalist state.

Catharine MacKinnon's thoughtful analysis of the problems imposed by the new rape legislation in Canada poses fundamental questions. She demonstrates that the term "assault" may be inappropriate for rape, since violence can claim a gender neutrality, while rape or sex cannot be described in that way. She advocates the reintroduction of the term "sexual" with all forms of assault in order to reclaim the nature of the crime. Consent is the essential factor in all forms of rape, and so the crime of rape should be redefined as "intercourse with force."

Another issue relating to women and knowledge was the recurring discussion of "credentialism." While many speakers and interveners stressed that there was much to be learned and much valid research being conducted outside of officially "accredited" institutions, members of the privileged white academic bourgeoisie were warned that, while it was all very well for them to spurn male-stream knowledge, credentialization is often the first step of empowerment for oppressed women.

The theme of women's resourcelessness tolled throughout this conference. In terms of women's knowledge this means the under-capitalization of women's organizations, women's studies programs, and women's presses and journals, and our lack of any real ongoing access to the media.

The discourse on knowledge reflected most of the central areas of unity and division within the entire conference. While on the one hand it is clear that there is a large shared history of coming to intellectual consciousness within the area of women's studies and community-based feminism, there is also a certain mistrust and divisiveness brought on by the hierarchical nature and arrangement of those institutions and organizations which house feminist scholars and researchers. The attribution of values in the patriarchy determines the hierarchy; hence, one of the factors which divides women is the extent to which we are validated, empowered, and economically supported by men in power. We can be united only in so far as we understand the nature of the contradictions in which we live and in so far as we are able to admit them to ourselves and one another. We must collectively find ways of flourishing within these contradictions through choices which reflect good faith.

WHERE DO WE GO FROM HERE?

While there may not have been as much interchange as desired at this conference on the American and Canadian women's movements, there was certainly a mirroring quality in some of the summary statements on the state of the struggle. Micheline Dumont quoted the words of the Ligue des droits des femmes in the 1940s: "Our full work has not yet begun." Jo Freeman said, about the Equal Rights Amendment, "The struggle is not over; it has barely begun." It is this urgency, this knowledge that there is so much left to be done in the advocacy of women's rights in every realm of our experience, that should inform our individual and collective choices of political engagement in the future.

This conference provided an important opportunity for the kind of forum that gets things moving, that makes people crystallize, share, and often revise their ideas as a result of the dialogue in which they participate. The conference covered a breadth of ideas, and there was much original thought available to the participants. However, the old patriarchal authoritarian "talking heads" model was the pattern of interaction at the conference. The experts hold forth, and the rest listen and pose a few questions. The only opportunity for lateral discussion was at those meals we shared, where the topics of conversation were most likely to be determined by the composition of the party at particular tables.

We must learn to design more interactional feminist meetings whose structure is appropriate to dialogue and collective exploration. Sometimes there seemed to be a "tension of credentialism" about who is most worth hearing. What about "ordinary mortals" who work in the front lines in our community? Where is their voice, the necessary ingredient to complete our theoretical speculations? Is it possible to present research and scholarship in the kind of language which more adequately reflects the unity of feminist scholarship with everyday feminist experience? I think it is possible to build those bridges at conferences. It is important that conferences experiment with models of appropriate discourse to encourage dialogue between all feminists. Presenters should be asked to focus on their *modes* of communication as well as their material, working to achieve a unity of theory and praxis.

It is glib to tax with these omissions the conference organizers who must fit so much activity into so little time. However, it should be said that Third-World North America, an important locus for feminist intervention, was not accorded sufficient attention in this conference. Neither were the issues of our founding peoples in Canada, the First Nations, and the Québécoises. There was little discussion of lesbianism and compulsory heterosexism. While it is difficult to fulfil all these needs in a single conference, not addressing these concerns renders organizers vulnerable to accusations of oppressing others. Including these concerns, on the other hand, could evoke accusations of co-opting the causes of others.

These are all potentially divisive issues, whether they are ignored or overtly addressed. We must not become disillusioned and hopeless at our difficulties at achieving unity. No group of men has been sufficiently foolhardy to attempt to embrace their entire gender in one homogeneous consensus (except, perhaps, misogyny) and political will. Rather, they have always created various echelons of "the other" to be turned into enemy or ally. Women are struggling for something untried and for new forms of interaction, and we have a right to our mistakes and problems.

A conference organized to address those matters which most divide us would have to be planned in such a way that all participants would get the time and space to listen, to learn, and to respond directly to one another. There would have to be a shared will to deal with feelings of defensiveness and rejection and to try to avoid personalizing criticism and accusing one another. This is a risky business which requires a high degree of courage and trust, as well as the desire to engage viscerally with others.

Most of the presenters at this conference are engaged in education within or out of school. It is of the utmost importance that we share our ideas and highlight the important issues raised in this conference for our students. I think this is especially important for those of us working with young women who think that the battle is won. They must be exposed to the process of consciousness-raising so important in understanding that women still have a long road not only to equality, but towards identifying and celebrating those areas of discourse and experience which unify us and resolving those inequities which divide us.

It is important, as we redefine the world for ourselves, that we differentiate clearly between solidarity and unanimity. Women have been very good at rallying with great immediacy and solidarity when there are obvious enemies and issues for struggle. We have more difficulty with the long-term struggle. To this end, we must develop coalitions on the numerous issues which concern us all, such as classism, racism, heterosexism, ethnicity, and all the injustices women suffer. None of us has the understanding, the skill, or the inclination to fight on all fronts. What feminists of good faith must do, then, is to identify their individually chosen arenas of struggle and work from there to form meaningful coalitions, and thence strong networks of solidarity.

The struggle for solidarity in this world is a difficult one requiring the willingness to identify common cause, the willingness to give up privilege, and the willingness to action. We must not forget Mariana Valverde's dictum that "inertia is political ... the politics of inertia is the politics of privilege." Feminist educators have an obligation not only to study, to communicate, and to learn but also to become dynamic examples of the possibility of unifying theory and praxis with the will for solidarity.

Patricia Monture-OKanee concluded her talk with these words: "A Nation is not conquered until the hearts of its women are on the ground. My heart is not on the ground." In solidarity with her passion and her example, we must all undertake the homework of an unflinching analysis of our own roles in the global network of injustice. We must further strategize for modes of systemic redress. Thus in our comings together and our partings, we will forge the continuity and solidarity to keep all our hearts off the ground.

Notes

CHAPTER ONE

1 The sole exception was Marjorie Heins, who presented her paper somewhat earlier in the academic year, as a distinguished visitor to the
Centre for American Studies at the University of Western Ontario.
2 This last reference is, of course, from Gloria Steinem, *Outrageous Acts
and Everyday Rebellions* (NY, 1983).
3 Nancy F. Cott, *The Grounding of Modern Feminism* (New Haven 1987), 3, 283.
4 Sheila Jeffreys, *The Spinster and Her Enemies: Feminism and Sexuality
1880–1930* (London 1985).
5 *City of Richmond* v. *J.A. Croson Company* 109 S.Ct. 706 (1989).
6 For a more detailed discussion, see *Edwin Roberts* v. *Her Majesty the Queen
in Right of Ontario and the Ministry of Health*, 10 Canadian Human Rights
Reporter at D/6353 (1989), (Ont. Board of Inquiry, C. Backhouse).
7 *California Federal Savings and Loan* v. *Guerra* 479 U.S. 272 (1987).
8 *Roe* v. *Wade* 410 U.S. 113, 93 S.Ct. 756 (1973); *R.* v. *Morgentaler*, [1988] 1
SCR 30; Report of the Committee on the Operation of the Abortion Law
(Ottawa 1977).
9 Shalumith Firestone, *The Dialectic of Sex* (NY 1970); Marge Piercy, *Woman
on the Edge of Time* (NY 1976).

CHAPTER TWO

1 *Report of the Royal Commission on the Status of Women in Canada* (Ottawa
1970).

2 *Toronto Star*, 8 December 1970.

3 In addition to material found in subsequent notes, see Nancy Adamson, Linda Briskin, and Margaret McPhail, *Feminist Organizing for Change: The Contemporary Women's Movement in Canada* (Toronto 1988), chapters 2, 5, 7 and appendix A; Sylvia Bashevkin, *Toeing the Lines: Women and Party Politics in English Canada* (Toronto 1985), chapter 2; Florence Bird, *Ann Francis: An Autobiography* (Toronto and Vancouver 1974); Sandra Burt, "Women's Issues and the Women's Movement in Canada since 1970," in A. Cairns and C. Williams, *The Politics of Gender, Ethnicity and Language in Canada* (Ottawa 1986), 111–179; The Clio Collective, *Quebec Women: a History* (Toronto 1987); Penney Kome, *Women of Influence: Canadian Women and Politics* (Toronto 1985), 67–99; Judy LaMarsh, *Memoirs of a Bird in a Gilded Cage* (Toronto 1969), chapter 10; Alison Prentice, Paula Bourne, Gail Cuthbert Brandt, Beth Light, Wendy Mitchinson, and Naomi Black, *Canadian Women: A History* (Toronto 1988); Barbara Roberts, "Women's Peace Activism in Canada," in Linda Kealey and Joan Sangster, eds., *Beyond the Vote: Canadian Women and Politics* (Toronto 1989), 276–308; and Carolle Simard, "Les Femmes dans l'État," in Y. Bélanger and Dorval Brunelle, eds., *L'Ère des Libéraux: Le Pouvoir fédéral de 1963 à 1984* (Quebec 1988), 357–381.

4 It was created by Order in Council PC 1967–312, approved by the Governor-General on 16 February 1967. The Terms of Reference appear at the beginning of the *Report of the Royal Commission on the Status of Women in Canada*.

5 One such example is E. Forbes, compiler, *With Enthusiasm and Faith: History of the Canadian Federation of Business and Professional Women's Clubs, 1930–1972* (Ottawa 1974), 95–107.

6 Margaret Mead and Frances Balgley Kaplan, eds., *American Women: The Report of the President's Commission on the Status of Women and Other Publications of the Commission* (New York 1965).

7 Naomi Black, "The Canadian Women's Movement: The Second Wave," in Sandra Burt, Lorraine Code, and Lindsay Dorney, eds., *Changing Patterns: Women in Canada* (Toronto 1988), 80–102.

8 First elected in 1961, Kirkland-Casgrain served in different portfolios from 1962 to 1973. She became a symbol for Quebec women by sponsoring Bill 16, in 1964, giving married women legal capacity.

9 Cerise Morris, "Determination and Thoroughness: The Movement for a Royal Commission on the Status of Women in Canada," *Atlantis* 5, no. 2 (1980): 1–21.

10 Further to the Mulroney government's first budget on 23 May 1985, universal old age pensions were to be partially de-indexed. Although a majority of senior citizens had consistently voted for the Progressive Conservatives through the years, their unexpected, rapid, and general

mobilization reached such proportions that the government backtracked on 27 June, a very short period of time indeed for an immensely popular new government.

11 The directors of the Women's Bureau (Department of Labour) since its foundation have included: Marion V. Royce, 7 Sept. 1954–1966; Jessica Findlay, 23 Jan. 1967–25 March 1968; Sylva M. Gelber, 15 Oct. 1968–1975; Blanche Borkovic, Sept. 1976–June 1979 (with the title of Head); Ratna Ray, July 1979–1984; Linda Geller-Schwartz, 26 March 1985–Jan. 1989, temporarily replaced by Paula Bernet.

12 In 1964, for example, immediately before the so-called second wave of feminism, the bureau released solid documents entitled respectively: *Job Training for the Mature Woman Entering or Re-entering the Labour Force*; *Les Conséquences de la distinction traditionnelle entre les emplois masculins et les emplois féminins dans notre société*; and *Fields of Work for Women: Physical Sciences, Earth Sciences, Mathematics*.

13 Morris, "Determination and Thoroughness," 19.

14 John Humphrey decided at the end that he could not sign a report which advocated quotas as a measure of correction, although he agreed with our analysis.

15 MacGill's separate statement (she did not want to weaken the report by signing a minority report), which appears on p. 429 of the report, recommended that abortion be left as the sole decision of the woman and as a private matter outside of any legal framework.

16 House of Commons Debates, 28 January 1975, 2685.

17 "Really in this case (abortion) I think that it should be essentially the women who would have the louder say in this because they are the ones who are carrying the foetus." Pierre Elliott Trudeau, *Conversation with Canadians* (Toronto 1972), 38.

18 We recommended the appointment of two women from each province to the Senate, when there were vacancies, more women judges, and the amalgamation of women's political associations within their respective political parties (*Report of the Royal Commission on the Status of Women in Canada*, 414–15).

19 Texts by Margaret Benston, from Vancouver, or Marlene Dixon, then living in Montreal.

20 *Report of the Royal Commission on the Status of Women in Canada*, 226.

21 The first university courses on women were offered in Canada in 1970, with historian Natalie Davis at the University of Toronto and sociologist Greta Nemiroff, who co-taught with philosopher Prudence Allen, at Concordia University in Montreal. At Carleton University, historian Deborah Gorham started a course on "Women in Society" in 1971. At the University of Ottawa, professor of literature Marie-Laure Girou-Swiderski taught her first officially feminist course in 1978. (Somer

Brodribb and Micheline de Sève, *Women's Studies in Canada*, RFR/DRF (Toronto 1987).

22 Reviews of the literature, background research papers from secondary sources, and original research projects were written by staff as well as by outside consultants. The commission published eleven of the thirty-four studies completed for us.

23 Lionel Tiger, *Men in Groups* (NY 1969).

24 The ministers for the status of women have included Robert K. Andras, minister of consumer and corporate affairs, 7 May 1971–30 November 1971; Bryce Mackasey, minister of manpower and immigration, 1 December 1971–26 November 1972; John Munro, minister of national health and welfare, 27 November 1972–7 August 1974; Marc Lalonde, minister of national health and welfare, 8 August 1974–3 June 1979; David MacDonald, minister of social development, 4 June 1979–2 March 1980; Lloyd Axworthy, minister of employment and immigration, 3 March 1980–21 September 1981; Judith Erola, minister of state (mines), then minister of consumer and corporate affairs, 22 September 1981–9 September 1984; Walter McLean, secretary of state, 17 September 1984–29 June 1986; Barbara McDougall, minister of state (privatization and regulatory affairs), then minister of employment and immigration, from 30 June 1986 to 30 February 1990; Mary Collins, 30 February 1990 to the present.

25 Robin F. Badgley, Denyse Fortin-Caron, and Marion G. Powell, *Committee on the Operation of the Abortion Law* (Ottawa 1977). This committee had been appointed by the Trudeau government in September 1975 to deflect some of the anger of organized medicine at minister of justice Otto Lang and his criticisms of physicians performing (too many) abortions. The report was tabled in March 1977.

26 Sue Findlay and Melanie Randall, eds., *Feminist Perspectives on the Canadian State*, RFR/DRF 17, no. 3 (Sept. 1988).

27 See, in particular, Sue Findlay, "Feminist Struggles with the Canadian State, 1966–88," ibid. One has the feeling that only the Women's Programme of the Department of the Secretary of State "did something" for women. It is true that this locus defined itself by a feminist activism which surely sent shock waves elsewhere in the bureaucracy, educating people and speeding up action. But numerous individual women, and some men, in other government offices, who, alone or in small, almost secret networks, used any opportunities to exercise a reformist feminist role, also made an important contribution to social change.

28 Rosalie Silberman Abella, *Equality in Employment: A Royal Commission Report* (Ottawa 1984).

29 *R. v. Morgentaler*, [1988] 1 SCR 30.

30 House of Common Debates, 9 March 1971, 4106.

CHAPTER THREE

1 Samuel Clark, J. Paul Grayson, and Linda Grayson, *Prophecy and Protest: Social Movements in Twentieth-Century Canada* (Toronto 1975), 373.

2 The "second wave" periodization only applies to the movement which relates to the federal state. Earlier manifestations of the Native women's movement have not become visible in current feminist scholarship; the Quebec movement's "first wave" lasted until 1940.

3 My colleague Patricia Smart, who was involved in the Waffle, notes that its members did not see themselves as New Left, which they viewed as American in nature. Clearly the Waffle *was* part of the international renewal of the non-communist Left. In Canada, however, it was in opposition to a largely non-Marxist tradition. In consequence, it was significantly more Marxist than its u.s. counterpart. I have retained the terminology "New Left," although it is clear that the Waffle movement was quite distinct from its u.s. and European counterparts. There was also a u.s.-style New Left in Canada prior to the development of the Waffle. The evolution of the Waffle as an anti-American force was in opposition to it. Jim Laxer, "The Americanization of the Canadian Student Movement," in Ian Lumsden, ed., *Close the Forty-Ninth Parallel* (Toronto 1960), 275–86.

4 Jill Vickers, "Politics as if Women Mattered: The Institutionalization of the Canadian Women's Movement and Its Impact on Federal Politics, 1965–1988," Association for Canadian Studies in Australia and New Zealand, 1988 Conference, Canberra, Australia, June, 1988; Lynn MacDonald, "Evolution of the Women's Movement in Canada. Part 1", *Branching Out* 6, no. 1 (1979); and Joan Thro Richardson, "The Structure of Organizational Instability: The Women's Movement in Montreal, 1974–1977," Ph.D. thesis, New School for Social Research 1985.

5 Micheline Dumont, "The Origins of the Women's Movement in Quebec," in this volume.

6 Richardson, "The Structure of Organizational Instability."

7 Caroline Andrew, "Women and the Welfare State," *Canadian Journal of Political Science* 17, no. 4 (1984); Vickers, "Politics as if Women Mattered"; Vickers, "Feminist Approaches to Women in Politics," in Linda Kealey and Joan Sangster, eds., *Beyond the Vote: Canadian Women and Politics* (Toronto 1989).

8 Monique Bégin, "Debates and Silences – Reflections of a Politician," *Daedalus* 117, no. 4, (Fall, 1988): 343–9.

9 Nancy Adamson, Linda Briskin, and Margaret McPhail, *Feminist Organizing for Change: The Contemporary Women's Movement in Canada* (Toronto 1988), 53. These authors assert an ideological distinction between "institutionalized" and "grass-roots" groups which ignores the ideological diversity in nac and the ffq.

10 Women Unite Collective, *Women Unite* (Toronto 1972), 9.

11 Bonnie Kreps, "Radical Feminism!" in *Women Unite*, 75.

12 Ibid., 74–5.

13 Lucy Garretson, "American Women in Politics: Culture, Structure and Ideology," in Dana Raphael, ed., *Being Female: Reproduction, Power and Change* (The Hague 1975).

14 Richardson, "The Structure of Organizational Instability."

15 Chris Appelle, "The New Parliament of Women," MA thesis, Carleton University 1987, 26.

16 Ibid., passim.

17 Richardson, "The Structure of Organizational Instability," 28, 29.

18 Roberta Hamilton and Michele Barrett, *The Politics of Diversity* (Montreal 1986), 2, 11.

19 Ibid., 4.

20 Lynn McDonald, "Evolution of the Women's Movement in Canada. Part 1," 39.

21 Gillian Riddington, personal communication, April 1988.

22 Andrew, "Women and the Welfare State."

23 Frances Fox Piven, "Women and the State: Ideology, Power and the Welfare State," *Socialist Review* 74 (1984): 14.

24 Interestingly, it is in the area of services created by feminists to help alleviate the effects of rape and battering that a more critical appraisal of state involvement has emerged.

25 Richardson, "The Structure of Organizational Instability," 28.

26 Adamson et al, *Feminist Organizing for Change*, 179.

27 Cerise Morris, "Pressuring the Canadian State for Women's Rights: The Role of the National Action Committee," *Alternate Routes* (Ottawa 1983); Appelle, "The New Parliament of Women"; Vickers, "Politics as if Women Mattered."

28 Adamson et al, *Feminist Organizing for Change*.

29 Clio Collective, *Quebec Women: A History*, trans. Roger Gannon and Rosalind Gill (Toronto 1987), 364.

30 Marlene Dixon, "Where Are We Going?" in Edith Altbach, ed., *From Feminism to Liberation* (London 1971).

31 Ibid., 53, 56.

32 Ellen Willis, "Radical Feminism and Feminist Radicalism," in *The Sixties without Apology; Social Text* 3, no. 3 and 4, no. 1 (Spring-Summer, 1984).

33 Richardson, "The Structure of Organizational Instability," 14, 15.

34 Francie Ricks, George Matheson, and Sandra W. Pyke, "Women's Liberation: A Case Study of Organizations for Social Change," *Canadian Psychologist* 18 (Jan. 1972).

35 Ibid., 32, 33.

36 Ibid. Kreps described this group in somewhat different terms. See Anne Koedt, Ellen Levine, and Anita Rapone, eds., *Radical Feminism* (NY 1973).

37 Richardson, "The Structure of Organizational Instability"; Ricks et al., "Women's Liberation."

38 Dixon, "Women's Liberation: Opening Chapter Two," *Canadian Dimension* 10, no. 8 (June 1975): 57, 58–60, 61.

39 Dixon, "Where Are We Going?" 61.

40 Stanley Aronowitz, "When the New Left Was New," in *The Sixties Without Apology*, 19.

41 Ibid., 21.

42 Ibid., 24, 32.

43 Tong, 1988.

44 Ellen Willis, "Radical Feminism and Feminist Radicalism," in *The Sixties without Apology*, 94, 95.

45 Belden Fields, "French Maoism," in *The Sixties without Apology*.

46 Richardson, "The Structure of Organizational Instability," 411.

47 Jo Freeman, *The Politics of Women's Liberation* (NY 1975), 143.

48 I use "socialist feminist" without the hyphen to identify feminism with socialist parties, unions, etc. not the current academic hybrid of Marxist feminism and radical feminism.

49 M.L. Carden, *The New Feminist Movement* (NY 1974), 49 (my emphasis).

50 Donna Hawhurst and Sue Morrow, *Living Our Visions: Building Feminist Community* (Tempe, Arizona 1984).

51 Ibid, 73.

52 Jill Vickers, "Feminist Approaches to Women in Politics," in Kealey and Sangster, eds. *Beyond the Vote*.

53 Joan Sangster, *Dreams of Equality: Women on the Canadian Left, 1920–1950* (Toronto 1989).

54 Kay Macpherson, "The Seeds of the Seventies," *Canadian Dimension* 10 (June 1975): 101.

55 Sharleen Bannon, "The Women's Bureau Is Twenty-One," *Labour Gazette* (1975).

56 MacPherson, "The Seeds of the Seventies," 10.

57 Kay Macpherson and Meg Sears, "The Voice of Women: A History," in Gwen Matheson, eds., *Women in the Canadian Mosaic* (Toronto 1976), 72.

58 Clio Collective, *Quebec Women*, 286.

59 Muriel Duckworth, "Voice of Women Dialogue," *Atlantis* 6 (Spring, 1987): 172.

60 Macpherson and Sears, *"The Voice of Women"*, 86.

61 Duckworth, "Voice of Women Dialogue," 173.

62 Macpherson and Sears, "The Voice of Women," 88.

63 Sangster, *Dreams of Equality*, 1989; Kealey and Sangster, eds., *Beyond the Vote*.
64 Ibid., 108.
65 For this paragraph, see John Manley, "Women and the Left in the 1930's: The Case of the Toronto CCF Women's Joint Committee," *Atlantis* 5 (Spring, 1980):, 103, 108, 110, 112, 116.
66 Ibid., 101.
67 Laxer, "Americanization of the Canadian Student Movement."
68 National Archives of Canada (NAC), Manuscript Group (MG) 28–IV-I, vol. 446, Waffle 1969 Convention.
69 NAC, MG 28–IV-I, vol. 446, Waffle 1969 Convention.
70 NAC, MG 28–IV-I, vol. 1, Waffle Conference Agenda Study Papers, 1970.
71 NAC, MG 28–IV-I, vol. 446, Ontario Waffle 1970–72.
72 NAC, MG 28–IV-I vol. 446, Ontario Waffle 1970–72 (my emphasis).
73 NAC, MG 28–IV-I, vol. 446, Saskatchewan-Manitoba Waffle Resolutions 1970.
74 NAC, MG 28–IV-I, vol. 446, Waffle-Ontario Debate, 1971–72.
75 NAC, MG 28–IV-I, vol. 446, *Waffle News*.
76 Jean Burgess, "Power Is Not Electoral," *Branching Out* 4, no. 5 (1977).

CHAPTER FOUR

1 See Sara M. Evans, *Born for Liberty: A History of Women in America* (NY 1989), chapters 10 and 11.
2 Elaine Tyler May, *Homeward Bound: American Families in the Cold War Era* (NY 1989).
3 See Leila Rupp and Verta Taylor, *Survival in the Doldrums: The American Women's Rights Movement, 1945 to the 1960s* (NY 1987).
4 Amy Swerdlow, "Ladies' Day at the Capitol: Women Strike for Peace versus HUAC," *Feminist Studies* 8 (1982): 493–520.
5 Ibid., 510.
6 Helena Lopata, *Occupation: Housewife* (NY 1971), 376.
7 The following account is based on Cynthia E. Harrison, "A 'New Frontier' for Women: The Public Policy of the Kennedy Administration," *Journal of American History* 67 (1960): 630–46; and Jo Freeman, *The Politics of Women's Liberation: A Case Study of an Emerging Social Movement and Its Relation to the Policy Process* (NY 1975), 52–3.
8 Harrison, "A 'New Frontier' for Women," 640.
9 Betty Friedan, *The Feminine Mystique* (NY 1963).
10 See May, *Homeward Bound*, for a discussion of these letters.
11 Rupp and Taylor, *Survival in the Doldrums*, 176–7.
12 *New York Times*, Editorial, 21 August 1965.
13 Judith Hole and Ellen Levine, *Rebirth of Feminism* (NY 1971), 84.

14 Freeman, *Politics of Women's Liberation*, 73–4.
15 See Sara Evans, *Personal Politics: The Roots of Women's Liberation in the Civil Rights Movement and the New Left* (NY 1979).
16 See Nancy Cott, *The Grounding of Modern Feminism* (New Haven 1987).
17 For example, the art of Judy Chicago, or the writings of Carol Gilligan and Nancy Chodorow.
18 John D'Emilio, *Sexual Politics, Sexual Communities: The Making of a Homosexual Minority in the U.S., 1940–1970* (Chicago 1983), 236.
19 Arvonne S. Fraser, "Insiders and Outsiders: Women in the Political Arena," in Irene Tinker, ed., *Women in Washington: Advocates for Public Policy* (Beverly Hills 1983), 122.

CHAPTER FIVE

1 Karen Offen, "Defining Feminism: A Comparative Historical Approach," *Signs* 14, (1988): 119–57.
2 Ibid., 153.
3 Sara Evans, *Born for Liberty* (NY 1989), 264.
4 Nancy Partner, as cited in Carroll Smith-Rosenberg, "Writing History: Language, Class, and Gender," in Theresa de Lauretis, ed., *Feminist Studies: Critical Studies* (Bloomington, Indiana 1986), 31.
5 See Micheline Dumont, "The Influence of Feminist Perspectives on Historical Research Methodology," in Winnie Tomm, ed., *The Effects of Feminist Approaches on Research Methodologies* (Waterloo 1989), 111–29.
6 One recent example: in Nancy Adamson, Linda Briskin, and Margaret McPhail, *Feminist Organizing for Change: The Contemporary Women's Movement in Canada* (Toronto 1988), Quebec is mentioned three times, each mention specifying that it will not be considered.
7 Other Quebec feminist magazines have included: *RAIF* (since 1973); *Des luttes et des rires de femmes* (1978–1981); *La Gazette des femmes* (since 1979); and *La Vie en rose* (1980–85).
8 One example is the disappearance of the debate on the "salary for domestic work" from issues discussed among feminists. Another one is abortion, of course.
9 Micheline de Sève stated the main thrust of these debates in *Le Féminisme libertaire* (Montreal 1985).
10 Collectif Clio, *Histoire des femmes au Québec depuis quatre siècles* (Montreal 1982); translated as *Quebec Women: A History* (Toronto 1987).
11 Sylvia B. Bashevkin, *Toeing the Lines: Women and Party Politics in English Canada* (Toronto 1985).
12 Jean Hamelin, *Histoire du catholicisme québécois: Le XXe siècle, vol. 2: De 1940 à nos jours* (Montreal 1984), 71–82.

13 Ghislaine Desjardins, "Les Cercles de fermières et l'action féminine en milieu rural, 1915–1944," in *Travailleuses et Féministes: Les femmes dans la société québécoise* (Montreal 1983), 217–44.

14 Archives de l'AFEAS. See Léon Lebel, *Pourquoi l'Union catholique des fermières?* (Montreal 1946), 31.

15 Louise Leblanc, "La Scission des fermières: Dissidence et autonomie, 1937–1950," Mémoire de maîtrise en histoire, Université de Sherbrooke, 1987.

16 Micheline Dumont, "La Parole des femmes: Les Revues féminines, 1938–1968," in *Idéologies au Canada français: 1940–1976* 2, (Quebec 1981): 5–46.

17 Micheline Dumont and Nadia Fahmy-Eid, "Les Rapports femmes/famille/éducation au Québec: Bilan de la recherche," in Micheline Dumont and Nadia Fahmy-Eid, eds., *Maîtresses de maison, maîtresses d'école* (Montreal 1983), 25–34.

18 Many bibliographies on the question of ideologies in Quebec have been published, but they do not take account of ideologies by and about women. See Dumont, "La Parole des femmes," 40, n. 10.

19 Lucia Ferretti, "La Philosophie de l'enseignement," in Micheline Dumont and Nadia Fahmy-Eid, eds., *Les Couventines: L'Éducation des filles au Québec dans les congrégations religieuses enseignantes, 1840–1960* (Montreal 1986), 143.

20 Mona-Josée Gagnon, *Les Femmes vues par le Québec des hommes: Trente ans d'histoire des idéologies 1940–1970* (Montreal 1974).

21 Thivierge, *Ecoles ménagères et instituts familiaux: Un modèle féminin traditionnel* (Quebec 1982), 275–304.

22 *La Signification et les besoins de l'enseignement classique pour les jeunes filles: Mémoire des collègues classique de jeunes filles du Québec à la Commission Royale d'enquête sur les problèmes constitutionnels* (Montreal 1954).

23 Ferretti, "La Philosophie de l'enseignement," 143–66.

24 See Nadia Fahmy-Eid, "Les Revues et journaux étudiants 1870–1960," in Dumont and Fahmy-Eid, eds., *Les Couventines*, 167–88.

25 Danielle Juteau, "Les Religieuses du Québec: Leur influence sur la vie professionnelle des femmes 1908–1954," *Atlantis*, 5, no. 2 (1980): 29–33.

26 Marta Danylewycz, *Taking the Veil: An Alternative to Marriage, Motherhood and Spinsterhood in Quebec, 1840–1920* (Toronto 1987).

27 Nadia Fahmy-Eid and Aline Charles, "Savoir confisqué ou pouvoir contrôlé: L'Éducation des filles dans trois disciplines du paramédical à l'Université de Montréal: 1940–1970," *Recherches féministes* 1, no. 1 (1988): 5–30.

28 Micheline Dumont, "Vocation religieuse et condition féminine," in *Travailleuses et Féministes: Les Femmes dans la société québécoise*, 271–92; Dumont, "L'Instruction des filles avant 1960," *Interface* 7, no. 2

(1986): 22–9; Dumont and Fahmy-Eid, eds., *Les Couventines*; Francine Barry, *Le Travail de la femme au Québec: L'Évolution de 1940 à 1970* (Montreal 1977).

29 Simone de Beauvoir published *Le Deuxième Sexe* in 1949. At that time, women born between 1930 and 1945 (the present generation of "older" feminists) were not likely old enough to read that book, in French or in its 1952 English translation. Young women of Quebec discovered it as they reached university. I read it myself in 1957. I suggest that Beauvoir, like Mary Beard, was really discovered in the mid-1960s.

30 Dumont, "La Parole des femmes;" Collectif Clio, *Histoire des femmes au Québec depuis quatre siècles*.

31 Micheline Dumont, "Historienne et sujet de l'histoire," in *Identités féminines: Mémoire et création*, Questions de culture, no. 8 (Quebec 1986), 21–34.

32 On the occasion of the celebration of the feast of "Saint Jean Baptiste," on the theme "Hommage à la femme canadienne française," *Le Devoir*, 25 June 1961, published a special section filled with declarations from various women.

33 Collectif Clio, *Histoire des femmes au Québec depuis quatre siècles*.

34 Groupe de recherche sociale, *Les Électeurs québécois: Attitudes et opinions à la veille de l'élection de 1960* (Montreal 1960), 25. The survey was held in the fall of 1959 during the short term of Paul Sauvé as premier of Quebec.

35 Vincent Lemieux, *Parenté et politique: L'Organisation sociale dans l'Ile d'Orléans* (Quebec 1971).

36 Thérèse Casgrain, *Une Femme chez les hommes* (Montreal 1971).

37 Sylvia B. Bashevkin, "Social Change and Political Partisanship: The Development of Women's Attitudes in Quebec, 1965–1979," *Comparative Political Studies* 16, no. 2 (1983): 147–72.

38 Political scientists are not unanimous about the political attitudes of Quebec women. See Bashevkin, "Social Change and Political Partisanship"; Jerome H. Black and Nancy McGlen, "Male-Female Political Involvement Differentials in Canada, 1965–1974," *Canadian Journal of Political Science* 12 (1979): 3; André Blais, "Le Vote: Ce que l'on en sait ... Ce que l'on n'en sait pas," in *Québec: un pays incertain: Réflexions sur le Québec post-référendaire* (Montreal 1980), 159–82; Francine Fournier, *La Participation politique des femmes du Québec*, Etudes préparées pour la Commission royale sur la situation de la femme au Canada (Ottawa 1969); Lemieux, *Parenté et politique*; Evelyn Tardy, "Les Femmes et la campagne référendaire," in *Québec: Un pays incertain*, 185–203; and Carole J. Uhlaner, "La Participation politique des femmes au Québec: 1965–1977," in Jean Crete, ed., *Comportement électoral au Québec* (Montreal 1984), 201–42.

39 Naomi Black, "'The Child Is Father to the Man': The Impact of Feminism on Canadian Political Science," in Winnie Tomm, ed., *The Effects of Feminist Approaches on Research Methodologies* (Waterloo 1989), 225–43.

40 Joan Kelly, "The Social Relations of the Sexes: Methodological Implications of Women's History," in Joan Kelly, *Women, History and Theory: The Essays of Joan Kelly* (Chicago 1984), 1–18.

41 Johanne Daigle, "Une révolution dans la tradition: Les Réformes dans le champ de la santé au cours des années 1960 et l'organisation du travail hospitalier," in Robert Comeau, ed., *Jean Lesage et l'éveil d'une nation* (Sillery, Quebec 1989), 148–54.

42 Florence Howe, *Myths of Coeducation* (Bloomington, Indiana 1984).

43 V. Brodeur et al., *Le Mouvement des femmes au Québec* (Montreal 1982).

44 Diane Lamoureux, *Fragments et collages: Essai sur le féminisme québécois des années 1970* (Montreal 1986).

45 Québec, Conseil du Statut de la femme 1979.

46 Renée Dandurand and Evelyn Tardy, "Le Phénomène des Yvettes à travers quelques quotidiens," in Yolande Cohen, ed., *Femmes et politique* (Montreal 1981), 21–54.

47 Tardy, "Les Femmes et la campagne référendaire," 185–203.

CHAPTER SIX

1 Jim Bearden and Linda Jean Butler, *Shadd: The Life and Times of Mary Shadd Cary* (Toronto 1977), 160–1; Paula Giddings, *When and Where I Enter: The Impact of Black Women on Race and Sex in America* (NY 1984), 59–60.

2 Alison Prentice, Paula Bourne, Gail Cuthbert Brandt, Beth Light, Wendy Mitchinson, and Naomi Black, *Canadian Women: A History* (Toronto 1988), 131, 172.

3 Doris Anderson, "Women's Magazines in the 1970s," *Canadian Women's Studies/Les cahiers de la femme* 2, no. 2 (1980): 16.

4 Jo Freeman, *The Politics of Women's Liberation: A Case Study of an Emerging Social Movement and Its Relation to the Policy Process* (NY 1975), 59, 107.

5 Judy Bernstein, et al., "Sisters ... Brothers ... Lovers ... Listen ... " in *Women Unite! An Anthology of the Canadian Women's Movement* (Toronto 1972), 168.

6 Phyllis Waugh, "Movement Comment: Choice Description," *Broadside* 9, no. 2 (November 1987): 6.

7 Naomi Black, "'The Child Is Father to the Man': The Impact of Feminism on Canadian Political Science," in Winnie Tomm, ed., *The Effects of Feminist Approaches on Research Methodologies* (Waterloo 1989), 225–43.

8 Mary Gray Peck, *Carrie Chapman Catt: A Biography* (NY 1944), 283.

9 Susan J. Pharr, *Political Women in Japan: The Search for a Place in Political Life* (Berkeley 1981), 29.

10 The following discussion draws on the notions of "equity feminism" and "social feminism" developed in Naomi Black, *Social Feminism* (Ithaca 1989).

11 Heather Jon Maroney, "Using Gramsci for Women: Feminism and the Quebec State," *Resources for Feminist Research/Documentation sur la recherche féministe* 17, no. 3 (September 1988): 27.

12 Ibid., 29

13 Compare Warren Magnusson, who cites the marginalization of feminism as part of the socialist acceptance of bourgeois definitions and bourgeois focus on the state. Warren Magnusson and Rob Walker, "De-Centring the State: Political Theory and Canadian Political Economy," *Studies in Political Economy* 26 (Summer, 1988): 71, fn. 22.

14 The tensions built into this approach show clearly in Mariette Sineau's interviews of leading political women in France, *Des femmes en politique* (Paris 1988).

15 A few analyses have attempted to discuss the women's movement in the context of "normal" politics. Some have finally examined suffragism and enfranchisement in this context: e.g. Martin D. Pugh, "Politicians and the Women's Vote, 1914–1918," *History* 59, no. 197 (1944): 358–74; David Morgan, *Suffragists and Democrats: The Politics of Woman Suffrage in America* (East Lansing, Michigan 1972). More recent cross-national studies of the influence of the women's movements in various coutries include Drude Dahlerup, ed., *The New Women's Movement: Feminism and Political Power in Europe and the USA* (Beverly Hills 1986); Mary Fainsod Katzenstein and Carol McClurg Mueller, eds., *The Women's Movements of the United States and Western Europe: Consciousness, Political Opportunity, and Public Policy* (Berkeley 1989).

16 Some feminist analysts now prefer terminology such as the movement of women or women's feminist movement (e.g. bell hooks, *Feminist Theory: From Margin to Center* [Boston 1984]), thus directing attention away from organized social groups and social or political structure. This strategy also has the effect, as intended, of delegitimizing the historical women's movements we know.

17 Katzenstein and Mueller, *The Women's Movements of the United States and Western Europe*, 3, 4; emphasis added in last citation.

18 There is now a fairly substantial literature on each of these episodes. For the u.s. and the ERA, I found particularly useful the essays edited by Joan Hoff-Wilson, *Rights of Passage* (Bloomington, Indiana 1986); Jane Mansbridge, *How We Lost the ERA* (Chicago 1986); and Cynthia Harrison, *On Account of Sex: The Politics of Women's Issues, 1945–1968* (Berkeley 1988); for Canada and the Charter of Rights and Freedoms, I have

relied on the account given in Prentice, et al., *Canadian Women: A History*.

19 *Reed* v. *Reed* overruled by *In re Lockwood* (Hoff-Wilson, *Rights of Passage*, xiv).

20 Mansbridge, *How We Lost the* ERA, 56–9.

21 Hoff-Wilson, *Rights of Passage*, 41.

22 M. Elizabeth Atcheson, Mary Eberts, and Beth Symes, with Jennifer Stoddart, *Women and Legal Action: Precedents, Resources and Strategies for the Future* (Canadian Advisory Council on the Status of Women, Ottawa 1984), 12–26.

23 The so-called Persons' Case of 1929, decided on appeal by the Judicial Committee of the Privy Council in Britain, included Canadian women among the "persons" who, if qualified, could be appointed to the Senate. Canadian feminists have tended to interpret the case more widely, as recognizing the legal "personhood" of women.

24 Penney Kome, *The Taking of Twenty-Eight: Women Challenge the Constitution* (Toronto 1983), 23.

25 Jean Chrétien, *Straight from the Heart* (Toronto 1985), 189. Roy Romanow, who as attorney-general of Saskatchewan was central to the process, gives more space – and more credit – to women's groups (Roy J. Romanow, John Whyte, and Howard Leeson, *Canada–Notwithstanding: The Making of the Constitution, 1976–1982* [Toronto 1984]), as does Bruce P. Elman in "Altering the Judicial Mind and the Process of Constitution-Making in Canada," *Alberta Law Review* 28 (1990), 521–34.

26 The tension between the rights of Quebec and the rights of women continued as the Meech Lake Accord, intended to reinclude Quebec, was debated until its defeat in June 1990; see Lynn Smith, "Could the Meech Lake Accord Affect the Protection of Equality Rights for Women and Minorities in Canada?" *Constitutional Forum* (Centre for Constitutional Studies, University of Alberta) 1, no. 1 (Winter, 1990): 13–16.

27 Gwen Brodsky and Shelagh Day, *Canadian Charter Equality Rights for Women: One Step Forward or Two Steps Back?* (Canadian Advisory Council on the Status of Women, Ottawa 1989).

28 But see Mansbridge, *How We Lost the* ERA, on the debilitating struggles in the key state of Illinois.

29 The major exception here is, of course, the campaigns related to abortion, part of the federal Criminal Code.

CHAPTER SEVEN

1 Nancy Adamson, Linda Briskin, and Margaret McPhail, *Feminist Organizing for Change: The Contemporary Women's Movement in Canada* (Toronto 1988), 28.

2 Penney Kome, *The Taking of Twenty-Eight: Women Challenge the Constitution* (Toronto 1983), 101; and *Women of Influence: Canadian Women and Politics* (Toronto 1985), 45.

3 Renée Dandurand and Evelyne Tardy, "Le Phénomène des Yvettes à travers quelques quotidiens," in Yolande Cohen, ed., *Women and Politics* (Montreal 1981) (English edition available).

4 Montreal *Gazette*, 9 April 1980.

5 See Sylvia B. Bashevkin, "Independence versus Partisanship: Dilemmas in the Political History of Women in English Canada," in Veronica Strong-Boag and Anita Clair Fellman, eds., *Rethinking Canada: The Promise of Women's History* (Toronto 1986), 270.

6 Clio Collective, *Quebec Women: A History* (Toronto 1987).

7 Article 28 reads: "Notwithstanding anything in this Charter, the rights and freedoms referred to in it are guaranteed equally to male and female persons."

8 See Barbara Roberts, *Smooth Sailing or Storm Warning? Canadian and Quebec Women's Groups and the Meech Lake Accord*, (Ottawa, CRIAW 1988).

CHAPTER EIGHT

1 Marie France, "Why Women's Studies?" *Women's Studies International Forum* 7, no. 3 (1983): 305–8, quote p. 305; see also Nancy Adamson, "One in Ten," *Feminist Review* 15 (1983): 88–93; Marilyn J. Boxer, "For and about Women: The Theory and Practice of Women's Studies in the United States," *Signs* 7 (1982): 661–95; Marion Colby, "Women's Studies: An Inclusive Concept for an Inclusive Field," *Canadian Women's Studies* 1 (1978): 4–6; G. Payeur, "Women's Studies: The Search for Identity," *Canadian Issues* 6 (1984): 74–83; Mary Evans, "In Praise of Theory: The Case for Women's Studies," *Feminist Review* 10 (1982): 61–74; Renate D. Klein, "The Dynamics of the Women's Studies Classroom: A Review Essay of the Teaching Practice of Women's Studies in Higher Education," *Women's Studies International Forum* 10, no. 2 (1987): 187–206; Susan Magarey and Susan Sheridan, "Women's Studies in Northern Europe," *Hecate* 9, nos. 1–2 (1983): 183–91; Paige Cousineau, "Changing Society with Women's Studies," unpublished paper presented to the International Conference on Research and Teaching Related to Women, Simone de Beauvoir Institute, Montreal, 1982; Hanna-Beate Schoepp-Schilling, "Women's Studies, Women's Research and Women's Research Centres: Recent Developments in the U.S.A. and in the F.R.G.," *Women's Studies International Quarterly* 2, no. 1 (1979): 103–16; Veronica Strong-Boag, "Mapping Women's Studies in Canada: Some Signposts," *Journal of Educational Thought* 17 (1983): 94–111; Fanny Tabak, "UN Decade and Women's Studies in Latin America," *Women's Studies International Forum*

8, no. 2 (1985): 103–6; and Sheila Tobias, "Women's Studies: Its Origins, Its Organization and Its Prospects," *Women's Studies International Quarterly* 1, no. 1 (1978): 85–98.

2 Robyn Rowland, "What Are the Key Questions Which Could Be Addressed in Women's Studies?" *Women's Studies International Forum* 10, no. 5 (1987): 521. An alternative formulation is that women's studies itself constitutes a movement; see, for example, Barrie Thorne, "Contradictions, and a Glimpse of Utopia: Daily Life in a University Women's Studies Program," *Women's Studies International Quarterly* 1, no. 2 (1978): 201: "In a nutshell, women's studies is a social movement – committed to social change."

3 We will examine women's/feminist studies as a paradigmatic shift in a separate publication. In this essay, I simply assume that this is a reasonable view rather than examine the evidence. In any case, there is no question that women's/feminist studies constitute a major challenge to mainstream academic thought. See, for example, Ruth Bleier, *Science and Gender: A Critique of Biology and Its Theories on Women* (NY 1984); Margrit Eichler, *The Double Standard: A Feminist Critique of Feminist Social Science* (London 1980); Margrit Eichler, *Nonsexist Research Methods* (Winchester, MA 1988); Mary McCanney Gergen, ed., *Feminist Thought and the Structure of Knowledge* (NY 1988); Sandra Harding, *The Science Question in Feminism* (Ithaca 1986); Everlyn Fox Keller, *Reflections on Gender and Science* (New Haven 1985); Marian Lowe and Ruth Hubbard, *Woman's Nature: Rationalizations of Inequality* (NY 1983); Julia A. Sherman and Evelyn Torton Beck, *The Prism of Sex: Essays in the Sociology of Knowledge* (Madison 1979); and Winnie Tomm, ed., *The Effects of Feminist Approaches on Research Methodologies* (Waterloo 1989).

4 As Lorraine Greaves notes in her contribution to this volume, our group is restricted to university professors only, which therefore excludes those academics who teach in community colleges and CEGEPS.

5 Various aspects of the overall project have been financially supported by the following grants: Social Science and Humanities Research Council of Canada (SSHRCC) grants #482–86–0007 and #482–88–0016 (M. Eichler and R. Lenton); (OISE) SSHRCC grant #0920 (M. Eichler); grant #234.02 of the Ontario Women's Directorate (M. Eichler); a McMaster Arts Research Board grant (R. Lenton); and a grant from the Université du Québec à Montréal (L. Vandelac).

6 See the following articles, all in *Atlantis* 16, no. 1 (1990): Margrit Eichler, "On Doing the Splits Collectively: Introduction to the Canadian Women's Studies Project," 3–5; Eichler, "What's in a Name? Women's Studies or Feminist Studies," 40–56; Eichler with the assistance of Rosonna Tite, "Women's Studies Professors in Canada: A Collective Self-Portrait," 6–24; Eichler with the assistance of Louise Vandelac, "An

Awkward Situation: Men in Women's Studies – Part 1, 69–91; Rhonda Lenton, "Academic Feminism and the Women's Movement in Canada: Continuity or Discontinuity," 57–68; Lenton, "Influential Feminist Thinkers for Academics in Canadian Women's Studies," 92–118; Tite with the assistance of Margaret Malone, "Our Universities' Best Kept Secret: Women's Studies in Canada," 25–39.

7 Eichler, with the assistance of Vandelac, "An Awkward Situation."

8 In our study, we consistently used the formulation women's/feminist studies so as to be inclusive. The respective meanings of the terms have been explored in a separate paper: see Margrit Eichler, "What's in a Name?" In brief, the label "women's studies" denotes a subject area, while the label "feminist studies" denotes a perspective. This has some rather important consequences in terms of what is included or excluded. The label "women's studies" may (and does) include non-feminist approaches, while excluding men's studies as well as some other subject areas, while a feminist perspective is applicable to all subject areas, including men's studies, while by definition excluding non-feminist approaches.

9 The exact wording was: "Prior to teaching your first course(s) in women's/feminist studies at a university or college, had you ever worked with somebody actively involved with women's concerns and/or research?" Response categories were no or yes. If yes, respondents were asked to circle all of the following categories that applied: Student(s); A part-time faculty member in my department; A full-time faculty member in my department; Faculty member outside the department; Women's group; Other, please specify. Up to three responses were coded.

10 One might expect that the importance of a woman's consciousness-raising group as a motivating factor would be strictly related to when the women first started teaching in women's/feminist studies, assuming that such groups were a phenomenon of the late 1960s and early 1970s. A comparison between whether respondents checked this answer and when they taught their first course in women's/feminist studies reveals no such pattern. Of the 172 women who indicated that a woman's consciousness-raising group was one factor in motivating them to teach in the area, 68 taught their first course between 1969 and 1979 and 104 started teaching in the area between 1980 and 1988. This could either mean that consciousness-raising groups were (and possibly are) operating in 1980 and later, or that the effect of having participated in one carries through over the years.

11 The exact wording was: "Since your initial involvement in women's/feminist studies as an academic perspective in a Canadian university or college, have you been involved in women's concerns and/or research on

an on-going basis?" Response categories were no or yes, and if yes, respondents could indicate which of the following responses applied: Teaching in the area; As a researcher; Active in women's groups; Politically active; Through publishing/editing; As a public speaker; Other, please specify.

12 The exact wording was: "Have you ever been a member or held an organizing/co-ordinating position in any women's organizations?" Response categories were: No, I have never been a member or held an office; Yes, I have been a member of a women's organization, but I have not held a co-ordinating position; Yes, I have held an organizing/co-ordinating position in a women's group or organization. These percentages omit 10 missing cases.

13 The exact wording of the question was: "In relation to how you view yourself, which of the following statements is most appropriate? I define myself as a feminist; I would define myself as a non-feminist but I am concerned about women's issues; I would define myself as a non-feminist who is not concerned about women's issues; I am an anti-feminist; Other, please specify." The total percentages omit 13 missing cases.

14 We used a total of 6 indicators with yes-no responses: 1. Had they ever been a member or held an organizing/co-ordinating position in a women's group? 2. Since their initial involvement in women's/feminist studies as an academic perspective, had they been involved in a women's group on an ongoing basis or 3. been politically active on an ongoing basis with respect to women's concerns? 4. Was one of their motivations in teaching their first women's/feminist studies course a women's consciousness raising group or 5. political motivations aimed at improving the position of women? 6. Were they a member of a women's group prior to teaching their first course? Any yes response resulted in a score of 1, a no response in a score of 0. In testing the reliability coefficients, we found that the reliability coefficient alpha was 0.65.

15 The first question was: "At the time you taught your first course in women's/feminist studies, how would you describe the centrality of the area in relation to your entire work (including teaching, research, as well as other activities)? How about now?" The exact wording of the second question was: "Overall, how would you rate your initial as well as your most recent experience in teaching in the area of women's/feminist studies? [Circle the one response which best reflects your experience.]" Response categories, for the first course and the most recent course, were: Very positive experience; Somewhat positive; Somewhat negative; Very negative; Very mixed. We asked for further elaboration of their answers, which will be considered on another occasion.

16 These numbers do not correspond to those contained in table 3 because the numbers of missing cases are different. We included in our female population a number of former professors no longer teaching at a university; indeed, we made a special effort to locate these people. In any comparisons, however, these respondents do not appear, since they are no longer teaching. The percentages are, of course, always calculated on the basis of the various applicable totals.

17 These figures are derived from table 4 by adding together those applicable cells that indicate a shift in the centrality of interest between the first and last course.

18 The suggested probes were as follows: What events or persons or situations prompted you to work in this area? Where were you at the time? How did things develop from there on? What was the first involvement with respect to women for you? Was it teaching, political activity (what?), a study group? Please tell me about your teaching history with respect to women. Have you supervised student theses related to women? Have there been any problems? What year was that? It must be kept in mind, however, that the actual wording varies slightly from case to case, since these were open-ended interviews in which interviewees might, for instance, answer one of the probes before it was asked.

19 This is an estimate, rather than a count. Quotations from French-speaking respondents have been silently translated here and below.

20 This is an estimate rather than a count.

21 There are, of course, important feminist thinkers who are not attached to any university and who may have quite a different vision; see our list of feminist thinkers, which includes a large proportion of non-academics. Nevertheless, academics are supposed to publish, are therefore placed in a position where it is generally easier for them to publish than for non-academics, and are therefore likely to produce the greater bulk of our common literature.

22 See Eichler, with the assistance of Tite, "Women's Studies Professors in Canada," table 7.

23 Grudging seems to be the appropriate term: in phase two of the study, respondents were asked to indicate, in the order of their importance, the factors which influenced their decision to teach their first course in women's/feminist studies. Out of twelve possible factors, the item "Administration outside the department was promoting the area" was ranked twelfth and last.

24 Thelma McCormack, "Becoming a Women's Studies Scholar: From Stardust to Section Fifteen," *Canadian Woman Studies* 6, no. 3 (1985): 7, notes a "growing separation between feminist politics and feminist scholarship."

CHAPTER NINE

1 *Signs: Journal of Women in Culture and Society.*

2 Elizabeth Janeway, *Man's World, Woman's Place: A Study in Social Mythology* (NY 1971); Kate Millett, *Sexual Politics* (NY 1971).

3 Elizabeth Minnich, Jean O'Barr, and Rachel Rosenfeld, eds., *Reconstructing the Academy: Women's Education and Women's Studies* (Chicago 1978).

4 Carol S. Pearson, Donna L. Shavlik, and Judith G. Touchton, eds., *Educating the Majority: Women Challenge Tradition in Higher Education* (NY 1989).

5 Mariam K. Chamberlain, ed., *Women in Academe: Progress and Prospects* (NY 1988); Alice S. Rossi, *Academic Women on the Move* (NY 1973).

6 Susan Hardy Aiken, Karen Anderson, Myra Dinnerstein, Judy Nolte Lensink, and Patricia MacCorquodale, eds., *Changing Our Minds: Feminist Transformations of Knowledge* (Albany 1988).

7 Peggy McIntosh, "The Study of Women: Processes of Personal and Curricular Re-vision," *Forum for Liberal Education* 6, no. 5 (April 1984): 2–4.

8 Adrienne Rich, "Resisting Amnesia: History and Personal Life," in *Blood, Bread and Poetry: Selected Prose, 1979–85* (NY 1986), 143.

9 Micheline R. Malson, Jean F. O'Barr, Sarah Westphal-Wihl, and Mary Wyer, eds., *Feminist Theory in Practice and Process* (Chicago 1989).

10 Marilyn Frye, *The Politics of Reality: Essays in Feminist Theory* (Freedom, California 1983), xii.

11 Sandra Harding, "The Instability of the Analytical Categories of Feminist Theory," in Malson, et al., eds., *Feminist Theory in Practice and Progress*, 17.

12 Editorial, *Signs* 12, no. 4 (Summer 1987): 619–20.

13 Deborah K. King, "Multiple Jeopardy, Multiple Consciousness: The Context of a Black Feminist Ideology," in Malson, et al., eds., *Feminist Theory in Practice and Process*, 75–106.

14 Elisabeth Young-Bruehl, "The Education of Women as Philosophers," in Malson, et al., eds., *Feminist Theory in Practice and Process*, 263.

15 Nannerl O. Keohane and Barbara C. Gelpi, Foreword, to Nannerl O. Keohane, Michelle Y. Rosaldo, and Barbara C. Gelpi, eds., *Feminist Theory: A Critique of Ideology* (Chicago 1981), vii.

16 Linda Alcoff, "Cultural Feminism versus Post-Structuralism: The Identity Crisis in Feminist Theory," in Malson, et al., eds., *Feminist Theory in Practice and Process*, 315.

17 Alice Walker, *The Color Purple* (NY 1982), 15.

18 Adrienne Rich, *Blood, Bread and Poetry*, 1–2.

CHAPTER ELEVEN

1 Mariana Valverde, "'The Mothers of the Race': Race in the Sexual and Reproductive Politics of First-Wave Feminism," in F. Iacovetta and

M. Valverde, eds., *Gender Conflicts: New Essays in Women's History* (Toronto 1992).

2 Mariana Valverde, *Sex, Power, and Pleasure* (Toronto 1985, and Philadelphia 1987).

3 Mary Daly, *Pure Lust* (Boston 1984).

4 Gayle Rubin, "Thinking Sex," in C. Vance, ed., *Pleasure and Danger* (Boston 1987).

5 See, for instance, the collection edited by H.L. Gates, *Race, Writing and Difference* (Chicago 1988).

6 The latter point is argued by Jenny Bourne in *Towards an Anti-Racist Feminism* (London 1984).

CHAPTER TWELVE

1 Although "women of colour" is used as a unitary term to describe these different groups of non-white women, it, like any other unitary term, has the tendency to erase the particularities of women grouped under this nomenclature. We must always remember that "women of colour" does not refer to a monolithic group and those subsumed under it do not produce a unitary discourse. However, opposition to racism does appear as a common thread in their variegated concerns.

2 Elizabeth V. Spelman's *Inessential Woman: Problems of Exclusion in Feminist Thought* (Boston 1988) is a detailed analysis of exclusion of race-related concerns in the work of major feminist theorists.

3 Catharine R. Stimpson, "Nancy Reagan Wears a Hat: Feminism and Its Cultural Consensus," *Critical Inquiry*, 14, no. 2 (Winter 1988): 241. Although Audre Lorde also appeals for an appreciation of "difference," she is not talking about the postmodern "difference" which refrains from privileging one discourse over any other discourse, thus relativizing all truth claims. Lorde, instead, appeals to white women to take into account their race privilege and the racist oppression suffered by women of colour: "Poor women and women of Color know there is a difference between the daily manifestations of marital slavery and prostitution because it is our daughters who line 42nd Street. If white american [sic] feminist theory need not deal with the differences between us, and the resulting difference in our oppressions, then how do you deal with the fact that the women who clean your houses and tend your children while you attend conferences on feminist theory are, for the most part, poor women and women of Color? What is the theory behind racist feminism?" See Audre Lorde, "The Master's Tools Will Never Dismantle the Master's House," in *Sister Outsider: Essays and Speeches* (Trumansburg, NY 1984), 112.

4 Marcia Ann Gillespie, "My Gloves Are Off, Sisters: Power, Racism, and That 'Domination Thing,'" *Ms*, April 1987, 19–20. Also see Combahee River Collective, "A Black Feminist Statement," in Cherríe Moraga and Gloria Anzaldúa, eds., *This Bridge Called My Back: Writings by Radical Women of Color* (NY 1981; rpt. 1983), 218.

5 See Angela Y. Davis, *Women, Race and Class* (NY 1981), chapters 11 and 12. Also see Brenda Eichelberger, "Voices on Black Feminism," *Quest* 3, no. 4 (Spring 1977): 16–28.

6 bell hooks, *Ain't I a Woman: Black Women and Feminism* (Boston 1981), 121–2.

7 Following is a list of some of the well-known feminist theory books that I was using in this course: Nancy Chodorow, *The Reproduction of Mothering: Psychoanalysis and the Sociology of Gender* (Berkeley 1978); Geraldine Finn and Angela Miles, eds., *Feminism in Canada: From Pressure to Politics* (Montreal 1982); Alison M. Jaggar and Paula Rothenberg Struhl, eds., *Feminist Frameworks: Alternative Theoretical Accounts of the Relations between Women and Men* (NY 1984); Annette Kuhn, *Women's Pictures: Feminism and Cinema* (London 1982).

8 Alice Walker, "One Child of One's Own: A Meaningful Digression within the Work(s)," in *In Search of Our Mothers' Gardens: Womanist Prose* (NY 1983), 372.

9 Gayatri Chakravorty Spivak, "Three Women's Texts and a Critique of Imperialism," in Henry Louis Gates, Jr, ed., *"Race," Writing and Difference* (Chicago 1986), 270.

10 Patricia Meyer Spacks, *The Female Imagination: A Literary and Psychological Investigation of Women's Writing* (London 1976); Ellen Moers, *Literary Women: The Great Writers* (NY 1976); Elaine Showalter, *A Literature of Their Own: British Women Novelists from Brontë to Lessing* (Princeton 1977); Sandra M. Gilbert and Susan Gubar, *The Madwoman in the Attic: The Woman Writer and the Nineteenth-Century Literary Imagination* (New Haven 1979) and *No Man's Land: The Place of the Woman Writer in the Twentieth Century*, vols. 1 and 2 (New Haven 1988–89).

11 Barbara Smith, *Toward a Black Feminist Criticism* (Trumansburg, NY 1977); Hazel V. Carby, *Reconstructing Womanhood: The Emergence of the Afro-American Woman Novelist* (NY 1987).

12 For example, Sandra Gilbert and Susan Gubar have complained that they are being denied the right to speak out of a secure female identity by those who charge their theory of being "essentialist." Gilbert and Gubar, thus, want to be above criticism because they have the authority of "experience." See Bruce Robbins, "The Politics of Theory," *Social Text* 18 (Winter, 1987/88): 11.

13 Carby, *Reconstructing Womanhood*, 53–5.

14 Gillespie, "My Gloves Are Off, Sisters," 19.

15 See Nancy A. Hewitt, "Beyond the Search for Sisterhood: American Women's History in the 1980s," *Social History* 10, no. 3 (1985): 299–321. Cora Kaplan's *Sea Changes: Essays on Culture and Feminism* (London 1986), 3, also cautions against taking "a purely celebratory stance" towards women's writing which is "painfully class-bound and often implicitly or explicitly racist".

16 Kate Millett, *Sexual Politics* (NY 1978), 68.

17 Ibid., 50, 56, 68.

18 Spelman discusses the insidious racism of such comparisons in her chapter on Simone de Beauvoir. See *Inessential Woman*, especially 64–79.

19 Kum-Kum Bhavnani, "Complexity, Activism, Optimism: An Interview with Angela Y. Davis," *Feminist Review* no. 31 (Spring, 1989): 68.

20 Cherríe Moraga's excellent bibliography of writings by women of colour, "Third World Women in the United States–By and about Us: A Selected Bibliography," in Moraga and Anzaldua, eds., *This Bridge Called My Back*, 251–61, lists most of the major works published up to 1980. The important work of writers like Angela Davis and bell hooks, however, was published after that date. The following titles should be of interest to those wanting to explore further: Paula Giddings, *When and Where I Enter: The Impact of Black Women on Race and Sex in America* (NY 1984); Nila Gupta and Makeda Silvera, eds., *The Issue Is 'Ism: Women of Colour Speak Out* (Toronto 1989; reprinted from *Fireweed* 16); bell hooks, *Feminist Theory: From Margin to Center* (Boston 1984); Barbara Smith, ed., *Home Girls: A Black Feminist Anthology* (NY 1983); Jesse Vorst, et al., eds., *Race, Class, Gender: Bonds and Barriers* (Toronto 1989).

21 Lorde, *Sister Outsider*, 131–2.

22 hooks, *Feminist Theory*, 12.

23 Gail Pheterson, "Alliances between Women: Overcoming Internalized Oppression and Internalized Domination," in Elizabeth Minnich, Jean O'Barr, and Rachel Rosenfeld, ed., *Reconstructing the Academy: Women's Education and Women's Studies* (Chicago 1988), 139–53.

24 bell hooks, "Giving Ourselves Words: Dissident Black Woman Speech," *Zeta Magazine* 2, no. 1 (January 1989): 39–42.

25 Toril Moi, *Sexual/Textual Politics: Feminist Literary Theory* (London 1985), 86. Moi's assumption of total similarity between "black" and "lesbian" positions is remarkable in terms of the postmodern valorizing of "difference."

26 Maxine Baca Zinn, Lynn Weber Cannon, Elizabeth Higginbotham, and Bonnie Thornton Dill, "The Cost of Exclusionary Practices in Women's Studies," in Minnich, et al., eds., *Reconstructing the Academy*, 128.

27 Lorde, *Sister Outsider*, 117.

28 Virginia Woolf, "Women and Fiction," *Collected Essays*, vol. 2, ed. Leonard Woolf (London 1967), 142. Showalter quotes this passage approvingly in *A Literature of Their Own*, 9.

CHAPTER THIRTEEN

1 John Samuels, "Immigration and Visible Minority in the Year 2000: A Projection," *Canadian Ethnic Studies* 20, no. 2 (1988).
2 Michele Wallace, *Black Macho and the Myth of the Superwoman* (NY 1979).
3 bell hooks, *Talking Back: Thinking Feminist, Thinking Black* (NY 1984).
4 Heleieth I. B. Saffioti, *Women in Class Society*. Translated from the Portuguese by Michael Vale (NY 1978).
5 See Dionne Brand's discussion in "A Working Paper on Black Women in Toronto: Gender, Race and Class," *Fireweed* (Summer/Fall, 1984).
6 Maxine Tynes, *Borrowed Beauty* (Porters Lake, Nova Scotia 1987).

CHAPTER FOURTEEN

1 Diana Russell, *The Secret Trauma* (NY 1986), 20–37, and Diana Russell, *Rape in Marriage* (NY 1982), 27–41.
2 Susan Brownmiller's *Against Our Will: Men, Women and Rape* (NY 1975) is the classic articulation of this position.
3 I never did this in my own work but am attempting to comprehend and credit feminists who did.
4 In Canada, the specific changes discussed below are traced by Christine Boyle, *Sexual Assault* (Toronto 1984), with references to the sections of the Criminal Code before and after.
5 See Russell, *Rape in Marriage*, 375–81; Patricia Searles and Ronald Berger, "The Current Status of Rape Reform Legislation: An Examination of State Statutes," *Women's Rights Law Reporter* 10 (1987): 25.
6 The sexual history exclusions in the Canadian Criminal Code were eliminated by the Supreme Court of Canada after this speech was given, eliminating even this formal improvement. *Seaboyer* v. *The Queen, Gayme* v. *The Queen* (1991). Legislation has been introduced to attempt to reinstitute at least some protection for victims of sexual assault in this area. C–49 [An Act to Amend the Criminal Code (sexual assault)]. This legislation makes sexual history inadmissible to support an inference that the complainant is likely to have consented to the abuse or should not be believed.
7 This argument is made more fully and footnoted in my *Toward a Feminist Theory of the State* (Cambridge, MA 1989), chapter 9.
8 A different but creative solution emerging from this critique is reflected in Canada's new proposed sexual assault law, C–49, which takes the

approach of providing a meaningful legal definition of consent centring on "voluntary agreement" (section 273.1(1)). No consent exists where another person purports to consent for the woman, where she is rendered incapable of consenting, where a position of trust or authority has been abused, or where she said or indicated "no."

CHAPTER FIFTEEN

1 Catharine MacKinnon, "Feminist Approaches to Sexual Assault in Canada and the United States: A Brief Retrospective," in this volume.
2 For a lengthier discussion, please see Osennontion (Marlyn Kane) and Skonaganleh:rá (Sylvia Maracle), "Our World," *Canadian Woman Studies* 10, nos. 2 and 3 (Summer/Fall, 1989): 7–19.
3 Race (as well as colour, creed, national or ethnic origin) is a Western European and now, Euro-Canadian construction. My people speak of nations, in a holistic sense. My race can never transcend my colour, or creed, or ethnic origin. My race is always inclusive of those characteristics, and as well includes my spirituality and my culture. Since this is a difficult construction to grasp, interested readers are referred to Mary Ellen Turpel, "Aboriginal Peoples and the Canadian Charter: Interpretive Monopolies, Cultural Differences," *Canadian Human Rights Yearbook 1989–1990* (Ottawa 1990), 3–45.
4 See Arun Mukherjee, "A House Divided: Women of Colour and American Feminist Theory," in this volume.
5 This reminds me of how pornography dissects women's bodies, exposing a limb or torso, here and there. What I cannot understand is how feminists continue to fail to learn the lessons which they purport to teach others.
6 Verna Kirkness, "Emerging Native Women," *Canadian Journal of Women and the Law* 2, no. 2 (1986): 408–15.
7 As the "MicMac" refer to themselves.
8 In the 1960s and 1970s we heard all about the "Indian" problem. Today, I hear "What do you Indians/Natives/Aboriginals want anyway?" This is not just my problem. Nor can First Nations in isolation be charged with the authorship of the solution. What is required is *mutual respect* for all good ways of life and sincere commitments to finding solutions. Canadian political will and judicial recognition still eludes us. A further discussion is found in Osennontion and Skonaganleh:râ, "Our World," 10.
9 My first article is a story about law student experiences, racism, anger, and pain. See Patricia A. Monture, "Ka-Nin-Heh-Gah-E-Sa-Nonh-Yah-Gah," in *Canadian Journal of Women and the Law* 2, no. 1 (1986): 159.
10 This is an exceptionally important consideration as universities, law schools, and other programs fling their doors open to First Nations and

minority students. It must be accepted that these programs do not benevolently offer us an opportunity that is special or undeserved. These programs ought not be established to "help" us. Reshaped admission standards for First Nations and minority students are *not* lesser standards, just (merely) different. Different because our experience in this country is different. Different does not automatically mean lesser. It must be recognized that through our participation and sharing of our unique experience, there is a general benefit to all involved. Finally, university administrators, teachers, and students must also be aware and accepting that our mere presence will change the basic nature of these institutions.

11 Not all law schools, however, can still be criticized for this failure. Citing only from my personal experience (which is unfortunately not a complete canvas of all Canadian law schools), law schools at Dalhousie University, Osgoode Hall, Queen's University, the University of British Columbia, and the University of Ottawa have been actively pursuing minority recruitment and establishing formal programs. Further, the College of Law at Saskatoon offers a law preparation and access program recognized by all Canadian law schools.

12 As Rudolph C. Ryser explains: "The new European nations have worked diligently to wipe out indigenous history and intellectual thought. The great lie is simply this: If indigenous peoples will only reject their own history, intellectual development, language and culture and replace these things with European values and ideals, then indigenous people will survive. It is from this twisted thinking that European nations have convinced millions of indigenous people all over the world to surrender their freedom and accept subjugation as a way of life." (Rudolph C. Ryser, "Nation-States, Indigenous Nations and the Great Lie," in Leroy Little Bear, Menno Boldt, and Anthony Long, eds., *Pathways to Self-Determination* [Toronto 1984], 28).

13 An honest (a task Canadian courts and lawyers have generally failed to achieve) interpretation of treaties and their provisions demonstrates this point. The Two Row Wampum Belt of my people (the first treaty we signed with the Europeans) guarantees that our nations will develop side by side. The two paths are parallel, separated only by kindness, respect, and sharing. Yet these paths never cross or become one.

14 Rights philosophy with particular reference to the Canadian constitution is discussed in Turpel, "Aboriginal Peoples and the Canadian Charter."

15 This is not to say that a just settlement of First Nations claims is that all peoples descendant of the settlers must go home. That is not our expectation or even desire. The settlers were welcomed here in the spirit of

unity (that is kindness, sharing, truth, and strength). That is the true immigration law of this land. That law has never been rescinded.

16 The 1986 census data regarding aboriginal post-secondary school education have not been introduced in the publication by Gilles Y. Larocque and R. Pierre Gauvin, *1986 Census Highlights on Registered Indians: Annotated Tables* (Ottawa: Indian and Northern Affairs Canada 1989). The statistic cited was provided by Indian and Northern Affairs Canada based on 1986 census data. Further, I was advised that there are currently eighteen thousand Registered Indians attending post-secondary institutions.

17 Pamela M. White, *Native Women: A Statistical Overview* (Ottawa: Native Citizens Directorate 1986), 16, uses 1981 census figures.

18 The E-12 education policy of Indian Affairs is allegedly an innovative new policy but is really only a disguised cutback policy. It was supported by the new minister of Indian and northern affairs. In the spring of 1989, the general dissatisfaction with the package erupted when outraged First Nations communities, led by students, marched on Ottawa. Despite the dissatisfaction in our communities, the minister has *not* rescinded or shifted his policy.

19 A fast is *not* a form of hunger strike to gain public and political attention. Put simplistically, a fast is a spiritual ceremony in which individuals sacrifice food and/or drink in order for their prayers to be carried forward. Fasting is not meant to be fully explained here. The media and the government chose to misunderstand the students' fast, characterizing it as a threat and a ploy. Using our own cultural beliefs against us is one of the most damaging forms of racism. Those young students acted in a good way following the traditions of their ancestors.

20 Personal conversation with one of the women who was arrested.

21 Please do not tell me you were there for section 12(1)(b) (an old section of the *Indian Act*, which disenfranchised only Indian women and not Indian men who married non-Indians). The 1985 amendments to the *Indian Act* allow such women to be reinstated and their children get a limited reinstatement, but their grandchildren get nothing. This does not happen to the men. Their children and grandchildren and great-grandchildren still maintain full status. Some feminist groups were there for a while (perhaps it suited their own constitutional amendment mandate for all women), but now as we try to publicize the issue, there is only silence. Sometimes, it feels like so much has been built on our brown backs.

22 Canadian Human Rights Commission, *Annual Report 1988* (Ottawa 1988), 19.

23 Michael Jackson, *Locking Natives Up in Canada* (Ottawa 1988), 3.

24 See an expanded discussion of this topic in Patricia A. Monture, "A Vicious Circle: Child Welfare and the First Nations," *Canadian Journal of Women and the Law* 3, no. 1 (1987): 1–17 at 4.

25 A copy of this report, "Breaking the Cycle of Aboriginal Family Violence: A Proposal for Change," is available from the Ontario Native Women's Association, 101–115 North May Street, Thunder Bay, Ontario, P7C 3N8.

26 I am aware that I have not included definitions of certain important concepts such as racism. That is principally because I have not had the opportunity to spend energy doing necessary definitional work but must first clear out the old definitions and understandings. To date, I have not discovered a definition of racism which works for me in both theory and practice.

27 This is not an argument that asserts that women are to be relegated to the private sphere. In fact it is the opposite. As first teachers of all people not just the children, it is essential that women are involved in politics and nation building.

28 Mohawk thanks.

CHAPTER SIXTEEN

1 Some of the material in this essay is derived from Francine D. Blau and Marianne A. Ferber, *The Economics of Women, Men, and Work* (Englewood Cliffs, NJ 1986); and Marianne A. Ferber, "What Is the Worth of 'Comparable Worth'?" *Journal of Economic Education* 17, no. 4 (Fall, 1986): 267–82.

2 It is interesting to note that in recent years the labour force participation of both women and men has been very nearly the same in Canada and the U.S.

3 Marianne A. Ferber, "Labor Market Participation of Young Married Women: Causes and Effects," *Journal of Marriage and Family* 44, no. 2 (May 1982): 457–68.

4 William B. Johnston and Arnold E. Packer, *Workforce 2000. Work and Workers in the Twenty-First Century* (Indianapolis 1987).

5 The most common measure of occupational segregation, developed by Duncan and Duncan (1955) is $S = \frac{1}{2}\Sigma i |Mi - Fi|$, where Mi = the percentage of males in the labour force employed in occupation i, and Fi = the percentage of females employed in the same occupation. Otis Dudley Duncan and Beverly Duncan, "A Methodological Analysis of Segregation Indexes," *American Sociological Review* 20, no. 2 (1955). The indices reported in this essay are based on this formula, using the approximately four hundred detailed occupations generally employed by the U.S. Bureau of the Census. If more detailed categories were used,

the figures would be considerably higher. One study of four hundred California firms, using employers' job classifications, found that 51 per cent of the firms were completely sex-segregated by job category, so that no men and women shared the same job title. In addition, 8 per cent of the firms had an entirely single-sex labour force. The mean index in the remaining firms was 84 per cent. William T. Bielby and James N. Baron, "A Woman's Place is with Other Women: Sex Segregation within Organizations," in Barbara F. Reskin, ed., *Sex Segregation in the Workplace: Trends, Explanations and Remedies* (Washington, DC 1984), 27–55.

6 Edward Gross, "Plus Ça Change ... ? The Sexual Structure of Occupations over Time," *Social Problems* 16, no. 1 (Fall, 1968): 198–208.

7 Francine D. Blau and Wallace E. Hendricks, "Occupational Segregation by Sex: Trends and Prospects," *Journal of Human Resources* 14, no. 2 (Spring, 1979): 197–210; Andrea H. Beller, "Changes in the Sex Composition of U.S. Occupations, 1960–1981," *Journal of Human Resources* 20, no. 2 (Spring, 1985): 235–50.

8 Blau, "Occupational Segregation by Gender: A Look at the 1980's," Paper presented at the annual meetings of the American Economic Association, New York, December 1988.

9 Donald J. Treiman and Heidi I. Hartmann, *Women, Work, and Wages: Equal Pay for Jobs of Equal Value* (Washington, DC 1981).

10 It is interesting that as of the 1980 census, the earnings gap between men and women was smaller among all minority groups than among whites, and particulary so among Blacks, where women earned fully 73 per cent as much as men. Black women earned 93 per cent as much as white women, while Black men earned only 69 per cent as much as white men. Asian men earned about the same as white men, and Asian women actually earned 111.3 per cent as much as white women.

11 James P. Smith and Michael Ward, "Women in the Labor Market and in the Family," *Economic Perspectives* 3, no. 1 (Winter, 1989): 9–24.

12 Jonathon S. Leonard, "Women and Affirmative Action," *Economic Perspectives* 3, no. 1 (Winter, 1989): 61–75.

13 June O'Neill, "The Worth of 'Comparable Worth,'" Paper presented at the meetings of the International Personnel Management Association, October 1983.

14 Edward P. Lazear, Symposium on Women in the Labor Market, *Economic Perspectives* 3, no. 1 (Winter, 1989): 3–8.

15 Morley Gunderson and W. Craig Riddell, *Labour Market Economics: Theory, Evidence and Policy in Canada* (Toronto 1988).

16 George Johnson and Gary Solon, "Pay Differences between Women's and Men's Jobs: The Empirical Foundations of Comparable Worth Legislation," National Bureau of Economic Research, Working Paper #1472 (1984). It

might be noted that if their objection is sound, the fear that comparable worth would disrupt the economy is not likely to be justified.

17 Barbara R. Bergmann, "Why Wage Realignment under the Rubric of 'Comparable Worth' Makes Economic Sense," in Heidi I. Hartmann, ed., *Comparable Worth: New Directions for Research* (Washington, DC 1989).

18 Treiman and Hartmann, *Women, Work, and Wages*.

19 Ronald G. Ehrenberg and Robert S. Smith, "Comparable Worth in the Public Sector," National Bureau of Economic Research, Working Paper no. 1471, 1984.

20 Paula England, "Explanations of Job Segregation and the Sex Gap in Pay," in *Comparable Wealth: Issue for the 80's*. A Consultation Paper of the U.S. Commission on Civil Rights, 1984.

21 Donald J. Treiman, Heidi I. Hartmann, and Patricia A. Roos, "Assessing Pay Discrimination Using National Data," in Helen Remick, ed., *Comparable Worth and Wage Discrimination: Technical Possibilities and Realities* (Philadelphia 1984).

22 Robert Gregory and Vivian Ho, "Equal Pay and Comparable Worth: What Can the U.S. Learn from the Australian Experience?" Australian National University, Centre for Economic Policy Research, Discussion Paper no. 123. Further evidence that higher wages for women do not have a negative effect on their employment is provided by Sweden, the country with the smallest earnings gap, where the ratio of women's to men's hourly earnings is 90 per cent, and 66 per cent of women are in the labour force. It is interesting, however, that an unusually large proportion of these women work part-time, providing support for the conclusion of Nakamura and Nakamura that higher wages do not necessarily increase the amount of labour supplied by women (Alice Nakamura and Masao Nakamura, "Predicting the Effects of Comparable Worth Programs on Female Labour Supply," unpublished paper, April 1988).

23 One reason for this may be that there appears to be little substitution in the labour market between women workers and mature men, though there is some between part-time women workers and young men. Maureen Pike, "The Employment Response to Equal Pay Legislation," *Oxford Economic Papers* 37, no. 2 (June 1985): 304–18.

24 Joseph Pleck and James Levine, *Research Report* 4, no. 1 (Fall, 1984).

25 F. Thomas Juster, "A Note on Recent Changes in Time Use," in F. Thomas Juster and Frank P. Stafford, eds., *Time, Goods, and Well-Being* (Ann Arbor 1985).

CHAPTER SEVENTEEN

1 *Report of the Royal Commission on the Status of Women in Canada* (Ottawa 1970).

2 Interview with Madeleine Parent.

3 Lorna R. Marsden, "The Role of the National Action Committee on the Status of Women in Facilitating Equal Pay Policy in Canada," in Ronnie Steinberg Ratner, ed., *Equal Employment Policy for Women: Strategies for Implementation in the United States, Canada, and Western Europe* (Philadelphia 1980), 242–60.

4 Gail C.A. Cook, ed., *Opportunities for Choice: A Goal for Women in Canada* (Ottawa 1976).

5 Statistics Canada, *Historical Labour Force Statistics* (Ottawa 1988), cat. 7201.

6 Pat Armstrong, *Labour Pains: Women's Work in Crisis* (Toronto 1984).

7 Duncan Cameron and Daniel Drache, eds., *The Other Macdonald Report* (Toronto 1985).

8 *Report, Royal Commission of the Economic Union and Development Prospects for Canada* (Ottawa 1985).

9 Marjorie Cohen, *The Macdonald Report and Its Implications for Women* (Toronto, NAC 1985).

10 For an analysis of the impact of free trade on women, see Marjorie Cohen, *Free Trade and the Future of Women's Work: Manufacturing and Services Industries* (Toronto 1987).

11 For an analysis of NAC's political action on free trade, see Sylvia Bashevkin, "Free Trade and Canadian Feminism: The Case of the National Action Committee on the Status of Women," *Canadian Public Policy* 15, no. 4 (1989): 363–75.

12 Canadian Labour Congress et al, *A Time for Social Solidarity* (Toronto 1987).

CHAPTER EIGHTEEN

1 *Frontiero* v. *Richardson*, 411 U.S. 677, 684 (1973).

2 *City of Richmond* v. *J.A. Croson Company*, 109 S.Ct. 706 (1989).

3 Ibid., 713, 728.

4 Ibid., 720–23, 728.

5 Ibid., 723–28.

6 Ibid., 714.

7 *Harris* v. *McRae*, 448 U.S. 300, 348 (1980) (Blackmun, J., dissenting), quoting *Beal* v. *Doe*, 432 U.S. 438, 462 (1977) (Blackmun, J., dissenting). *Harris*, like *Beal* before it, upheld the constitutionality of laws excluding payments for abortions from otherwise comprehensive medical assistance plans for the poor.

8 See *Craig* v. *Boren*, 429 U.S. 190, 204 (1976).

9 *Weinberger* v. *Wiesenfeld*, 420 U.S. 636, 648 (1975).

10 For a general description of the background of affirmative action, see Marjorie Heins, *Cutting the Mustard: Affirmative Action and the Nature of Excellence* (Winchester, MA 1988), 14–19.

11 See Heins, *Cutting the Mustard*.

12 107 S.Ct. 1442 (1987).

13 Ibid., 1448 note 5.

14 See Heins, *Cutting the Mustard*, 191–2.

15 Justice Scalia, however, made a "less qualified" argument in his angry dissent, 107 S.Ct. at 1467–69, 1474.

16 *Price Waterhouse* v. *Hopkins*, 109 S.Ct. 1775, 1782 (1989).

17 Ibid.

18 Carol Gilligan, *In a Different Voice* (Cambridge, MA 1982).

19 479 U.S. 272 (1987).

20 The heat of the debate is reflected, for example, in Linda J. Krieger and Patricia N. Cooney, "The Miller-Wohl Controversy: Equal Treatment, Positive Action, and the Meaning of Women's Equality," *Golden Gate University Law Review* 13, no. 513 (1983): 545–6; and Wendy Williams, "Equality's Riddle: Pregnancy and the Equal Treatment/Special Treatment Debate," *New York University Review of Law and Social Change* 13, no. 332 (1984–85): 347–63. The latter accuses Krieger and Cooney of "engag[ing] in some ill-considered rhetoric about how the equal treatment approach has served the needs of economically privileged employed women and left lower income women by the wayside" (ibid., 350, note 102).

21 479 U.S. at 284–90.

22 *Mississippi University for Women* v. *Hogan*, 458 U.S. 718, 727–31 (1982).

23 *Michael M.* v. *Superior Court of Sonoma County*, 450 U.S. 464 (1981).

CHAPTER NINETEEN

1 Barbara Katz Rothman, remarks at a conference on "Legal and Ethical Aspects of Human Reproduction," Canadian Institute of Law and Medicine, 2 December 1989.

2 Christine Overall, *Ethics and Human Reproduction: A Feminist Analysis* (Boston 1987), chapter 8.

3 *R.* v. *Morgentaler*, [1988] 1 SCR 30, 172.

4 Ibid., 56–61, 64–73.

5 Ibid., 90.

6 Ibid., 173.

7 Ignoring the Criminal Code provisions on abortion, community health clinics in Quebec had already been providing abortions for more than a decade before the Supreme Court decision.

8 *R.* v. *Morgentaler*, [1988] 1 SCR 32.

9 See George J. Annas, "Webster and the Politics of Abortion," *Hastings Center Report*, 19 (March/April 1989): 36–8. In July 1989 the United States Supreme Court ruled that the state of Missouri had the right to

ban public hospitals and public employees from performing abortions. It is anticipated that the court may in future uphold additional state-imposed restrictions on abortion services, with a resulting serious erosion in access to abortion, particularly for poor women. See *Webster* v. *Reproductive Health Services*, 109 S. Ct. 3040 (1989).

10 For example, Brenda Large's editorial, "If Sex-Based Abortions Are Wrong, So Are All," *Kingston Whig-Standard*, 11 February 1989.

11 Mark I. Evans, John C. Fletcher, Evan E. Zador, Burritt W. Newton, Mary Helen Quigg, and Curtis D. Struyk, "Selective First-Trimester Termination in Octuplet and Quadruplet Pregnancies: Clinical and Ethical Issues," *Obstetrics and Gynecology* 71, no. 3, pt. 1 (March 1988): 291.

12 "Multiple Pregnancies Create Moral Dilemma," *Kingston Whig-Standard*, 21 January 1989, 3; Dorothy Lipovenko, "Infertility Technology Forces People to Make Life and Death Choices," *Globe and Mail*, 21 January 1989, A4.

13 *Borowski* v. *Canada (Attorney-General*, [1989] 1 SRC 342.

14 *R.* v. *Morgentaler*, 181, 183.

15 Ibid., 76.

16 Ibid., 82–3, 110, 113, 124.

17 Neil Reynolds, "Fetal Status Cannot Depend on Momentary Opinion," *Kingston Whig-Standard*, 16 March 1989, 6.

18 Law Reform Commission of Canada, Working Paper 58, *Crimes against the Foetus* (Ottawa 1989), 64.

19 Ibid., 42, 56, 64.

20 A. Johnson, "Clinic Fights to Survive in B.C.," *Rites*, (March, 1989): 4; and Helen Armstrong, Debi Brock, and Jennifer Stephen, "'Operation Rescue' Turns into Fiasco," *Rites* (March 1989): 5.

21 Joseph Borowski, quoted in the *Toronto Star* and the *Globe and Mail*, 10 March 1989.

22 Caroline Whitbeck, "The Moral Implications of Regarding Women as People: New Perspectives on Pregnancy and Personhood," in William B. Bondeson, H. Tristram Engelhardt, Jr, Stuart F. Spicker, and Daniel H. Winship, eds., *Abortion and the Status of the Fetus* (Boston 1984), 251.

23 This is the argument of Sanda Rodgers, "The Future of Abortion in Canada," in Christine Overall, ed., *The Future of Human Reproduction* (Toronto 1989). This argument in no way endorses the use of abortion for supposed eugenic purposes. As disabled women and their allies have pointed out, feminists should be highly critical of the use of reproductive technologies to discriminate among human beings on the basis of their physical or mental condition, or to promote the notion of human perfectibility. See March Saxton, "Prenatal Screening and Discriminatory Attitudes about Disability," in Elane Hoffman Baruch, Amadeo F. D'Adamo, Jr, and Joni Seager, eds., *Embryos, Ethics, and Women's*

Rights: Exploring the New Reproductive Technologies (NY 1988), 217–24, and Ruth Hubbard, "Eugenics: New Tools, Old Ideas," in ibid., 225–35.

24 In my view, this is the effect of the proposal of the Law Reform Commission of Canada's *Crimes against the Foetus*, which would require "medical authorization" of an abortion by one "qualified medical practitioner" before fetal viability, and by two such practitioners after the fetus is capable of independent survival (64).

25 In North America there is a long history of the forced sterilization of Native women and women of colour.

26 John A. Robertson, "Procreative Liberty, Embryos, and Collaborative Reproduction: A Legal Perspective," in Baruch, et al., eds., *Embryos, Ethics and Women's Rights*, 180. Compare Lori B. Andrews, "Alternative Modes of Reproduction," in Sherrill Cohen and Nadine Taub, eds., *Reproductive Laws for the 1990s* (Clifton, NJ 1989), 364.

27 Robertson, "Procreative Liberty, Embryos, and Collaborative Reproduction," 181.

28 Ibid., 180, 186, and 190.

29 Lori B. Andrews, *New Conceptions: A Consumer's Guide to the Newest Infertility Treatments* (NY 1985), 138.

30 From this point of view, then, IVF with donor gametes is more problematic than IVF in which a woman and a man make use of their own eggs and sperm.

31 Genoveffa Corea, "Egg Snatchers," in Rita Arditti, Renate Duelli Klein, and Shelley Minden, eds., *Test-Tube Women: What Future for Motherhood* (London 1984), 37–51.

32 News release, Office of the Prime Minister, Ottawa, 24 October 1989.

33 Renate Duelli Klein, quoted in Christine St Peters, "Feminist Discourse, Infertility, and the New Reproductive Technologies," *National Women's Studies Association Journal* 1, no. 3 (Spring, 1989): 358.

34 See, for example, Susan Sherwin, "Feminist Ethics and In Vitro Fertilization," in Marsha Hanen and Kai Nielsen, eds., *Science, Morality and Feminist Theory* (Calgary 1987), 265–84.

35 Janet Ajzenstat, "The Sexism of Pro-Choice," paper presented at Queen's University, Kingston, 14 March 1989. Ajzenstat is a member of the Department of Political Science, McMaster University.

36 John Robertson claims that "[e]xtra-corporeal conception seems to promote choice, to promote the autonomy of women (and men) in helping them overcome infertility, which for many women (and men) is a very serious problem." It "makes possible new, partial reproductive roles for women" as "egg and embryo donors and surrogates" (Robertson, "Procreative Liberty, Embryos, and Collaborative Reproduction," 192–3).

CHAPTER TWENTY

1 Exceptions to this generalization may be found in Fay Ginsburg, *Contested Lives: The Abortion Debate in an American Community* (Berkeley 1989); Kristin Luker, *Abortion and the Politics of Motherhood* (Berkeley 1984); and Connie Paige, *The Right-to-Lifers: Who They Are, How They Operate, Where They Get Their Money* (NY 1983).

2 Barbara Ehrenreich, *Fear of Falling: The Inner Life of the Middle Class* (NY 1989); and Eric O. Wright, *Classes* (NY 1985).

3 Barbara Ehrenreich and John Ehrenreich, "The Professional-Managerial Class," in Pat Walker, ed., *Between Labor and Capital: The Professional Managerial Class* (Boston 1979); and Wright, *Classes*.

4 410 U.S. 113 (1973).

5 Lyle Denniston, "Supreme Court Reduces Abortion Rights," *Baltimore Sun*, 4 July 1989, 1A; *Webster v. Reproductive Health Services*, 109 S. Ct. 3040 (1989).

6 Allison Jaggar, *Feminist Politics and Human Nature* (Totowa, NJ 1983).

7 Rosalind P. Petchesky, *Abortion and Woman's Choice: The State, Sexuality, and Reproductive Freedom* (Boston 1985).

8 Jaggar, *Feminist Politics and Human Nature*.

9 Veronica Beechey, "On Patriarchy," *Feminist Review* 3 (1979): 78–9; and Zillah Eisenstein, *Capitalist Patriarchy and the Case for Socialist Feminism* (NY 1978).

10 Heidi Hartmann, "Capitalism, Patriarchy and Job Segregation by Sex," in M. Blaxall and B. Reagan, eds., *Women and the Workplace* (Chicago 1976).

11 Patricia Fernández Kelly, "Broadening the Scope: Gender and the Study of International Economic Development," *Sociological Forum* 4, no. 4 (1989): 611–36.

12 Barbara Ehrenreich, *The Hearts of Men* (NY 1983).

13 Jane Mansbridge, *How We Lost the ERA* (Chicago 1986).

14 Louise Tilly and Joan W. Scott, *Women, Work, and Family* (NY 1987).

15 Alice Kessler-Harris, "Stratifying by Sex: Understanding the History of Working Women," in Robert Edwards, Michael Reich, and David M. Gordon, eds., *Labor Market Segmentation* (Lexington, MA 1975).

16 Larry Griffin, Michael Wallace, and Beth A. Rubin, "Capitalist Resistance to the Organization of Labor before the New Deal: Why? How? Success?" *American Sociological Review* 51 (1986): 147–67.

17 John Kenneth Galbraith, *The Affluent Society* (Boston 1958).

18 Todd Gitlin, *The Sixties: Years of Hope, Days of Rage* (NY 1987); and Albert O. Hirschman, *Shifting Involvements: Private Interest and Public Action* (Princeton, 1982).

19 Ehrenreich, *The Hearts of Men*.

20 Ibid.

21 Mansbridge, *How We Lost the* ERA.

22 Donald Granberg, "Pro-Life or Reflection of Conservative Ideology? An Analysis of Opposition to Legalized Abortion," *Sociology and Social Research* 62 (April, 1978): 421–3; and Dana Naparsteck, "The Politics of the Right-to-Life Movement," *Interchange* (Washington, DC 1979).

23 Mansbrige, *How We Lost the Era.*

24 Patrick J. Buchanan, "Liberalism's Anti-Catholic Bias," *Conservative Digest* (July 1978): 43.

25 Michael Novak, "The Abortion Fight: It's Not Just a Matter of Religion," *Washington Post*, 20 November 1989, A15.

26 John Lippis, *The Challenge to Be "Pro Life"* (Santa Barbara 1978).

27 Luker, *Abortion and the Politics of Motherhood*; and Paige, *The Right-to-Lifers.*

28 These too are characteristics that pro-life activists attribute to contemporary feminist movements. Such attribution is the result of complex processes involving the rise of "neo-conservatism" and "the new Right," but also the result of tactical failures on the part of the "assimilationist" segment of the women's movement.

29 Fay Ginsburg, *Contested Lives: The Abortion Debate in an American Community* (Berkeley 1989); and Luker, *Abortion and the Politics of Motherhood.*

30 Rosalind P. Petchesky, *Abortion and Woman's Choice: The State, Sexuality and Reproductive Freedom* (Boston 1985), and Laurence H. Tribe, *Abortion: The Clash of Absolutes* (NY 1990).

31 Petchesky, *Abortion and Woman's Choice.*

32 Ibid. During much of the nineteenth century, the Roman Catholic church held that "animation"–not fertilization–marked the beginning of human life, and that a male fetus "animated" at forty days, while a female one did not become human until eighty days' gestation. The method by which sexual identity of the fetus could be determined remained a mystery (Anna Quindlen, "The Issue That Defies Agreement," *New York Times Book Review*, 3 June 1990, 7).

33 Peter Singer and Deane Wells, *Making Babies: The New Science and Ethics of Conception* (NY 1985).

34 Granberg, "Pro-Life or Reflection of Conservative Ideology?"

35 Part of a statement at a pro-life demonstration, 29 April 1990.

36 Linda Gordon, *Woman's Body, Woman's Right: A Social History of Birth Control in America* (Harmondsworth, England, and Baltimore 1977); Grandberg, "Pro-Life or Reflection of Conservative Ideology?"; and Carole Joffe, *The Regulation of Sexuality* (Philadelphia 1986).

37 Tribe, *Abortion.*

38 Patricia Fernández Kelly, "International Development and Industrial Restructuring: The Case of Garment and Electronics Industries in Southern

California," in Arthur MacEwan and William K. Tadd, eds., *Instability and Change in the World Economy* (NY 1989).

39 Katherine L. Bradbury, "The Shrinking Middle Class," *New England Economic Review* (September/October 1986): 41; and Isabel V. Sawhill and Charles F. Stone, *Economic Policy in the Reagan Years* (Washington, DC 1984).

40 Saskia Sassen, *The Mobility of Labor and Capital* (NY 1989).

41 Bennett Harrison and Barry Bluestone, *The Great U-Turn: Corporate Restructuring and the Polarizing of America* (NY 1988).

42 Alan Crawford, *Thunder on the Right: The "New Right" and the Politics of Resentment* (NY 1980); and Granberg, "Pro-Life or Reflection of Conservative Ideology?"

43 Naparsteck, "The Politics of the Right-to-Life Movement."

44 Luker, *Abortion and the Politics of Motherhood.*

45 For examples, see Buchanan, "Liberalism's Anti-Catholic Bias"; and Jack Kemp, "Wide Support for the Populist Revolution," *Conservative Digest* (October 1982): 8–9.

46 Carol Felsenthal, *The Sweetheart of the Silent Majority: The Biography of Phyllis Schlafly* (NY 1981); and Kevin P. Phillips, *Post-Conservative America: People, Politics, and Ideology in a Time of Crisis* (NY 1983).

CHAPTER TWENTY-ONE

1 This essay is primarily derived from the notes I took at the conference and from my notes for my own final remarks. In what follows, all quotations from written texts are fully cited. Those taken from oral presentations will be attributed to their authors within the text of this essay. Although I have since reviewed copies of several of the presentations upon which this essay is based, I have found myself most frequently drawing upon verbatim quotations noted at the time. The freshness of those words lingers with me like a faint and evocative scent.

2 Marilyn Frye, *The Politics of Reality: Essays in Feminist Theory* (Trumansburg, NY 1983), 118.

3 Ibid., 126, 127.

4 Nadya Aisenberg and Mona Harrington, *Women of Academe: Outsiders in the Sacred Grove* (Amherst, MA 1988), 28, 32.

5 Ibid., 52, 56.

6 Ibid., 137.

7 In the summer of 1989, Canadians saw two cases of ex-boyfriends taking out injunctions to prevent their pregnant ex-girlfriends from having abortions. In Toronto, the injunction was not granted. In Quebec, the Superior Court upheld a judge's injunction preventing Chantal Daigle from having an abortion in July, 1989. Although the Supreme

Court of Canada overturned this ruling, making third-party intervention impossible, Chantal Daigle obtained an abortion in Boston in her
twenty-second week while the court was deliberating. The Canadian
and Quebec's women's movements were active in supporting both
women.

Index

Abella, Rosalie, 36
Ablebodyism, 279
Aboriginal women, 103;
 oppression of, 176–7.
 See also Native women.
Abortifacients, 261
Abortion: access to, 13–
 14, 239, 241–7; Montreal
 protest, 29; and RCSW,
 30, 36–7, 291n; Badgley
 report on, 35; Bill C-43,
 37; splits over, 68; late
 in pregnancy, 246;
 polarization of dis-
 courses, 256–67; argu-
 ments against, 256–62;
 and economic restruc-
 turing, 265–6; symbolic
 meaning of, 266
Abortion Caravan, 55,
 96
Abortion law, Canada,
 241–7
Abstinence, 261
Adamson, Nancy, 45
Ad Hoc Committee (1981),
 104–5, 108
Advisory Councils on the
 Status of Women, 36,
 104, 105

Affirmative action, 203,
 204, 212, 232; pro-
 grams, 11–12, 115
Africa, 139, 175, 180
African-Americans, 8, 226
Agriculture, Quebec Min-
 istry of, 79
Air Canada, 222
Aisenberg, Nadya, 282
Alberta, 37, 177, 216
Alcoff, Linda, 147
Amalgamated Carpenters
 of Canada, Women's
 Guild, 56
American Civil Liberties
 Union (ACLU), 233–4
American Council on
 Education, 138
American Express, 224
Anderson, Doris, 23, 44,
 95–6, 114
Anderson, Jacqueline, 276,
 277
Andrew, Caroline, 44
Andrews, Lori B., 248
Androcentrism, 97
Anti-abortion movement,
 245, 251
Anti-communism, 55–6
Anti-Semitism, 171

Arizona, University of,
 142
Asia, 175, 187
Assault, 188
Assembly of First Nations,
 5–6, 116, 183, 198
Association des femmes
 autochtones, 114
Association des femmes
 diplômées des univer-
 sités, 25, 82
Association féminine
 d'éducation et d'action
 sociale (AFEAS), 25, 80–
 1, 85, 113
Association of Women
 University Graduates,
 82
Athletics, 232
Atlantic provinces, 220
Australia, 209, 213

Barrett, Michele, 43, 44
Bashevkin, Sylvia B., 78,
 85
Battered women's shelters,
 10, 183
Beard, Mary, 32, 299n29
Béchard, Monique, 81–2
Beetz, Jean, 242–3, 244–5